Celebrating Tolkien's Legacy
Essays by Nancy Bunting, Seamus Hamill-Keays,
and Toby Widdicombe

Celebrating Tolkien's Legacy

Essays by Nancy Bunting, Seamus Hamill-Keays, and Toby Widdicombe

2024

Cormarë Series No. 52

Library of Congress Cataloguing-in-Publication Data

Nancy Bunting, Seamus Hamill-Keays, Toby Widdicombe:
Celebrating Tolkien's Legacy. Essays by Nancy Bunting, Seamus Hamill-Keays, and
Toby Widdicombe

ISBN 978-3-905703-52-8

Subject headings:
Tolkien, J.R.R. (John Ronald Reuel), 1892-1973
Middle-earth
Biography
The Lord of the Rings
The Hobbit

Cormarë Series No. 52

First published 2024

Set in Adobe Garamond Pro and Shannon by Walking Tree Publishers

Cover art by Stefan Honegger (with the help of Adobe Firefly).
Picture of the Tolkien bust (artist: Faith Tolkien) by Julian Nyča (2012, CC).

Board of Advisors

In our preface to *The Gallant Edith Bratt* (2021) we expressed our hope that the example of the authors' investigation into the first decades of Edith's life would inspire other researchers to look into the biographies of other 'neglected' women such as Mabel Tolkien or Jane Suffield. It is, of course, too early to have any substantial results from that front. However, there exist a plethora of articles and papers authored by Nancy Bunting (sometimes co-written with Seamus Hamill-Keays) that look into various aspects of JRR Tolkien's life and investigate the possible effects of crucial events, such as Mabel Tolkien's diabetes, or discuss some of his 'neglected' relatives, such as May Incledon.

A selection of these articles, often published before (see 'Acknowledgments'), were chosen for inclusion in this volume. They have been revised and expanded for re-publication, and supplemented by contributions that were written purposely for this volume (cf. 'The Interlace of Autobiography' and the three papers by Toby Widdicombe). We hope that they provide inspiration for further research into the complex relationship between JRR Tolkien's life and work.

Lastly, we would like to thank all those who worked on this project: our peer-reviewers who read and commented on the original manuscript, Larissa Zoller, who layouted the text, Peter Buchs who proofread the text with a 'critical historian's eye', Andrew Moglestue who smoothed the wrinkles of the layout and, of course, the authors themselves, Nancy Bunting, Seamus Hamill-Keays, and Toby Widdicombe, who invested so much time and energy into uncovering new apects of Tolkien's life and work.

June 2024
Walking Tree Publishers

Table of Contents

Future: New Directions

Acknowledgements

"Tea in Hay"

A revised and expanded version of the paper first published as "A Hobbit Hole Means Comfort" in *Beyond Bree* (May 2015).

Our appreciation to Paul Collins for permission to reproduce a photograph from his research, the 1903 photograph of the typical one-decker "toastrack" cars.

The 1897 Diamond Jubilee and the Long Awaited Party

A revised and expanded version of the paper first published in *Beyond Bree* (June 2019)

Many thanks to the Moseley Society History Group for help, especially Fiona Adams and Jan Berry.

May Incledon, the Other Suffield Aunt

A revised and expanded version of the paper first serialized in *Beyond Bree* (May, July, August 2019).

Many thanks also to Maggie Devos-Vaughn at the church office of Christ Church, Lille, France. Our appreciation to Dale Heath who helped with the correct description of architecture and décor.

J.R.R.Tolkien: Ambidexter

A revised and expanded version of the paper first published in *Beyond Bree* (October 2017)

1904: Mabel Tolkien, Living and Dying

A revised and expanded version of the paper first published as "'All the Days of Her Life Are Utterly Forgotten': Scenes from Mabel Tolkien's Last Year" in *Lembas* (June 2021)

Seamus Hamill-Keays who was able to obtain the copy of Mabel Tolkien's will from https://www.gov.uk/search-will-probate.
Thanks to Ruth and Reginald Lacon for information on Edwardian housekeeping.
Thanks to Mark Hooker for help with Catholic resources.

Nancy Bunting wishes to thank Vincent Anderson who provided invaluable assistance for years with tracking down resources and then finding a copyeditor. In this context, she also wishes to thank Faith Collins for carefully proofreading and copyediting the entire manuscript.

Seamus Hamill-Keays has been a mentor in the arcana and wonders of internet research and a resource for all things military. He has been a guide to the store of information available from maps, a revelation for a person with left-right confusion. His knowledge of British culture, geography, and custom saved me from many false steps. He was unfailing available for consultation, advice, and helpful suggestions.

Without Seamus, neither *The Gallant Edith Bratt* nor many of the essays in this collection would exist.

Mark Hooker has had the patience to help me improve my writing and think through the implications of what I have written. He was always available for linguistic explorations and elaborations.

We are greatly indebted to Andrew Comptom for access to Angela Gardner and Neil Holford's *Wheelbarrows at Dawn: Memories of Hilary Tolkien* from ADC Publications Ltd. 2010.

We owe a great debt again to Walking Tree Publishers. They have shepherded this manuscript expertly from draft to final version. Their many suggestions and corrections and their knowledge of all facets of the publishing process have improved this collection in so many ways.

List of Illustrations

Introduction

Toby Widdicombe

John Ronald Reuel Tolkien died on September 2, 1973. His youngest son, Christopher, died on January 16, 2020. His last surviving child and only daughter, Priscilla, died on February 28, 2022. The torch has definitively been passed to a new generation, his grandchildren, and to a new era of scholarship. This collection of essays, both new ones and those that have been significantly revised, recognizes the fiftieth anniversary of the older Tolkien's passing. It reassesses his achievement; it suggests some fruitful ways forward in scholarship; it celebrates the complex history of Tolkien's relation to fiction and epic as something tantamount to his being the founder of modern fantasy.

This festschrift is divided into two sections: the first examines the past; the second, the future. The first section, "Biographical Explorations," focuses on the historical context in which Tolkien grew up. The second, "New Directions," asks the reader to consider where Tolkien studies may go in the next few decades and what issues it needs to address.

Let's dwell for a little on what each section has to offer the reader.

The first section consists of seven essays. Chapter One, "Tea in Hay," explores the likelihood of a 1904 excursion by the Tolkien brothers with Father Francis Morgan to the popular destination of Kinver to have "Tea in Hay." The rock homes of Kinver Edge were "curious, warm and commodious and the garden extremely pretty" and could easily have been the model for hobbit holes, including Bilbo's green-painted front door. The town of Kinver has roots in Celtic and early Catholic Britain that Tolkien was probably already familiar with and which resonated with his pride in his Hwiccian and Mercian ancestry.

Chapter Two, "The Diamond Jubilee," presents the multiple parallels between Queen Victoria's "long-expected" 1897 Diamond Jubilee and Tolkien's description of Bilbo Baggins's "long-expected" party in *The Lord of the Rings*.

Tolkien's statement that he lived in an "'almost rural' village of Warwickshire on the edge of the prosperous bourgeoisie of Birmingham (about the time of the Diamond Jubilee!). "I take my models like anyone else—from such 'life' as I know" (*Letters* 235) seems more true than many readers may have realized. Bilbo Baggins's birthday party features a gathering of relatives, from near and far, and in 1897, Tolkien had lots of family who would have come, including Tolkiens, Suffields, Incledons, and so on. Both occasions featured fireworks, food and drink, singing and music, and children's toys and games as if it were a birthday party.

Chapter Three, "May Incledon, the Other Suffield Aunt," introduces the life of Tolkien's aunt, Edith Mary "May" Incledon (née Suffield), immortalized as one of the "three remarkable daughters of the Old Took" in *The Hobbit* (*Bio* 175). Given a new understanding of the social and financial standing of the Incledons, the presence of May Incledon forms a recurring background to her sister Mabel Tolkien's life in South Africa and then their simultaneous conversion to Catholicism on June 28, 1900 (Ordway, *Tolkien's Faith* Figure 5). After Mabel died in 1904, May Incledon came gradualy to act as a substitute or proxy mother for the Tolkien boys as they were growing up. Tolkien appears to have lovingly commemorated his aunt's warmth and their relationship in scenes from his impromptu story, *Roverandom*. As typical for an extended family, after their mother's death the Tolkien boys spent time with their Incledon cousins, Marjorie (1891-1937) and Mary (1895-1940), who appeared to have spurred Tolkien's interest in invented languages with their *Animalic* and later *Nevbosh*, and to have shared his interest in painting. A final coda in the essay explores the possible contribution of the Incledon cousins to the genesis of *The Lord of the Rings*.

Chapter Four, "J.R.R. Tolkien: Ambidexter," considers how unique Tolkien was and how his probably being ambidextrous contributed to his distinctive imagination and rare command of languages. Being ambidextrous would have given Tolkien a facility with visual and linguistic reversals that paves the way for one of the hallmarks of fantasy: the reversal in the narrative of the everyday world's perspective. Evidence of Tolkien using mirror writing and reversals, scattered throughout his works, is reviewed.

Chapter Five, "For Want of a Biography, a Story was Lost," examines how the attempts to document Tolkien's life have run an obstacle course, if not a gauntlet, beginning with Tolkien's own attitude to biography. The Tolkien family and the unstinting efforts, in particular, of Tolkien's third child, Christopher, to guard his father's extraordinary—frankly, *sui generis*—achievement complicate the situation. The essay then offers possible remedies for the accidents of history and circumstance that have so far dominated how Tolkien is remembered.

Chapter Six, "1904: Mabel Tolkien, Living and Dying," opens new perspectives on the last year of Mabel Tolkien's life beginning with the publication of her will and a consideration of the significance of its signing on Sunday, November 6, 1904. A re-evaluation of the evidence for the isolation of Mabel and her sons follows. The Tolkien brothers' responsibilities for the reality of maintaining an Edwardian household are detailed along with new information about when they became ill and what that meant in terms of their daily lives. The historical context of Mabel's hospitalization and the Suffield family's actions raise questions about the meaning of Mabel's convalescence in Rednal. The previously overlooked complications of Mabel's diabetes are also reviewed to complete the picture of this difficult year.

Chapter Seven, "The Interlacing of Autobiography and Faërian Imagery in *Smith of Wootton Major*," takes a biographical view of the study of Tolkien's last short story. Tolkien appears to reconceptualize his life in the character of Smith and to include a true faërian drama with Nokes. In this valedictory tale, Tolkien appears to also include cameos, or guest appearances, by the important people in his life including his mother, Father Francis Morgan, and his Suffield grandfather. Tolkien's lifelong themes of exile and loss are now centered on a faërian Living Flower, with some consolation but without recovery or eucatastrophe as found in "On Fairy-stories."

The second section, on the future direction of Tolkien studies, consists of two essays.

Chapter Eight, "Tolkien as Forgotten Utopian," proposes that in the process of developing his mythology, Tolkien created a remarkable number of pocket eutopias and dystopias—communities of betterment or deterioration—within a larger, even epic, landscape. Tolkien had a vision of utopia that developed throughout the almost sixty-year life of the legendarium. Tolkien's own view that his is "not a Utopian vision" or an "ideal" represents a not-uncommon misunderstanding on his part (based on the OED) of More's original meaning.

Chapter Nine, "Christopher Tolkien as Editor: The Perils of Kinship," ponders how Christopher Tolkien, the literary executor of his father's estate—who seems to have had the perfect match of experience, training, and knowledge of his father's work for the job he was called to do through love—was caught in the conflicting demands and duties of editor, guardian of his father's reputation, and custodian of his family's estate. Christopher Tolkien was placed in an unenviable—even impossible—position: editor of another's man's literary achievement, a role in which disinterestedness coupled with a wish to judge and preserve an achievement is foremost; guardian of his father's legacy, a position informed by love and duty; and, lastly, a concern (unusual for most academic publishing) created by the unprecedented success of and profits from the Tolkien legacy. The essay chronologically tracks Christopher's changing editorial choices and the results of those choices that have produced a range of problems partly because of the distorting quality of all mediation. Consistent with the direction established by Christopher Tolkien before his death, the Tolkien Estate continues its control over information about what manuscripts have or have not been published, over use of the materials in many of the archives where they are stored, and even precisely what documents exist. This is something about which most Tolkien readers are, I suspect, wholly unaware.

So, why another collection of essays on Tolkien—this particular collection, in fact—and why now? This introduction has, in a way, come full circle. I began by pointing out that the last of Tolkien's children died in 2022. As a result, in a sense, Tolkien now belongs to the reading public in a way he did not, could not, before. In such a situation, it is essential that the variety of perspectives on his work be preserved, indeed widened, and at the same time his legacy not become (as it is in danger of doing) the preserve of professional linguists. Yes, Tolkien's work on Elvish and numerous other Middle-earth tongues was extraordinary, but it is not that which has given his work worldwide fame and literary immortality. Rather, it is the depth of the stories he tells and their resonance with readers that matters. In this regard, it is his life and his retelling of that life that created Middle-earth and not his talents as a philologist. This collection dwells at length on the life and not the academic profession. At the same time, it points out how complicated that retelling was and how fraught with distortion and lacunae. Perhaps this is like the white spaces on Victorian maps of Africa that needed to be filled in.

With the passing of the torch to a new generation of the family, something else has started to happen which renders collections of well-thought-out and detailed essays even more essential than they have been since Tolkien shot to fame in the 1960s. It is becoming clear that those now in charge of the rights to Tolkien's work are less interested in verity and ever more interested in preserving the biographical legend and in profits. When Tolkien's son Christopher was in charge, he scrupulously defended the accurate portrayal in film of his father's achievement. Even so, one can see cracks beginning to develop in such a focus as Christopher moved into his late eighties. Peter Jackson's *The Hobbit* (2012-2014), as a three-film epic version of a *children's* story, takes liberties with its source material when compared with Jackson's earlier three-film treatment of *The Lord of the Rings* (2001-2003), an epical treatment of a manifest literary epic. The earlier trilogy was remarkably faithful to *The Lord of the Rings*. The later trilogy was markedly *un*faithful even to the spirit of *The Hobbit*. The best-known examples of such a lack of fidelity are its category error of creating an epic out of a fairly brief there-and-back-again quest tale for children and its crass invention of an attractive she elf (Tauriel) presumably to bolster the appeal to a youth demographic. Now, we have recently had *The Lord of the Rings: The Rings of Power* (2022-2024?) presented to us by Amazon Prime. It is based on the events of the Second Age ("loosely based" would be the operative phrase), and again does not show the fidelity to the original (in this case the Númenor saga) which Jackson's *Lord of the Rings* two decades earlier did. Instead of three films, we will now have sixteen episodes by the time this visually stunning but inaccurate series is over.

With this sort of development and its preference for the visual over the written, as is common in this post-literate age, it has become more important than ever to explore Tolkien's *written* legendarium and the complexities of its origins and background. This collection of nine essays represents part of that effort. The films and multimedia versions of Tolkien's mythology have a place in Tolkienian secondary creation but not primacy. Primacy necessarily belongs to Tolkien's written achievement and, hence, to the sort of scholarship this collection represents.

Preface

Nancy Bunting

"Doubt is not a pleasant condition, but certainty is." Voltaire

In examining ideas, we all love the "easy case" where a document pins down a particular 'fact,' e.g. a birth certificate, a marriage certificate, or a death certificate. 'Proof' and its resulting certainty are concepts which create comfortable states of mind. However, when faced with gaps in the documentation and accessible information, the reader or curious observer is not helpless and without tools or skills with which to reconstruct the missing information. An attitude of scepticism or critical thinking, one which cautiously tests and waits for the elaboration of a complete context so that the relationship of the parts and the whole can be understood in a new way, challenges and clarifies the nature of the facts, reality, and previous assumptions. This is what historical philologists, like Tolkien, did and do.

The inquiring mind can collect, survey, and analyze all the available evidence, including contradictory, disconfirming, inconvenient, previously overlooked, or ignored facts. A collection of this type of information or facts makes it possible to define a reality that gives a consistent context to the claims made. For example, in law, preponderance of the evidence (American English), also known as balance of probabilities (British English), is the standard required in most civil cases. The standard is met if the proposition is more likely to be true than not true or "more probable than not." A higher standard is needed for clear and convincing proof, also known as "clear, convincing, and satisfactory evidence," "clear, cognizant, and convincing evidence," or "proof beyond a reasonable doubt." This sort of proof of such a convincing character that one would be willing to rely and act upon it without hesitation in the most important of one's own affairs, despite the fact no absolute certainty exists.

Most people would be willing to say that they are "certain" that J.R.R. Tolkien lived and that he wrote books, including *The Hobbit* and *The Lord of the Rings*. That is due to the preponderance of evidence and the clear, convincing and satisfactory evidence that supports those statements. Many of the essays in this collection, however, deal with matters that are not completely certain or lack documentary evidence which can support a claim of truth. Consequently, these issues require critical thinking that weighs the probabilities or likelihood that the claims or conclusions are true and relevant and then evaluates the context created by new explanations or implications of previously assumed 'facts.'

Many of the essays in this collection present new explanations or interpretations of previously known facts that provide the reader with a new understanding of Tolkien's life and works. This new understanding may lead to different conclusions about what is or is not true. Consequently, 'proof' depends not only, or even necessarily, on the existence of particular documents, but also on the logical evaluation of all the available facts tested in light of the best understanding or explanation available. Because so much documentation in Tolkien Studies is lacking, an appropriate inquiry into the specifics of comparable, contemporary circumstances, similar to Tolkien's, has the capacity to advance of our understanding of Tolkien. As a result, logically justified 'speculation,' based on the best available evidence of life at the time in which Tolkien lived, can be used to learn more about Tolkien's life given the absence of specific documentary evidence about that life. The type of critical thinking about Tolkien's life leads to an accumulation of findings which build one on another.

What is true is independent of and separate from what we know. The earth revolved around the sun for a long time before Copernicus advocated that position in a culture that viewed the cosmos as geocentric. If one demands certainty or incontestable evidence, then a lack of such evidence closes the path forward. The path forward remains open for those who apply a sceptical attitude of critical thinking: interrogating supposed facts as well as one's beliefs or assumptions and what those beliefs are based on and why those beliefs are compelling. This is the kind of thinking Copernicus used to reimagine the earth revolving around the sun. An inquiry into and exploration of what can be reasonably and probably expected to have happened in the past can generate reliable and accurate information when there is a lack of documentation and certainty. These essays invite the reader to embark on a journey of discovery which seeks to break the magic spell of preconceptions and assumptions, to summon and cultivate disbelief and critical thinking, and to explore and test ideas, both new and old. *Bon Voyage!*

Turning to the mechanics of this book, the editor of Walking Tree Publishers kindly allowed the writers to use American or British spelling conventions as they chose. The authors are very grateful for this flexibility.

The Tolkien Estate graciously gave permission for the reproduction of three of J.R.R. Tolkien's drawings. Unfortunately, the budget for this book has not allowed us to include them. To understand the full range of Tolkien's work as an artist, the reader may wish to consult Hammond and Scull's *Artist and Illustrator*, McIlwaine's *The Maker of Middle-earth*, and the Tolkien Estate website for reproductions of his artwork.

One final note: Throughout this book, wherever clarity of reference is needed J.R.R. Tolkien is called "Ronald," his preferred Christian name.

Past:

Biographical Explorations

Chapter One

"Tea in Hay"

Nancy Bunting

J.R.R. Tolkien, also referred to as Ronald Tolkien, wrote that words like 'gamgee' and 'cotton' "like most of the Shire [are] derived from [my] childhood."[1] In a 1968 BBC interview, he also said:

> But, of course, in the process of writing *The Hobbit* [...] an awful lot gets tied up; your own present situation, your past, the things you would like to do, the things you have done, and so that it's simply full, of course, of memories for me (Lee, "Tolkien in Oxford" 140).

Those memories would include Belladonna Took, her sisters, and the Old Took in *The Hobbit* who were all characters based on Mabel Tolkien and her Suffield family of origin (*Bio* 175). In addition, Ronald reports that the number of Thorin and company's members and the "thunder-battle" in *The Hobbit*'s Misty Mountains came from his 1911 Swiss walking tour (*Letters* 309). Since the Shire is "full, of course, of memories for me," a consideration of other possibilities seems warranted. One of the memories, which contributed to the Shire, appears to be "Tea in Hay" from 1904 (*Bio* 30).

In late June of 1904, Ronald Tolkien and his younger brother, Hilary, were reunited at Rednal with their mother who had been released from the hospital after being diagnosed with diabetes—a disease that was untreatable at the time. Their mother, Mabel, would have known that she was under a death sentence and that the amount of time remaining for her to be with her sons was precious and unknowable. Her boys were all that was left to her. Much of what is known about Mabel's last year comes from her letters to her widowed mother-in-law, Mrs. John B. or Mary Tolkien, who was the same age as Mabel's father, both having been born in 1833.

Mrs. Mary Tolkien (1833-1915) was John Benjamin Tolkien's (1807-1896) third wife.[2] In 1835, the widower John Benjamin Tolkien married Jane Holmwood (1806-1854). They had four children: three daughters and a son. By 1845, the family moved from London, where John B. was born, to Birmingham. His company, Tolkien and Co. Music and Musical Instruments, on New Street was dissolved in 1847. In 1849, John Tolkien was listed as a music seller and professor of music at Bristol Road, Hemlingford, Edgbaston. He also composed music. After his second wife's death in 1854, the forty-eight year old John B. Tolkien married, in 1856, the twenty-three year old Mary Jane Stowe, who was only three years older than John Tolkien's oldest daughter. The couple had eleven children, with the eldest being Arthur Reuel, J.R.R. Tolkien's father.

In 1875, John B. Tolkien's business, J. B. Tolkien–Music Warehouse, was at 87 New Street, Birmingham. Mr. Tolkien attended the United Brethren Church from the 1850s to the 1870s, and was known as a philanthropist in Birmingham. In a letter to a Florence Tolkien in the United States, Ronald Tolkien wrote:

> He [John B. Tolkien] was once a wealthy man, but not one of business and a rigidly religious Baptist and would not deal with music halls or theatres. He was a dear old and poor man in the [eighteen] nineties when I knew him.[3]

After her husband's death at the age of eighty-nine in 1896, Mary Tolkien went to live with her daughter, Grace Bindley Tolkien Mountain (1861-1947), and her son-in-law, William Charles Mountain (1868-1928)—an industrialist, engineer, and a Justice of the Peace (J.P.) (1891 census). Until 1901, the Mountains lived in a twenty-room mansion in Gateshead named 'The Hermitage', and Grace's brother, Laurence, lived there too for a while (Ahmed 12). Laurence and Charles Mountain were both members of the Literary and Philosophical Society. By 1901, the Mountains moved to a large, terraced house in Sydenham Terrace, Newcastle, less than one mile from the City Center (Ahmed 11-12).[4] In 1901, this was where Mary Tolkien was living as a "visitor." It is likely that Mabel Tolkien, wanting to spare Mary Tolkien any alarming or difficult news, would have focused on sharing positive, upbeat stories from Birmingham and Rednal.

In particular, Mabel appears to have made the most of that 1904 summer when she enjoyed her sons' activities including: "Bilberry-gathering—Tea in Hay—

Kite-flying with Fr. Francis—sketching—Tree Climbing" (*Bio* 30). This is from a letter to Mary Tolkien which appears to have been written in late July 1904.

Of the boys' activities, "Bilberry-gathering—Tea in Hay—Kite-flying" are likely to have all been in the company of Fr. Francis, because Mabel Tolkien was in the final stages of diabetes. She had previously become housebound due to weakness from this disease in late November 1903 (*Bio* 28). Tiredness or weakness is a frequent and prominent symptom in end-stage diabetes.[5] Her physical condition was not likely to permit her to have been out roaming hills looking for berries. By September 1904, she "was unable by this time to venture out at all and was very weak" (Gardner/Holford 48). Fr. Francis was spending a lot of time in Rednal with the two Tolkien boys because he was tutoring both of them (Bridoux, "Letting Images" 1): Ronald to be ready to resume classes at King Edward's and Hilary to pass the entrance examination for King Edward's—which he did in the fall of 1904.

The phrase, "Tea in Hay," could refer to an outing in a town by the name of 'Hay'.[6] In the county of West Midlands, which contains Birmingham and Rednal, there is a town, Hay Mills, which is an industrial area on the River Cole—an unlikely destination for a picnic. The nearby county of Warwickshire has no villages with 'Hay' in their name. It may, however, refer to Iverley Hay which is an area directly adjacent to Kinver, a popular tourist destination at the turn of the century. Iverley Hay in Staffordshire was one of three hays—hunting areas enclosed in hedges—in Kinver Forest. Forests were usually divided into hays for administrative purposes. The only other 'Hay' near this area is Beach-Hay well beyond Kidderminster and close to the Wyre Forest.[7]

There is also Boney Hay, a mining town near Lichfield, and Cheslyn Hay, another mining town, near Cannock, both in Staffordshire. Two other Staffordshire villages, the small villages of Offley Hay—Offleyhay—and Scot Hay, the last near Newcastle-under-Lyme, are not known as picnic venues. There are also three villages by the name of 'Hay Green': in Norfolk, Hertfordshire, and Essex counties, respectively. There is the well-known Hay on Wye in Wales. All of these towns are quite far from Rednal. "Tea in Hay" or nearby Kinver would have been a possible holiday excursion of Fr. Francis with the Tolkien brothers.

Kinver

On April 4, 1901, an electric tram-line, the Kinver Light Railway, was inaugurated to Kinver, and the rock houses there became an immediate tourist attraction with their residents serving teas and other refreshments. One of these teas may have been part of what Mabel Tolkien reported in her letter to Mary Tolkien about her sons' day trip. An outing to Kinver was very popular on bank holidays.[8] At one point, Martindale's Tea Gardens at Kinver's Edge, across from the town of Kinver, advertised it could provide "covered accommodation" for two hundred people.[9] Hundreds of thousands of people were carried on the railway each year—as many as 20,000 on a single day. The line, which was unique because it was developed for tourism, was also successful in developing other traffic including a daily milk service and the transportation of parcels, livestock, and other goods (Collins). Two books have been written about this uncommon tram: Collins's *The Kinver Light Railway* (2012) and Bills and Griffith's *By Tram to Kinver: 1901-1930* (1980).

Kinver, by the River Stour, lies about fifteen miles west of Birmingham and ten miles south of Wolverhampton. From Rednal where Mabel Tolkien and her sons were living, the easiest route to Kinver would have been to take the train at Rednal toward Birmingham to Dudley and pick up the connecting line to Amblecote. The Kinver Light Railway ran from Amblecote to Kinver—a distance of about four-and-a-half miles. Kinver was advertised as the "Switzerland of the Midlands," a perfect getaway from the dirty skies of the industrial heartland of Birmingham and the Black Country—the local name for the polluted and grimy industrial area of Birmingham and its environs. In Kinver and its pastoral environs, travelers could enjoy countryside walks, family picnics, teas, and fresh air.[10] From the top of the hill above the rock houses, now revealed as harboring the remains of an Iron Age hill fort, the Malvern Hills to the south-west and the Cotswold Hills to the south can be seen. The tramway company offered a guidebook with a choice of eight walks of varying length and difficulty.[11]

If Mabel Tolkien did not go on the excursion to Kinver due to her weakness, then the excited reports from the two boys may have been a jumble of information that included the name 'Iverley Hay'. The Iverley area was not on

1. 1903 photograph of the typical one-decker "toastrack" cars that plied the line fully loaded

the Kinver tramline. The site was approximately three miles east, south/east from Kinver. Iverley took its name from Iverley or High house, built by Edward Millward, Esq. of Wollescot at the top of "Hay-hill" (Wi. Scott 183). The Hay is described as a "pleasant and desirable site" (Wi. Scott 77).

The town of Kinver dates to at least Anglo-Saxon times, and the earliest form of the name, as 'Cynibre', appears in a charter of 736 AD. The first element is commonly, but probably incorrectly, derived from *cyne-* 'royal' (Old English) or possibly a Celtic root *cuno-* 'dog'. Following this view of the Old English origin of Kinver, the second element of the name was then assumed to be *-bre* (Middle English) referring to a steep hill, probably Kinver Edge (Watts 349).[12] The possible 'royal'/*cyne* part of the name might have been understood to refer to Eanberht, one of the last kings of the Hwicce (Wiccia) nation before the rule of King Offa of the Mercians.[13] This type of etymology based on Anglo-Saxon is likely to be what Ronald would have heard or inferred at the time in the early 1900s when Britain's nationalistic and patriotic view of its origins was strong. This Anglo-Saxon etymology would resonate with the interest in Anglo-Saxon which Ronald Tolkien's teacher, George Brewerton, had already awakened (*Bio* 27-28).

After the Norman conquest of England in the eleventh century, Kinver, which was surrounded by productive farmland and which was on the main route from Bristol to Chester, began to grow and become an important market town.[14]

Kinver Edge is the massive sandstone escarpment just west of Kinver, on the border between Worcestershire and Staffordshire, England. This soft Triassic-era stone is very easily quarried and natural caves can be quickly enlarged to form habitats. When the first caves at Kinver Edge were carved is unknown, but similar rock-cut chambers in the neighboring county of Shropshire were made as early as 700 AD. Although there are also rock houses at Nanny's and Vale's Rock at Kinver Edge, the houses at Holy Austin are the better-known ones. These houses were arranged in three layers around a knob of rock called the Holy Austin (Johnson 604). Local tradition holds that an Augustine monk once had his hermitage here. It seems likely that the first permanent inhabitants of the Rock Houses were the descendants of the local quarrymen from Kinver who began quarrying rock in the middle of the seventeenth century.[15]

In his 1777 guide book, Joseph Heely of Birmingham published the first description of the modern homes at Kinver Edge. Heely describes the rock home, where he took shelter from a storm, as "curious, warm and commodious and the garden extremely pretty." The owners were proud of their pleasant homes, which were well furnished. Most of the houses had only two rooms, as was typical for working-class people, with one for living in and one for sleeping, with a storeroom at the back. Each room had a fireplace cut into the rock, with a slanted chimney flue taking the smoke towards the outer wall.[16] The interior walls were generally whitewashed or plastered (Johnson 604), and niches could easily be carved for cupboards, windows, or doorways.[17] Rooms could be larger and ceilings higher than in the cottages in town and could be divided as families grew or lodgers were taken in.[18] Rent reportedly varied from one [shilling]-and-sixpence to two [shillings]-and-sixpence weekly (Johnson 604). Ceilings sometimes showed the cross-stratification of the ancient sand dunes that created the Kinver Sandstone. Some residences had wooden flooring laid down (Johnson 604), and some floors were tiled. Rooms could run completely through the rock so that there was a front and back view (Johnson 604).[19]

Kinver Edge provided fresh air and open space and was considered better than the Kinver village with its smoke and risk of river flooding. The rock houses stayed dry due to the impermeable, dull reddish-purple Bunter Pebble Beds that overlay the red Lower Mottled Sandstone.[20] A deep well provided water for the rock houses, and sanitation was by earth closets.[21] By the nineteenth century, the dwellings were improved by the addition of brick walls.[22] The rock houses stayed cool in the summer and warm in the winter. There was almost no problem with cave-ins and pegs driven into the wall held securely (Johnson 604). "Most of the dwellings had a modern stove or kitchen range sunk into the rock" (Johnson 604). Some rock houses were owner-occupied, but most were rented to farm laborers, tradesmen, or workmen in local industries. They kept "sloping gardens" that were "neatly kept" (Johnson 604). Inside the restored Fletcher's Cottage, the main living area includes a large fireplace, a dining table, a bathtub, and a few traditional toys.

The serving of teas to visitors by local inhabitants from their rock homes was one of the special attractions and pleasures of a visit to Kinver.[23] The 1861 census lists eleven families living here, totaling forty-four people, across the three levels.[24] When families entertained visitors, certainly the views from the windows over the valley would have been admired and the furnishings would have been inviting and comfortable. The orchards of apple and pear trees provided the fruits the Kinver cave dwellers made into jam for the teas they offered.[25]

"Comfort" is the distinguishing mark of a hobbit home. Although Ronald Tolkien was likely to have been aware of the cave dwellings of Nottingham and Shropshire, as well as prehistoric pit dwellings and *fogous*, none of these would have been as personally memorable as the homey, comfortable rock dwellings at Kinver. "Comfort" was not a quality of the souterrain near the village of Naours in Picardy, near the staging area of the Battle of the Somme in World War I, or even the German dugouts that Tolkien saw during that battle. The enlarged caves of Picardy were a bare "refuge," more in keeping with the Caves of Aglarond behind Helm's Deep in Rohan or the cave behind the waterfall in Ithilien used by Faramir's rangers (*TT* III vii 526; IV v 659).

Several considerations point to the likelihood that the Kinver Rock Houses served as a possible model for hobbit holes. The first is the popularity and easy access of this tourist attraction for the Birmingham area at a time when Ronald and his brother were spending time with Fr. Francis. Another consideration is the many parallels of these residences with hobbit holes. Although there are no round doors or windows; tiled floors, a soot-free habitat, cupboard-like storage in pantries and wardrobes, and windows that "look[ed] over his garden and meadows beyond, sloping down to the river [...] that ran at the foot of The Hill" are all details redolent of the Kinver rock houses (*H* I). When the hobbits repair the damage of Sharkey and his gang, "the bricks were used to repair many an old hole, to make it snugger and drier" (*RK* VI ix 999), just as bricks were used at Kinver. The restoration of the rock houses at Holy Austin "was accurately based on the many photographs from times past and the many memories buzzing to be heard."[26] Bilbo's front door was painted green (*H* I), like the doors and shutters of Kinver Edge based on this historical research. The families who lived in the Kinver rock houses were noted for their longevity, like certain hobbit families.[27]

Bilbo Baggins's hobbit hole is the reader's introduction to the concept of hobbits. A hobbit hole is a smial: "A word peculiar to hobbits (not Common Speech), meaning 'burrow'; [...] It is a form that the Old English word *smygel* 'burrow' might have had, if it had survived. The same Old English word appears in Gollum's real name, *Sméagol*" (Lobdell, "Guide to the Names in *The Lord of the Rings*" 214; *RK* Appendix F "On Translation" 1110). The Kinver rock houses were definitely burrowed into the sandstone. Bilbo's hobbit hole was specifically excavated for Belladonna by Bilbo's father (*H* I).

Belladonna Took, the mother of Bilbo Baggins, is modeled on Mabel Tolkien, Ronald's mother (*Bio* 175). Given that Mabel was in the terminal stages of diabetes and was not likely to have been able to handle the effort that such a jaunt would require, she could still have enjoyed the boys' recounting their adventures and discoveries and perhaps even their enthusiasm for living in such a residence. The special summer of 1904 was associated with Mabel being able to enjoy both of her sons as witnessed in her letter to her mother-in-law.

The Tolkien brothers' special, final summer with their mother in Rednal can be seen in Hilary's recall of his childhood in his notebook. Late in life, Hilary began recording in a notebook memories from when he lived in Sarehole in 1899, but then he skipped four or five years to make a series of observations specific to the stay at Rednal including "Tree Climbing." He wrote that "[w]e used to live a big part of the summer up trees, particularly a certain sycamore" where they enjoyed pulling up a basket full of "nice things to munch" (H. Tolkien 28). Perhaps Ronald incorporated these happy memories into the character of the Galadhrim who live in Mallorn trees which, like the sycamore, are very tall.

Ronald Tolkien seems to have kept alive the memories of this summer respite, before his mother's death that following November, not only in his evocative creation of Belladonna Took's hobbit hole, but perhaps also through his life-long and well-known habit of pipe smoking, copied from Fr. Francis Morgan's habit of pipe smoking at Rednal (*Bio* 30). Ronald's pipe smoking did not, in fact, include actual smoking because he never inhaled, except by accident (S. Tolkien). The idiosyncratic view that pipe smoking is a way to remember someone comes to the fore in Ronald Tolkien having three characters in *The Lord of the Rings*—Théoden, Aragorn, and Bilbo—who recommend pipe smoking as an act of commemoration (*RK* V vi 824, *RK* V viii 851, *RK* VI vi 965). The memory of this brief, final time with his mother and a lovely summer outing, "Tea in Hay," which Ronald could share with his mother for her enjoyment, may be linked here. After all, what does Bilbo do, but invite Gandalf to tea in his hobbit hole?

Catholicism and Tolkien's Mercian Roots

In 1904, with Fr. Francis as their chaperon, the party was more than likely to stop at the church of St. Peter in Kinver and ponder its roots in early Catholic history. A long-standing, local tradition holds that the parish church of St. Peter was dedicated by Wulfere, King of Mercia (succeeded 657), in memory of his sons, Wulphad and Ruffius, whom he killed in anger when they converted to Christianity (Seisdon Council Guide, 1966). This legend may have resonated with Ronald. Not only his mother, but also Ronald, one of two brothers, faced hostility and family ostracism because of a conversion to Catholicism.

Ronald had already read Rhŷs's *Celtic Britain* by the time of this likely visit to Kinver (*C&G* 2.214). He would have known from Rhŷs that Bede records that in 627 the Northumbrian King converted to Christianity when he married his queen who was a Christian from Kent (128). Bede also reports that the rulers and people of the Hwicce kingdom were Christian (193). Kinver was part of this Hwicce kingdom. The Celtic tribe of Hwicce, or Huicii of Bede, was earlier known as the Jugantes in Tacitus. They were early converts to Christianity, possibly converted during the Roman occupation or later by Celtic Christians, rather than by missionaries from Pope Gregory I (Manco). A twelfth-century chronicler of Worcester comments that Worcester was selected as the seat of the bishop because it was the capital of the Hwicce ("Chronicle" 379), and there are probable, early Christian burials beneath Worcester Cathedral (C. Thomas 253-71).

In a letter of January 1945 to his son Christopher, Ronald Tolkien wrote that things of ancestral or ethnic and linguistic significance "attract me and stick in my memory." He then reminded Christopher that "you are a Mercian or Hwiccian" (*Letters* 108). In 628, according to the *Anglo-Saxon Chronicle*, the kingdom of the Hwicce, established in 577, became an allied or client state of Mercia after Penda of Mercia's success at the Battle of Cirencester. Mercia, led by Earl Æthelred, whose name points to a possible Hwicce origin, submitted to King Alfred about 877–883. Memories of the Hwicce lingered in place names like 'Wychwood' or 'wood of the Hwicca' by the Rollright Stones in the Cotswold Hills at the edge of Warwick (Hooker, *Tolkien and Welsh* 172), which must have piqued Tolkien's scholarly interest (Shippey, *Road* 266).

Although the doings of little kingdoms in the seventh century seem obscure to modern readers, for Ronald Tolkien, this was the "age of Bede," meaning The Venerable Bede, an English monk and chronicler (672/3–735). Tolkien explicitly stated that the *Beowulf* poet, author of the greatest poem in Old English and the earliest vernacular European epic, lived in the "age of Bede" or approximately 700-730 AD (*The Monsters* 20). Ronald Tolkien felt a closeness to this poet to such an extent that he felt he "*knew what the poet had been thinking*" (Shippey, "*Beowulf*-poet" 2, italics in original). As a descendent of a long line of Mercians from his mother's Suffield family, who had lived on the same soil and had spoken the same ancestral language as the *Beowulf* poet, Ronald Tolkien believed he had a "privileged insight" into the poet's intent (Shippey "*Beowulf*-poet" 5). Tolkien saw the *Beowulf*-poet as an early Catholic looking back at a heathen age. The Hwiccian past and its language and the history of Catholicism present in Kinver, along with memories of his mother's vicarious pleasure from an outing with Fr. Francis, could become part of the "leaf mould of his mind" "what you might call the heart, the emotional side" that Tolkien used in his writing (*Bio* 126; Lee, "Tolkien" 158-59). Ronald Tolkien "nourished the seeds of his imagination" "almost exclusively upon *early* experience, sufficiently broken down by time" (*Bio* 126, italics in the original).

Carpenter wrote that he left out "*several* difficult issues" in the Tolkien biography ("Cover book," italics added). Given the lack of specific details for the important year of 1904 (e.g. when the two Tolkien boys became sick, how long they were sick with each disease, and who became sick first), one of these "difficult issues" may include other events of the year of 1904 when Mabel Tolkien died. Consequently, it is reasonable to wonder if a memory of Ronald Tolkien's childhood, like a daytrip with Fr. Francis Morgan in 1904 to "Tea in Hay," could be part of the "leaf mould" that was used to create the Shire (*Bio* 126; Lee, "Tolkien" 158-59).

End Notes

1 "Important letter regarding the publication of The Lord of the Rings on auction (11.02.14)." Pieter Collier, https://tolkienlibrary.com/press/1142-tolkien-letter-to-cotton-minchin-regarding-publication-of-the-lord-of-the-rings.php, accessed on 6/19/2022. Underlining is in the original.
2 Derdziński, Ryszard, "John Benjamin Tolkien (1807-1896): a grandfather, a philanthropist, a religious man" Friday, January 5, 2018, http://tolkniety.blogspot.com/, accessed on 10/5/2023.
3 Derdziński, Ryszard, "John Benjamin Tolkien (1807-1896): a grandfather, a philanthropist, a religious man" Friday, January 5, 2018, http://tolkniety.blogspot.com/, accessed on 10/5/2023.
4 Ronald and Hilary Tolkien spent school holidays with the Mountain family and their children, Dorothy and Kenneth (*C&G* 2.814).
5 "Caring for Someone with End-stage Diabetes." https://santecares.com/2019/10/07/caring-for-someone-with-end-stage-diabetes/, accessed on 5/29/2022.
6 "Tea in Hay" could possibly suggest a meal or picnic in a hayfield or more likely a field enclosed by a hedge or 'hay'. The fact 'Hay' is capitalized does not mean it is a proper name, given Mabel Tolkien's idiosyncratic and variable orthography, which Carpenter appears to have tried to reproduce accurately.
7 "Kinver Rock Houses-The Original Hobbit Holes?" *Britain Explorer.com*, accessed on 5/1/2015, no longer available.
8 These are public holidays in the United Kingdom, like federal holidays in the United States, as well as other days when banks are closed
9 Paul Collins's *The Kinver Light Railway Facebook page*: https://www.facebook.com/people/The-Kinver-Light-Railway/100057309954187/, accessed on 5/30/2022.
10 The rock houses of England's last cave people: Kinver Edge, Staffordshire." accessed on 5/29/2022. https://www.theguardian.com/travel/2020/oct/02/kinver-edge-black-country-to-tea-englands-last-cave-people.
11 Collins's *The Kinver Light Railway* https://www.facebook.com/people/The-Kinver-Light-Railway/100057309954187/.
12 The –bre root is found in the name of Ronald Tolkien's village, 'Bree'. Given that the Hwicce were a Celtic tribe, a Celtic origin for the name 'Kinver' should be considered. KINVER or KINFARE in "Welsh Cefn *mawr* [is] 'great ridge', the m in mawr is sounded like v or is in Cornish *Cein* or Irish *Ceann* 'head, great head'" (Duignan 121). Given the presence of Celtic people in the area, this gloss may be more historically appropriate. The Anglo-Saxon invaders commonly took over earlier names, like 'Kinver', not knowing their meanings. They then may have reinterpreted the name, perhaps with a slight change in pronunciation, to create a suitable meaning in Old English, a linguistic process known as hyper-correction. The Celtic provenance of 'Kinver' would probably not have been acknowledged in the early 1900s given the history of opposition to and dislike of the Welsh. Only later in Ronald Tolkien's career as a philologist, armed with a knowledge of Welsh, would Ronald have understood the complexities of this kind of British place-name.
13 Kinver Rock Houses-The Original Hobbit Holes?" *Britain Explorer.com*. No longer available.
14 "The rock houses that inspired Tolkien." https://www.amusingplanet.com/2017/10/the-rock-houses-that-inspired-tolkien.html, accessed on 5/29/2022.
15 "The rock houses that inspired Tolkien." https://www.amusingplanet.com/2017/10/the-rock-houses-that-inspired-tolkien.html, accessed on 5/29/2022.
16 "The rock houses that inspired Tolkien." https://www.amusingplanet.com/2017/10/the-rock-houses-that-inspired-tolkien.html. accessed on 5/29/2022.
17 "The Black Country Geological Society Newsletter No. 35, October 1982,

accessed on 5/29/2022. https://bcgs.info/pub/wp-content/uploads/newsletters/BCGS_Newsletter035.pdf.

18 "Kinver Edge and the Rock Houses." https://www.nationaltrust.org.uk/kinver-edge-and-the-rock-houses, accessed on 5/29/2022.

19 "The Black Country Geological Society Newsletter No. 35, October 1982, accessed on 5/29/2022. https://bcgs.info/pub/wp-content/uploads/newsletters/BCGS_Newsletter035.pdf.

20 "The Black Country Geological Society Newsletter No. 35, October 1982, accessed on 5/29/2022. https://bcgs.info/pub/wp-content/uploads/newsletters/BCGS_Newsletter035.pdf.

21 "Kinver Edge and the Rock Houses." https://www.nationaltrust.org.uk/kinver-edge-and-the-rock-houses, accessed on 5/29/2022.

22 "The Black Country Geological Society Newsletter No. 35, October 1982, accessed on 5/29/2022. https://bcgs.info/pub/wp-content/uploads/newsletters/BCGS_Newsletter035.pdf.

23 "Teas and tourism." "Kinver Edge and the Rock Houses." https://www.nationaltrust.org.uk/kinver-edge-and-the-rock-houses, accessed on 5/29/2022.

24 "Kinver Edge and the Rock Houses." https://www.nationaltrust.org.uk/kinver-edge-and-the-rock-houses, accessed on 5/29/2022.

25 "The rock houses of England's last cave people: Kinver Edge, Staffordshire," accessed on 5/29/2022. https://www.theguardian.com/travel/2020/oct/02/kinver-edge-black-country-to-tea-englands-last-cave-people.

26 "Restoration of Holy Austin Rock." https://www.nationaltrust.org.uk/kinver-edge-and-the-rock-houses/features/life-in-a-rock-house, accessed on 6/1/2022.

27 "Kinver Rock Houses-The Original Hobbit Holes?" *Britain Explorer.com* no longer available.

Chapter Two

The 1897 Diamond Jubilee and the Long Awaited Party

Nancy Bunting & Seamus Hamill-Keays

Ronald Tolkien wrote he was "brought up in an 'almost rural' village of Warwickshire on the edge of the prosperous bourgeoisie of Birmingham (about the time of the Diamond Jubilee!) I take my models like anyone else—from such 'life' as I know" (*Letters* 235). Ronald had an excellent memory for childhood events, recalling images from just before the age of three when the family lived in Bloemfontein (*Bio* 15, also *TFA* 18). Tolkien wrote that words like 'gamgee' and 'cotton' are "like most of the Shire derived from [my] childhood."[1]

Ronald did witness the Diamond Jubilee celebrations because he could recall coming up the hill from Sarehole to the Moseley Botanical Gardens, the site of the fireworks, located on the corner of Wake Green and College Roads on the grounds of Pine Dell Hydropathic Establishment (previously Spring Hill College) (W. Foster "An Early History").[2] The Botanical Gardens were not a public park and charged a small admission fee.

Although Ronald would have been only five at the time, the drama and excitement of this unique and "long-expected" event appear to resurface in Ronald Tolkien's description of Bilbo Baggins's "long-expected" party in *The Lord of the Rings*, because, as stated in the quote above, he took his models from such 'life' as he knew. He called his years at Sarehole "the longest-seeming and most formative part of my life" (*Bio* 24). In *The Lord of the Rings*, Tolkien easily evokes the flavor of the time of the Jubilee with its intense anticipation, gossip, and speculation about the preparations and entertainments to be provided as well as the anxiety surrounding the possibility of bad weather (*FR* I i 24-26). £250, equivalent to £34,622.83 or $43,736.57 in 2022, was allocated for the Queen's Diamond Jubilee in Moseley, and festoons and bunting decorated the shops near Moseley Green and the church (Hewston 39-40).[3]

In 1897, an exciting event like this would be treated as a day-long entertainment, much like the guests at the long-expected party who showed up by "elevenses" and stayed through the various meals until the fireworks. For the Diamond Jubilee in Moseley, six hundred children from St. Mary's Day and Sunday Schools and Oxford Road Sunday School sang the national anthem on the Moseley Green and then formed a procession to the large meadow Moor Green for sporting activities and a meal while the "elderly ate theirs at home" (Hewston 39-40). After planting two trees, singing the national anthem again, and having a tea; "Mrs. Heaven gave each child a medal" and "a toy." Given that children received toys (if at all) only on their birthdays and Christmas, many of the young participants may have felt that this was like a giant birthday party.[4] Certainly there was a gathering of friends and families to witness and admire the children's parade and games and to enjoy such a spectacle.

2. Moseley Botanical Gardens probably in 1893

Each Sunday since her husband's death, Mabel Tolkien had been attending the 'high' Anglican church, which was "a long walk" from Sarehole (*Bio* 23).[5] This would be St. Mary's in Moseley. Mabel had been baptized at the Anglican cathedral of St. Andrew and St. Michael in Bloemfontein on May 24, 1891 by William Crisp, the Archdeacon of the cathedral, with Arthur Tolkien as one of the two witnesses.[6] Ronald was baptized on January 31, 1892 in Bloemfontein Cathedral, and his godfather, G. Edward Jelf, was the son of Canon G.E.

Jelf. Canon Jelf was associated with the Oxford Movement, which sought to introduce earlier, and consequently Roman Catholic traditions, into Anglican liturgy and orthodoxy (Ordway, *Tolkien's Faith* 15).

Church attendance was the only exception to the rule that no lady in "deep" or full mourning, like Mabel Tolkien, attended social events.[7] As a likely attendee of the St. Mary's Sunday School, young Ronald Tolkien would have been included in the sports or games, marched with the procession which may have had some musical accompaniment that would have also backed the singing of the national anthem, and have received a toy. Ronald shared his mother's enthusiasm for marching band music, pageants, parades, fireworks, and love of the Queen (Grotta-Kurska 19). Like Bilbo's birthday party, the Diamond Jubilee celebration had at times "merely lots of people eating and drinking" and also "songs, dances, music, games" in the children's activities as Hewlett records (*FR* I i 27).

Tolkien wrote the "presents were unusually good" at Bilbo's party and some of the toys had "been ordered a year before." Birmingham was touted as the "Toy Shop of the World," or at least of Europe, in the nineteenth century because the city was known not so much for great factories but for many small workshops producing crafts by skilled artisans (Burns, "local habitation" 30, 28). The residents of Moseley were likely to know the best local toymakers resulting in "unusually good" presents. To provide toys for six hundred children in 1897, the organizers would have needed to order the toys the preceding year.

At Bilbo's party, "Many young hobbits [like Ronald Tolkien, and probably some of his cousins, like Marjorie and Mary Incledon, Eric Mitton, and the Hadley children] were included and present by parental permission; for hobbits were easy-going with their children in the matter of sitting up late, especially when there was a chance of a free meal" (*FR* I i 28).[8] The parade participants had lunch and tea provided and did stay up late because the fireworks did not start until after dark (which would mean, in modern terms, after 9 pm American Central Daylight Time, with daylight savings) because the June 20, 1897 date coincided almost exactly with the summer solstice, the longest day of the year.

The Jubilee's date of June 20, 1897 may have posed certain problems for Mabel Tolkien due to her husband's death on February 15, 1896. Victorian mourning etiquette was very strict, especially for widows, and mourning lasted for more than two years. In contrast, children only dressed for mourning for a period of six months. After one year and a day, Mabel Tolkien no longer wore "full," "deep," or "first" mourning. During that period, her black dress, preferably of a dull material like bombazine, was entirely covered by dull black crepe and she wore a white widow's cap indoors. In "second" mourning (during the time of the Jubilee), she still would have dressed all in black or "widow's weeds" (from the Old English *waed*, meaning 'garment'), but the black crepe veil, which previously covered her face in public, was now lifted and worn back over the head and her dress was only trimmed with crepe. Second mourning lasted six months. This was followed by "ordinary" mourning for six months when black or black-and-white dresses in any fabric were allowed as well as ribbons, jet (black) jewelry, and buttons (Flanders 340-46, 378-79). Attendance at a public celebration might have bordered on social impropriety, but Mabel's willingness to exchange secret letters with her eventual fiancé, Arthur Tolkien, and later to accompany her husband on business in South Africa indicates that social norms were not always compelling for her (*Bio* 9, McIlwaine 116). The unique circumstance of the Jubilee may have also given Mabel Tolkien some leeway.

Bilbo Baggins's birthday party in *The Lord of the Rings* features a gathering of relatives: "Practically everybody living near was invited," and the few overlooked ones "turned up all the same" (*FR* I i 26, 29). In 1897, Ronald Tolkien had lots of relatives who would have come to see the children's parade and the attendant games and celebrations. May and Mabel's father, John Suffield, Mabel's sister Jane, and the boarder, Edwin Neave, Jane's future husband (perhaps one of the overlooked ones?), lived nearby in King's Heath. It is uncertain if May (née Suffield) Incledon and her children were back from South Africa in 1897, though the directory of 1895 and 1897 lists Walter Incledon. (They certainly would have been in Moseley by October 1899, when the Second Boer War started.) Walter's parents and two brothers lived close by in Moseley. Mabel was in contact with her husband Arthur's widowed mother, Mrs. John B. or Mary Tolkien, who was the same age as Mabel's father. According to 1897 *Kelly's Directory*, Mary Tolkien was living at "Beachwood" on Church Road and almost certainly would have come by to see her grandchildren in the parade and to have a fine view of the fireworks.[9]

Arthur Tolkien had five siblings who survived into adulthood. Mabel's brother-in-law, T.E. Mitton with his wife, Mabel Mitton (née Tolkien), and family would have been likely to be present. In 1896, they were living on Anderton Park Road in Moseley. T.E. Mitton ran a successful brass foundry and was a member of the Central Literary Association. He probably knew John Suffield from both of these activities (Burns "Jane Suffield," "John Suffield"). His oldest son, Eric, who was four years older than Ronald Tolkien, and his younger son, Ewart, five years younger than Ronald, would attend King Edward's School as did Ronald (Burns "Thomas Ewart Mitton"). Arthur Tolkien, Mabel's deceased husband, had also been a member of the Central Literary Society and a student at King Edward's School, like T.E. Mitton.

Arthur Tolkien's brother, Laurence Tolkien, lived on Middleton Hall Road in King's Norton, five miles southwest of Chantry Road, Moseley in 1904 and could have come (*C&G* 1.12). He had a continuing interest in Ronald because Laurence paid the fees for King Edward's School in 1900 and appears to have briefly given the Tolkien brothers a home in 1904 after Mabel's death (McIlwaine 132, *C&G* 1.12).

In the 1891 census, Arthur Tolkien's sister, Florence Tolkien Hadley, her husband, and two children, one and two years older than Ronald, lived very close to John Suffield's home at 9 Ashfield Road, just off of Cotton Lane on Grove Avenue. Tom Hadley was a solicitor and later a commissioner (or notary as an American would say) and could afford such a fine neighborhood. Tolkien noted that "*Cotton Lane* was a name of importance in my early childhood" and "[d]own Cotton Lane I used to walk as a child to my [Tolkien] grandmother's house." [10]This last is an accurate description because one actually walks downhill from Ashfield to Church Road on Cotton Lane on a long slope. Also, Ashfield Road, where the Suffield grandparents lived, was a continuation of Cotton Lane and was called Cotton Lane at one time (Burns "Jane Suffield"). By 1897, the Hadleys were living close to one end of Cotton Lane at "Glenthorne" at the corner of Wake Green and Mayfield Roads.

John Suffield, Mabel Tolkien's father, was one of nine siblings, some of whom would have been expected to come. His brother, Mark Oliver, had been a partner in John Suffield's failed brass foundry of the 1880s as well as a student at King Edward's. In 1897, Mark Oliver was living nearby at 6 Brighton Road, Moseley. Another brother, Joseph, was a 'victualler'. That is, he ran a restaurant, at Union Passage Hotel, Birmingham.[11] He could have provided some catering for the festivities. William, May and Mabel's younger brother, was living in Acocks Green in 1897 and 1899, and Ronald recalled walking to visit an uncle in Acocks Green (*C&G* 2.8). And those are just the relatives that we know of. Like the guests of the long-expected party, the crowd at the 1897 Jubilee would include some who "had hardly ever been in Hobbiton [read Moseley] before, as they lived in remote corners of the Shire" (*FR* I i 28).

Gandalf's fireworks were the principal attraction at Bilbo's birthday party. Tolkien loved fireworks, and the spectacular display for the Diamond Jubilee seems to have lingered in his memory (Lee, "Tolkien in Oxford" 149). Although we do not have a report of the Moseley fireworks, the Jubilee fireworks over Birmingham's Calthorpe park started with "an aerial maroon [a firework that makes a loud bang] exploding at an immense height with a loud report" like Gandalf's thunderclaps and the "deafening explosion" of the dragon at the end of the Hobbiton display. The maroon was followed by "a shower of electric rain" comparable to Gandalf's "red thunderstorm and a shower of yellow rain" (*FR* I i 27). A "glowing palm tree of the tropics, spreading golden branches springing from a stem with revolving centre of iridescent hues" resembles Gandalf's "green trees with trunks of dark smoke" and "shining branches;" and "fiery snakes, silver streamers." "A revolving wheel of golden fire [...] terminating with the explosion of fiery serpents, cobras, and scorpions" recalls the "forest of silver spears" that dissolve with "a hiss of a hundred hot snakes" at Bag End.[12]

Bilbo's birthday party also features a sudden burst of light, which covers Bilbo's escape, courtesy of Gandalf. Birmingham began to have electricity after 1882, and the Moseley Botanical Gardens had electricity in time for the Jubilee and displayed "fairy lights"—the small colored electric lights used at festivals (e.g. Christmas lights)—as part of the celebration (Blackham 26-27, *C&G* 1.6). Although Gandalf is responsible for the sudden blinding burst of the illumination at Bilbo's birthday party, the Moseley Garden's "fairy lights" could have been dramatically extinguished for the best view of the fireworks. Although shutting electric lights off may seem unremarkable to the jaded mind of the twenty-first century, this would have been truly impressive when Tolkien was five years old. In Sarehole, he would have been familiar with candles, oil lamps, and a fireplace or stove. Ronald Tolkien wrote, "[m]y memory is pictorial" (*Letters* 343). Tolkien's approach to creating a fictional Secondary World was often the result of reversing language and experiences from the Primary World, here a fictional burst of light in *The Lord of the Rings* as opposed to the dousing of a light so strange and unique to a five year old in 1897.[13]

In the 1968 BBC interview, Ronald Tolkien said:

> But, of course, in the process of writing *The Hobbit* [...] an awful lot gets tied up; your own present situation, your past, the things you would like to do, the things you have done, and so that it's simply full, of course, of memories for me (Lee, "Tolkien in Oxford" 140).

The only specifically documented memories that contributed to *The Hobbit* come from Ronald Tolkien's report that the number of Thorin and company's members and the "thunder-battle" in the Misty Mountains originated from his 1911 Swiss walking tour (*Letters* 309). In addition, Carpenter reveals that Belladonna Took, her sisters, and the Old Took in *The Hobbit* were all characters based on Mabel Tolkien and her family of origin (*Bio* 175). Since The Shire is "full, of course, of memories for me [Ronald]," other undocumented possibilities seem likely. One compelling candidate for an undocumented childhood memory that supplied material not only for *The Hobbit*, but also for "New Hobbit or *The Lord of the Rings* is the "long expected" Queen Victoria's 1897 Diamond Jubilee as a potent source for Bilbo's "long expected" birthday party. The catchphrase "long expected" was applied to both events, and the parallels between the two feature fireworks, presence of many family members and friends, food and drink, singing and music, and children's toys and games as if it were a birthday party.

End Notes

1 "Important letter regarding the publication of The Lord of the Rings on auction (11.02.14)." Pieter Collier, https://tolkienlibrary.com/press/1142-tolkien-letter-to-cotton-minchin-regarding-publication-of-the-lord-of-the-rings.php, accessed on 6/19/2022. Underlining is in the original.

2 Scull and Hammond (2017) state: Tolkien "will later recall walking through the river-meadows up the hill to the old college, Moseley Grammar School" (1.6). The old college did not become Moseley Grammar School until 1939.

3 "CPI Inflation Calculator." https://www.in2013dollars.com/uk/inflation/1897?amount=250 and "CPI Inflation Calculator." https://www.officialdata.org/uk/inflation/1897?amount=250. Convert to dollars with "XE Currency converter." https://www.xe.com/currencyconverter/convert/?Amount=34622.83&From=GBP&To=USD, accessed 5/5/2022.

4 Since 1903, with 1911 as the only exception, the monarch's birthday (actual or official) and the trooping of the color have occurred in June to take advantage of better weather. In the year 1897, the trooping of the color for Queen Victoria's birthday was held on May 24. Looking back, Tolkien could easily conflate the pageantry of the monarch's birthday celebration, typically held in June, with the June 1897 Jubilee so that the 1897 festivities were a function of a birthday celebration.

5 Mabel Suffield married Arthur Tolkien in the Anglican Cape Town Cathedral on April 16, 1891 (*Bio* 10). She may have associated the 'high' Anglican Church service with her husband so that she did not consider the nearby Anglican St. Agnes's church, also in Moseley. Going to church in central Moseley may have also given her the opportunity to visit family members after the church service.

6 Derdziński, Ryszard, "Mabel Tolkien baptized in …1891!" Friday, January 5, 2018, http://tolkniety.blogspot.com/, accessed on 9/24 2023.

7 Victorian Era: Victorian Era Mourning Period Rituals, clothes to wear." http://victorian-era.org/victorian-era-mourning-period.html, accessed on 5/5/2022.

8 The modern reader has difficulty appreciating the relative cost of food at the turn of the twentieth century: "At the start of the First World War, food purchases consumed half the average paycheck; today the figure is six percent. According to the federal statistics, an American in 1919 had to work for two and a half hours to earn enough money to buy a chicken; these days it would take less than fifteen minutes of labour" ("Freedom from Fries." *The New Yorker*. November 2, 2015, p. 58). These figures are for Americans, but the figures should be comparable in England. The Federal Reserve Bank of Dallas published a table on the high cost of living in 1897 as compared to 1997 based on Sears Catalog prices (https://www.dallasfed.org/-/media/documents/fed/annual/1999/ar97.pdf). There is also a table on food prices. In the 1860s and 1870s, a British lower middle-class family with an income of £140 yearly spent £30 on rent, property taxes and water. Nearly £80 was spent on food (Flanders 224).

9 *Kelly's Directory* or, more completely, *Kelly's Office and Harrod & Co. Directory* was a trade directory in England that listed all businesses and tradespeople in a particular city or town, as well as a general directory of postal addresses of local gentry, landowners, charities, and other facilities. In effect, it was a Victorian version of the twentieth century's Yellow Pages. This house appears in *The Book of Ishness* in Tolkien's drawing, *Memories of My Grandmother's House*, drawn in January 1914 (*A&I* 66).

10 Hammond and Scull, *LotR, A Reader's Companion* 56; http://tolkiengateway.net / wiki/Letter to H. Cotton Minchin_(16_April_1956, accessed on 5/5/2022.

11 http://sueyounghistories.com /archives/2009/11/21/ john-suffield -1802-1891/, accessed on 5/5/2022.

12 "Historic England: Jubilee-ation: A History of Royal Jubilees in Public Parks"

by David Lambert, https://historicengland.org.uk/images-books/ publications/ jubilee-ation/jubilee-parks/, accessed on 5/5/2020.

13 Ronald Tolkien could call these "Mooreeffoc," originally a word created by Chesterton, "to denote the queerness of things that have become trite, when they are seen suddenly from a new angle" (OFS 146). See "J.R.R. Tolkien: Ambidexter" this volume for more examples of reversals.

Chapter Three

May Incledon, the Other Suffield Aunt

Nancy Bunting & Seamus Hamill-Keays

Edith Mary "May" Incledon (née Suffield) (1865-1936) was one of the three daughters of J.R.R. Tolkien's maternal grandfather, John Suffield, and his wife Emily Jane (née Sparrow). J.R.R. Tolkien, also referred to as Ronald Tolkien, used these three sisters as the source of the "three remarkable daughters of the Old Took" in *The Hobbit* with their father John Suffield as the Old Took (*Bio* 175). May Suffield was the eldest, with Mabel Suffield—Ronald Tolkien's mother—the middle one, and Emily Jane, or Jane, the youngest sister. Although new information and interest have emerged about Ronald Tolkien's relationship with his Aunt Jane (Morton, Morton/Hayes, Gardner/Holford), there has not been an effort to assess the importance of Mabel and Ronald Tolkien's relationships with May Incledon, the other Suffield aunt.

May and Mabel's outlooks appear to have converged in their simultaneous conversion to Catholicism on June 28, 1900 (Ordway, *Tolkien's Faith* Figure 5). Given that Mabel began instructing her sons in Catholicism almost immediately, and given that May had previously been Ronald Tolkien's godmother when he was baptized in the Church of England or Anglican Church, May is likely to have resumed these responsibilities as his Catholic godmother.[1] May's husband Walter, as would befit the son of a Church of England clergyman, intensely disapproved of the Catholic Church, and May appears to have coped with his outrage by not attending a Catholic church (*Bio* 24).

Before Mabel's death, the Tolkien boys spent time with their Incledon cousins, Marjorie (1891-1973) and Mary (1895-1940), which Ronald Tolkien recalled when writing his notes for "On Fairy-stories" (*TOFS* 234) and which Marjorie recalled late in life as "red letter days" (McIlwaine 164). Also, before Mabel's death, Ronald's Aunt May appears to have arranged a seaside holiday for the Tolkien brothers in 1902 at Torquay—a treat that she was financially equipped to subsidize.

After Mabel's death in 1904, when Ronald was only twelve, May appears to have gradually begun to act as a substitute mother for the Tolkien boys as they grew up. The boys spent holidays with their Incledon cousins, and the girls appeared to have shared Ronald Tolkien's interest in painting and spurred his interest in invented languages with their *Animalic* and later *Nevbosh*.

May Incledon, whose wealth can be seen in the Incledons' increasingly well-to-do address of "The Cottage" in Barnt Green in 1907, seems to have been the person most likely to have underwritten the expenses of Tolkien's rather lavish lifestyle, for a poor orphan, with inclusion on art tours in 1910 and 1912, a walking tour of Switzerland in 1911, membership in King Edward's Horse at Oxford in 1911, and the "expensive dinners" at Oxford University of 1913-1914 (*Bio* 59). May repeatedly appears during the crucial years of World War I: writing not only to Ronald, but also to Ronald's friends; hosting him and his fiancée Edith Bratt in 1915 before Ronald joined the military; almost certainly visiting him in the hospital in Birmingham on his return from the Western Front in 1916; and being present for Edith when their first son John was born in November 1917 when Ronald's military duties would not release him. Ronald appears to have lovingly commemorated his aunt's warmth and their relationship in scenes from his impromptu story, *Roverandom*.

Humphrey Carpenter's official Tolkien biography has limited information on Ronald Tolkien's Aunt May. Ronald identified himself with his mother's Suffield family, who came to Birmingham from Worcestershire: "I am a Suffield by tastes, talents, and upbringing, and any corner of that county [Worcestershire] (however fair or squalid) is in an indefinable way 'home' to me" (*Letters* 54). Exploring Ronald's relationship with his Aunt May and the Incledons, leads to a new understanding: of the social and financial standing of the Incledons, and of Ronald's relationship with his cousins as seen in the following sections on "The Suffields" and "The Incledons." In the section "Roman Catholicism," Walter Incledon's rejection of Mabel Tolkien's Catholicism seems pivotal to Ronald's view of what led to his mother's death and Ronald's solidarity with his cousin, Mary Incledon, who joined the Catholic Church and became a godmother to his first child. Aunt May seems to be a likely source of Ronald's familiarity with Jung and psychical research, which is apparent from his years at Oxford and possibly earlier. Finally, in "Roverandom and the Incledons,"

Ronald's visit to Torquay in 1902, a holiday likely to have been hosted by the Incledons, appears to supply models for his artwork as well as for incidents and characters in *Roverandom*. A final coda explores the possible contribution of the Incledon family to the genesis of *The Lord of the Rings*.

The Suffields

When May Suffield was born, her father John Suffield was probably thirty-two years old and her mother Emily Jane (née Sparrow) was twenty-seven. May had two older brothers: John, who was six years older than she, and Roland, who was a year older. Her sister Mabel was born in 1870 so she was five years younger than May, and Emily Jane was born two years later. The next child was William, who was nine years younger than May. He died at the age of thirty on February 27, 1904, and Mabel died on November 14 of that same year at the age of thirty-four. The youngest child was Rose, born when May was fourteen, and who died in 1886. The 1911 census shows that there had been ten children in all, with three dying in infancy (Burns, "Roland Suffield" 16).

We know nothing about May's early years except that when she was born, her father was managing his father's drapery business at Old Lamb House in central Birmingham and her mother was "kind and understanding" (*Bio* 16). The family drapery business went through several transformations. In 1881, May's father, known as "John Suffield the younger," his younger brother Mark Oliver Suffield, and Hector Coiwell—"all of Birmingham"—owned the "trade or business of Wholesale Drapers [...] at Union-passage and Crooked-lane, in Birmingham." That year, this business was transferred "to John Suffield the younger and Mark Oliver Suffield," thereby keeping it completely within the Suffield family (August 19, 1881 notice, *London Gazette*). On April 18, 1884, the Partnership among "John Suffield the elder, John Suffield the younger, and Mark Oliver Suffield, carrying on business as Wholesale Drapers, at Crooked-lane and Union-passage, Birmingham" was transferred to "John Suffield the younger and Mark Oliver Suffield in copartnership" (April 18, 1884 notice, *London Gazette*).

May's father went through several businesses with concomitant financial ups and downs. As a result, at the time of May's marriage to Walter Bury Incledon in the second quarter of 1890, May's family was probably living in a rental house at 90 Trafalgar Road, Moseley as reported in the 1891 census. Moseley was then still in the countryside, on one of the hills immediately south of Birmingham—a pleasant suburb with trees and large gardens including the Moseley Botanical Gardens. Moseley was part of the rural county of Worcestershire until 1911 (Burns "Jane Suffield").

Based on the 1891 census, the 1890 Suffield household included: May's parents, John and Emily Jane Suffield; her younger sister Jane, who was attending King Edward's School; her younger brother, seventeen-year-old Willie, listed as a clerk; and one live-in servant. Charles R. Helley, a brassfounder, was a boarder. Mr. Helley's presence shows that John Suffield maintained contact with the brass foundry industry as Mr. Suffield had owned a brass foundry, John Suffield and Co., in partnership with his brother Mark Oliver. This business failed in the late 1880s as did his drapery business. John Suffield then declared bankruptcy.[2] The 1891 census lists Mr. Suffield as a "commercial traveler," a position perhaps equivalent to a manufacturer's representative, for Jeyes Fluid. He enjoyed travel, and worked as a commercial traveler until the age of eighty-six (Burns "John Suffield"). However, in 1892, Emily Jane listed her father's occupation as iron founder on a form for Mason College (a forerunner of Birmingham University).

John Suffield was also a Unitarian preacher, but May Suffield does not appear to have married in the church of her local congregation as was traditional. May Suffield married in King's Norton, Birmingham probably at the local Anglican St. Nicholas church. It would not be surprising if Walter's father, Rev. Charles Incledon, a Church of England clergyman, presided because the Rev. Incledon was living in Moseley by 1895. Rev. Incledon's presence would have bolstered his son's opposition to Catholicism that so affected his wife May and her sister Mabel. Rev. Incledon was living with the Incledons at King's Norton in 1911 according to census data. He died in June, 1918 at King's Norton, Worcestershire.

At the time of the wedding, May would have been approximately twenty-five, an age when she was just beginning to be considered "old" for the marriage market. Walter would have been thirty years old. Because he would need to provide a home for wife and children, thirty was an expected age for a Victorian man to marry. Humphrey Carpenter reports that Walter had interests in the diamond and gold business in the Transvaal and the Orange Free State in 1893 (*Bio* 14). Although Walter was a definite "catch," that information is misleading, as we will see.

The Incledons

Walter Incledon was born February 19, 1860 in Sheffield, Yorkshire, England, and had at least six siblings (1939 Register). When Walter was born, his father Rev. Charles Porter Incledon was thirty-five years old, and his mother Eleanor W. was thirty. The records show that Walter's parents had married in 1852, and this was followed by the birth of an older brother, Charles Leonard, in 1853. Walter had two younger brothers, George Herbert (1873-1905) and Arthur (1871-1960) who were later associated with Walter's business. He had three younger sisters: Lilias (1867-1960), Eleanor Eliza (1865-1910), and Emily Mary (b. 1863-?).

Walter's father, Charles P., had a substantial resume. According to the records of Oxford University, Charles P. matriculated in 1844 at the age of eighteen, obtained a B.A. in 1847 and a M.A. in 1850. After graduating, he held various teaching jobs, but from 1870 to 1879, Rev. Incledon was the chaplain at Christ Church in Lille, France.[3]

Lille was a busy industrial city and river port, and the Anglican congregation there was composed mainly of British residents, employed in commercial or manufacturing businesses. According to the "History of Christ Church, Lille," Rev. Incledon was present for the opening of Christ Church, newly built in modern Gothic, on Ascension Day, 1870. In 1874, the parsonage was completed, with Rev. Incledon responsible for its design because no architect was hired. He also oversaw the 1877 remodeling of the space under the church that created a reading-room, library, lecture space, and Sunday School. As a result, from the age of ten until nineteen, Walter would have had considerable exposure to French language and culture even if he had been sent back to England for some of his schooling and left home before the age of nineteen.

The census of 1891 lists Walter Incledon as a "foreign accounts manager." Walter was probably working at Lloyd & Lloyd Ltd., Birmingham, one of the largest iron and steel makers in Britain. This is because when his brother George Herbert Incledon died in January 1905 and left his brother, "Walter Bury Incledon," in charge of his new and very profitable business, Walter is identified as a foreign accounts manager at Lloyd & Lloyd.[4] George Herbert was the founder of Cape Incledon, a manufacturer of steel pipe and tube in Cape Town, South Africa, and he too had previously worked at Lloyd and Lloyd.

By 1899, Lloyd & Lloyd Ltd. was the premier manufacturer of industrial pipes and tubes in England. By 1903, Lloyd & Lloyd Ltd. had technically become Stewarts & Lloyds due to its acquisition of one of the other largest iron and steel makers in Britain—A. & J. Stewart & Menzies Ltd. of Coatbridge, North Lanarkshire, Scotland. Walter's likely familiarity with French language and culture, gained during his years in Lille, would have been an asset in his role as a foreign accounts manager. Although English was the language of trade, French long retained the prestige as the language of diplomacy which might influence transactions of many kinds.

In 1893, Walter Incledon, as a probable Lloyd and Lloyd foreign accounts manager, "had interests in the diamond and gold business in the Transvaal and the Orange Free State" (*Bio* 14). At that time, Walter was accompanied by his wife May and their sixteen month old daughter Marjorie (born 11/10/1891, 1939 Register) when they visited Mabel, Arthur, and Ronald Tolkien in Bloemfontein, then the capital of the Boer Republic, the Orange Free State. In the 1901 census, Walter describes himself as "commercial manager wrought iron tube works," (i.e. of Lloyd and Lloyd).

Consequently, when Walter married May in 1890, he was already a "captain of industry." Moreover, when he took over his brother's booming business in 1905, the market for iron and steel pipe for South Africa's gold and diamond mines was taking off after the disruption of the Second Boer War of 1899-1902. Walter then might qualify as a "baron of industry." His managerial skills created the basis for his nephew, Gerald, to expand and reorganize the company in 1947 as Incledon and Lamberts so that this company has survived and thrived for more than one hundred years. These skills may reflect that Walter inherited his father's competent managerial abilities as seen in the building projects at Christ Church, Lille.

May evidently did not have the striking good looks of Mabel, nor the education of Jane; so her marriage was something of a social and financial coup for the Suffield family and père John Suffield. This impressive marriage may have fueled John Suffield's reluctance to accept more ordinary suitors.

Suitors were calling on the other two Suffield sisters in the 1890s. In 1894, Edwin Neave was already courting Jane, and Carpenter reports the family "thought him common" and was "horrified when she [Jane] became engaged to him" (*Bio* 18). By the time they married in 1905, Edwin was an established business man—an insurance inspector. Carpenter also reported that the "proud" John Suffield "tolerated" Mabel's husband, Arthur Tolkien (*Bio* 10). This attitude may have partly been the residue of Arthur Tolkien's inappropriate contact with Mabel in 1888 or Arthur's status, at that time, as only a bank employee and not a manager (*Bio* 9). Mabel daringly and immodestly arranged to have her sister Jane pass secret letters to Arthur when they were both on the platform of Birmingham's New Street Station. British sensitivity and routine scrutiny of status, class differences, and long-term financial prospects would have been relevant to any marriage opportunities for the Suffield daughters.

In 1891, Walter and May were living at 81 Gough Road, Moseley with one servant. This house was only a short distance from 69 Gough Road where Walter's mother and his two younger brothers, Arthur and George Herbert, ages twenty and eighteen, lived. Arthur and George are listed as "clerks," but we do not know if that was with Lloyd and Lloyd. Walter's father is listed as living there in 1895 and 1897. In the meantime, Walter was clearly keeping an eye on his mother and brothers.

In *Kelly's Directory* of 1895 and 1897, Walter is listed at 'Woodville'—the name of the house at 56 Chantry Road in Moseley. The name can still be seen above the door. In 1901, the Incledon household included a cook and a nursemaid—standard staff for a prosperous middle-class household. This is where May and Walter lived when Mabel Tolkien could walk up from Sarehole with her children to visit May and May's children—Marjorie, not quite two months older than Ronald Tolkien, and Mary (1895-1940), a year younger than Ronald's younger brother Hilary. The walk was about 1.75 miles or 2.8 km, but the Tolkien family may have taken a horse-drawn cab to Chantry Road. The most likely routes are shown on the map.

The residence at 56 Chantry Road is a brick, Victorian, semidetached house. Its paneled entrance or front door features a vertical stained glass transom and a portico with a carved and peaked pediment. This house was built in the 1890s along with the houses numbered 54 to 64.[5] The typical layout would have the front door opening onto a foyer with a handsome staircase to the first floor (English designation with American use labeling this the second floor) facing the door. There may have been decorative tile set in the foyer floor. From the foyer, one entered the front parlor on the left. It features a three-window bay. The windows are single-hung with a geometric pattern outlined with stained glass inserts in the top half. On the exterior, there are carved, decorative rectangular inlays over these windows. In its heyday, this room probably had cornices or other decorations on the ceiling and an ornately carved fireplace. The large chimney probably serviced this room and at least one other ornate fireplace in the dining room. The kitchen and servant quarters probably occupied the rest of the ground floor. Upstairs there is again another three-window bay. The windows are again single hung, with fifteen mullioned panes over three windows. The Incledons occupied this floor. On the second floor (i.e. attic), there are windows for what would have been the nursery suite. The dormers are half-timbered construction topped by a finial with a cross. There is a large backyard which was likely to have included a lawn and flower garden.

The house was strategically located near the tram line that could take Walter into Birmingham for business, as shown in the accompanying map. However, it was not so close that the loud and frequent noise of the trains, or of the sometimes-boisterous crowds, was a problem. This house was also clearly in the "better" part of town as it is adjacent to the private Moseley Park, which opened in 1899 to subscribers only. It was close to the heart of the Moseley village where the retail shops were.

Ronald's cousin Marjorie, whom he seems to have seen as a peer, wrote in 1971:

> throughout the whole of my life, from the nursery days in Chantry Road when we pressed our noses against the windows watching for the tram which would bring the happy moment of your arrival, up to my last visit to you at Poole—all the days we ever met were red letter days. No other days came up to them ever (McIlwaine 164).

Marjorie is recalling a specific memory here as, in the years 1896 to 1900, a steam tram from Birmingham's New Street came to Moseley. There are no similar tramlines on the Sarehole map, but there was a tram terminus, probably horse-drawn, at the eastern end of College Road before 1900, feeding into central Birmingham. This means that for that specific visit the Tolkien family had traveled into Birmingham first, probably by horse-tram, and then out to Chantry Road by steam-tram.

Marjorie's delight was the result of the typical Victorian treatment of girls. In general, well-to-do, Victorian and Edwardian girls were sequestered in the attic nursery suite containing the following: a day nursery, a bedroom, the nanny's room, and maybe a schoolroom (Rose 223). Their diet was generally plain and monotonous in contrast to their parents' lavish meals. Any toys were locked away and carefully rationed, and many comfortable homes provided few toys (Rose 225). Nannies and governesses were expected to teach "etiquette," and for girls this included that they could never admit to needing to use the toilet and that they had to use the toilet in secret after making sure there were no males present (Rose 229, 227). Many nurseries were dreary and girls were virtual prisoners (Rose 223, 225, 227), allowed only to go on walks chaperoned by the nanny or governess or perhaps lessons at a dancing academy or a rare gymnasium for children (Rose 165). In middle-class homes, time with parents was rationed. Although the visits might be relaxed, they were within a definite framework of discipline (Rose 228). The restrictions and boredom of nursery life, especially for girls, inspired a minor genre of children's literature, expressing wishes to break free as in the opening scene of *Peter Pan*, set in the nursery at the top of the house, or in the magical interventions of Mary Poppins (Rose 228).

This environment drove intelligent children to "compensate for a lack of toys with make-believe games, and even concoct their own sub-culture of a secret language that kept the adult world at bay" (Rose 227-228). In fact, by 1905 when Ronald and his brother resumed regular visits to the Incledon family following the death of their mother, Mary and Marjorie had invented *Animalic*, probably a code language. The model of their grandfather, John Suffield—known for his puns, jokes, and doggerel—would have encouraged this kind of language play (*Bio* 16, Morton/Hayes 12). Ronald, however, denies that the inventors of *Animalic* used their language to "bewilder or hoodwink the adult" (*Bio* 36, "Secret Vice" 201). Mary and Ronald later collaborated on *Nevbosh* or New Nonsense, a language made mostly of disguised English, French, and Latin words (*Bio* 36). In a similar way, the six Mitford sisters, born between 1907 and 1920 in an upper-class British household, invented the languages *Boudledidge* and *Honnish* (Pryce-Jones 31).

Middle-class Victorian girls were far more likely to be taught at home by governesses, than to attend the new female academies or boarding schools. Governesses were poorly paid and not highly qualified, though they were of "genteel" background (Rose 165). "The education methods were standard: memorizing tables, dates and passages from literature and the Bible, and practicing copperplate" [handwriting] (Rose 165). They taught a range of subjects including arithmetic, history, needlework, drawing, French, and botany; but Latin, algebra, chemistry, and physics were "masculine" and not taught to girls (Rose 165). Mabel followed this curriculum with Ronald, teaching him Latin, botany, handwriting, and drawing (*Bio* 23).[6] Ronald Tolkien added he learned history, astronomy, grammar, and etymology as well as geometry (OFS 135). Above all, governesses taught ladylike deportment and speech.

In 1939, at the age of forty-seven, Ronald Tolkien wrote:

> I can vividly remember, re-feel, the vexation (such emotions bite deep and live long) caused me in early childhood by the assertions of instructive relations (in their gift-books) that e.g. snowflakes were (or were more beautiful than) fairy jewels, or that the marvels of the ocean depths were more wonderful than the strangest creatures of Fairyland. [...] The beauty and wonder seemed of two quite different kinds.
>
> I thought early about these things (and was not exceptional in that) before I was eight (when my childhood reading or hearing of fairy-stories ceased) the question of belief had a matter not only of personal [pondering?] but of debate with fellow children (*TOFS* 233-34, underlining in original).

The "fellow children," who would have shared this debate "before I was eight," would have included Ronald's cousins, Marjorie and Mary. Before the age of eight, Ronald lived in Sarehole and was not yet in school. "Fellow children" would not refer to the local children in Sarehole as Ronald and Hilary, dressed in their fancy clothes and with strange accents, had little contact with them (*Bio* 21). Ronald's lack of interaction with other children is probably part of why he was absent "much of the first term" at King Edward's school due to ill health (*Bio* 25). That is, having only rarely been exposed to other children's germs previously, Ronald was likely to have become repeatedly sick once he began to attend school.

The interactions of the Tolkien and Incledon children were set in the context of Walter Incledon's being a successful provider for his wife and children and shaped by Victorian attitudes and expectations about newly created fortunes. The Victorians had complicated views about the display of wealth: "Not living up to one's income was bad; trying too hard was worse; the greatest sin of all was living above one's means" (Flanders 132). A granddaughter of Charles Darwin, Gwen Raverat, recalled her aunt and uncle who lived in Southampton: "They were well off and lived in style and comfort; but it was neither for style or comfort that Aunt Sara really cared. Her religion was Duty, and it was her duty to her position and her kind to keep a carriage and horse" (Flanders 132). Charles Dickens echoes this sentiment precisely in *Our Mutual Friend* (1864-1865) when a dustman and his wife receive a great inheritance. Mrs. Boffin states: "We have come into a great fortune, and we must do what's right by our fortune; we must act up to it" (Flanders 132-33). This would include: living in the best house one could afford; buying the best furnishings; dressing in a way that displayed one's fortunate and blessed status; the quality, quantity, and variety of food and drink on the table; traveling first-class; and taking holidays in the 'best' places and for extended periods of time.

The Victorians experienced an unprecedented wave of peace, prosperity, and technological progress. The prosperous were expected and had a "duty" not only to live in style, but also a "duty" to take care of their community and family. For example, all Victorian and Edwardian hospitals in Britain were created and funded by the middle and upper classes to serve the medical needs of the working-class population without charge.[7] In this spirit, Andrew Carnegie endowed libraries throughout the United States. J.R.R. Tolkien's grandfather, John Benjamin Tolkien, was known as a philanthropist in Birmingham.[8]

In his 1843 novella, *A Christmas Carol*, Charles Dickens, a man with his finger on the pulse of Victorian society and sentiment, portrays the prevailing cultural beliefs about the proper use of money in the creation of his character, Ebenezer Scrooge. Dickens first presents the reprehensible nature of the hard-hearted, penny-pinching misers, Scrooge and his business partner, Marley; Dickens then shows how Scrooge's life has shriveled from the effects of greed and selfishness, rendering him pitiable; and finally, Ebenezer reforms and redeems himself: making a large donation to charity; reconciling with his only family, his disinherited nephew, Fred; and taking an open-hearted and financially generous interest in his employee, Bob Cratchit, and the welfare of his family. Similarly, on the 1911 Swiss walking tour, James and Ellen Brookes-Smith, who were described as having "lived in some style" (Morton/Hayes 40), were joined not only by Ronald and Hilary Tolkien and their Aunt Jane Neave, but also by Rev. C. Hunt, Vicar of Hurst Green where the Brookes-Smiths resided, and his wife. The stipend of a country parson would not have covered the costs of an extended holiday in Switzerland so it is likely the Brookes-Smiths paid the travel expenses of the vicar and his wife.

Walter Incledon seems to have accepted his role in the Victorian spirit of *noblesse obligé*. 69 Gough Road, where Walter's mother and his two younger brothers, Arthur and George Herbert, lived was in an upscale neighborhood that they could hardly afford on the salary of Walter's father, a country curate. Walter was likely to have been the person who made that residence possible. Mabel's generous stipend from her brother-in-law appeared to have allowed the Tolkiens to have lived in "genteel poverty," prior to her conversion to Catholicism (Grotta-Kurska 17). Mabel maintained her middle-class status by having enough money to hire a working-class maid to do the physically taxing household chores of dishwashing, cleaning, and cooking (Gardner/Holford 270-72). Walter directed his nephew, Leonard, son of Walter's older brother, Charles Leonard Incledon (b. 1853), to a reputable boarding house, the one maintained by Walter's sister-in-law, Beatrice Suffield (1911 census). He also gave Hilary Tolkien his first job as a hardware merchant's clerk in a successful and expanding business when he left King Edward's in July 1910 (*C&G* 1.24, 1.820). Herbert's son, Gerald, who joined the Durban branch of Cape Incledon during the Depression and led the company's expansion at that period (ABOUT "Cape Incledon"), was sponsored and encouraged by his uncle. In 1911, Walter established the private company, Electrical Conduits, Ltd., with a capital of £20,000. This would be equivalent to £1,946,335.92 in September 2023 or $2,402,537.64.[9] The directors were W.B. Incledon, A.K. [brother Arthur Kingsley] Incledon, S.V. Reynolds and L. [nephew Leonard] R. Incledon. It is worth noting that this company was not Walter's main commercial enterprise and source of income. Rather what became Cape Incledon was his main business.

Given Walter's largesse to Mabel Tolkien and the rest of his Incledon family, it is not surprising he would be willing to foot the bill for Ronald Tolkien accompanying his daughters on holidays in Torquay, as discussed below, and on art tours in 1910 and 1912. Walter would certainly appreciate the importance of entertaining to make contacts, network, and close business deals. May Incledon's likely bankrolling of Ronald's entertaining at Oxford would make sense to Walter as part of his nephew's establishing himself among socially prominent peers.

Roman Catholicism

On June 28, 1900, Ronald's Aunt May and his mother became Catholics after receiving instruction at the Catholic St. Anne's church on Alcester Street, Birmingham (Ordway, *Tolkien's Faith* Figure 5). Although St. Anne's was in the Digbeth district of Birmingham, a working–class slum full of poor Irish immigrants (Ordway, *Tolkien's Faith* 24), this church could be reached easily by taking the tram. When Walter Incledon, whose father Rev. Incledon was then living nearby, returned from his overseas business, it is not surprising that Walter forbade May from entering a Catholic church again (*Bio* 24). His anti-Catholic fervor was not unusual for the time, and Birmingham had been a stronghold of puritanical Protestantism since the English Civil War (1642-1651) with a virulent hatred of "popery" that fueled riots as late as 1867 (Grotta-Kurska 19). The prevalence of this prejudice, fed by the belief that Catholics owed their primary allegiance to the Papacy and not the English Crown, reappears when Edith Bratt's "Uncle" Charles H. Jessop required her to leave his house in 1913 where she had stayed as a guest for three years. This was at least part of the price of Edith's conversion to Catholicism for her fiancé, Ronald.

The strength of Walter's anti-Catholic feelings can also be judged from the fact that when his daughter Mary converted to Catholicism, she no longer lived with the family, but lived by herself in a London flat two blocks from the Catholic Westminster Cathedral in London. Evidently, she chose to attend mass, unlike her mother, who bowed to Walter's demand that she not enter a Catholic church. In contrast, her sister Marjorie continued to live with her father until he died in 1950. On Mary's death in 1940 from cancer, she left "a large number of shares in her father's business" to the Catholic Archbishop of Liverpool. When Walter learned of this, he bought back the shares, presumably of Cape Incledon, "at great expense," rather than have the profits go to Papists (*C&G* 2.568).

Until the confrontation in the Incledon household over Roman Catholicism, Walter had been helping "occasional[ly]" to support Mabel and her sons financially since the death of Arthur Tolkien in 1896 (*Bio* 4, 23). Given his longstanding employment with Lloyd and Lloyd, Walter could easily afford to do this. Without his financial provision, the Tolkien family spiraled into poverty with multiple moves and a loss of furniture (*Bio* 29). Later in life, Ronald Tolkien strongly felt, and repeatedly stated, that his mother's death from diabetes was "hastened by persecution of her faith" and the resulting "hardships of poverty" (*Letters* 54, 172, also *Letters* 354). Repeated statements point strongly to the conclusion that Ronald, at some level, fairly or unfairly, laid the blame for his mother's suffering at least partly on Walter whom Ronald may have consequently seen as an accessory or a contributor to his mother's death.[10]

A letter, from May to her sister Mabel, that appears to have somehow escaped Beatrice Suffield's incineration of Mabel's letters and papers (*Bio* 33), reveals May's commitment to Catholicism, her affectionate nature, and her awareness of her husband's impending opposition (*Bio* 33):

> Dear old Darling, I did try to say my prayers, and it came to me absolutely certainly that I *must* obey my conscience come what may, and I feel *sure* we are right to do this [...] Oh Pet my heart feels like a huge cabbage—does yours? But my mind is clear as crystal & happy because it feels *sure* (Priestman 12, italics in original).

Seemingly or partly, as a result of her husband Walter preventing her from following her religious preference, May eventually became an "enthusiastic member" of the International Club for Psychical Research (Priestman 36). The International Club for Psychical Research (ICPR) was a short-lived psychical organization that Annie Besant, the heir of Madame Blavatsky's Theosophy, formed in May 1911. This organization grew out of dissatisfaction with the more scientific focus of the English Society for Psychical Research (SPR) founded in 1882. The ICPR was considered a rival organization to the SPR, and its membership mainly consisted of spiritualists and occultists. Sir Arthur Conan Doyle, the author of Sherlock Holmes, contributed to their journal, *Psychic Gazette*. Mrs. Faulkner, who presided over the boarding house where Ronald and Hilary Tolkien lived from January 1908 to December 1909, was previously the manager of the Dorothy Restaurant on Oxford Street, London (1891 census). This restaurant was owned by several of Madame Blavatsky's Theosophy disciples and was used to promote Theosophical doctrines from 1890 until 1895 (A.L.C. 533). The restaurant was unique and almost-revolutionary in serving only women. *The Theosophist* reports that Mrs. Faulkner joined the movement, illustrating the widespread dissemination of Theosophy which originated in America.

Because the ICPR splintered off from the SPR, May was likely to have been familiar with the SPR also. The SPR was the first organization of its kind in the world, and it proposed the radical agenda of scientifically studying phenomena such as hypnosis, dissociation, trance writing, telepathy, poltergeists, ghosts and haunted houses, dreams, and the physical phenomena associated with séances. Much of its early work involved investigating and exposing fake phenomena in séances and fraudulent mediums. Sigmund Freud responded to this society's 1912 request with the essay, "A Note on the Unconscious in Psycho-Analysis." At the turn of the twentieth century, psychical research was both respectable and intriguing.

Frederick W.H. Myers of Cambridge (1843-1901) was one of the SPR's most prominent members and an influential theorist. Based on his research, Myers proposed the most respected model for psychical phenomena, the "subliminal self" (Noll 32). F.W.H. Myers borrowed the term "mythopoetic" from the philologist Müller to describe the apparent myth-making functions of the subliminal self. This "mythopoetic" or myth-making function was similar to Jung's later conception of a collective unconscious (Noll 343). Jung was well acquainted with Myers. He cited Myers in his 1902 doctoral dissertation on hypnotically induced trance states (Noll 32). Ronald Tolkien famously used the term "mythopoeia," in his poem stemming from the September 19, 1931 conversation, which was instrumental in persuading C.S. Lewis to return to Christianity (*C&G*.2.683, *TOFS* 113). Tolkien's use of this sense of the word may have been due not so much to his study of the philologist Max Müller, with whom Tolkien strongly disagreed (*C&G* 2.610), but rather to his contact with the widespread ideas coming out of the psychical research with which his aunt was familiar.[11]

Psychical research was a subject of interest at the university level. Andrew Lang, the folklorist and chronicler of fairies, and fellow of Merton College Oxford, was President of the SPR in 1911—the year Ronald went up to Oxford (*C&G* 2.610). The surprising overlap in subject matter and interests can be seen in Lang's publication of *The Book of Dreams and Ghosts* (1897).[12] Consequently, Ronald, with his interests in philology and fairy tales, could easily be drawn to a topic like ghosts. At a June 15, 1912 meeting of the Apolausticks, a literary group Ronald organized at Oxford, Ronald proposed that "a belief in ghosts is essential to the welfare of a people" (*C&G* 1.40). Again, on October 20, 1914, at a meeting of the Stapeldon Society—a debate and discussion society of Tolkien's Exeter College—Ronald proposed, "This House believes in ghosts" (*C&G* 1.53). The fact that Ronald proposed a topic twice suggests that he had the intellectual ammunition and background to both present, and rebut, objections. Ronald's familiarity with and interest in this subject may be reflected in his arguing, at the April 2, 1912 Open Debate at King Edward's on the topic 'That it is better to be eccentric than orthodox.' He claimed that there was no "true opposition between the orthodox and the eccentric, and [he] maintained the possibility of a man's being both at the same time" (*C&G* 1.39). This point of view might be useful for discussing psychical research topics. Consequently, ghosts, as well as fairies, could mesh with Ronald's interests in philology.[13]

Ronald proposed debate topics that were of interest to him—as seen in his November 3, 1914 proposal at the Exeter College Stapeldon Society that "This House approves of spelling reform" (*C&G* p. 1.63). This reflected Ronald's interest in Esperanto (*C&G* p. 2.628). Ronald's support of the motion "This House deplores the signs of degeneracy in the present age" (*C&G* 2.1228) aligns with the later statements of the T.C.B.S., the literary society composed of Ronald's friends from King Edward's that reformed in late 1914 with its the purpose to "reestablish sanity, cleanliness and the love of real and true beauty in everybody's breast" (*C&G* 2.1285). In a similar vein, in a letter of February 12, 1916, Ronald wrote that he wanted "more than anything" for his writing "'to make England Catholic' again" so that "beauty, purity, and love" could return to England (McIlwaine 157).

During the time Ronald attended King Edward's, by 1907, the Incledons moved to a very exclusive area in Barnt Green outside Birmingham (*C&G* 2.568). Their house no longer exists, but their next-door neighbor was a diamond merchant, a Mr. Jack Cohen (whose original name was probably Jacob Cohen). In the 1911 census, Walter Incledon described himself as "Hardware Merchant." In accordance with the family's more affluent address, they now had two live-in servants: a cook and a housemaid. Though named 'The Cottage', this house would have been a step up from the 56 Chantry Road address and would have been commensurate with Walter's increased status and income as manager of H. Incledon (*A&I* 22). In 1910, H. Incledon was incorporated as a private company.[14] Like the residence on Chantry Road, the new home was near a station with a railroad line that could take Walter quickly into central Birmingham for business at the red-painted Town Hall Chambers (1895-1940), at 86 New Street (Gardner/Holford 62). Ronald painted the Incledons' lovely garden at Barnt Green in July 1913, with its foxgloves and delphiniums (*A&I* 20). He was so taken with this garden that he produced at least four versions from different vantage points (*A&I* 33).

Ronald was in regular contact with his Aunt May and his Incledon cousins, although few specifics about this appear in the Carpenter biography or in Scull and Hammond's *Chronology and Guide*. Nevertheless, two areas seem to indicate involvement with the Incledon family. One area was painting and art which were shared interests among Ronald and both Marjorie and Mary. The sisters are described as "both amateur artists" (McIlwaine 164). In the 1911 census when Marjorie was nineteen, she was listed as an art student. She possibly attended the respected Birmingham Government School of Design—founded in 1843, and renamed the Municipal School of Art in 1885. It became the leading center for the Arts and Crafts Movement.[15] Marjorie also trained in "late middle age," probably following her mother's death in 1936, at the Brighton School of Art, which was near the Incledons' Rottingdean house. She specialized in landscapes and portraits. She continued to paint at her residence in Ditchling until the age of eighty (*C&G* 2.568).

In 1910, Ronald took a holiday which included visiting Whitby where he drew several landscapes (*A&I* 16). Again, in the summer of 1912 after his first year at Oxford, Ronald went on a walking tour with a new sketchbook in Berkshire. He drew various landscapes with three ink drawings of Eastbury (August 27-8 1912), three watercolors of the Lambourn countryside, and two pages of ink drawings of the Lambourn church (August 21, 23, 30-31) (*C&G* 1.40). The tour also included sites in Buckinghamshire (*A&I* 17).

Ronald was unlikely to have simply been wandering by himself. The alternative was for him to have had a benefactor along helping to pay for art supplies and travel expenses, both part of the activities of the privileged and leisure class. Given Aunt May's affluent lifestyle, she is a likely candidate, who could have acted as a chaperone, companion, and benefactor. The delicacy and finish of Ronald's *Eastbury, Berkshire* drawing is almost at the professional level indicating he was a very active artist at the time and was creating a large number of works (Ellison 22). Such skill suggests some training or supervision which he, Marjorie, and Mary might have shared. In a 1917 letter from Mary, she asks about the relationship of the 'ishnesses' that Ronald had been painting and John Ruskin, a leading nineteenth-century art theorist and critic (McIlwaine 164).

Also, Aunt May's generosity could have covered the expenses of Ronald's wonderful Swiss walking tour of 1911—a seven-week excursion organized by the Brookes-Smiths (Lewis/Currie, *Switzerland* 269-70). Ronald's Aunt Jane Neave had become a business partner with Ellen Brookes-Smith in the Phoenix and Manor Farms in July 1911 (Morton and Hayes 34), and this association seems to have led to this exciting opportunity and adventure.

While living at Barnt Green outside of Birmingham, May continued the Suffield family tradition of putting on dramatic programs at Christmas, for which the programs of 1872 and 1883 survive (Burns "Jane Suffield"). May's father would have fostered this tradition because he was an active member of both the Birmingham Dramatic and Literary Club and the Central Literary Association (Burns, "An unlettered peasant" 18-20). Both of Ronald's parents had participated in amateur theatricals as young people (Priestman 23). Mabel also participated in an amateur theatrical in Bloemfontein, South Africa (Gorelik 7). In 1912, when Ronald's maternal grandparents were likely to have been at Barnt Green at the Christmas festivities—as well as Ronald's literary friends such as Christopher Wiseman, Rob Gilson and Geoffrey Smith—Ronald contributed a play, *The Bloodhound, the Chef, and the Suffragette*, for the Christmas entertainment at Barnt Green (*Bio* 59). A December 1913 letter from the Tolkien brothers' maternal Suffield grandmother to Hilary Tolkien implies this was a long tradition because she writes that "I missed you at our Christmas Gathering at Barnt Green, but memory brought [your] face near" (Gardner/Holford 72).

May appears to have acted as a surrogate mother to Ronald in relation to his friends. Given Ronald's regular involvement with his Aunt May and his Incledon cousins, his Aunt May seems to have met young Ronald's friends from King Edward's and was in contact with them because Christopher Wiseman wrote Ronald by October 10, 1917 that "he has heard from Mrs. Incledon that Tolkien is still in hospital in Hull" (*C&G* 1.209). May's contact with Ronald's friends in the T.C.B.S. (Tea Club Barrovian Society) literary group may have been part of the reason that Ronald omitted Edith Bratt's name when announcing his betrothal to his close friends in late December and early January 1914 (*Edith* 100-101). Young Ronald probably did not want his aunt to know about the betrothal until the deed was done because of the likely previous family shock over his clandestine relationship with Edith Bratt in 1909-10 (*Edith* 101-02). This discretion may be why one of the T.C.B.S. members, Rob Gilson, wrote to ask if Ronald would "reveal the lady's name" (Garth, *Great War* 33).

Aunt May's likely financial support is apparent not only in her continuing contact with Ronald (*C&G* 1.61), but also in her generosity that funded a surprisingly lavish lifestyle that Ronald had at Oxford. During Ronald's freshman year at Oxford, his social activities included joining the Exeter College unit of King Edward's Horse—a unique and prestigious organization with units in London,

Liverpool, Oxford, and Cambridge. King Edward's Horse was administered directly by the Horse Guards in London and had the cachet of royal patronage. It was only open to "Colonials"—those born in the colonies—like Ronald, who was born in what became South Africa. King Edward's Horse's most attractive quality was likely to be that it functioned as a dining and drinking club (*Edith* 73-74). This organization had fees which Ronald would be ill-prepared to pay. Ronald had only £20 to £40 of yearly income (*Letters* 53). While Ronald was at Oxford, Fr. Francis Morgan, Ronald's guardian, supplemented the scholarship that Ronald won. However, Ronald "regularly overspent his meagre income and the allowance that Father Francis gave him" (Priestman 24). Aunt May appears to have been acting like an indulgent parent for the first Suffield family member to have the honor of going up to Oxford.

Following his passing the Honour Moderations with a Second Class in the spring of 1913, Ronald's lifestyle became rather well-heeled in the Michaelmas term of 1913. His expenses seem to have exceeded any earnings that he had made as a tutor and escort to some Mexican boys on tour in France in the summer of 1913. In the fall of 1913, Ronald indulged in a spending spree which included two tailored suits, furniture, Japanese prints for his rooms in Oxford, and custom rugby boots (*Bio* 68).[16] Ronald's college bills for food and coal showed a debt of £8 9s 7d for the 1913 Michaelmas term (Garth, *Tolkien at Exeter* 35). The food and drink brought to his room had to be paid for on a weekly basis (*C&G* 2.921). When Michaelmas Term at Oxford ended on December 6, 1913, Ronald went to Birmingham to visit friends, participated in Old Edwardian activities at King Edward's High School, and visited his cousins and Aunt and Uncle Incledon at Barnt Green in late December and early January (*C&G* 1.55).

The exponential increase in bills at Oxford continued for the rest of the academic year with expenses of £26 8s 3d for the 1914 Hilary term and £25 16s 6d for the Trinity term (Garth, *Tolkien at Exeter* 35). This appears to be the result of the Sub-Rector giving Ronald and Cullis permission "to have supper for nine on Sat. nights in the rooms of one or the other this term" (*C&G* 1.57). These dinners seem to be the "expensive dinners" (*Bio* 59) and "dinner parties" (*Bio* 69) that Carpenter intimates Ronald gave when he entertained beyond his means (*Bio* 53). The debt of £60 14s 4d for the 1913-1914 academic year is equivalent to at least £5,786.57 in September 2023 goods and services or $7,075.13.[17] May

Incledon's deep pockets could cover these expenses and express her support for her nephew and godson during Ronald's years at Oxford.[18]

Interrupting the idyll at Oxford, Britain declared war on August 4, 1914, and young men had choices to make. Aunt May, like most women in Britain, would have been concerned about the choices and fates of family who were near kin. Aunt May's youngest brother, William, had no children. Her older brother, Roland had a son, Roland Hind, born in 1894, who died in early 1914 at the age of nineteen (Burns, "Roland Suffield" 16). Roland's second son Frank was born in 1904 so he was too young for the war. May's oldest brother John had two sons, John, born in 1891 and Rupert in 1893 (Census 1901). There are no records that John served in World War I, but a Rupert Suffield was a gunner in the Royal Field Artillery from 1914 to 1920.[19] Walter's nephew, Leonard R. Incledon, joined The Royal Warwickshire Regiment as a Second Lieutenant, but relinquished "his commission on account of ill-health" by February 9, 1916, so he had been in danger early in the war.[20] By October 3, 1914, twenty-year old Hilary Tolkien joined the 3rd Birmingham Battalion (Gardner/Holford 78). Aunt May would have wanted to know what Ronald's course would be.

On August 23, 1914, Ronald wrote to his Aunt May from Warwick where he had been seeing his fiancée Edith (*C&G* 1.61). Aunt May would have been eager to see her nephew and find out his plans in the face of Britain's declaration of war. Ronald later wrote that his poem, "The Lonely Harebell", was "insp[ired] Cromer 1914" (*C&G* 1.103). Cromer is a coastal town on the north coast of the English county of Norfolk. It became a resort for the wealthy in the nineteenth century and known for its gardens, ornate Victorian houses and hotels, and the late-Victorian Cromer Pier—home to the Pavilion Theater. Cromer was the type of fashionable resort the Incledons would favor, and September would have been an optimal time at the seashore where Ronald would have seen the well-known harebells (*campanula*) of Cromer blooming (Pigott 71). An inferred visit to Cromer in September to see the Incledons could easily fit in the noticeable gap in the *Chronology* before Ronald's Michaelmas term at Oxford began on October 11, 1914.

After Ronald passed his Examinations for the Honours School on June 10-15, 1915 and then applied on June 28 for a commission with the Army, he spent some time in Warwick with Edith. By July 9, 1915, the couple was in Birmingham, probably visiting Fr. Francis Morgan (*C&G* 1.76-78). Edith and Ronald stayed at Ronald's Aunt and Uncle Mitton's house, 'Abbotsford', in Moseley. Arthur Tolkien's sister, Mabel, married T.E. Mitton, and Ronald and Hilary had previously spent school holidays with the Mitton family (*C&G* 2.791). Ronald and Edith then stayed with his Aunt May and probably saw his Uncle Walter, Marjorie, and Mary, in Barnt Green on July 13-14, 1915 (*C&G* 1.78). Ronald would be taking leave of May, who may have been, like Jennie Grove for his fiancée Edith Bratt (*TFA* 36), a "substitute mother." Ronald then left to report for duty to Col. Frederick J. Tobin at 20 de Parys Avenue, Bedford (*C&G* 1.77).

By November 10, 1916, Ronald returned from the Western Front to the 1st Southern General Hospital in Birmingham with a stubborn case of trench fever. Edith, accompanied by Jennie Grove, hurried to Birmingham and stayed initially with the T.E. Mittons in Moseley where she had visited in the summer of 1915.[21] This was Ronald's address for his correspondence in November 1916. The hospitalized 2nd Lt. Tolkien was likely to have attracted little attention because he had not been wounded and was only sick (Carden-Coyne 235). He would have been placed in an "Officers [Only]" ward. His Aunt May certainly would have come with Marjorie and Mary, not to mention Fr. Francis Morgan, his guardian.

In late November 1917, May visited Edith when she gave birth to her first child, John. May wrote to Ronald, reassuring the anxious new father, who was prevented by his military duties from being present. May's affectionate and warm greeting to Ronald, "Dear old Pet and ancient Lamb," seems to express well the close and caring relationship between May and Ronald (Priestman 36). Ronald's cousin, Mary Incledon—who had converted to Catholicism after coming of legal age in 1916—and his brother Hilary became John's godparents. Aunt May was probably accompanied by, or soon joined by, Mary and her sister Marjorie, because Mary was to be godmother at the christening. Mary, in a letter postmarked November 23, 1917, refers to a conversation between Ronald and her sister Marjorie about art—Ruskin and Ronald's 'Ishnesses' (McIlwaine 164). This was presumably a recent conversation which would have been on November 22, 1917 or before, when John's baptism was celebrated and documented that Mary was present.

The Father Christmas letter of 1920 is addressed to "Dear John" with "Love to Daddy, mummy, Michael & auntie Mary." This suggests that "auntie Mary" was present at Christmas. The most likely candidate for "auntie Mary" was Mary Incledon. As John's godmother, she was obligated to support her godchild's faith experience.

Roverandom and the Incledons

Despite Ronald Tolkien's repeated protests concerning the irrelevance of biography to his writings, he appears to have drawn on readily available interests and memories from his life as a source for his oeuvre. The use of his life experiences may or may not have been a conscious strategy. This began at least as early as the age of twenty in his play, *The Bloodhound, the Chef, and the Suffragette*, a thinly-disguised recital of his anticipated reunion with his soon-to-be fiancée, Edith Bratt (*Letters* 257, 288; *Bio* 59). Ronald Tolkien also saw himself as the character Beren with his wife as Lúthien in the legendarium, and he had these names carved on their headstones (*Letters* 420).

This pattern appears to be true of Tolkien's 1925 spur-of-the-moment story *Roverandom*, told during a storm in order to comfort and distract his two oldest sons—then ages seven and four (Bunting, "*Rover* Part I;" R xi, xvi-xvii). Ronald Tolkien had to spin a yarn on the spot that could engage his own children. In particular, in this story, Tolkien needed to sympathetically address the grief of his four year old son Michael who had just lost a black-and-white toy dog, to which he was so attached that he ate with it, slept with it, and could hardly put it down to wash his hands (*R* ix). To effectively use a story to comfort his son, Tolkien would have to recall what it was like and how it felt to experience the loss of such an important attachment at that age (i.e. around the age of four). While Tolkien did not articulate his theory of fairy-stories stories until 1939, he knew that a fairy tale, besides being entertaining, must make a child feel understood and show that his or her deepest feelings, hopes, and anxieties are taken into account (*TOFS* 15; Bettelheim 19). The fairy tale can give "consolation" because it deals with the truth of the child's feelings and is true to the child's inner situation at that moment (Bettelheim 50, 58).

Although this story may have been told over several nights and there were later elaborations to this story, e.g. wordplay and a lunar eclipse of 1927 were added, the basic plot was complete the night of the storm because the last part of *Roverandom* attributes the storm, which kept the children awake, to the story's fictional Sea-serpent (*R* xii-xiii, xi). In the story, the Sea-serpent causes "terrible tides" and "the water heaved and shook and bent people's houses and spoilt their repose for miles and miles around" (*R* 77, 76). In this way, the destructive high tide during the Tolkiens' holiday stay at Filey and the inability of the Tolkien children to sleep in such a storm were "explained" (*R* xi).

In something of the manner of a *roman à clef*, Ronald Tolkien appears to have taken various characters in *Roverandom*, including the wizards Artaxerxes and Psamathos, largely from his own life (Bunting, "*Rover* Part I and II"): "For creative Fantasy is founded upon [...] a recognition of fact, but not slavery to it" (OFS 144). In *Roverandom*, Psamathos, a sand fairy, clearly lifted from *Three Children and It* by the admired Edith Nesbit (*TOFS* 251) is likely to be based on Ronald's grandfather, John Suffield. After the puppy Roverandom returns from his adventures on the Moon, Psamathos arranges the marriage of the "elderly" daughter of the mer-king, a likely alias for Aunt May to Walter Incledon, who is seemingly impersonated by the magician Artaxerxes (*R* 50). John Suffield (the likely model for Psamathos) and Walter Incledon (the likely model for Artaxerxes in the second part of *Roverandom*) shared business interests and contacts in iron manufacturing (Morton/Hayes 11, *C&G* 2.568). May was the oldest or "eldest/elderly" Suffield daughter, and getting just a bit old for the prime marriage market. The beautiful setting of Ronald's lovely watercolor, *The Garden of Mer-king*, from September 1927 (*A&I* 81) appears to be a transformation of May and Walter Incledon's impressive Barnt Green garden which Ronald had repeatedly painted in 1913 (*A&I* 20).

In July 1913, when Ronald painted watercolors of the garden at the Incledons' cottage, it was "glorious in its full bloom," with colorful "delphiniums and still more foxgloves" (*A&I* 20). Analogously, Ronald Tolkien painted the September 1927 gorgeous watercolor, *The Garden of Mer-king* (*A&I* 81), where the palace of the mer-king is defined by its beautiful garden setting. The watercolor is "a vision of pastel pinks, greens, blues, mauve, and yellows, against which the tendrils of plants and sea anemones, the tentacles of an octopus, and the pennon flying from the tallest dome of the palace curve and curl in Art nouveau splendor" with the palace shining "as if made of porcelain" (*A&I* 81). The range of colors in both watercolors is similar, although the earlier pictures emphasize more upright forms and have less profusion of curves.

With new information on Walter and May Incledon, more parallels emerge between Ronald Tolkien's story and his history with the Incledons.

In *Roverandom*, the newspapers, satirically titled *The Illustrated Weekly Weed*, *Ocean Notions*, *The Mer-mail*, *The Conch*, and *The Morning Splash*, all have pictures of Artaxerxes's wedding with Psamathos "grinning in the background" (*R* 52). The Incledons wed in 1890, and photographs of local society events did not appear in newspapers in Britain until the twentieth century. There were private photographers in Birmingham starting in the 1870s, and the Incledons would have posed for photographs for a family album. Ronald appears to use a contemporary 1925 detail to play with his memory of the 1890 wedding pictures he would have seen.

Ronald Tolkien's method here was the same as his approach in "The Notion Club Papers" of approximately 1946, when he took selected aspects of the Inklings and then recombined them as the starting point or models for characters in "The Notion Club Papers." Tolkien cautioned: "the mirror is cracked, and at the best you will only see your countenances distorted, and adorned maybe with noses (and other features) that are not your own" (*SD* 148-49). He appears to follow the same approach in *Roverandom* and revises the expected stereotype of a happy wedding picture.

Given that a proper, formal wedding photograph in 1890 would not have had any participant smiling, much less grinning, Ronald Tolkien is imagining that Psamathos/John Suffield is "grinning in background" not only because of the coup of such a socially prestigious wedding for a daughter who was a bit "old" for the marriage market, but also perhaps in relief. That is because in 1888, Mabel exchanged secret letters with her eventual fiancé, Arthur Tolkien (*Bio* 9). For this breach of respectable conventions, John Suffield was very likely to have separated the pair just as, in 1909, the guardian Fr. Morgan separated Ronald and the object of his affection, Edith (*Edith* 102).

Carpenter supports this likely scenario with his explicit identification of Mabel Tolkien with Belladonna Took in *The Hobbit* (*Bio* 175). In *The Hobbit*, "once in a while members of the Took-clan would go and have adventures" and "they discreetly disappeared and the family hushed it up." The narrator adds, "Not that Belladonna Took [if read as Mabel Suffield] ever had any adventures after she became Mrs. Bungo Baggins [if read as Mrs. Arthur Tolkien] (*H* I). By 1889, Arthur Tolkien had left for South Africa to advance his career at the Bank of Africa, a subsidiary of Lloyd's Bank, and Mabel was free to return to her family in the Birmingham area and attend her sister's 1890 wedding. John Suffield would have been relieved this "hushed up" "adventure," or rather scandal, did not prevent May marrying the respectable and successful son of an Anglican minister.

Although in the first part of *Roverandom*, Ronald Tolkien appears to have focused on Artaxerxes as a representation of his mother, once the puppy Rover goes under the sea to the mer-king's palace, the characterizations of Artaxerxes shift and seem to reflect characteristics of Walter Incledon (Bunting, "*Rover* Part II"). Tolkien gives the impression of venting his dislike of his Uncle Walter in a lively parody with a transformation of the knowledgeable manager into the incompetent wizard, Artaxerxes. As reviewed above, Ronald's dislike of his Uncle Walter rested on: his preventing May from attending the Catholic Church with her sister Mabel and his cutting off much-needed financial support to Mabel. In addition, by 1925 when *Roverandom* originated, Uncle Walter evidently refused to allow his daughter Mary to practice her chosen religion of Catholicism while living in his house.

Ronald Tolkien trenchantly depicts Artaxerxes, a likely parody of Uncle Walter: "He had become rather full of his own importance [... due to] his appointment to the post of Pacific and Atlantic Magician (the PAM)" (*R* 61). The nickname, the PAM, could be another lampoon of Walter's self-importance because it was the nickname of the British Prime Minister, Lord Palmerston (*R* 102). Tolkien continues by describing Artaxerxes as "too big for his boots" which could be another dig at his Uncle Walter (*R* 71). Walter may have come by this habit of self-importance honestly as his father, the Rev. Incledon, impressed the 1861 census taker with his credentials to such an extent that an unheard-of four lines are taken up listing his occupation as "Clergyman without cure (i.e. parish); School Master; Master of Arts, Worcester College Oxford."

Walter Incledon as Artaxerxes, or the PAM, receives lots of complaints by mail, especially on Mondays (*R* 71), and this was probably true of the real Walter due to his position as a foreign accounts manager at Lloyd and Lloyd and then for his own prosperous and growing iron and steel tube or pipe business. If one is willing to allow that Ronald Tolkien might have been enjoying a send-up of his uncle, he seems to have spun impromptu complaints that cleverly echo and satirize Walter's business woes "that not even the best PAM in the ocean could prevent, and some of which he is not even supposed to have anything to do with:

> Wrecks come down plump now and again on the roof of somebody's sea-house [read mine cave-ins]; explosions occur in the sea-bed [mine explosions] [...] savage fish have a fight in the highway and knock mer-children over [Native African workers, virtually imprisoned by the 1895 Pass Law, riot]; or absent-minded sharks swim at the dining-room window and spoil the dinner [read wandering lions, etc. disrupt work or transportation] (*R* 70-71).

Concocting an entertaining and diverting story to occupy his sons during their holiday at the beach in Filey, Ronald apparently recalled his own visits to the beach. In 1902 at the age of ten, Ronald Tolkien "felt rather grand" making a train trip by himself to Torquay on the 'English Riviera', as reported by his grandson, Simon Tolkien.[22] It had become a holiday destination, especially after Queen Victoria in 1846 praised its natural beauties. Ronald certainly would have gone to the beach there and appreciated how fine it was in contrast to the "ghastly sea-side resorts" in Wales which he had previously visited (*Letters* 289, *C&G* 1.5). In 1902 at Torquay, the young Ronald must have had a host who could afford such a renowned resort.

In 1902, Marjorie would have been ten, like Ronald, and Mary, seven. In the Edwardian era (1901-1910), there was a gradual relaxing of restrictions on middle-class children. Around the age of twelve, children were given more freedom to go on chaperoned outings to zoos, the Crystal Palace, pantomimes, and public exhibitions. They could join guests at the lunch table, speaking when spoken to (Rose 229). Edwardian schoolgirls could now play "sedate" games like tennis, cricket, and hockey, but only in "liberty" bodices, stockinette knickers, flannel petticoats, and often high-necked woolen "spencers" as underclothing in summer (Rose 230). By 1905, children talked more to adults, helped at bazaars and charity concerts, and cycled in the parks (Rose 231-232). This more liberal attitude toward children coincided with the 1902 advent of the first advertising campaign to bring healthy visitors to Torquay, so that Torquay changed from being solely a winter holiday resort for invalids to also being a summer holiday resort aimed at families from the industrial Midlands and the north of England seeking fresh air and recreation.[23]

Taking into account Ronald's train trip to Torquay, his artwork as discussed below, the age of Marjorie and Mary, and the new attractions and amenities of Torquay, it could be inferred that May arranged a holiday for her daughters at this newly fashionable summer resort and somehow managed to call a truce with her husband so that Ronald could be included and add to the girls' enjoyment. The girls looked forward so much to their Tolkien cousins' visits to break the monotony of their socially isolated and limited life.

In *Roverandom*, Mrs. Artaxerxes, or in this off-the-cuff *roman à clef*, Aunt May, greets Rover with "What a sweet little dog!" (*R* 62), reminiscent of Aunt May's salutation in her 1917 letter: "Dear old Pet and ancient Lamb" (Priestman 36). Mrs. Artaxerxes is "fond" of Rover and "knew how to manage the PAM [i.e. Walter] in any mood" (*R* 72). Also, the PAM is "very anxious to oblige his wife" (*R* 64). Perhaps she argued the sins of Mabel, the Catholic apostate, should not be visited on innocent children who might yet return to the fold of Protestantism. The Incledons could certainly afford a fine holiday in Torquay and include a guest or guests.

Ronald must have just been finishing his summer or Trinity term at St. Philip's Grammar School and may have followed the Incledons to Torquay when his school let out. Ronald would have felt "grand" indeed if he rode in first-class—a rail ticket that Uncle Walter could easily afford. His aunt may have insisted on this given the unsavory or dubious individuals that rode in second- and third-class carriages. Hilary was not with his brother on the train, but there may be other evidence that he was included on this holiday.

In *Roverandom*, Tolkien appears to identify with the puppy Rover, who experiences a version of Ronald's traumatic dream of the Great Wave (*R* 12).

Rover's having that dream is strong evidence that the puppy is an avatar for Ronald Tolkien because he wrote: "As far as any character is 'like me' it is Faramir," and Faramir also has the dream of the Great Wave (*Letters* 232, *RK* VI v 941). At the beginning of the story, the "very small, and very young" puppy Rover is in the yard of a grandmother's house. Like the small, young puppy, at the age of three and four, Ronald visited his Tolkien grandmother (*Bio* 18). Ronald recalled his memorable visits there in the unpublished 1914 drawing *Childhood Memories of My Grandmother's House* (*A&I* 66, also *Bio* 17). In Ronald's memories of his grandmother and her house, he was approximately the same age as his very distressed son Michael whom he was trying to comfort. These parallels are evidence of Ronald Tolkien's intention to use autobiographical elements in *Roverandom*, both for himself and the other characters. In addition, a puppy or pup is a term that can refer to a young man or boy, especially one who is conceited or impertinent, as in a line from Irving Berlin's song of his time in World War I: "And then I'll get that other pup, the one who wakes the bugler up." Ronald's Aunt May called him "Pet" which would be expected for a puppy (Priestman 36).

Mrs. Artaxerxes shares parallels with May in terms of her relationship with Ronald and May's later disabling condition of Parkinson's disease discussed below. Mrs. Artaxerxes, [presumably May Incledon] and some of the mer-children [which can be read as Marjorie, Mary and possibly Hilary] "visited the Great White Caves" (*R* 72). One of Torquay's premier attractions was Kent's Cavern, then part of Lord Haldon's estate. In the mid-1800s, the Torquay Natural History Society obtained permission from Sir Lawrence Palk to have scientists explore the caves to obtain fossils and artifacts for the then-planned Torquay Museum. These important finds were exhibited at the Museum. In 1903, the caves were opened to the public as a tourist attraction with concrete paths, electric lighting, and visitor facilities. However, there is no doubt that the well-to-do and well-connected could get private tours in 1902 when these improvements were being put in place. Kent's Cavern is full of white stalactites and was famous for a large stalagmite formation known as "The Wedding Cake," named for its successively smaller, white tiers. Kent's Cavern makes a likely model for the "Great White Caves."

The Torquay Natural History Museum, founded in 1844, was also a likely destination for a children's holiday. It had special collections of shells, seaweed, and marine plants, as well as insects, butterflies, birds' eggs and nests, and minerals. In *Roverandom*, the puppy, now named Roverandom, and some of the mer-children "went too, another time, to visit the smaller sea-fairies in their little *glass houses*" (*R* 72-73 italics added). Tolkien, the narrator, also mentions tiny fishes, crabs, shells, and sea-horses seen on this visit, likely to be found at the Torquay museum. Tolkien wrote: "the marvels of the ocean depths" could be compared to "the strangest creatures of Fairyland." As a result, Tolkien could take a short step and call the exhibited wonders of the natural world "sea-fairies" (*TOFS* 234). Given that the specimens at the Torquay Natural History museum would have been *housed* in *glass* cases or *glass houses*, Ronald Tolkien could imagine sea-fairies living in glass houses. An early notebook contains Ronald's drawings of plants and a starfish created during an "early seaside holiday" (Priestman 10, 11). These drawings are not dated, but they would be consistent with the interest in natural history and the sea that the Torquay museum visit would have fostered.

Even as a child, Ronald Tolkien had a strong grounding in natural history.[24] The Torquay area is on Lyme Bay and is well-known for its fossils, many of which are in the Torquay museum. In the 1937 Christmas Dragon lecture, in an aside, Tolkien said: "I [*added*: once as a boy] found a saurian jaw myself with nasty teeth at Lyme Regis—and thought I had stumbled on a bit of petrified dragon" (Rateliff, *History* 539, italics in original). If the fossil was found at Lyme Regis, it can only date from the summers of 1905, 1906, or 1907 when Ronald was between thirteen and fifteen years old. It seems unlikely that he, at that age, had a "literal belief in dragons" (Rateliff, *History* 539). Rateliff proposes the 1902 date is more likely.

Ronald Tolkien's statement about a saurian jaw was probably only a playful remark suitable for his audience of children. Nevertheless, if Ronald, who as a boy "desired dragons with a profound desire," found a fossil that he could imagine to be the remains of a dragon, then that experience would have marked that seaside holiday as very memorable (OFS 135). Ronald may have conflated Lyme Bay with Lyme Regis where he spent a number of holidays because the ages of thirteen through fifteen do seem late for a belief in dragons.

Art was an activity that both of the Tolkien brothers shared with the Incledon sisters (H. Tolkien 69). All four of them were quite likely to have spent time drawing at Torquay.

Hammond and Scull reproduce the drawing, *Two Boys at the Seaside*, and an untitled drawing they call *Ship at Anchor* with a background of a curved beach with a distinctive hump of headland (*A&I* 11, 12). They imply that these two sketches were done about the same time, and this seems reasonable. They write:

> [the] picture of two boys on a beach [5] probably [shows] Tolkien himself and Hilary at about the ages of ten and eight years. If those ages are correct, then the drawing was made about 1902, possibly at Bournemouth or Poole where the boys spent seaside holidays with Tolkien's godfather (*A&I* 13).

When Ronald Tolkien was christened in 1892, his godparents were Aunt May Incledon; George Edward Jelf, Assistant Master at St. Andrew's College, Bloemfontein (an Anglican high school for boys); and Uncle Tom Hadley, the husband of Arthur Tolkien's sister, Florence (*C&G* 1.2). The unidentified godparent, who might have taken the Tolkien brothers on multiple "seaside holidays," is not likely to have been Fr. Francis Morgan, Ronald's eventual guardian—who took the boys to the beach at Lyme Regis in 1905, 1906, and 1907—because the Tolkien family only met Fr. Francis in early 1902 and there is no mention that he was ever Ronald's godfather (*Bio* 26). Although there is information on Ronald spending holidays with the Mitton and Mountain families (*C&G* 2.791, 2.814), as well as the Incledons, there is no information on his spending time with the Hadley family.[25]

Though there is no published information to identify Tolkien's Catholic godparent(s), May would have been the obvious choice for a godparent as she would be continuing in her previous role.

Scull and Hammond's 1902 date matches Ronald Tolkien's report of a trip to Torquay. The scene of the two boys at the beach with rocks or islands in the background appears similar to the view from Meadfoot Beach near Torquay, showing Ore Stone and Thatcher's Rock. The beach was already popular by the turn of the twentieth century judging from period photographs on the internet. It cannot have been drawn based on the coast at Lyme Regis or Bournemouth because those harbors do not have the rocks or islands that match Ronald's drawing. Although Monet may have painted haystacks *en plein air*, drawing at the beach was not practical for children, given the erratic and brisk sea breezes ruffling paper and getting sand in everything. Ronald's drawings were done from memory and approximate the view as seen in his reversal of the slope on Ore Stone.

Hammond and Scull's identification of the context of the drawings appears to be a slip-up.[26] Although the ages and the date for *Two Boys at the Seaside* are correct, as is the general location on the southern coast of England, their identification of the boys' chaperon as a godfather is likely to be incorrect. Rather, the boys' chaperon is likely to be Aunt May. In addition, the report of multiple seaside visits with an unknown godparent may be the result of confusing the multiple seaside visits with Fr. Francis, Ronald's later guardian, and Ronald's visit to Torquay with the Incledons, or possibly just referring to Walter as a godfather since May was Ronald's godmother.

In the *Two Boys at the Seaside*, both boys are well-protected from the sun with long sleeves, long pants, and wide-brimmed sun-hats. The one boy, who is facing the viewer, has a fair likeness to Hilary Tolkien—as seen in the 1905 photograph found in Carpenter's biography. This drawing strongly suggests that Hilary was included in the Torquay trip. He may have traveled with the Incledon family to Torquay since at that time he was still being schooled at home. Meanwhile, his brother Ronald had to wait for his school term at St. Philip's to end before joining the party. The other figure, presumably Ronald, is wearing part of the classic Edwardian sailor suit as seen in his flared bell bottom pants, derived from those worn by the common sailor or "Jack Tar." Queen Victoria started the sailor suit fashion craze for boys when she dressed her eldest son, Albert, in a sailor suit. A photograph from 1899 shows Ronald wearing a variant of this sailor suit with the insignia of authority, the bosun pipe, in his front pocket (McIlwaine 112).

Ronald Tolkien rarely drew people, and when he did, he was not skillful. The drawings from the age of twelve are not accomplished. These include: *What is a Home Without A Mother (or A Wife)* (Priestman 15, McIlwaine 133), *They Slept in Beauty Side by Side* (*A&I* 10), *For Men Must Work* (McIlwaine 134), and *Working Over Time* (Henry 32). Later drawings of human figures during

Ronald's time in college tend to be stick figures or cartoonish, including: the card for the Exeter College Smoker (Priestman 26), *End of the World* (*A&I* 40, McIlwaine 37), *The Back of the Beyond* (McIlwaine 41), and *Grownupishness* (*A&I* 39). Ronald Tolkien drew the people in 1918 *High Life at Gipsy Green* (*A&I* 27; Priestman 36, 38) from the rear as he did with *Two Boys at the Seaside.* A rare profile portrait of Jennie Grove (*A&I* 28) is detailed and persuasive, but this may be the result of her being older and willing to sit for the drawing. Marjorie's interest in portraiture may have sparked Ronald's attempt to draw his brother in 1902.

The landscape, *Ship at Anchor*, shows better control and more confident technique. Ronald Tolkien enjoyed creating landscapes all his life. This drawing is likely to be the result of a separate excursion to the popular Redgate Beach in Anstey's Cove close to Torquay.[27]

Ronald's picture focuses on a steam trawler, a fishing vessel, with its red hull showing. Earlier trawlers used sails, but this vessel has a steam stack in addition to the two masts. Trawlers from the nearby, important port of Brixham were painted red below the water line.[28] The red hull allows a quick judgment of how high a boat is riding in the water. With so much of her red hull showing, the boat appears to have been driven ashore by a storm and is not at anchor. A ship beached by a storm was likely to have attracted Ronald's attention. Further, there is no room for an anchored vessel pictured that close to the shore to swing with winds and tides. Ronald carefully records the sand bars visible in the foreground showing the tide is out, although the map of this cove shows there is little difference between the high and low water marks. The pier behind the trawler was probably used to load stone from Comfort's quarry and quarries at the top of Wall's Hill on to stone barges moored there.[29]

In his drawing, Ronald added the pronounced summit above and to the right of the trawler and omitted the two stacks on Long Quarry point, either for dramatic effect or because of his uncertain memory of the odd hump at the end of the point. (One of these "Rhino Horns" recently fell in a storm.) He also has the two masts in front of the steam stack on the trawler, instead of one mast before and after. Ronald evidently learned about the limitations of memory from this experience, and the August 1906 view, *Lyme Regis Harbour*, done from the drawing room window of the Cups Hotel, let Ronald use direct observation away from the disruption of the elements (*A&I* 14).

It seems likely that the pictures Ronald drew during his Torquay holiday functioned as picture postcards, or even the more recent selfie, with known landmarks in the background identifying the popular beaches of Meadfoot and Redgate by Anstey's Cove. He would have been likely to have shared these with his mother on his return home.

Returning to the Incledon family who appears to have sponsored the Torquay holiday, *Roverandom* contains more parallels and apparent references to that family and particularly the relationship between Ronald and Marjorie. When the puppy Roverandom finds another Rover, a mer-dog, the two exchange insults. Ronald Tolkien, the narrator, comments, "you can see that they took rather a fancy to one another at first sight. Indeed, they soon made great friends" (*R* 63). This friendship would fit Marjorie's view of Ronald's visits as "red letter" days. The beautiful Mrs. Artaxerxes is kind. She encourages their play telling them, "Now swim away and amuse yourselves! [...] Don't worry the fire-fish, don't chew the sea-anemones, don't get caught in the clams; and come back to supper!" (*R* 62, 63).

Ronald's visits with his cousin were limited in time, just like Roverandom's short time in the undersea world, and both Ronald's and Roverandom's visits were limited by the "dangerous environment." The sea was "full of dark and awful places where light has never been and never will be, because they will never be uncovered till light has all gone out" (*R* 63). This last may refer to what Ronald would view as his Uncle Walter's benighted Church of England religion. Tolkien called this organization "a pathetic and shadowy medley of half-remembered traditions and mutilated beliefs" (*Bio* 65) and averred that "hatred of our [Catholic] church is after all the real only foundation of the C[hurch] o[f] E[ngland]—so deep it remains when all the superstructure seems removed" (*Letters* 95-96). Uncle Walter, with the religious zeal common at the time with many Church of England members, may have tried to impress his religious views on the young Ronald. In his later writings, Tolkien uses the imagery of light and darkness as a way to express moral/religious/spiritual dichotomies and their significance.

This reading is supported by a limerick that Ronald Tolkien wrote about his Uncle Walter :

> This is an old fellow called "Parkin"
> (His wife simply would not be called "Markin")
> The organ on Sundays
> And business on Mondays
> Don't leave much time over for larkin! (Gardner/Holford 251).

Parkin is a gingerbread cake traditionally enjoyed in the United Kingdom on the 5th of November, also known as Guy Fawkes Night. In 1605, Guy Fawkes was a member of the Catholic conspiracy which had intended to assassinate the Protestant King James I and his parliament by placing explosives/gun powder beneath the House of Lords to blow it up. Although, initially, November 5th was a celebration of the king's survival, Gunpowder Treason Day, as it was named, soon carried strong Protestant religious overtones and was a focus of anti-Catholic sentiment—including burning the Pope in effigy and even rioting. Consequently, Ronald Tolkien's view of "Bonfire Night," or the night of November 5, focused on this tradition of anti-Catholic propaganda from "that abominable business of 1605 [the year of Guy Fawkes's arrest] [...] Certainly one of the wickedest, cleverest and most successful pieces of Government propaganda in history!" (H. Tolkien 71).

Having identified Walter with the parkin cake, representative of anti-Catholic bigotry and prejudice, which Ronald abhorred; the second line notes how Edith Mary—called 'May'—did not use the name 'Mary' because Markin is a pet form of or nickname for 'Mary'. In line three, Ronald observes that in the Church of England on Sunday, there is only "the organ," implying that true religion is not found there.

Further, Walter's surname, 'Incledon', would have spoken to the philologist Ronald Tolkien because he was not only interested in the origins and meanings of place names (Shippey, *Road* 266), but in the origins and meanings of surnames. Using his own name, Ronald identified and calqued his surname 'Tolkien' in English as 'Rashbold' in "The Notion Club Papers" (*SD* 150). Again, he created a Gothic calque of the name 'Tolkien' in 'Dwalakonis' (*Letters* 357).[30] In his notes to "The Notion Club Papers," C. Tolkien "presumes" the names 'Ramer' and 'Dolbear' are significant. He writes, "*Dolbear* is an uncommon surname, but there was a chemist's shop in Oxford called Dolbear and Goodall" with which J.R.R. Tolkien was familiar. Tolkien found this name "engaging" (*SD* 150).

For a man as fascinated by languages and names as Ronald Tolkien was, the first syllable of 'Dolbear' could be read as a cognate with the first syllable in the name 'Tolkien'. The first syllable, 'Dol' or 'Tol', can be read as not only 'foolhardy', but also 'crazy' as in 'bananas' or 'nuts'. The second syllable, 'bear' can be read as *bær* or 'berry' in Danish, Norwegian, and Old Swedish. When read in this manner, 'Dolbear' means crazy, or narcotic, or hallucinatory berry. 'DolBear' is not found in Bosworth-Toller, but the Frisian *Dolkäärs* (literally 'crazy cherry') and the German *Tollkirschen* (literally 'crazy cherry') show the same pattern of syllables using *Dol-* and *Tol-*. These names identify *atropa*, a plant family which includes belladonna or deadly nightshade from which scopolamine is derived. This plant could be appropriately characterized as 'crazy berries'. The second name at the chemist shop, 'Goodall' contributes to the joke because Goodall derives from 'good ale'. The druggists were, therefore, crazy berry/belladonna (or perhaps in modern terms peyote button) and beer—druggists indeed.[31]

Ronald Tolkien, as he became an experienced and accomplished linguist, would have been sensitive to the origins and implications of the name 'Incledon'. Incledon was one of the many new names that came to England following the Norman Conquest of 1066. Robert de Incledon was the first recorded member of the family living in the parish of Braunton, North Devon in 1160 (Vivian 497-99). Ronald's very strong opinions—including "his almost inexplicable" "Gallophobia" which "made him angry not only about what he considered to be the pernicious influence of French cooking in England but about the Norman conquest itself, which pained him as if it had happened in his lifetime" (*Bio* 129)—may have partly expressed a reaction to the name 'de Incledon' associated with the Norman conquest. This Norman association could elaborate another reason for Ronald to dislike his uncle.

Although Ronald Tolkien's dislike/hatred of the Norman Conquest may have been a part of the British mindset at the turn of the twentieth century, the personal connection to his mother would have been likely to be a stronger determinant. Prior to World War I, dating from The Hundred Years War (1337 to 1453) dislike of the French and all things French, if not Gallophobia, was very common in England. The brief rapprochement between the two countries during the Crimean War (1953-1856) in the face of their common enemy, Russia, did little to change this attitude. The World War I alliance between France and England, which buried centuries of traditional animosity between the two countries, was slow to make a dent in this long-standing prejudice. The belief, that the Norman Conquest enabled the destruction of Old English (also known as Anglo-Saxon) and its literature, certainly contributed to Ronald's grudge.

Ronald Tolkien repeatedly expressed dislike of the French language (*Letters* 288). His difficulties speaking fluent French, as opposed to reading it—in the summer of 1913—as a chaperon probably did not improve this view because the French are notoriously and reliably prompt in letting foreigners know when they have not mastered the intricacies of the French language (*Bio* 67). Tolkien admitted that the only foreign language he had ever been fluent in, and then only briefly, was Spanish ("Tolkien in Oxford" 134). During this 1913 visit to France, when Ronald served as the chaperon, he had the unexpected and difficult responsibilities of dealing with the accidental death of one of the boys' aunts: making arrangements for the return of the aunt's body to Mexico, consoling three shocked and grieving boys, and making unanticipated return-travel arrangements (*C&G* 1.51). All of these considerations may have contributed to Tolkien's "almost inexplicable" Gallophobia, but for the linguistically attuned and sensitive Tolkien, the addition of the Norman-French origin of the name 'Incledon' may have been an indelible black mark, adding a possible "French Connection" to Tolkien's belief that his Uncle Walter contributed to his mother's death.

Ronald Tolkien, seemingly recalling his Incledon cousins, pokes fun at the rote memorization of isolated facts—typical of the poor education that Victorian and Edwardian girls received—in the mer-dog's (Marjorie's) responses to Roverandom's question about where a ship was going:

> O! Japan or Honolulu or Manila or Easter Island or Thursday or Vladivotok [*sic*] or somewhere or other I suppose,' said the mer-dog, whose geography was a bit vague, despite hundreds of years of boasted prowlings. 'This is the Pacific, I believe; [...] a warm part, by the feel of it. It's a rather large piece of water (*R* 70).

Although the wizard Mr. Artaxerxes is willing to entertain "little mer-children" by turning "bubbles into red balls," Tolkien, the narrator, later comments: "occasions like the bubbles had been rare" (*R* 68, 81). This would have been true of Walter Incledon, the busy entrepreneur, and fit with the turn-of-the-century model of rationing time with children (Rose 228). Ronald's limerick about Walter, highlighting that he does not have "much time for larkin," indicates that this is because of "business on Mondays" (Gardner/Holford 251).

In addition, the puppy Roverandom, as an apparent expression of part of Ronald Tolkien's experience, "in spite of all these varied sight-seeings and these astonishing journeys" [read trip to Torquay], kept the memory of an injury—the PAM's throwing "ill-tempered lumps of rock" at him (*R* 74). Perhaps Ronald was thinking of some sharp or cutting remarks about his and his mother's Catholicism. In retaliation, Roverandom bites the tail of one of the PAM's sharks which draws the PAM's chariot—"For fun! What fun!"—and precipitates a disaster: the Sea-serpent's turning, causing "terrible tides" so that "the water heaved and shook and bent people's houses and spoilt their repose for miles and miles around" (*R* 77, 76). This part of the story "explained" the frightening high tide and its devastation (*R* xi, 76-77).

The PAM has to return to put the Sea-serpent back to sleep, "and Mrs. Artaxerxes was obliged to stay and watch the wizard" (*R* 79). This could be a reference to May and the sixteen-month-old Marjorie accompanying Walter Incledon, when in the fall and winter of 1893, they stayed with the Tolkiens while Walter was prospecting for contracts in the South African gold and diamond mines (Gardner/Holford 16). Ronald Tolkien may also be thinking of the way his mother, Mabel, not only hosted the expected dinners and parties for Arthur in Bloemfontein, but "was also intrepid enough to accompany Arthur when he went on lengthy business trips across the rugged terrain" (McIlwaine 116).

Ronald Tolkien appears to use the Incledons' 1907 move to Barnt Green, pointedly writing that "Artaxerxes [read Walter Incledon] said goodbye to his father-in-law [read John Suffield] rather coldly." "Some of his [Artaxerxes's] countless sisters-in-law tried to be polite [read Jane Suffield], especially if Mrs. Artaxerxes [read May Suffield Incledon] was there; but everybody was impatient to see him going out of the gate" (*R* 81). Although John Suffield may have been philosophical about May's move to Barnt Green, as other of his children had moved away, "everybody else was sorry [Mrs. Artaxerxes was leaving] and [...] especially her mer-nieces and mer-nephews," which could stand in for Ronald and Hilary (*R* 82).

"The sorriest of all and the most downcast was the mer-dog," which can be read as Marjorie and perhaps also Mary Incledon in this extended amplification of family history: "'Just drop me a line whenever you go to seaside', he [the mer-dog] said 'and I will pop up and have a look at you" (*R* 82). This could be an accurate reflection of the two cousins' separation, given Marjorie's sentiments expressed in her 1971 letter. Ronald "stayed often" at the house in Barnt Green, though the frequency and duration are not specified (*A&I* 20).

By 1918, the Incledons had moved to London in the Chelsea area (voter listing). This move probably was good in terms of Walter's international business and also to make sure May had the best doctors to monitor her symptoms of Parkinson's disease.[32] Also, May and Marjorie could visit Mary—though it is an open question whether Walter joined them. The residence in Chelsea is in a very "upscale" or "posh" neighborhood, and the Incledons had the famous Margaret Haig Mackworth (née Thomas)—2nd Viscountess Rhondda (1883-1958), a Welsh peeress, businesswoman, and a leader in the women's suffrage movement—as their neighbor (phone listing). May Incledon may have been quite impressed by this neighbor because she registered to vote in 1918, which was the first opportunity for women in England. However, she did not re-register until 1933, suggesting that Walter may have expressed his views on this matter. By 1933 with the emergence of the Socialists and Communists and the growing Labour Party, Walter may have felt the Conservatives could use every vote they could get and encouraged May's registration. Walter's practical and conservative mind may have found his wife's openmindedness to seemingly "cock-eyed" ideas—including Roman Catholicism, psychical research, and women's suffrage—trying. The Incledons moved several times in London and were still listed there in 1939.

Even the ending of *Roverandom* may reflect the Incledon family. By 1925, a wheelchair may have been needed at times for May because of her Parkinson's disease. This wheelchair and the effects of Parkinson's disease seem to have been incorporated into the *Roverandom* story. In the story, Roverandom later finds that Artaxerxes and his wife have settled in a seaside town. In reality, the Incledon family moved to Little Barn, Rottingdean, Sussex—a coastal village near Brighton and Hove, a seaside town as specified in *Roverandom* (*R* 86). We do not know when the Incledons bought this country home. During the 1920s, they may only have had regular visits to the fashionable Brighton resorts. However, Ronald Tolkien's story indicates a seaside setting.

Mr. Artaxerxes "purchased a bath-chair" (i.e. wheel-chair) for Mrs. Artaxerxes as her mermaid's tail would not permit walking. However, Mrs. Artaxerxes's, now known as Mrs. PAM, riding in her bath-chair/wheelchair, may reflect Aunt May's use of a wheelchair that protected her from falling due to her Parkinson's disease. Also, bathing in the ocean water could have been beneficial to her Parkinson's disease because the buoyancy of the water eliminates the fear of falling and thus can help to relax muscles and diminish tremors—allowing for easier and larger movements. Ronald appears to have created a Faërian solution for his beloved aunt's condition because her disability would have been greatly reduced, if not resolved, in the form of a mermaid.

Mrs. PAM or rather May Incledon, if this in another of Tolkien's *roman à clef*, "wore the mer-king's jewels in the afternoon, and became very famous, so that no one ever alluded to her tail" (*R* 87). Dijkstra notes that in the nineteenth market society, part of the role of the middle-class wife was as a status symbol of virtue and as a mannequin whose expensive dress advertised the husband's financial success and credit rating (6-7, Flanders 255). Ronald's description of Mrs. Artaxerxes "wearing the mer-king's jewels in the afternoon" fits this pattern, and some of these jewels might have been selected by the Incledons' neighbor in Barnt Green, the knowledgeable Mr. Cohen (*R* 87). With such a display of jewelry, no one ever alluded to Mrs. Artaxerxes's tail—suggesting a reading of May's tremors from Parkinson's.

Coda: A Final Possible Incledon Legacy to Tolkien's Art

May Incledon died in 1936, but her influence persisted in Ronald's continued contact with her daughters, Marjorie and Mary. Marjorie sent Christmas presents and wrote when she heard a broadcast in 1953 of Ronald's translation of *Sir Gawain and the Green Knight* (*C&G* 1.441).[33] Following May's death, her sister Jane Suffield Neave lived at Rottingdean for a short time with "Wink" (Walter) and "Mink" (Marjorie) Incledon and then returned to Dormston in 1936/7 (Morton/Hayes 22). From the 1939 Register, it appears that Walter remarried. Adele Hastings, two years younger than Walter, has her occupation listed as "unpaid domestic duties"—a code for a wife.

By the time the bombing of London started in September 1940, there were concerns about a coastal invasion so the Rottingdean house may not have been considered safe. Marjorie and Walter moved to Worcester for four years during the war. Marjorie had contact with the Tolkien brothers because Ronald and his family came to Hilary's nearby farm, outside of Evesham, and Ronald Tolkien's son, Michael, spent time in the hospital in Worcester during World War II (*C&G* 2.1414).

In Ronald Tolkien's July 31, 1947 letter to his publisher, he lists the occupations of six people who had read *The Lord of the Rings* (*Letters* 122). Carpenter's commentary on this list positively identifies the first three, but "the others cannot be certainly identified, though the artist may have been Tolkien's first cousin Marjorie Incledon, who was a painter" (*Letters* 441).

Marjorie continued to live with her father Walter after he retired to Rottingdean. The Rottingdean phone listings place Walter there from 1946 to the year of his death, 1950. In early September 1947, Ronald visited Marjorie and her father at Rottingdean for a few days (*C&G* 1.341), and Marjorie traveled with Ronald and Edith Tolkien to Ireland more than once (*C&G* 1.851).

Marjorie appears to have continued to live at the Rottingdean house, as indicated by phone listings from 1951 through 1954, until moving to nearby Ditchling in 1955—again according to her phone listings. Edith Tolkien visited Marjorie in Ditchling in late June 1955 (*C&G* 1.483). In January 1956, Ronald sent Marjorie a copy of the just-published *Return of the King* (*C&G* 1.510). A letter of October 23, 1958 to Marjorie from Ronald contains a relaxed and comic update of his latest difficulties with examining in Ireland and getting remodeling done on the new house (*Revised Letters* 410). On June 7, 1960, Marjorie—along with Ronald, Edith and Fr. John Tolkien—attended the wedding of Hilary's son, Julian, in Blackminster (Gardner/Holford 223-24). Ronald first shared his new story *Smith of Wootton Major* with his wife Edith (*Bio* 158), and then by mid-February 1965 with Marjorie (*C&G* 2.1216). On March 22, 1966, Marjorie—as well as Fr. John Tolkien, Michael and Joan Tolkien, Christopher and Priscilla Tolkien, Hilary Tolkien, and Sir Stanley and Rayner Unwin—attended a luncheon for Ronald and Edith's fiftieth wedding anniversary (Gardner/Holford 248). Marjorie had a visit with Ronald in August 1973, shortly before his death (*C&G* 1. 814).

An overlooked, but significant, Incledon contribution may have come from Ronald Tolkien's cousin Mary.

In December 1937, after considerable urging from his publisher for a sequel to *The Hobbit*, Tolkien began writing what would become *The Lord of the Rings*. Ronald Tolkien admitted that *The Hobbit* contains: "your [Ronald's] own personal situation, your past, the things you would like to do, the things you have done, and so that it's simply full, of course, of memories for me" (Lee "Tolkien in Oxford" 140). Similarly, using memories from his childhood in Sarehole—specifically the celebrations for Queen Victoria's 1897 Diamond Jubilee in Moseley—he created the initial scenes from Bilbo's birthday party ("The Diamond Jubilee" this volume). He then appears to have drawn on memories of his 1905 visit to Buckland Hall in Wales, at the age of thirteen, with Fr. Francis Morgan and his brother Hilary to create the Shire's Buckland (Hamill-Keays "Tolkien in Buckland").

Ronald Tolkien then wrote his publisher on February 17, 1938, that he had stopped at what would eventually become Chapter V (*Letters* 29)—although he seems to have made various notes until March 4, 1938 (*RS* 108). Ronald appeared to have writer's block, stating on July 24, 1938, "the pressure of work as a 'research fellow' [...] has taken all my time, and also dried up invention. [...] I have no idea what to do with it [i.e. the sequel to *The Hobbit*]" (*Letters* 38).

On August 9, 1938, Tolkien wrote to his publisher that he was summoned to Walthamstow "on a melancholy errand to the Connaught Hospital only a few hours earlier" and he would go to Walhamstow on August 10 (*C&G* 1.234). This immediate response and required change of plans indicate this was an important call. Ronald had just handled the death of his colleague and collaborator, E.V. Gordon, on July 29, 1938. Tolkien appears to have taken that in stride because he was able to perform five days later on August 3, 1938, in the Oxford Summer Diversions, giving a recitation of Chaucer's "The Nun's Priest's Tale" in fourteenth-century costume and beard (*C&G* 1.233). Earlier in January 1938, Tolkien learned that his son Christopher's x-rays showed heart irregularities. Ronald was understandably perturbed about his son's bad heart, but he was able to continue working and carrying out his responsibilities (*C&G* 1.225). Nevertheless, a peremptory need to visit a hospital does not presage positive news.

Following the August 10, 1938 hospital visit, the "melancholy errand to Connaught Hospital," Ronald was apparently so distressed that he "collapsed" on "the edge of a nervous breakdown" and was "unable" to work for two weeks. Twenty-year-old John Tolkien, thirteen-year-old Christopher and his sister, nine-year-old Priscilla, were all living at home and would have witnessed this. In a letter of August 31, 1938, written three weeks after this visit, Ronald Tolkien writes that

> I am not so much pressed, as oppressed (or depressed). [...] I have been unwell [...] In the last two or three days [...] I have begun again on the sequel to the 'Hobbit'—The Lord of the Ring. It is now flowing along, and getting quite out of hand. It has reached about Chapter VII and progresses toward quite unforeseen goals (*Letters* 40).

On April 1, 1944, a similar situation appears to have occurred when Tolkien, who was stuck in Book Four of *The Lord of the Rings*, visited his old school, King Edward's in Birmingham (Garth, "As Under a Green Sea" 9-10). There, the memories, or possibly visions, of "ghosts that rose from the pavements," the ghosts of healthy young men and friends who had died in World War I, triggered Tolkien to draw on his own painful war experiences (*Letters* 70). This crisis of 1938, following the Connaught Hospital visit—like the visit of 1944—seems to have suddenly released his writer's block. It seems to have precipitated Ronald Tolkien's burst of writing the three Bombadil chapters in August 1938, chapters he basically never revised (*RS* 110, 112, 120, 127)—unlike much of the rest of *The Lord of the Rings*, which was rewritten and re-plotted ceaselessly. This surge follows the method Carpenter reports:

> When in a black mood he [Tolkien] would feel that there was no hope, either for himself or the world; and since this was often the very mood that drove him to record his feelings on paper, his diaries tend to show only the sad side of his nature (*Bio* 129).

The most likely candidate for a distressing event at Connaught Hospital was the revelation of the diagnosis of cancer, a death sentence, in Mary Incledon. After converting to Catholicism, Mary lived alone for many years in a London flat (1B Carlisle Place, Victoria SW1P 1BX in Gardner/Holford 193) two blocks from the Roman Catholic Westminster Cathedral. Connaught Hospital in Walthamstow is in the greater London area, a likely medical facility that Mary might use (*C&G* 2.568).

Mary no longer lived in her family's comfortable residence, but lived in seemingly modest accommodations, paid for by income from shares of her father's business, because of her conversion to Catholicism and insistence on attending Mass (*C&G* 2.568). Ronald Tolkien was likely to have seen a parallel between the "persecution" of his mother Mabel for becoming a Catholic, by Walter's discontinuance of financial support (*Bio* 24) and Mary's suffering similar treatment with living on a limited income. Ronald keenly felt that his mother's death at the age of thirty-four was the result of poverty and "of a disease hastened by persecution of her faith" (*Letters* 54). Ronald might have understandably felt the *déjà vu* of history repeating itself. He could have easily seen his young cousin, Mary, around the age of forty-three, enduring merely a different deadly disease with Mary's end "hastened by persecution of her faith." Further, Mary was the godmother to Ronald's eldest son, John, so she and Ronald had a common bond in their commitment to Catholicism.

Mary and Ronald also shared childhood memories. Mary was part of the "debates" concerning the relation of fairies and real life (*TOFS* 233-234) and was a co-inventor with Ronald of *Nevbosh* (*Bio* 36). Mary, like Ronald, had a deep interest in art (McIlwaine 164). Mary was living in Moseley and was in contact with Ronald when he experienced a trauma that led to the dream of the Great

Wave during the "sad and troublous" time in Sarehole (*Bio* 23, OFS 135). She was likely to have known the circumstances that led to that calamity, as well as Ronald's loss of the Sarehole willow for which he mourned in *Leaf by Niggle* (*Bio* 22, Ready 141). She would have known about the destruction of Ronald's first invented languages when he failed to pass the entrance examination for King Edward's School (Plimmer/Plimmer, Grotta-Kurska 18). The two cousins had much in common and knew each other's trials and sufferings.

Ronald Tolkien was likely to have felt "the shadow of the past" after a hospital visit with a dying childhood friend and cousin who knew of the "sad and troublous" years in Sarehole—a fellow Catholic who had also weathered family prejudice. He then "collapsed" on "the edge of a nervous breakdown," "unable" to work for two weeks. His response was to finally set course on the voyage of *The Lord of the Rings* and the crown of his life's writings. The hospital visit, probably to Mary, is one more debt to May Incledon and her family that seems to have been unnoticed.

Ronald Tolkien wrote: "I feel it is better not to state everything (and indeed it is more realistic, since in chronicles and accounts of 'real' history, many facts that some enquirer would like to know are omitted, and the truth has to be discovered or guessed from such evidence as there is)" (*Letters* 354). The authors have followed his method of discovering or guessing the truth "from such evidence as there is." Researching May's family background and life, her influence on and involvement with her nephew and godson Ronald Tolkien, and the longstanding effects of her daughters on him uncovers some new and interesting aspects of J.R.R. Tolkien.

Carpenter, who had access to all of Tolkien's letters, diaries, and papers, certainly knew about the significance of the Incledons in Tolkien's life, writing, and artwork. However, Carpenter "castrated" his original draft of the Tolkien biography and "cut out everything which was likely to be contentious" ("Learning about Ourselves" 270, 271). This redaction seems to include the Incledons and in particular the disliked Uncle Walter. Carpenter promised "if the Bodleian is ever able to open its Tolkien coffers fully" a "magnificent new biography [...] could be written" (Carpenter, "Review: Cover Book"). The role of the Incledons will be part of that new biography.

End Notes

1 Mabel, May, Ronald, and Hilary's Church of England baptisms would have been accepted by the Catholic Church so that they were said to have been "received" into the Catholic Church after proper instruction.

2 "Sue Young Histories." http://sueyounghistories.com/archives/2009/11/21/john-suffield-1802-1891/, accessed on 5/5/2022. This site lists the brass foundry offices at 1, 2, and 3 Crooked Lane, and 29, 30 and 31 Union Passage, Birmingham.

3 By 1881, Walter was no longer living with the family according to the census.

4 ABOUT page "Cape Incledon." http://www.incledoncape.co.za/html/about.php, accessed on 4/11/2022. Victorian white-collar, salaried managers had coveted jobs so they tended to stay with the same business for their entire working lives.

5 The Chantry Road and Park Hill Residents' Association website documents the origin of Chantry Road: "Nos 54-64 were also built at this time [1890s]—the house names are still inscribed above the doors in identical letters" (http://craph.org.uk/ about/downloaded 2/25/2019).

6 Given that Mabel was able to teach Latin, French, and German to Ronald, she certainly was given a more than traditional education by her nonconformist family that valued education for women.

7 "Paying for healthcare: life in Britain before the 'free' NHS." HistoryExtra, official website of the BBC Magazine. https://www.historyextra.com/period/20th-century/nhs-history-pay-healthcare-free/, accessed on 12/3/2020.

8 Derdziński, Ryszard, "John Benjamin Tolkien (1807-1896): a grandfather, a philanthropist, a religious man" Friday, January 5, 2018, http://tolkniety.blogspot.com/, accessed on 10/5/2023.

9 "Bank of England Inflation Calculator." https://www.bankofengland.co.uk/monetary-policy/inflation/inflation-calculator, accessed on 11/6/2023. "X E Currency Converter, accessed on 11/6/2023. https://www.xe.com/currencyconverter/convert/?Amount=1946335.92&From=GBP&To=USD. "Grace's Guide to British Industrial History," accessed on 5/5/2022. https://www,gracesgruide.co.uk/1922_Who%27s_Who_In_Engineering:_Company_E.

10 The first two chapters of Carpenter's first draft of the biography contained paragraphs that differed from the published version: "most notably one that describes the family's reaction to Mabel's becoming a Catholic and the religious leanings of Walter Incledon and his family" (Gardner/Holford 286).

11 J.S. Ryan reports that Jungian philosophy and its implications for literature was "a topic known to have been much aired by the Inklings" (*Cult or Culture?* 89). Jung's ideas, which grew out of psychical research, would have fit well with the Inklings's interest in myths and the place of the Christian story in relation to myth. Tolkien used the concept of the Jungian unconscious when he rewrote material from the abandoned 1936-37 "The Lost Road" in "The Notion Club Papers" written around 1946.

12 Lang was not the only one. Professor C.D. Broad of Cambridge was the President of the SPR in 1935 and 1958, and Professor H.H. Price of Oxford was the President in 1939 and 1960.

13 These interests may have resurfaced years later in *The Lord of the Rings* in the episodes of the Barrow-wight (Burns "Night-wolves, Half-trolls" 189-93) and Aragorn's summoning the ghosts on the Paths of the Dead.

14 "Grace's Guide to British Industrial History: 1922 Who's Who in Industrial Engineering: Company L," accessed on 5/5/2022. https://www.gracesguide.co.uk/1922 _Who's_Who_In_Engineering:_Company_L.

15 Hammond and Scull note Tolkien's familiarity with the Arts and Crafts movement's decorative style (*A&I* 9, 10, 43).

16 "On 11 October 1913, an Oxford undergraduate bought a pair of black leather football [rugby] boots for 14 shillings and sixpence and spent an extra sixpence on a pair of brown laces." "Rare ledgers reveal shoe-buying habits of Tolkien and Waugh," accessed on 6/9/2020. https://www.theguardian.com/uk-news/2017/mar/22/rare-ledgers-shoe-buying-habits-of-tolkien-waugh-ducker-son.

17 "Inflation Calculator. Bank of England." https://www.bankofengland.co.uk/monetary-policy/inflation/inflation-calculator and "XE Currency Converter." https://www.xe.com/currencyconverter/convert/, both accessed on 11/9/2023.
18 This debt would have had to have been paid for Tolkien to graduate, and there are no indications that there were impediments to his obtaining his degree.
19 https://discovery.nationalarchives.gov.uk/results/r?_q=rupert+suffield&_sd=1914&_ed=1920&_hb=, accessed on 9/20/2022.
20 *THE LONDON GAZETTE*, 8 February 1916.
21 Documentation of Edith staying with the Mittons in Birmingham is courtesy of David Robbie from information from the Tolkien Estate.
22 Simon Tolkien's website, www.simontolkien.com/author.html.
23 "Torquay's history as a tourist destination." https://www.tlh.co.uk/blog/torquays-history-tourist-destination/, accessed on 5/6/2022. "Torquay-the evolution of a tourist resort." https://wearesouthdevon.com/torquay-evolution-tourist-resort/, accessed on 5/6/2022.
24 Tolkien wrote he liked "history, astronomy, botany," as well as or better than fairy tales as a child (OFS 135). "History" here could imply natural history given the other two subjects.
25 Ronald Tolkien's Aunt Grace Bindley Tolkien married William Charles Mountain. Ronald learned about his Tolkien family from his Aunt Grace (*Bio* 16, 18). The Tolkien brothers had holidays with the Mountain family after their mother's death in 1904 (*C&G* 2.814), and would have seen their Tolkien grandmother during their visits, see "Tea in Hay" in this volume.
26 Hammond and Scull's *A&I* was published in 1992, and a number of details have been learned since that time.
27 Wikipedia commons also contains many photographs showing a good match to the central part of Tolkien's drawing of the beach with the escarpment of Wall's Hill in the background. The photographs also show the "hump" or "rhino horn" that Tolkien tried to reproduce.
28 "History and Restoration of Brixham Trawler Pilgrim." https://classic-sailing.com/article/history-and-restoration-brixham-trawler-pilgrim/, accessed on 5/17/2022.
29 This is documented in a July 11, 1884 inquest (https://www.genuki.org.uk/big/eng/DEV/CourtRecords/Inquests TT1846). This quarry was closed by 1886 so this pier was no longer in use.
30 Ronald Tolkien grew up being told 'Tolkien' derived from *tollkühn* in German meaning 'foolhardy' (*Bio* 19). In 1967, Tolkien signed a poem that he had written to congratulate W.H. Auden on the occasion of Auden's sixtieth birthday ("For W.H.A."). Tolkien used an Old English calque of his name: *Rægnold Hrædmoding*. The first name (*Rægnold*) is the Old English equivalent of Tolkien's second name Ronald, and the surname (*Hrædmoding*) is a calque of the sense of *Tolkien* < *Tollkühn*. It is parsed as: *Hræd* (*rash*) + *Moda* (personal name = *courageous*) + *–ing* (*descendants of* …) (Hooker, *Translating 'The Hobbit'* 106). Other calques include in 1909 *Spurius Vectigalius Acer, Haruspex,* in1910 *Eisphorides Acribus Polygloteus* (*C&G* 1.22), in 1911 *T. Portorius Acer Germanicus*, and in *The Hobbit*, Tolkien appears to again play with his name when he describes Bilbo Baggins as 'audacious' (Hooker, *Translating 'The Hobbit'* 104-10) because Bilbo Baggins was based on Ronald Tolkien (*Bio* 175).
31 Spelling variations of 'Dolbear' include: Dolberg, Dölberg, Dolben, Dahlberg, Dalberg and many more. https://www.houseofnames.com/dolbear-family-crest, accessed on 11/6/2023.
32 May Incledon died August 22, 1936 from "paralysis agitans"—or what we would now call Parkinson's disease—at the age of 70 (death certificate). Parkinson's is a chronic, slowly-progressive disease of the nervous system that is characterized by slowly-spreading tremors; muscular weakness and rigidity; and an increasing risk of falls.
33 Relatives do not begin sending Christmas presents at the age of sixty-one. Presumably, Christmas greetings and presents were a longstanding tradition for the cousins.

Chapter Four

J.R.R. Tolkien: Ambidexter

Nancy Bunting

J.R.R. Tolkien was a unique individual. He was not quite like other people. In the 1911 photograph of the Exeter College freshmen, Ronald Tolkien stands properly lined up with the rest of the incoming freshmen (McIlwaine 161). By the time of the Exeter Sexcentenary in 1914, however, Ronald expresses himself by hanging at an angle from a vine, while all the other proper and upright Oxonians line up decorously (Garth, *Tolkien at Exeter* cover). It is unlikely that the photographer would have asked Ronald Tolkien to perch at an angle in the 1914 Exeter group photograph; rather, it is more likely Ronald had the idea and persuaded the photographer into letting him have the pose of his choice. Although Ronald was obviously quite intelligent, as seen in his academic career; and had good social skills, as evidenced in his many long-term friendships and ability to negotiate syllabus reform in his department at Oxford; and had a deep and serious view of religion like many of his contemporaries, as seen in his involvement with the T.C.B.S. and the Inklings; his imagination and dazzling command of languages set him apart. This paper proposes that this difference was at least partly based on something that has not been considered previously, namely that Ronald Tolkien was an ambidexter—a person with the ability to use both left and right hands easily.[1] This paper discusses the evidence that would support this description of Ronald Tolkien as ambidextrous and the implications of that designation.

Ronald Tolkien showed the behaviors and had the background and interests found in ambidexters. Ronald wrote with his right hand (*TFA* 6), but in the late nineteenth century when Ronald grew up, he would not have been allowed to write with his left hand.[2] He also used silver ware like a right-handed person (BBC documentary "In Their Own Words"). However, a number of photographs show Ronald Tolkien with his pipe in his left hand when his right hand does not appear encumbered or occupied (google. Images of J.R.R. Tolkien). Video clips of Ronald Tolkien show him repeatedly pointing with his left, as well as his right, hand when his right hand appears to be free (YouTube: BBC documentary "In Their Own Words, J.R.R Tolkien"). Although we cannot request Ronald Tolkien to answer the standard questionnaires on laterality that ask which hand you use to throw a ball or tie shoelaces, Tolkien's pointing with his left hand and holding his pipe in his left hand are not the actions of the predictable 90% of the population who are right-handed.

Ronald Tolkien's Suffield family had a history of "engravers and plate-makers," which is consistent with the inheritance of ambidextrous ability (*Bio* 18). Several occupations, including those of etchers, who do engravings, and lithographers, exploit the ability to do mirror-writing. Mirror writing or *Spiegelschrift* is a neurological phenomenon that can appear in entirely normal people, is inherited, and is most often seen in left-handed or ambidextrous people (Schott, "Mirror writing: reflections" 5-6). Ronald Tolkien cited the mirror writing of Mooreeffoc or Coffee-room in his 1939 lecture "On Fairy stories" (OFS 146). This word was originally created by Chesterton, and Tolkien used it "to denote the queerness of things that have become trite, when they are seen suddenly from a new angle" (OFS 146). Ronald Tolkien, however, is using a literal mirror image or reversal, an example of *Spiegelschrift*, to express a metaphor or concept about reversal. The hallmark of fantasy is the reversal in the narrative of the everyday world's perspective (Rabkin).

Ronald's awareness of and familiarity with this phenomenon may have come from his Aunt Jane, his mother's younger sister. Ronald's Aunt Jane Suffield was "the first [female] pupil to attend extra physiology classes at Mason College," the forerunner of Birmingham University (Burns "Jane Suffield"). Frank James Allen was the professor of Physiology at Birmingham. At the age of thirteen, he accidentally discovered he could do mirror writing with his left hand, and he published an article on mirror writing in the prestigious medical journal *Brain* in 1896 (Schott, "Mirror writing: Allen's self observations" 2159).

A small college is not likely to have more than one instructor in physiology, and professors have always talked about their own research interests to their students. It is very likely that Allen shared his views of ambidexters with his students, including Ronald's Aunt Jane who appears to have attended classes at Mason from 1891 until 1895, when she obtained her degree in Botany from the University of London by means of its correspondence school (Burns, "Jane Suffield;" Gardner/Holford 55). Aunt Jane moved to Liverpool in 1896 to teach science in a girls' high school but then returned to the Birmingham area in 1899 when she again taught at King Edward's Girls' Grammar School at Bath Row (Burns, "Jane Suffield"). On her return, in 1900, she tutored the eight year old Ronald Tolkien in geometry to prepare him for taking the King Edward's School entrance exam (*Letters* 377).

Mirror writing is a variant of the standard handwriting taught in school. Ronald Tolkien "had a different style of handwriting for each of his friends," and Ronald's interest in handwriting as well as languages, etymology, and alphabets began in childhood (*Bio* 57, *Letters* 377). Mirror writing is almost always carried out by the left hand because this appears to be the "natural script" for the left hand (Schott, "Mirror writing: reflections" 7, 10). In respect to handwriting, Ronald Tolkien can be compared to Charles L. Dodgson, the Oxford mathematician and author who wrote *Alice's Adventures in Wonderland* and *Through the Looking-Glass* under the pseudonym Lewis Caroll. He may have been left-handed, though he wrote with his right hand, and composed "looking-glass" letters to amuse young acquaintances. Caroll also wrote a rebus letter with pictures inserted in the text (Schott, "Mirror writing: Allen's self observations" 2159). The twelve year old Ronald wrote a rebus letter to Fr. Francis Morgan on August 8, 1904 with a dazzling display of visual and language play (Priestman 17; *TFA* 33; Bridoux, "Letting Images Speak" 11-12). Dodgson, like Tolkien, is famous for his word play, and recent studies show that around 20% of left-handed (and this is likely to be applicable to ambidexters) people show bilateral or right hemisphere dominance in language, as opposed to the typical left hemisphere dominance of right-handed people (Szaflarski, Binde, Possing, McKiernan, Ward, Hammeke). That is, ambidexters have brains that are organized differently than the 90% of the population who are right-handed. They are consequently likely to process and think differently than the majority of other people.

The evidence of Ronald Tolkien using mirror writing and reversals is scattered throughout his works. Being ambidextrous may be reflected in Ronald's interest in reversals that began as a teenager with his invented language *Nevbosh* in which he reversed 'cow' to become *woc* around 1905-6 (Bio 36). Ronald's late 1913 or early 1914 monogram on the back of *The Book of Ishness* is an example of mirror writing (*A&I* 43). His monogram with the Rs mirror-reversed is evident in the August 1912 drawing *Keystone of Door* (*A&I* 18) and in the watercolor *Eeriness* of January 1914 (*A&I* 43, McIlwaine 169). From his studies, Ronald would have been familiar with the fact that Ogham and other languages are written right to left, but his lifelong play with reversals and mirror images suggests more than academic interest. In *Roverandom*, a story created in September 1925, but only committed to paper in perhaps late 1927 (*R* xii), Ronald Tolkien briefly called the character Psamathos a "nilbog" which is 'goblin' spelled backward (*R* 93).

Ronald Tolkien showed continuing interest in mirror-writing and reversals in his twenties and thirties. He appears to have used a mirror image of the map of India to generate some of the map of *The Silmarillion* (Hooker, *T&S*). There are also language reversals at the time of earliest stories of *The Silmarillion.* For example, in the "Qenya Lexicon," probably begun in the spring of 1915 (QL xii), the root SILI- is seen in words such as *sil* for 'moon' and *silwa* 'glossy' (QL 83). In the "Gnomish or Goldogrin Lexicon," begun between May and August 1917 (*C&G* 1.108), *sil* and *thil* were used for 'moon' (GL 67, 72). These invented roots appear to be a reversal of the Danish or Norwegian *lys*, meaning 'light' and derived from Old Norse (Hooker, *Glossology* 41). The Elves' names for the Sun and Moon (*S* 114), *Anar* and *Rana*, are the same name, but written backward (Hooker, Glossology 43). In 1918, when he was still working on the "Qenya Lexicon," Ronald spent time in the hospital and worked on languages: improving his Spanish and Italian and teaching himself some Russian (*Bio* 98). It appears that the Gnomish *rim* or 'peaceful, calm' (GL 65) qualifies as a reversal of Russian *mir* or 'peace' (Hooker, *Glossology* 43).

The map for *The Hobbit*, which was completed by 1931 when Tolkien was thirty-nine, appears to be based on reversals. Steve Ponty proposes that the Shire is a mirror image of the map of Wales, and this concept is elaborated by Mark Hooker in *Iter Tolkienensis.* In *The Hobbit*, Tolkien also seems to have borrowed from Jules Verne's *Journey to the Center of the Earth* which features true mirror writing on a map, just like the text written in moon letters on Thror's map (Hooker "Journey"). Tolkien created mirror-image writing on the reverse side of Thor's Map, but this was not used when *The Hobbit* was published due to the difficulties of reproduction (*C&G* 2.523).

Language reversals appear in Tolkien's *A Secret Vice* from 1931. Tolkien notes that 'scratch' can be reversed to create a seemingly alien word, although it only contains English sounds (*MC* 208-09, Fimi/Higgins 19, 21). This documents that Tolkien did language reversals, like those noted from the 1920s, deliberately. In the December 1946 "Notion Club Papers," Tolkien plays with the name, 'Basil Blackwell and Mott' transforming it into 'Whitburn and Thoms' (*SD* 149, 153). Part of this change is the phonetic reversal of 'Mott' to 'Thoms'.[3]

There are some indications in *The Lord of the Rings* for Tolkien's continuing interest in reversals. Ronald Tolkien's "pictorial" memory appears to have included vivid memories of the 1897 Queen Victoria's Diamond Jubilee which he used when writing about Bilbo's birthday party (*Letters* 343). For the grand finale of the 1897 fireworks, the electric "fairy lights," likely to have been a novelty for the young Tolkien, were abruptly shut off. Gandalf's sudden burst of light that covers Bilbo's escape would reverse that effect (see "Diamond Jubilee" in this volume).

Ronald Tolkien admitted to using memories of his expedition to Switzerland at the age of nineteen in 1911 not only for the "thunder battle" in *The Hobbit*'s Misty Mountains, but also for the background for the crossing of the Misty Mountains and the peaks of Moria in *The Lord of the Rings* (*Letters* 309, 391). The most prominent members of the 1911 walking party were the well-to-do Brookes-Smiths, who organized the trip. Ronald routinely abbreviated names, as seen in his letters (e.g. *Letters* 102), and the comic possibilities of abbreviating Brookes-Smith would have been immediately evident to him as Ronald had a pronounced sense of humor (*Bio* 130). If Ronald was going to poke fun at and parody the Brookes-Smiths, a surreptitious reversal of initials to S.-B. could discreetly veil his allusion. Bilbo and Frodo's distant relations, the Sackville-Bagginses, are known as the S.-B.s, as in "Whatever happens to the rest of my stuff, when the S.-B.s get their claws on it" (*FR* I iii 67). Given that the 'S.-B.s' have a pretentious hyphenated name, the name could have originated as Ronald's swipe at the ostentatiously rich Brookes-Smiths. This possibility is supported by Ronald's September 1911 parody of the Finnish *Kalevala*, *The New Lemminkainen goeth to his brother in the Southlands* or *Lemminkainen goeth to the Lands of Ima the Smith and Kemi the Brook* (Gardner/Holford 66). The second title plays with the Brookes-Smith name and the character of Ilma or

Ilmarinen in the *Kalevala*. The Sackville-Bagginses make their first appearance in the legendarium at Bilbo's auction in *The Hobbit* (xix). Ronald Tolkien was likely to have known that Hilary, as employee of the Brookes-Smith and his Aunt Jane, helped set up items and assist in February 1914, at the large auction which was held when the lease on the Brookes-Smith's residence, The Lodge, expired (Bunting/Currie "Swiss Walking Tour, Part I" 3).

In a February 23, 1941 letter to Christopher Tolkien, Ronald Tolkien casually refers to an "Ovenlid" in the choir gallery at church (*Revised Letters* 66). An explanatory note states this was Tolkien's "playful reversal" of the name 'DelNovo'. The Tolkien family was evidently familiar with Ronald's everyday propensity to alter and reverse names. This was not an activity limited solely to his invented languages or artwork.

Tolkien also reversed the compass rose in his drawing of Shelob's Lair (*WR* 201). Reversed compass directions are associated, in a distinctive way, with right and left hands in Elvish (Hooker, *T&S* 112-16). A compass would be an anachronism in Middle-earth.

Even in the late story, *Smith of Wootton Major*, published in 1965, Tolkien plays with name reversals. The smith of the title was known from "Far Easton" to "the Westwood" (*SWM* 17). In *Smith of Wootton Major*, Tolkien appears to be drawing on memories of being in the Staffordshire area as a young man in the Army, and there is a town near his training camp of Cannock Chase called 'Weston', a common English town name.[4] Although 'Easton' is also a common British place name with examples in Hampshire, Dorset, and Cambridgeshire, Ronald Tolkien appears to have reversed the directional portion ('West town') of the name 'Weston', that he knew in his youth, changing it to 'Easton' ('East town'). He then continued playing with reversal of directions by completing the image with the addition of 'Westwood'. Westwood is again another actual place name with an instance in Wiltshire. Reversing the directional part of the place names masks the biographical association of the town of Weston in Ronald's early life and demonstrates the linguistic playfulness of a man who could indulge in "a low philological jest" in the name of Smaug the dragon in *The Hobbit* (Letters 31) and create characters and their names, Bill Stickers and Major Road Ahead, from posted notices (*Bio* 161).

Ronald Tolkien wrote around 1968 that the Eldar or Elves are "ambidexters" and "the allocation of different habitual services or duties to the right or the left was a purely individual and personal matter, undirected by any general inherited racial habit. And Elda could usually write with either hand" ("Eldarin Hands, Fingers and Related Writings" [Eldarin] 9). Tolkien is clearly familiar with the concept of 'ambidexters', and one can only wonder how much this reflects Ronald's own experience. Tolkien added, "If written with left [hand] (as often in letters or private moods) the Tengwar were reversed, and were correct in a mirror," although this "changed later" (Eldarin 11).[5] In other words, Tengwar written with the left hand was *Spiegelschrift* or mirror writing.[6]

Ronald Tolkien's family history of "engravers and plate-makers" is consistent with the inheritance of ambidextrous ability. A number of photographs and video clips show Tolkien using his left hand in a way that right-handed people typically do not. Tolkien had a life-long interest in reversals of words and images as seen in his invented language *Nevbosh*, the map of *The Silmarillion*, the map and moon letters of *The Hobbit*, and a comment in "On Fairy-stories." This interest in reversals would be derived from and is consistent with the ambidextrous ability which reflects a unique brain organization. Tolkien's comments in the 1968 "Eldarin Hands, Fingers and Related Writings" probably reflect his own experience because the 90% of the population who are right-handed rarely consider the possibility of using either hand. In addition, being ambidextrous could have contributed to Ronald Tolkien's imaginative ability to see new connections among stories and patterns and his amazing ability to reverse and play with languages in new and surprising ways.

End Notes

1 Well-documented studies show differences in the brains of left- and right-handers, including areas involving language. See "Large Study Compares the Brains of Right-Handers and Left-Handers: Max Planck Institute for Psycholinguistics." November 17, 2021. https://www.mpi.nl/news/large-study-compares-brains-left-handers-and-right-handers, accessed on 10/12/2023 and "Handedness- and Hemispheric-Related Differences in Small-World Brain Network: A Diffusion Tensor Imaging Tractography Study." Meiling Li, Heng Chen, Junping Wang, Feng Liu, Zhiliang Long, Yifeng Wang, Yasser Iturria-Medina, Jiang Zhang, Chunshui Yu, and Huafu Chen. *Brain Connect.* 2014 March 1, 4(2), pp. 145-156. https://www.ncbi.nlm.nih.gov/pmc/articles/PMC3961786/, accessed on 10/12/2023.

2 Throughout the Middle Ages and continuing through at least the middle of the twentieth century, the use of the left hand had negative cultural connotations and was discouraged.

3 Language reversal courtesy of Mark Hooker

4 See also "The Interlace" in this volume.

5 Tengwar is one of Ronald Tolkien's invented scripts. Tolkien attributed this one to Fëanor, and it was originally used for the Elvish languages. Ronald Tolkien reports having to write with his left hand in 1953 at the age of sixty-one, due to pain in his right hand (*Letters* 173). Problems with pain in his right hand appear in letters from November 1961 and in 1963 (*Letters* 311, 325, 335). Later in 1969, he complained of trouble with his left hand (*Letters* 335, 397). The use of the left hand, in the 1950s and 1960s as compensation for pain in his right hand, is not evidence of any ambidextrous ability. However, if Ronald were ambidextrous, this switch to using his left hand would have been easier than it would have been for a right-handed person.

6 The possible sample of Tolkien's mirror writing with the left hand from approximately 1968-69 appears shaky ("Eldarin" 37). However, in Ronald Tolkien's letter of January 2, 1969, he complained of trouble with his left hand so that might have affected this isolated example (*Letters* 397). Also, given the many complaints from both Christopher Tolkien and Carl Hostetter concerning the inscrutability of Tolkien's handwriting, it is hard to say how much worse this sample might be than Tolkien's regular handwriting.

Chapter Five

For Want of a Biography, the Story Was Lost

Toby Widdicombe

On 2 September 1973, John Ronald Reuel Tolkien died at the age of 81 from pneumonia and complications of a stomach ulcer. The obituaries (history's first take on any biography) were mostly complimentary and balanced, but one can already see canards and significant errors creeping in. *The New York Times*, for example, propagates the myth of Tolkien as a harmless academic par excellence:

> He was a gentle, blue-eyed, donnish-appearing man who favored tweeds, smoked a pipe and liked to take walks and ride an old bicycle (though he converted to a stylish car with the success of his books) ("J.R.R. Tolkien Dead at 81").

No to the caricature of a don. No to when he bought his first car. (That was in 1932—fully five years before *The Hobbit* was published and 23 years before all of *The Lord of the Rings* appeared). And no—later on in the obituary—to Tolkien's mother, Mabel Suffield, serving "as a missionary in Zanzibar." The biographies, of course, took a little longer to appear, with one outlier: William Ready's *The Tolkien Relation: A Personal Inquiry* (1968).[1] First came Daniel Grotta's *J.R.R. Tolkien: Architect of Middle Earth* [sic] three years after Tolkien's death (1976) and then Humphrey Carpenter's *J.R.R. Tolkien: A Biography* a year later (1977), a biography which had been authorized by Tolkien's heirs. A decade later the floodgates opened, and I offer here only a selection of what has come out to date: Shorto's *J.R.R. Tolkien: Man of Fantasy* (1988); Collins' *J.R.R. Tolkien: Master of Fantasy* (1992); Neimark's *J.R.R. Tolkien* (1996); Moseley's *J.R.R. Tolkien* (1997); Pearce's *Tolkien: Man and Myth* (1998); Coren's *J.R.R. Tolkien: The Man Who Created The Lord of the Rings* (2001); White's *J.R.R. Tolkien. A Biography* (2001); Duriez's *Tolkien and the Lord of the Rings* (2001); Lynch's *J.R.R. Tolkien: Creator of Languages and Legends* (2003); Jones's *J.R.R. Tolkien: A Biography* (2003); Willett's *J.R.R. Tolkien* (2004); Scull and Hammond's Chronology volume in *The J.R.R. Tolkien Companion and Guide* (2006); Wheeler's *J.R.R. Tolkien* (2009); Needham's *Biography of*

J.R.R. Tolkien (2012); Elansea's *J.R.R. Tolkien: Codemaker; Spy-master; Hero. An Unauthorised Biography* (2015); McAlister's *John Ronald's Dragons: The Story of J.R.R. Tolkien* (2017); and Braun's *J.R.R. Tolkien: Epic Fantasy Author* (2022). And there's an important rivulet to complement this rushing stream: biographies about particular parts of Tolkien's life. John Garth seems to have specialized in these, with his *Tolkien and the Great War: The Threshold of Middle-earth* (2004); *Tolkien at Exeter College: How an Oxford Undergraduate Created Middle-earth* (2014); and *Worlds of J.R.R. Tolkien: The Places That Inspired Middle-earth* (2020).[2]

So, everything would seem to be doing well in the world of Tolkien scholarship. Lots of people have said lots of useful things about the most original writer Britain produced in the previous century. *It isn't doing well, however. Very far from it.* It is fair to say that of all the major British writers of the twentieth century—Ali, Byatt, Conrad, Eliot, Fitzgerald, Golding, Larkin, Lewis, Murdoch, Woolf, and the rest—Tolkien has been *the* most ill served by his biographers. One can see that at least one scholar knows this is the case but glosses over the fact. Take this comment from Colin Duriez in his *Tolkien and C. S. Lewis: The Gift of Friendship* (2003): "In composing this study of their relationship I owe an enormous debt to the main biographers—Humphrey Carpenter, Walter Hooper, the late Roger Lancelyn Green, George Sayer, and Andrew Wilson" (Preface, x). This list looks impressive, but there's a glaring problem with it: of these five names only one (Carpenter) refers to a biography of Tolkien. This 4:1 ratio holds for Duriez's bibliography too. There are about 30 titles in Duriez's bibliography for *Tolkien and C. S. Lewis* devoted solely to Tolkien, with very few of them (incidentally) just about Tolkien's life. The rest of the approximately 120 references are given over to C. S. Lewis or to the Inklings. The reasons for this failure of scholarship make up a complicated, fascinating, and convoluted tale of missed opportunities and poor decisions. It is a tale, however, which does not have to end, rather predictably, with a bathetic ending: the works remain and the great man dwindles and eventually vanishes. It only takes a change of heart to allow Tolkien to stand before us as he was and not as he has been carefully shaped to be. The tale begins at the beginning with Tolkien's own attitude to biography. It then moves on to the Tolkien family and the unstinting efforts, in particular, of Tolkien's third child, Christopher, to guard his father's extraordinary—frankly, sui generis—achievement. It ends with a plea of a sort for a better way forward. Along the way it shows how accidents of history and circumstance can play a role in how someone is remembered.

Tolkien's Attitude to Biography

In their remarkably comprehensive *Reader's Guide*, Christina Scull and Wayne Hammond begin their entry on "Biographies" with this assertion: "Tolkien held qualified views on biography and its uses, in particular when he was the subject" (108). As I see it, this assertion is not accurate at all. It turns as well on the meaning of "qualified," an unfortunate and ambiguous word under the circumstances. (Are we talking about *qualified* as in fit for something, or *qualified* as in having reservations about something?) In fact, Tolkien was adamantly opposed to anyone writing his biography besides the brief copy for dust jackets and the like. This opposition actually gets him into some logical problems unusual for him as a philologist, perhaps because he is so opposed to his life being picked over for whatever reason. As quoted by Scull and Hammond, in a 1957 letter to Caroline Everett (who had written an MA thesis on his fiction), Tolkien remarks: "I do not feel inclined to go into biographical detail. I doubt its relevance to criticism. Certainly in any form less than a complete biography, interior and exterior, which I alone could write, and which I do not intend to write" (*Letters* 257, qtd. in *Reader's Guide* 108). That would make Tolkien's book an *auto*biography and not a biography. A creature of quite a different colour. It would also make that autobiography subject to all sorts of biases as Tolkien probably knows. The temptation to embroider and the habit of forgetting primary among them. There is also an irony in Tolkien's response to Everett: he says he does not believe in biography and then proceeds to offer her a potted autobiography in the midst of which he unintentionally suggests why autobiography is often much less reliable than biography: "The chief biographical fact to me," he says, "is the completion of *The Lord of the Rings*, which still astonishes me" (*Letters* 257). With distance, that astonishment would turn into a decent explanation of some sort in the hands of someone other than the author, but Tolkien could never have that distance.

The Everett letter dates from 24 June 1957. A little over a year later (25 October 1958), Tolkien writes to a fan named Deborah Webster. Now he presents the argument against biography in different terms even as he remains much more opposed to its use than Scull and Hammond claim. His dislike of biography unless it is, illogically, autobiography is replaced by a different binary: "dry" facts and "juicy details." And the first term (facts) may be strung along a spectrum of significance. So, insignificant facts (by which he actually means, I think, "juicy details") include (rather alarmingly) "drunkenness, wife-beating, and suchlike disorders"—none of which, Tolkien says, afflict him. Then there are "more significant" facts such as his fascination with language because these facts bear relation to the works he (Tolkien) has produced. Last, there are a few "really significant" facts such as date of birth, religion, the place where one spends one's childhood, and so on (*Letters* 288).

I find myself disagreeing with Tolkien about the terms of his argument, but what matters here is not that disagreement (academics disagree so much more than they ever agree about anything) but how Tolkien presents the periphery of his argument. Here, he makes some comments which help to explain Tolkien's dislike of biography in terms other than those he himself constructs for the sake of argument, and this dislike, by the way, has nothing (or very little) to do with the different meaning of privacy in the days before the arrival of the internet, before the omnipresence of Facebook, Twitter, and the rest of those intrusive and ghastly wastes of time. Tolkien's framing of the periphery is a caricature by him, but it matters that he chooses to see the periphery in such terms.

He begins, in this letter to Webster, by complaining about the trend in academic criticism in the late 1950s towards an "excessive interest in the details of the lives of authors and artists" (*Letters* 288). As someone who has specialized in critical theory for several decades, I can only say that Tolkien is factually wrong—in part because Oxford University in the late 1950s and Tolkien himself were naïve about the subject.

Here, it is important to remember that Tolkien's field of study was Anglo-Saxon and Medieval literature and language. That period (from about 600 to 1400 CE) is marked by the anonymity of some of its greatest works. We know nothing about the composer of *Beowulf*; we know almost nothing about the writer of *Sir Gawain and the Green Knight.* Yes, about Chaucer we know quite a lot, but he is the great exception, and we know about him because he and his wife were employed by members of the royal family and were frequently at court. And when it comes to critical theory, as Scull and Hammond note in their *Chronology*, it was not until October 1948 than the English Department got around to appointing a Reader in Textual Criticism, with that discipline being in many ways a sibling subject to critical theory (342). The 1950s were still the era of Practical Criticism or New Criticism—two terms that are almost identical (the former being British and preceding the latter, which is American). That era deliberately ignored the life of the writer to focus on the work itself. It was replaced by structuralism in the early 1960s and by poststructuralism by the 1970s (the decade in which Tolkien died). However, Practical Criticism was still enough venerated that it was an essential part of the Oxbridge English curriculum into the 1970s. How do I know? Because I was a student reading English at Cambridge in the mid-1970s and we spent a great deal of time critiquing poetry in a way very familiar to the likes of I. A Richards, Cleanth Brooks, and the rest of those scholars who felt that the work alone was all that should be considered. There was always some interest in biography in the study of literature, true, but it was muted.

What *was* actually a constant during Tolkien's long academic life was something else: belletrism—the study of literature for its aesthetic qualities alone. It is in light of belletrism that Tolkien's dislike of "so-called 'psychologists'" must be read (*Letters* 288). Tolkien dislikes biography because he dislikes psychoanalytic criticism because he dislikes Freud, but Freud—even in the latter part of Tolkien's long life—was a straw man. Tolkien may fairly dislike "psychological" criticism inexpertly handled, but the majority of those who have found some use in the study of literature for Freud, Jung, Adler, Lacan and so on have written compelling criticism not biographical criticism designed to highlight the unpleasant parts of someone's life. It's almost as if Tolkien knows he is batting on a sticky wicket with the light beginning to fade as he transitions abruptly from his spectrum of significance to a closing paragraph which begins with the disarming and funny line: "I am in fact a *Hobbit* (in all but size)." So much for "dry" facts and "juicy details." Now we have fantasy dressed, humorously, as fact. Or, if it is fact, then we do need a radically new biography and we need it now.

Like Father Like Son

Before we look at how the Tolkien family treated the idea of a biography of their famous father in the aftermath of his death, I should briefly return to that long list of Tolkien biographies with which I began this essay. They would appear to offer prima facie evidence of the story of J.R.R. Tolkien being in great shape. As I said at the beginning, it is not. Not at all. Despite the score of biographical titles, the reality is we only have three biographies of any weight at all: Grotta (at 197 pages); Carpenter (at 288 pages); White (at 292 pages). Grotta did his best and was original but had little access to Tolkien's papers. Carpenter supposedly had free rein with everything that Tolkien produced over a lifetime, but he was just a young journalist for BBC Radio Oxford at the time of Tolkien's death. He still had the world to win. He was, frankly, boxing above his weight. White's book is entertaining and well written, but it is essentially a rehashing of Carpenter with a few added bells and whistles. Essentially all the biographies repeat what they find in Carpenter (as the authorized biography) or they focus on some narrow piece of his life (education; war service; contributions to philology; hiking tours; and so on) or they write a simplification for a specific audience (young adults or children, for example). They may add details from the press or from friends and acquaintances of Tolkien or even make up details that have no basis in fact.

The outlier is Scull and Hammond's Chronology (at an eye-popping 803 pages). However, the *Chronology* is only biography in the raw—a set of dates from 21 January 1889 to 17 November 1973 describing what Tolkien did day by day. All Scull and Hammond succeed in doing is underlining how much Carpenter left out and as a result how much later retellings of Carpenter's story have missed. Scull and Hammond even seem, paradoxically (and certainly unfairly), to blame those many biographers who came after Carpenter for being unable to find anything beyond the already known in Tolkien's life. They suggest Tolkien's readers have "perhaps [been] misled by the biographies of our subject [Tolkien] that have followed Carpenter (and are largely derived from his book)" into thinking he "lived in a simple circumscribed world in which little happened beyond his writing, his teaching, his immediate family, and the Inklings" (ix). Whence might they have got that idea? Perhaps the carefully controlled message coming from the Tolkien family, a message evident in Carpenter's anodyne authorized biography?

This situation is not remotely acceptable. It's not to this academic at least; it's not, I would have thought, to the millions of Tolkien fans. We are looking at the British writer (Tolkien would have said *English* writer) who routinely finishes at the top of reader polls for importance or popularity. *The Hobbit* has never been out of print over its 67-year life. It has sold more than 40,000,000 copies. That is impressive by any standards but is dwarved (or dwarfed) by *The Lord of the Rings.* That trilogy has likewise never been out of print since it was first published in 1954-1955 and has sold more than 150,000,000 copies. Tom Shippey is right to call his 2000 study: *J.R.R. Tolkien: Author of the Century.* (It seems almost an understatement as Tolkien was also the founder of the modern fantasy genre.) Despite the blandishments in Carpenter about Tolkien's routine—even boring—life, Tolkien actually led a long and difficult life.[3] That life, when described in adequate depth and detail, would help to explain the literary achievement in useful and important ways that have never been explored. The reasons for the shallowness of the biographical work on Tolkien have to do with decisions made by Tolkien's children (and, in particular, Christopher Tolkien as his father's literary executor) after their father died on 2 September 1973. I will now move on to look at those decisions.

In his *George Allen & Unwin: A Remembrancer*, Rayner Unwin, who (as a child) had responded so enthusiastically as a publisher's reader to the manuscript of *The Hobbit*, describes the Tolkien family's thinking in some detail. It is important enough for me to quote his account in full:

> I had long worried that without an authorised biography there would inevitably be ill-informed and tendentious writings about Tolkien over which neither he nor we [George Allen & Unwin, Tolkien's publishers] would have any control. In his lifetime Tolkien had brushed aside the fear, and for him indeed it would have been yet another distraction. But after his death it was one of the first matters I raised with the [Tolkien] family. They accepted the need for something to be done, but were doubtful about who could be entrusted with such a commission and what control there might be over what was written. As a stop-gap solution I suggested a pictorial biography, using family pictures for the most part, with extended captions as the text. [...] Priscilla [Tolkien], who lived in Oxford, knew a young man that she thought might be suitable. He worked for Radio Oxford, and I agreed to meet him. Humphrey Carpenter

> [...] was personable, eager, and willing to throw up his job on the radio to undertake our project. I didn't think a mixture of photographs and extended captions needed any great qualifications so I agreed to terms on the spot and encouraged him to get down to work. The material he needed for his research was stored in the converted barn next to the house that Christopher [Tolkien] was then living in outside Oxford, and Humphrey found himself working closely alongside Christopher.
>
> It soon became apparent that Humphrey had dug himself so enthusiastically into the project that a full-scale biography was in the making. Christopher seemed agreeable, and so was I (248-249).

This account (which I have never seen challenged by the Tolkien family) is very revealing. Shortly after Tolkien's death, the family decides they need to produce a biography over which they have some control. They are prompted to make this decision by a trusted family friend who also happens to be the son of the Unwin who published both *The Hobbit* and *The Lord of the Rings*. They are looking not just to control what is produced but how what is produced is broadcast to the world. It is Rayner Unwin who suggests a lightweight biography (a coffee-table book with lots of photographs) to satisfy Tolkien's fans and, presumably, to stymie the sort of biographical efforts of the likes of Ready (1968) and Grotta (1976) from becoming the norm. The suitability of Carpenter is that he is young and friendly and eager, controllable and unqualified (as in he needed "no great qualifications"). All he has to do is to choose some family photographs (under Christopher Tolkien's supervision, as in "working alongside") and write some sustained captions for text. What could go wrong? Then Carpenter goes off script in his eagerness (he had, after all, given up his day job at Radio Oxford to undertake this commission), and Christopher Tolkien appears to accept the inevitable. The result? The official biography of 1977.

In Scull and Hammond's *Reader's Guide*, right beneath this quotation from Unwin's memoir, we have a comment from the two compilers about the qualities of Carpenter's biography. As with Unwin's recollections, I shall quote this statement in full because it is so revealing:

> To date, only Carpenter among Tolkien's biographers has had full access to his subject's private papers. In addition, he [Carpenter] was able to interview members of Tolkien's family and many friends and colleagues, and he remains unsurpassed in personal knowledge of Oxford and understanding of university life. Although "authorized" by the Tolkien family, his book is by no means

> hagiography: it does not omit mention, for instance, of the younger Tolkien's occasional bouts of despair, or of tensions within his marriage. And having been vetted by Christopher Tolkien, it contains very few errors or misinterpretations. [...] [T]he biography serves its purpose well without verbosity (*Reader's Guide* 111).

Scull and Hammond make several comments that I consider tendentious (to echo Rayner Unwin, albeit in a different context). First, they say Carpenter had full access to Tolkien's papers, but that did not include (I assume) what Scull and Hammond refer to in the Preface to the *Reader's Guide* as the "most private of Tolkien's surviving papers" which "remain private" even to Scull and Hammond (x). They claim that Carpenter was "unsurpassed in personal knowledge of Oxford and understanding of university life." Carpenter's father was Warden of Keble College, Oxford during Carpenter's childhood before the older Carpenter was installed as Bishop of Oxford. The younger Carpenter was educated first at the Dragon School in Oxford, and then at Marlborough College in Wiltshire. He then read English at Keble.

Let me indulge in a little autobiography for a moment to suggest what Scull and Hammond mean by the latter phrase: "understanding of university life." I too grew up in Oxford and went to New College School and Magdalen College School before reading English at Fitzwilliam College, Cambridge. My father was a don at New College between about 1962 and 1972. He was—coincidentally—at New College at the same time that Christopher Tolkien taught there and met him a few times at cocktail parties and High Table. Carpenter went on to be a successful radio personality (principally on Radio 3) and an accomplished biographer. I have gone on to be an English professor in the United States. I have an understanding of life at Oxford the equal of Carpenter's, so it is important to understand what Scull and Hammond mean. The phrase denotes knowing how the university runs in a day-to-day sense, but it also connotes knowing not to rock the boat, not to make too eccentric or too troubled a senior professor such as Tolkien (who, after all, held professorships at Oxford for more than 30 years). As to the claim that Carpenter's biography is not hagiographic, I agree, but that is at the cost of making Tolkien's life (especially after the Great War) anodyne. It was anything but as we shall see. Notice, too, the peculiar construction of the phrase "does not omit mention" rather than the simpler "mentions." It is as if he and Christopher Tolkien had some discussions about whether Tolkien's "bouts of despair" (which were not just confined to Tolkien when he was young by the way) should be included in the book. Carpenter appears to have won that one.

And then there is that final phrase "serves its purpose well without verbosity." In one sense that means simply it is a good short biography; in another (in the sense that Rayner Unwin means in the quotation from his memoirs that immediately precedes these comments by Scull and Hammond), it means controlling the message and getting a brief biography out there before biographers more qualified than Carpenter undertake the task. In the 47 years since Carpenter's authorized biography was published, the Tolkien family's strategy has been remarkably successful. It is fascinating to see also that Rayner Unwin's germ of an idea led not just to an unsatisfactory biography but also to exactly the sort of coffee-table book he initially proposed: *The Tolkien Family Album* (1992). So, in place of a thorough biography of so important a writer (the kind exemplified for instance, by Hemione Lee's *Edith Wharton*), we have a short biography and lots of family pictures. On one level (the satisfaction of fans' demands) this pair of books is exemplary; in the pursuit of a fully developed picture of as complex a man as Tolkien it is anything but. What the Tolkien family has done with their father's life is entirely legitimate. It may even be morally defensible. *That doesn't make it right in a broader literary and cultural sense.*

Grotta to Carpenter to White

Let's turn to the three biographies I mentioned earlier to see what the family's decisions about their remarkable father have led to.

Daniel Grotta's *J.R.R. Tolkien: Architect of Middle Earth* is a remarkable achievement. It makes no major errors in the narrative of Tolkien's life. He says nothing about *The Silmarillion*, but then he couldn't have as his biography came out in 1976 (the year before Tolkien's account of the First and Second Ages as edited by his son Christopher was published). He does propagate the myth that Tolkien's mother was once a missionary in Africa (for which I have found no collaborating evidence). He does get the geography of Oxford wrong and misunderstands the differences between British and American universities.

He does mangle both the name and academic history of Joseph Wright. All true, but these are minor errors by someone who was very much on the outside looking in. After all, the Tolkien family was not about to edit Grotta's book for accuracy. What matters about Grotta's independent biography is what it reveals about the behaviour of Tolkien's heirs, and here Grotta is both indirectly and directly helpful in describing his situation. There are, for instance, omissions in the 1976 edition, each of which is labelled "deleted for legal considerations." I can only assume the Tolkien Estate intervened in these instances. In the Preface (dated September) to the 1991 edition (published to coincide with the centenary of Tolkien's birth), Grotta describes the situation in some detail:

> I had to contend with rather different—and difficult—circumstances [in comparison to the full access granted Carpenter for his authorized biography]. [...] Christopher Tolkien wished to keep independent biographers from writing *anything* about his father. As a result, I did most of my research in libraries and newspaper morgues [sic], and interviewed the relatively few of Tolkien's friends and associates who bridled at the kind of intellectual censorship that the Tolkien family tried to impose (ii).

In the Author's Note (168-176), Grotta talks of finding "considerable resistance to releasing information by the Tolkien family." Michael Tolkien refused to be interviewed and, helpfully from my point of view, goes on record why:

> I am well aware of the world-wide interest in my father's work and the great admiration for it that exists in almost every country where it has been published, and I am in fully [sic] sympathy with all this.

Then he continues (rather illogically given his "sympathy"):

> But it is my policy to keep all discussion about my father himself as far as possible strictly within the family, or those so long associated with it as to be virtually part of it. [...] [I]f people want to write about my father I cannot stop them (much as I would like to!), but all I have seen published so far seems to me to be extraordinarily inaccurate and ill-informed (Grotta 174).

Again, the illogic is disturbing (like father like son?), not to say breathtaking: Michael Tolkien dislikes the inaccuracy of what has thus far been published but is absolutely uninterested in doing the one thing for Grotta that would alter the situation: grant him access to Tolkien's papers. And the situation darkens when the web of silence extends beyond the family to its "close friends and associates," who have been "requested," according to Grotta, "to refrain from releasing information, out of respect for Tolkien's memory" (175).

To an unauthorized biography, then, the Tolkien family responds with silence and, possibly, a threat of legal action convincing enough for the publisher to remove some material from the 1976 Grotta book very late in production. With an authorized biography, the response is equally interesting but rather different: the appearance of freedom and cooperation but the actuality of deep influence. I have already indicated that Humphrey Carpenter was chosen because he was not a seasoned academic. Carpenter's remarks in his one-page "Author's note" (ix)—when taken in conjunction with his conclusion to the book proper and his Appendix D: "Sources and acknowledgments" (276-279)— reveal the naivete of a young journalist thrilled to have been chosen for the opportunity of his young life. (Carpenter was just 27 when Tolkien died and only 31 when his biography was published.) He begins by stating: "This book is based upon the letters, diaries, and other papers of the late Professor J.R.R. Tolkien, and upon the reminiscences of his family and friends." He then goes on to hope that "this book would not be entirely foreign to his [Tolkien's] wishes"—an odd idea given the fact that Tolkien had passed on, and odder still given the normal biographer's stance of independence and distance. He develops the note by indicating he has tried just to tell Tolkien's life story and to avoid literary judgments. He makes this claim even though the justification for understanding Tolkien's life is surely to make his remarkable achievement more explicable. He then undercuts the entire scholarly enterprise by suggesting "literary judgements" "reflect the character of the critic just as much as that of his subject." Yet, he seems to espouse something very close to exactly that sort of judgment when he finishes his note by hoping his book "may shed some light on his books" (ix).

The clarity of the opening paragraph of the "Author's Note" is fast disappearing and vanishes utterly when Carpenter finishes the book itself by undercutting his entire biography and all those months and, probably, years of work with these words: "He [Tolkien] disapproved of biography as an aid to literary appreciation; and perhaps he was right. His real biography is *The Hobbit, The Lord of the Rings*, and *The Silmarillion*; for the truth about him lies within those pages" (260). Then there is that appendix where he thanks Tolkien's literary executor, his son Christopher, who "made radical and invaluable suggestions, which have had a considerable influence on the final shape of this book" (279). How much did Tolkien's son influence Carpenter's biography? Consider this: the book was first published in 1977, but the "Author's note" dates from a year earlier, 1976, and perhaps early in that year, for in the note Carpenter calls his work "the first biography" even though Grotta's unauthorized biography also dates from 1976. It would seem the discussions between the two men may have gone on for some time. Consider this, too: Scull and Hammond (in their *Reader's Guide*) state that Carpenter's biography was "vetted" by Christopher Tolkien (112).[4] Had Carpenter's biography been unsatisfactory or intrusive, it would presumably not have been published. At any event, elsewhere Carpenter later claimed he had "virtually unrestricted access" to the Tolkien papers. A lot hangs on the meaning of that adjectival phrase!

The story with Michael White's 2001 biography is an easier one to tell. White was a more seasoned academic than Carpenter. He was a lecturer at an independent school in Oxford between 1984 and 1991 although oddly his field was science in general and chemistry in particular, and an Honorary Research Fellow at Curtin University in Australia in 2005. He was a seasoned biographer, beginning with an unauthorized biography of Isaac Asimov in 1994, and later a novelist. Like Grotta, he had no special access to Tolkien's papers or to his friends and colleagues. He "was approached to write this [the Tolkien] biography," but by the publisher in all likelihood and certainly *not* by the Tolkien Estate (3). Just as was Daniel Grotta, so is Michael White deeply unhappy about the Tolkiens' attitude to the life of their father and, by extension, family becoming common property. White devotes an entire paragraph to his concerns, and I quote it in full because it shows that by 2001 (almost a quarter of a century after the authorized biography was published) the family attitude of secrecy still prevailed:

> I consider myself a long-standing fan [of Tolkien], but I am dismayed by the over-protective stance of "official" or "authorised" material about Professor Tolkien. The published letters relate almost nothing of his private life. Veils of mystery are spread over anything personal, such as his relationship with his wife, Edith[,] and his friendship with C. S. Lewis and some of his fellow Inklings. No authorised description ever questions Tolkien's inner drives or tries to identify the man's personal demons. Worse still, his motivations and his opinions are rarely investigated. Tolkien was, as this book shows, a good man, a moral and upright, trustworthy and very intelligent man, but he was not in line for canonization (5).

Let me finish this section of my essay ("Grotta to Carpenter to White") by bringing back one more time the team of Christina Scull and Wayne Hammond, both seasoned Tolkien scholars. It doesn't matter that they claim on the dodgy ground of access that Carpenter's biography is "much to be preferred to Grotta['s]" (*Reader's Guide* 111). It does matter that even though they themselves are likely considered by the Tolkien family to be preferred researchers, even that preferential treatment has its limits. I mentioned earlier that "the most private papers remain[ed] private" even to them (with the adjectival phrase remaining unhelpfully undefined by the way). It is more complicated, however. They, even they, are not able to look at all of the rest of Tolkien's papers but just "a great deal else" "published and unpublished" (x). All this may amount to a "rich mine of data," but without knowing precisely what they could and could not see it is hard to say. It's as unhelpful, frankly, as Grotta's justification for his using a shoddy citation system in his biography: "I have not inserted textual or source footnotes. This biography is not written for scholars or academics alone, but for all these who enjoy and admire Tolkien" (176). So, admirers don't want or need to check the accuracy of statements? Still, Grotta is better than Carpenter. Grotta has 12 pages of what he terms "Reference Notes." Carpenter? He has merely three pages of "Sources and Acknowledgments" (276-279) and does not inform the reader why he is uninterested in accurate citation. That pales beside even White's derivative, unauthorized effort. At least White manages 10 pages of "Chapter Notes."

I indicated that it is unhelpful of Scull and Hammond not to be clearer about what papers of Tolkien's they did and did not have access to, but the *Chronology* (if you read it carefully) has levels of access to them that are strictly dependent on what Christopher Tolkien is willing to show them. So, on page 43, we have "(letter to Edith Bratt, 29 July 1913, courtesy of Christopher Tolkien)." Not one of the letters in *The Letters of J.R.R. Tolkien* (1981), then, even though it's worth quoting from in the *Chronology*? We have quotations from and references to assorted diaries (pages 81, 84, 106, 110, 134, 169, and so on) written by Tolkien during his life (some in code and some not, some merely engagement diaries and some more personal) but without any indication of provenance or location (as in "Since 5 June [1916] he has kept a concise diary [...]" ([81]). Sometimes Scull and Hammond quote directly from the diaries; sometimes Christopher

Tolkien will only quote from them in undated letters to Scull and Hammond: "(quoted by Christopher Tolkien in private correspondence)," for instance (110). There is even "a résumé of the year 1920" written by Tolkien, but again Scull and Hammond only come by this information in the same secondhand way: "(quoted by Christopher Tolkien in private correspondence)" (115). We have references to the Tolkien Papers at the Bodleian with no shelf number, yet, my electronic copy of the catalogue of Tolkien's Papers in the Reading Room of the Bodleian has such information. This absence of information for researchers is a marked and frustrating feature of Tolkien's legacy.

My educated guess is that Christopher Tolkien protected in particular the letters between Tolkien and Edith Bratt Tolkien during their courtship and the early part of their marriage as well as the many diaries Tolkien kept during his lifetime. I do understand the desire to protect loved ones and to hide the intimate details of their lives, but it would be helpful for those who regard Tolkien's work highly to have this information, this knowledge about Tolkien. It is my educated guess, too, that the Tolkien Papers were kept in the garage on Christopher Tolkien's property in Oxfordshire from 1973 (when his father died) or shortly thereafter until they were acquired by the Bodleian in 1979 on terms that are not, as far as I know, a matter of public record. The Tolkien family (even now that all of Tolkien's children have passed on to the next great adventure) will likely argue that access to such documents is not germane to understanding Tolkien's life. Few scholars or aficionados would agree, I think.

Bellamy or Morris Takes Charge

Imagine for a moment that like Julian West in *Looking Backward* or William Guest in *News from Nowhere* you are transported forward in time a hundred years or so to a better world. How might that better world be reflected in what those who admire Tolkien's work may read? Here is what I would suggest (perhaps fantasize would be a better word). First, at some point in the reasonably near future a scholar with a strong academic background is commissioned to write a biography of Tolkien without restrictions. All of the Tolkien Papers at the Bodleian would be available to her or him: *all* of the letters and not just those selected in 1981 by Humphrey Carpenter and Christopher Tolkien; all of the diaries; all of the manuscripts. (One could even crowd-source the discovery or recovery of Tolkien letters not known about.) These materials would, of course, complement an understanding of the legendarium based solely on materials at Marquette University and elsewhere.

How would the Tolkien family be assured that this scholar would not do a metaphorical hatchet job on the great man's legacy? Well, first of all, the family would have commissioned this individual, so she or he is highly unlikely to be a literary axe murderer. Second, John Milton was surely right in arguing in *Areopagitica* that censorship is "a dishonour and derogation to the author, to the book, to the privilege and dignity of learning" and that the only way to get to the truth is through open debate even if that debate includes falsehoods. To my mind, his argument covers the sort of censorship in a minor key as practised by the Tolkien family and the sort of foolish errors and imaginings we find in all of the biographies of Tolkien. In the absence of knowledge, we have Grotta's caricature of Tolkien at the beginning of his book (Prologue: The Old Professor), or Carpenter's downright strange section (Part Four, Chapter 1: Oxford Life) in which he imagines what a day in the life of the writer of *The Hobbit* might have been like in order to demonstrate something that was manifestly not true at even a casual glance: "And after this, you might say, nothing else really happened [in Tolkien's life]" (118). And in the absence of knowledge, we have White's really bizarre take on perhaps the most famous moment in Tolkien's long life when the first line in *The Hobbit* sprang wholly formed into his mind: "In a hole in the ground there lived a hobbit." We know from Tolkien's own account that he wrote the line on the blank page of an examination paper—one of those interminable exams he marked during the summer holidays because he needed the money to support his large family. White might have pointed out that the line is metrically beautiful with opening anapests and closing iambs, but, no, he goes off into his own fantasy ("as legend has it," he writes) and states that Tolkien writes about a hobbit and a hole in the ground because he "saw a hole in his study carpet" (150). Never mind that he didn't. Never mind that Bilbo Baggins would have been mortified at the idea of a hole in *his* carpet, and Tolkien was, after all, in spirit at least, a hobbit.

If we let a scholar write a detailed and comprehensive biography, then this question arises, of course: "What makes this scholar with backstage access (as we would say today) special? What about the rest of us?" (That's actually two questions, but never mind.) The answer is simple: digitize the entire Bodleian collection of Tolkien's papers according to a reasonable schedule and ask the Tolkien Estate to fund it. After all, the family has become fabulously wealthy off the genius of one man, John Ronald Reuel Tolkien. While you're at it include the materials housed in Special Collections at Marquette University and those the Tolkiens have themselves held back.

The remarkable thing about this glimpse into a Tolkien utopia is that we know what we will find—sort of. All we have to do is to look at Scull and Hammond's *Chronology* (that biography in the raw) and extrapolate. Absent any skeletons in the closet (that casual comment of Tolkien's about drunkenness and wife beating still rattles me a little), we already have the outline. A very intelligent person who led a terribly hard life until, unexpectedly for an orphan dogged by poverty but with a good education, he became a Professor at one of the most prestigious universities in the world by his early 30s. He had four children, was devoted to his wife despite some significant challenges, wrote two extraordinary works (*The Hobbit* and *The Lord of the Rings*) and most of a third (*The Silmarillion*) and a decent number of academic publications, and died. What the *Chronology* begins to show in a level of detail utterly missing from Grotta and Carpenter and White is how much his early life was affected by his mother's decision to convert to Catholicism, an episode glossed over in every biography. It shows how much Father Francis Morgan helped Tolkien after his mother's death *and* coercively hindered him. It shows how appalling the battle of the Somme was for him and the long period of convalescence that followed. We will see how much Tolkien needed Edith Bratt but how hard it was for her to have to convert from her Anglican faith to Catholicism. We will see how much Tolkien's career mapped the direction of their life together. We will see how frequently Tolkien was sick with the flu, with gastritis, with depression which led on a couple of occasions, at least, to nervous breakdowns, with other ailments sapping his strength at crucial times. We will see how much Edith suffered from rheumatism and arthritis (as physical ills) and from the omnipresence of her husband's career as an academic and a writer of his famous legendarium to be (as psychological ills). We will see how much his legendarium, *The Lord of the Rings* in particular, was wedged into the interstices of a life well lived. We will see the depth of his love for his children as well as the mundane aspects of any life that distract from what matters. Even senior and much-admired academics have to deal with burst pipes and medical bills. We will see how much of a perfectionist he was. We will see how he could be small minded and hurtful and stubborn and generous and kind.

None of this should cause the family alarm; all of this matters because one can map it onto the narrative of the legendarium. Tolkien is fascinated with power and suffering and love because he experienced all of these to an acute degree. As a man who was often sick and worried about the health of his wife and children, he describes the idyllic Rivendell, the Houses of Healing, and Lothlórien with extraordinary skill and depth and care. He tells his most beloved story from the First Age (of Beren and Lúthien) as if he had experienced it himself—as, in a sense, he indeed had. And last, we would come to understand, again in detail, how his love of language(s) drove him to create worlds in which those languages could live and how the drive to create such worlds in such depth came from the T.C.B.S. and the need to prove to himself, to his friends who died (Gilson and Smith) and his friend who survived (Wiseman), that they did have something important to say to the world. In all of Tolkien's long and fascinating life, we should never underestimate the power of survivor's guilt. It powered the legendarium for 60 years. As Tolkien put it when he wrote to Geoffrey Bache Smith during the battle of the Somme:

> What I meant, and thought Chris [Wiseman] meant, and am almost sure you meant, was that the TCBS had been granted some spark of fire—certainly as a body if not singly—that was destined to kindle a new light, or, what is the same thing, rekindle an old light in the world; that the TCBS was destined to testify for God and Truth in a more direct way even than by laying down its several lives in this war (which is for all the evil of our own side with large view good against evil) (*Letters* 10).

Surely that is the purpose of the legendarium and surely it is crucial that it be understood in all its stark beauty by fully understanding Tolkien's life—fully and not in the piecemeal way we have so far been allowed to view it. The last of Tolkien's four children died in 2022. That generation has gone; it is time to be open. If we do not get that chance (academics and fans alike) to know everything, then for want of a biography the story will surely be lost.

End Notes

1 Ready's account was aimed, presumably, at the American market in the wake of the popularity of Tolkien's epic on college campuses.

2 Rumour has it that John Garth would be the Tolkien family's choice to write a new biography of Tolkien. Garth is an assiduous researcher but a poor critic. His major books on Tolkien (about the Great War and about Tolkien's landscapes) cannot see the wood for the trees and inadequately connect life to work.

3 Nearly 20 years after he wrote his authorized biography of Tolkien, a somewhat chastened Carpenter offered a different perspective on the man. *The Art of Literary Biography*, edited by John Batchelor, includes an interview Carpenter gave to Lyndall Gordon. In it, Carpenter remarks that he first thought of Tolkien as a "rather comic Oxford academic—the stereotype absent-minded professor," but he came to see "he wasn't like that at all. He had had a very strange childhood. [...] And my caricature of the Oxford academic clashed with his [word or phrase missing?], and I never resolved it properly" (270).

4 In the interview in *The Art of Literary Biography*, Carpenter (after a gap of two decades) is much, much blunter than Scull and Hammond's "vetted." He remarks:

> The first draft of that life [his authorized biography of Tolkien] was a long sprawling thing, and was deemed unacceptable by the Tolkien family, or by the member of it [Christopher Tolkien?] who controlled permission to quote previously unpublished material. I went away and rewrote it, and it was then deemed acceptable. What I'd actually done was castrate the book, cut out everything which was likely to be contentious. I've therefore always been displeased with it ever since (270).

Chapter Six

1904: Mabel Tolkien, Living and Dying

Nancy Bunting

Mabel Tolkien, the mother of Ronald Tolkien, died of diabetes on November 14, 1904. Diabetes was an untreatable and always fatal disease before the discovery of effective insulin treatment in the early 1920s. This paper explores the implications of the date and circumstances surrounding Mabel's final will that granted full guardianship of her sons to Fr. Francis Morgan—ensuring that they would be brought up in the Catholic faith. For Mabel's sons, Ronald and Hilary, the last and, perhaps, most decisive act of her short life was the writing of her will. This discussion continues with a review of the events leading to the writing of the will and the likely impact of the gradual deterioration of Mabel's physical and mental health due to the chronic disease of diabetes.

Mabel Tolkien's Will and Death

In the summer of 1904, Mabel Tolkien and her sons moved to 'Woodside', a cottage in Rednal on the edge of the wooded grounds of the Oratory House. This was the home of Mr. Till, the local postman and his wife, the sub-postmistress, and it also served as the post office (Ferrández Bru 72, Gardner/Holford 45). Fr. Francis Morgan of the Birmingham Oratory arranged for Mabel and her boys to be reunited and live at 'Woodside' (*Bio* 29). The Tills provided room and board to the Tolkien family: a bedroom and a sitting-room and with meals prepared by Mrs. Till.

The nearby Oratory House served as a country retreat for the members of the Birmingham Oratory. Cardinal Newman built this modest country house with a chapel at Rednal with funds donated by the Catholic community of New York (Ferrández Bru 72). The cemetery for the Oratory was there, and it included Cardinal Newman's grave. When Fr. Francis Morgan made the short ride to Rednal on the Birmingham commuter line to visit, check on Mabel, tutor the boys, and relax with his dog, he stayed at the Oratory House (Bridoux, "Letting Images Speak" 1, *Bio* 30). The medical community and the public endorsed the powerful benefits of fresh country air for invalids like Mabel, and that would be found in Rednal (Nightingale, Saundby 1426).

Mabel Tolkien continued to stay at 'Woodside' when Ronald began school at King Edward's on Tuesday, September 20, 1904.[1] The family's continued residence in Rednal meant Ronald had to walk a mile (1.6 km) to the station to commute by train to King Edward's School (*C&G* 1.12). Ronald reported he had walked to school beginning at the age of eight so that would refer to the house in Moseley at 214 Alcester Road (Brace). The distance he walked then would have been between 0.81 or 0.96 miles (1.30 or 1.54 km).[2] When the family lived at 86 Westfield Road, King's Heath for the 1901 spring, summer, and fall terms, Ronald walked a distance of 3.68 miles (5.92 km).[3] At the time he lived in Rednal, Ronald was so poor he could not afford the school meals and had to get his lunch in Birmingham (Gardner/Holford 289).

Carpenter implies that Mabel remained at Rednal because of her distaste for the "smoke and dirt of Birmingham" (*Bio* 30). However, that is unlikely to be the most relevant reason for Mabel and her sons to stay in Rednal. Mabel was in the very end stage of chronic diabetes and would be dead in less than two months. By September 1904, Mabel was unable "to venture out at all and was very weak" (Gardner/Holford 48). By herself, Mabel would not have been able to manage and prepare the strict diabetic diet, recommended by her physician—the eminent Dr. Saundby (*C&G* 1.11). Mabel was almost certainly not able to do any physically taxing household chores that would be required in an independent household (e.g. laundry, dishwashing, cleaning, shopping, and cooking). The only realistic solution was for the family to stay where Mabel could continue to receive needed services from the postman's wife. The fact his mother was taken care of at 'Woodside' allowed Ronald to go back to school.

Although Mabel would have known since April 1904, when she was in the hospital in Birmingham, that she was dying, it was not until Sunday, November 6, 1904, that Mabel Tolkien dictated her last will and testament. The two witnesses to the will, Clement J. Haskew and Bertha Mary Newton have an address of "St. Peter's [Catholic Church] Bromsgrove." The Rev. Clement J.

Executor

This is the last Will and Testament of me Mabel Tolkien of Woodside Cottage Rednall in the County of Worcester Widow I appoint The Reverend Francis Morgan of The Oratory Edgbaston in the City of Birmingham Clerk in Holy Orders Executor and Trustee of this my Will and Guardian of my infant children I give devise and bequeath all and every my real and personal Estate whatsoever and wheresoever the same may be unto the said Francis Morgan Upon trust subject as hereinafter mentioned to pay and divide the same equally between my two Sons John Ronald Reuel Tolkien and Hilary Arthur Reuel Tolkien on their attaining the age of twenty one years or if there shall be only one of them who shall attain such age then the whole to go to such one absolutely and until my said Sons shall attain the age of twenty one years as aforesaid my wish and desire is that my said Trustee or the Trustee or Trustees for the time being of this my Will shall apply the income of my trust estate in and towards the support maintenance education and advancement in life business or profession of my said two Sons or the survivor of them in such manner and until such time as my Trustee or Trustees in his or their absolute discretion shall think fit but notwithstanding anything herein contained to the contrary I give my said Trustee or Trustees full and absolute authority in his or their absolute and uncontrolled discretion at any time to apply the capital of my said trust estate or any part or parts in and towards the support maintenance education and advancement in life business or any profession of my said Sons or either of them I direct that my said children shall be brought up and educated in the precepts and practice of the Faith and Religion which I profess and practice and of the Church of which I am a Member namely the Roman Catholic Church And for all the purposes aforesaid my Will and desire is that my said Trustee or Trustees shall have full power to sell realize and get in my said Estate or any part thereof as and when and in such manner as he or they shall in his or their discretion think fit In witness whereof I the testatrix have hereunto set my hand this 6th day of November One thousand nine hundred and four H.

CW

1

3. First page of Mabel Tolkien's will as indicated by the number "1" with the slash above it

Haskew was the priest for the church, and Bertha Mary Newton was probably a nun, who worked in the school attached to St. Peter's.[4]

St. Peter's in Bromsgrove, built in 1858, was the Catholic church which Mabel Tolkien and her sons attended when the Oratory clergy were not in residence at the Rednal retreat (H. Tolkien 26, *C&G* 1.11). When the Oratory clergy were in residence, Mabel and her boys would have attended Mass at the retreat.

To attend church in Bromsgrove, the Tolkiens traveled approximately six miles from Rednal to Bromsgrove in a pony-drawn buggy. In 1904, sixty-six year old George and fifty-nine year old Annie Church, the gardener and housekeeper at the Oratory House, drove the Tolkien family (Gardner/Holford 48). This would be a drive of approximately forty-five minutes allowing for road conditions, the age of the pony, etc.[5] The date and witnesses' signatures on the will indicate that this document was probably written just before or after Mass on Sunday, November 6, 1904.

Arthur J. O'Connor, the solicitor who wrote out the will, was a Catholic who had been a student at the Oratory school (Ferrández Bru 76). In that small community and school, O'Connor would have certainly known Fr. Francis. That a solicitor was willing to write a will on a Sunday suggests that he may have been contacted, possibly even by Fr. Francis, with an emergency request due to Mabel's deteriorating health and terminal diagnosis. The solicitor may even have been asked to write the will when he arrived as a worshipper at Mass at St. Peter's that day.

Solicitor O'Connor used standard "boilerplate" or stock phrases as can be seen in the reference-to twelve year old Ronald and ten year old Hilary as "infant children." The will was hand-written on commonly-available lined paper, further testimony to its impromptu composition. The text is repetitive and uses standard formulas—a conservative legal strategy. A knowledgeable solicitor would have followed this tact for a sudden consultation where little background information would have been provided.

We do not know what finally prompted Mabel Tolkien to arrange for the writing of her will. One possibility is that the man she trusted most, Fr. Francis Morgan, who visited regularly and was tutoring her sons, was able to persuade Mabel that only her written will would protect and ensure her sons' continued embrace within the Catholic Church. Fr. Francis Morgan, having had some experience as a priest with administering the sacrament of extreme unction, may have recognized the fragility and instability of Mabel's physical condition.

The next day, Monday, November 7, Mabel was lucid and competent. The following day, Tuesday, November 8, she went into a coma. She died on Monday, November 14 (*Bio* 30). This means Mabel Tolkien waited until almost literally the last opportunity to have a record made of her wishes for her sons' guardianship and education. The rapid decline in Mabel's health, as seen in her becoming comatose two days after the writing of her will, underscores the likelihood of a crisis that would have led to the contacting of a solicitor to write a will on a Sunday. The visibly poor state of Mabel's health on Sunday, November 6, would have eliminated any doubts in a solicitor's mind about the necessity of writing a will, without delay, on this very day.

Mabel's deferring the writing of her will should be seen in the context of her medical treatment. Mabel's doctor, Dr. Robert Saundby at the Birmingham hospital (*C&G* 1.11), would have been quite frank with her about her future prospects given the diagnosis of diabetes. Doctors, at the turn of the twentieth century, were quite accustomed to the duty of informing patients of terminal diagnoses and the inability of medicine at that time to treat or alleviate many illnesses.

"Before the discovery of insulin, diabetics were doomed. Even on a strict diet, they could last no more than three or four years."[6] The state of clinical knowledge around 1900 was that "where the disease attacked the thin and delicate [e.g. Mabel Tolkien] there was little hope" (Tattersall 24). Mabel would have definitely known her diagnosis by the last half of June 1904 when she left the hospital. Dr. Saundby and any other consultant on Mabel's case would have urged her to set her affairs in order, because she had young children, and also to think of making arrangements for her death. However, despite knowing that her days were numbered, Mabel postponed making out a will. Mabel's delaying or avoiding dealing with her most pressing responsibilities points to rather wishful thinking that she was not in immediate danger and that she still had hope for her future.

From the available information, it appears Mabel Tolkien did rally in the summer of 1904 in Rednal. Her letter to her mother-in-law, Mrs. Mary Tolkien, was upbeat and focuses on reporting her sons' happy activities (*Bio* 30).[7] Also, Hilary Tolkien, recalling the important events of his past, wrote three pages of text which refers to this special reunion at Rednal in the summer of 1904 with his mother and brother (H. Tolkien 26-30). However, this "holiday" did not last.

Mabel was at the cottage in Rednal when the Tolkien brothers witnessed her "sudden and terrifying collapse" into a diabetic coma (*Bio* 30). In a diabetic coma, Mabel would have had loud, rapid, labored breathing while in a stuporous, unresponsive state with her face and body pale and cool; a faint, fast pulse; and cold extremities (Tattersall 25). The Tolkien brothers would have witnessed this state for six days as they either shared a bedroom with their mother or slept in the sitting room (*Bio* 29). Fr. Francis and Ronald's Aunt May Incledon (née Suffield), a Catholic convert, kept vigil by Mabel's side awaiting her death (*Bio* 30).

Fr. Francis may have let May Incledon know about the will while they watched beside the comatose Mabel (*Bio* 30). The solicitor, A.J. O'Connor, would have been in communication with Fr. Francis, as the guardian and trustee of the Tolkien brothers. O'Connor had Fr. Francis's contact information at the Birmingham Oratory because it was given during the writing of the will.

The solicitor was very unlikely to have talked to any of the Tolkien or Suffield family members because he probably would have had no idea they were involved with Mabel Tolkien or how to contact them. This would have been the result of the solicitor having been summoned at the last moment for a client he was likely not to have known previously. If Mabel left the writing of her will to almost her last coherent and competent moment, it is little wonder that "already there had been some talk of contesting Mabel's will and of sending the boys to a Protestant boarding school" (*Bio* 32). This view is also probably a result of traditional family involvement with orphans because only after 1886 did a mother have the legal right to become the sole guardian of her children when the father died (Flanders 196). If the extended Suffield and Tolkien families heard about a will, they may have regarded the report of an alleged legal document written two days before Mabel lapsed into a coma as baseless hearsay. The two Tolkien brothers may or may not have been told the nature of the meeting between their mother and Mr. O'Connor, or who he was.

The widespread distrust of and hostility toward Catholicism and Catholics had a long history in England. Following King Henry VIII's separation from the Roman Catholic Church and the creation of the Church of England in 1534, in England Catholics were characterized as traitors and idolators. This situation had slowly begun to change in the 1800s when Catholics began to regain civil rights after an era of persecution and social marginalization. In nineteenth-century England, Catholics continued to have their doctrines misrepresented, were seen as obstacles to the English tradition of civil liberties, and were demonized in popular literature (Ordway, *Tolkien's Faith* 20). This negative view of Catholicism was the motivating pressure behind the possible legal maneuvering of the Tolkien brothers' extended family.

The probate of the will was two months later—on January 6, 1905. Fr. Francis Morgan may have felt it best to wait until the law declared his standing as guardian before pressing his rights, given the undoubted antipathy of Walter Incledon and the extended Tolkien families to Catholicism. Mabel's father, John Suffield, was not likely to contest the will due to his Unitarian beliefs as discussed below.

In the interim after Mabel's death, Arthur Tolkien's brother, Laurence, sixteen years younger than the Tolkien boys' father, appears to have given Ronald and Hilary a home. Laurence had a history of interest in and support toward Mabel and her sons. He was an insurance manager and paid the yearly £12 fee for King Edward's School for Ronald Tolkien in 1900 (McIlwaine 132). £12 in 1900 would be equivalent to £1468.04 in 2019 goods and services or $1957.16 in 2020.[8] The 1904 records of King Edward's School listed "John Ronald"'s address with Laurence Tolkien at Dunkeld, Middleton Hall Road in King's Norton (*C&G*.1.12). During the time with their Protestant uncle, it is unlikely that the boys attended Mass, except possibly for their mother's funeral and burial on November 14, 1904.

Probably sometime in November 1904, either shortly before his mother's death or after the move to his Uncle Laurence's, Hilary passed the entrance examination for King Edward's.

In a letter of January 1965, Ronald Tolkien recalled that his mother died "too ill for viaticum" and "alone" (*Letters* 354). However, Carpenter reports Mabel died on November 14, 1904, "with Fr. Francis and [Mabel's] sister May Incledon at her bedside in the cottage" (30). May was very likely to have been present because Barnt Green, where the Incledons lived, was the nearest station to Rednal where Mabel was living. Almost the only person who could have given Carpenter this information, which contradicts Ronald's recall of events as recorded in his letter, was his brother Hilary who was also there and was a known source for Carpenter. Fr. Francis, May Incledon, the postman, and his wife were all dead when Carpenter began writing in the 1970s, and we know of no other records of Mabel's death.

At that time, the generally accepted view of the Catholic Church was that the lack of viaticum was not likely to be a theological stumbling block for Mabel's eventual reception into Heaven to join Christ given that she had had Holy Communion on Sunday, November 6 with the coma starting on Tuesday, November 8. With Fr. Francis Morgan at her side, she was certain to have received the Last Rites or Extreme Unction.[9] The administration of Extreme Unction is meant to be done in the presence of family and/or friends who can participate as a server or with responses and prayers (Ordway, *Tolkien's Faith* 59). As part of the rite of Extreme Unction, Fr. Francis could give Mabel Tolkien conditional absolution of her sins. Fr. Francis could also give "the Apostolic blessing for the hour of death": "holy Mother Church lovingly grants such persons who are rightly disposed a plenary indulgence to be obtained at the approach of death, provided they regularly prayed in some way during their lifetime."[10]

According to Carpenter, Mabel was not, therefore, literally alone when she was dying or at the moment of her death. Perhaps the inaccurate description of "alone" and the comment, "too ill for viaticum," from the letter of January, 1965, reflect more of a summary statement or telescoping of Ronald Tolkien's experience of and anger at what he saw as his mother's road to martyrdom as she clung to her Catholic faith in the face of the financial disaster brought on by the withdrawal of Walter Incledon's (*Bio* 31) and also Laurence Tolkien's monetary support (McIlwaine 132). Because the viaticum, the food for the journey to Christ in Heaven, the final comfort before death, was denied to Mabel because she was "too ill," Ronald may have recalled the "persecution, [and] poverty" which he bitterly believed worsened her disease and led to her eventual death (*Letters* 354). Ronald made his First Communion at Christmas 1903 (*Bio* 28; see Ordway, *Tolkien's Faith* 23), and "fell in love with the Blessed Sacrament from the beginning" (*Letters* 340). Perhaps he wished for his mother the same "profound spiritual joy, a state of contentment" which he experienced when receiving the Blessed Sacrament to ease her transition to another world (*Bio* 128).

Her rejection by and isolation from her extended, previously supportive family in 1900 and after would have left her "alone" and found her turning more and more to her older son, Ronald, to bear the burdens created by financial hardship. Carpenter's omission of Mabel's probable contact with her Catholic sister May Incledon and Mabel's non-doctrinaire Unitarian Suffield parents underscore this separation of Mabel from her previous social network. As a result of the lack of other support and providers, Ronald Tolkien's feeling that all was "so empty and cold" after his mother's death is consistent with the experience of ever-vigilant caregivers who monitor and are ready to drop whatever they are doing to attend to the unpredictable needs of a fragile loved one with an unstable, chronic illness (*Letters* 416).[11] When life has revolved around meeting someone else's ever-changing needs for months and years, the abrupt cessation of external demands leaves the caregiver at a loss: "so empty and cold."

The probate notice of January 6, 1905 states that the estate was valued at £1261 16*s*. 10*d*. Part of this amount would have been used to cover the legal fees for A.J. O'Connor, the solicitor, as well as funeral and burial expenses for Mabel, room and board for the cottage in Rednal, and possibly medical expenses. Mabel Tolkien was buried at St. Peter's Bromsgrove three days after her death on November 17, 1904 (*Bio* 31, *C&G* 1.12). Other initial expenses incurred for the care of the Tolkien brothers are possible. However, these expenses may have been covered by the generous Fr. Francis who, beginning in 1905, paid Hilary's tuition at King Edward's and the cost of housing the Tolkien brothers. The probate notice of January 6, 1905 made clear that "reverend Francis Morgan clerk [cleric]" was in charge of the estate.

The Unstated Toll of Mabel Tolkien's Diabetic Disability

In the last year of Mabel's life, her increasing level of disability would have affected her sons. By at least late November 1903, Mabel, was so ill with undiagnosed diabetes that she was housebound (*Bio* 28). This limitation indicates that Mabel's disease had already progressed to a late stage. She would be dead a year later in November 1904. Her lack of mobility probably created a crisis in terms of household management. Mabel was likely to have turned to her family for help.

The redacted Carpenter biography highlights Mabel's ostracism and rejection by her family, especially her brother-in-law, Walter Incledon, a son of an Anglican minister (see "May Incledon" in this volume) who was quite anti-Papist, as were many of the Baptist Tolkiens (*Bio* 24). Carpenter's biography also records that John Suffield was "outrage[d] beyond belief by his daughter [Mabel's']" conversion to Catholicism (*Bio* 24), but Carpenter was not a witness to John Suffield's reaction nor does he give a source for this evaluation.[12] Further, the draft version of the first two chapters of Carpenter's biography had changes, including the presentation of "the family's reaction to Mabel becoming a Catholic" (Gardner/Holford 286).

If John Suffield was initially shocked, this may have had something to do with Mabel deceiving her father, as she had previously done with her clandestine letters to Arthur during their courtship (*Bio* 9). Also, John Suffield, who was probably well aware of Walter Incledon's antipathy to Catholicism, may have been "outraged" because Mabel had involved her sister May in this conversion to Catholicism thereby placing May's marriage and family in serious jeopardy. The wealthy Walter, a "pillar of his local Anglican church," could easily afford the litigation to separate from May, leave her without financial support, and not allow her to see their two daughters.

John Suffield was raised a Methodist, but he became a Unitarian preacher (Morton 3, *Bio* 24).[13] Mabel's mother is described as "kind and understanding" (*Bio* 16). Unitarians were in many ways the successors of the Deists, and they rejected many doctrines such as Original Sin, predestination, eternal damnation, or that one had to belong to a certain denomination to be saved. If John Suffield were true to his Unitarian principles, his two daughters' change of denomination would not have ruptured family relationships among the Suffields because Unitarians did not condemn Catholicism. Although Mr. Suffield may have been initially upset by Mabel's acceptance of Catholicism, Mabel's religion itself would not have fractured the family's connections. The Suffields' willingness to take in and care for Hilary shows that the Catholicism of Mabel and her sons was not an insurmountable obstacle to the Suffields.

Consequently, Mabel was likely to still be in contact with her parents, and some evidence for that is discussed below. There is also evidence that the two Tolkien boys had a holiday in 1902 with their Aunt May's (née Suffield) family in Torquay (see "May Incledon" in this volume).

The Short-Term Help of Jane Suffield

In 1903, Mabel's other sister, Jane Suffield, was still living at her parents' home in Moseley and was teaching at King Edward's Foundation Bath Row School. She took a leave of absence "for illness" (Morton/Hayes 12). Morton and Hayes suggest that it is likely that she was needed to help with Mabel's illness. In fact, Jane's only leave of absence as a school mistress at Bath Row School was during December 1903 due to "ill health," and she returned to her teaching duties in 1904. Jane Suffield would have left her teaching position from Thursday, December 1 to Friday, December 16 when King Edward's school closed for the holiday. Jane also had to pay for a replacement during her absence from King Edward's.[14] Jane's leave from teaching coincided with Mabel's becoming housebound. After December 16, Ronald was out of school and could attend to his mother on a full-time basis (i.e. he would be doing needed housework and running errands) (*Bio* 28). The timing of Jane's December leave of absence strongly supports the idea that she left to help Mabel, as opposed to Jane herself suffering from poor health.

In late November and December 1903, given how far her disease had progressed, in addition to weakness and fatigue, Mabel may have been experiencing one or more of the common complications of diabetes. Peripheral neuropathy is quite probable, because complications of various types of neuropathy can affect as many as 50% of people with diabetes.[15] The very common peripheral neuropathy of the foot results in the loss of normal sensation in the feet, which is replaced by feelings of tingling, numbness, or burning. This condition occurs because diabetes damages the nerves. Peripheral neuropathy of the foot is especially dangerous because the reduced sensation prevents the patient from knowing if there are any minor lesions—ranging from a stubbed toe to stepping on glass.[16] A minor injury to the foot, which would have only healed slowly due to the poor blood circulation that accompanies peripheral neuropathy, or increasingly frequent episodes of pain, would have compounded Mabel's weakness and fatigue, making it even more difficult for her to leave the house.

Given Mabel's debilitated state, she was no longer able to do the laborious, exhausting, and time-consuming chore of laundry, which had to be done to maintain a decent, respectable household. Many people sent their laundry out to be done commercially, but this was expensive (Flanders 118). There was no way the impoverished Tolkien family could afford that. Among other responsibilities, Jane was likely to have supervised the Tolkien brothers in managing the two-person job of laundry that could take all day (Flanders 122-29). Jane Suffield Neave was recalled as someone who "was capable of taking a stern view of matters concerning domestic order" (Morton/Hayes 23), and it can be assumed that Mabel's expectations of domestic routine would have been consistent with her sister's.

Mabel's physical limitations at that time can be gauged not only by the fact her sister Jane apparently had to take time off from work to help Mabel with shopping and managing the household, but also by the fact that Hilary did not enter King Edward's School in the fall of 1903. Seeing that her sons were educated at the prestigious and well-respected King Edward's High School, their father's *alma mater*, was important to Mabel. When Ronald failed, at the age of seven, his first attempt to pass the entrance examination for King Edward's in the fall of 1899, his mother made sure he was tutored in geometry by Jane (*Letters* 377), as well as probably increasing her own efforts. Ronald passed the examination in late June 1900 and entered in the fall of 1900 at the age of eight (*Bio* 4, *C&G* 1.7).

The tuition of £12 for King Edward's was a substantial expense. As a result, in January 1902, Mabel subsequently moved to the Ladywood district of Birmingham and placed both boys in St. Philip's grammar school, probably for financial reasons.[17] This is where the family was living when Jane came to help.

At that time, Fr. Robert Eaton was the headmaster of St. Philip's (Ordway, *Tolkien's Faith* 65)—a small Catholic school with less than a hundred students (Gardner/Holford 44). The majority of these students were probably the orphans from the Catholic orphanage next door to St. Philip's grammar school.

Mabel soon realized that her sons were not getting the same quality of education that King Edward's offered. She then schooled them at home until they could sit for the King Edward's entrance examination (*Bio* 27). Ronald passed his examination for King Edward's for the second time in November 1902 and re-entered there in January 1903 (*Bio* 27, *C&G* 1.9).

Hilary, then eight years of age, apparently failed what was presumably his first effort at the examination in November 1902, and could not matriculate with his brother in January 1903. What is unstated is how Mabel would have paid for Hilary's tuition if he had passed. Mabel must have had a plan for this if she had Hilary take the entrance examination. One can only wonder if Fr. Francis Morgan had already offered financial help. This seems likely because Fr. Francis paid Hilary's tuition beginning in 1905 (Gardner/Holford 52).

If Mabel had followed her previous pattern, she would have prepared Hilary for the next opportunity to enter King Edward's. We can infer that the next examination would have been in June 1903, and passing it would have allowed Hilary to enter in the fall of 1903. Hilary's failure to matriculate at King Edward's in the fall of 1903 suggests that his mother, who would have wanted to see him established in his father's school, was not able to prepare him in the way she had prepared Ronald earlier, due to her increasing debility. This may have been why both the boys were tutored by Fr. Francis in the summer of 1904 (Bridoux, "Letting Images Speak" 1). Hilary finally entered King Edward's in January 1905.

Part of the reason for Aunt Jane's presence in the Tolkien household in December 1903 may have been to help again with tutoring, but this time with tutoring Hilary, not Ronald. After Ronald's term ended at King Edward's School and he was able to take care of his mother, Jane took a trip to the Isles of Scilly on the coast of Cornwall during part of the Christmas holiday of 1903-04 (Gardner/Holford 45). She then returned to her teaching post in January 1904.[18]

The fact that Jane did not continue her leave of absence for the purpose of helping Mabel may have been due to Jane's financial reality of needing to continue in her job, or possibly Mabel was seen as not in need of so much help with Ronald being home from school and now helping regularly, or Mabel may have declined further family help, or Mabel's fluctuating cognitive state may have become evident in baffling, unaccountable, accusatory outbursts, which are discussed further below.[19]

Mabel's ability to deal with routine matters was slipping. In December 1903, Mabel was financially quite poor and had been "living at 26 Oliver Road, a house that was only one degree better than a slum" for almost two years (*Bio* 27, *C&G* 1.8). She had few possessions but somehow had misplaced "a postal order for 2/6" which she had received "at least" a year ago (*Bio* 28). This 2 shillings and 6 pence money order would amount to £10.61 in 2021 goods and services or $12.11 in 2022.[20] This was a meaningful amount of disposable income to a very poor family,[21] which Mabel could ill afford to mislay.

Ronald Tolkien's Responsibilities in Caring for His Increasingly Disabled Mother

"The King Edward's School class list dated July 1904, concerning the first half of the year, will list Ronald as 'absent'" (*C&G* 1.11). Being listed, even though absent, indicates that Ronald's tuition was paid by a Foundation Scholarship which he won in 1902. This scholarship was renewed in 1904, 1906, and 1908 (*C&G* 1.9), so each award must have covered two academic years. "The first half of the year" seemingly refers to the Hilary term, beginning in January and running to the Easter break, as well as the Trinity term. It is not clear from this summary if Ronald attended briefly or not at all in the term starting in January. He certainly was absent after April 1904 because he was residing in Hove with Edwin Neave.

Ronald probably started school on January 19, 1904, when King Edward's opened, given the evidence discussed below that the boys became ill with measles at the end of February.[22] Ronald would have had to manage not only his school work but also carry the weight of the necessary household chores. In addition, if Hilary had been the first one of the two brothers to have contracted measles, then Ronald would have been needed at home to help with the nursing.

Maintaining a house was physically heavy work in 1904, even with the convenience of the intermittently running water from the Edgbaston water works which were functioning by 1873. The usual location for the household tap was in the "scullery," located in the rear section of the Oliver Road house. Water did not run the whole day, as we expect of a tap nowadays, but rather for as little as two or three hours, one or two days a week. This is why the scullery contained a cold-water tank or cistern, which stored water for the whole household in-between times (Flanders 91-92). Water from the scullery had to be brought into the kitchen as needed in a bucket, and a gallon of water weighs 8.33 pounds or 3.78 kg. Saying the Oliver Road residence was "only one degree better than a slum" (*Bio* 27) probably meant that it was only a step away from a slum like the houses on Darley Street in the right-hand side triangle in the map above which probably shared taps somewhere in the back-yards.[23]

The small rear wing of the Oliver Road house would have contained not only the scullery, but also a toilet facility (water closet, also called a "WC") which would have had an outside entrance only (Flanders xxvi, 297). It would have been a very small room, "a closet," without a sink. Because the water supply was intermittent, one would either have to dump water from the cistern into the top tank of the toilet and then flush or wait to flush when the water was again running. The last was hardly the most sanitary or pleasantly aromatic option.

In addition to the exhausting job of hauling any water into the house in buckets for cooking and baths, someone would have had to have managed the constant need to haul coal from a "coal hole" into the house for cooking and heating. This was even heavier work than bringing in the water in buckets. Coal scuttles came in standard size. The smallest coal scuttles held approximately 1.75 to 3.55 cubic feet or 0.05 to 1.0 cubic meters of coal. Full, the smallest scuttle held approximately 82.25 pounds or 37.31 kilos.[24] Even half-full, that is 41.13 pounds or 18.66 kilos. This weight is substantially more than the weight of a two-gallon bucket of water: 16.6 pounds or 7.53 kilos. Reducing the amount of coal carried per trip to the weight of a bucket of water would require almost three times as many trips to bring in a small coal scuttle's worth of coal.

If the residence on Oliver Road had a "kitchener" or closed range, popular by the turn of the century, the stove included a hot-water tank (Goodman 160, Flanders 70). If the residence had an older open range, Ronald or his brother would need to put water buckets on the stove to heat water for washing dishes, doing laundry, and taking a bath. An older open range was simpler to use, had less that could go wrong, and was more likely in cheap housing (Goodman 160). The open range stoves required:

> the raking out the cold ashes from the previous day, brushing the range down vigorously with a stiff brush to remove burnt-on food and ash from all its surfaces, and black-leading (rubbing it all over with a greasy black graphite mixture) the whole thing. This was a filthy job but if you didn't do it the filth would spread during the day to all the pots and pans, cloths and aprons (Goodman 160).

A fire in the stove could be laid and lit only when this preparation of the stove was done. This cleaning eliminated smells, as well as the unending soot the coal fire created. The closed-in kitchener required more work than the open range because the soot in the flues also had to be brushed down and removed in order to maintain the proper conduction of heat (Goodman 161). A live fire would have needed tending in the coal stove, which was probably used for both heating and cooking.

In addition, the household's oil lamps and candles would need constant attention. Oil lamps needed to have their glass cleaned daily, and the wick and oil-reservoir adjusted using special tools on a tin tray—the last to avoid a fire hazard. The physical and emotional toll of household management, plus the strain of caring for sick family members, weakened the health and left Victorian and Edwardian caregivers vulnerable to disease (Flanders 304). This would have been true for the two Tolkien boys.

These grimy household chores may have been one reason why Ronald identified with Beren (*Letters* 420), who was condemned to be a kitchen scullion for Tevildo, Prince of Cats. Like Beren, Ronald's days in early 1904 may have "passed miserably in the washing of floors and vessels, in the scrubbing of tables [...] and the drawing of water" (*LT2* 15). Ronald would have known that Beren, doing household labor, would have become "haggard and unkempt" (*LT2* 15).

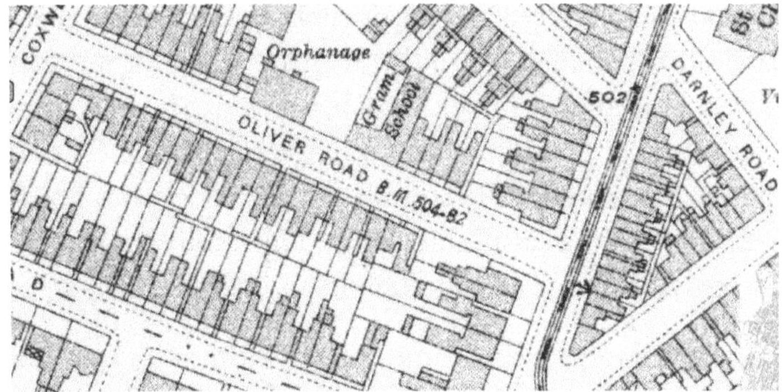

4. Oliver Road 1913-14 showing the entire length of Oliver Road

This household drudgery would have been in addition to any errands, like getting groceries for which Ronald would have been responsible after his mother became housebound. However, there may have been an additional duty as Mabel became weaker: cooking and meal preparation. When Mabel entered the hospital in late March 1904, she no longer prepared meals. Later, when she moved to Rednal, the postman's wife Mrs. Till prepared all the meals. The Tolkien boys may have already taken over preparing meals in February 1904, before the brothers became sick, because of their mother's slowly-increasing weakness and lethargy, as well as her difficulty standing for the length of time needed for food preparation. Meal preparation requires time and energy for the needed washing and cutting or chopping foods as well as cooking in heavy pots and pans, not to mention standing on diabetic feet that may have been affected by peripheral neuropathy. If the brothers bought staples, most cheap grocery staples were adulterated (e.g. alum, potatoes, or plaster of Paris in bread, or poisonous coloring agents) (Flanders 243-35).

Ronald may have been able to handle the responsibilities of both school work and household maintenance with the assistance of his younger brother, until he became ill himself and/or became burdened by caring for his brother and mother. Mabel's health, in particular, would have been expected to decline further by the start of 1904. Despite the value Mabel placed on education, Ronald may have found himself forced into the situation faced by many girls—helping in the house—that curtailed the ability to attend school. It was common for girls, who were needed to maintain the labor-intensive household routine, to be taken out of school when their help was needed at home. The continuing need for household help and the attitude that education was less important for girls were serious obstacles all through the nineteenth century and into the twentieth to girls' obtaining an education (Rose 192).

Which of the two brothers first came down with measles is unknown, but Ronald would have been either incapacitated by the illness himself or have been encumbered by nursing/household chores for the duration of both his and his brother's illnesses. Ronald and Hilary's illness can be more accurately dated now because "[a]t the time Hilary was ill with measles, uncle William Suffield had passed away suddenly" (Gardner/Holford 270).[25] Uncle William Suffield, Mabel's younger brother, died on February 27, 1904, at the age of 30.[26] That means that the whooping cough which "swiftly followed" Hilary's measles would have occurred in early March 1904 (Gardner/Holford 45). Measles usually last for one week, including the prodromal phase.[27]

A case of measles preceded Hilary's whooping cough—also known as pertussis. Clinically, the presenting symptoms of whooping cough in its first stage, which may look like the common cold, are the following: runny nose, sneezing, low-grade fever, and mild occasional cough. This first stage lasts one to two weeks. Stage two of pertussis can last from one to two months: the cough becomes more severe with coughing fits that can be followed by the defining high-pitched whoop that can lead to a cessation of breathing or to vomiting.[28] Coughing episodes are more likely at night, which means that the patient and other household members were kept from getting needed sleep. This is followed by a recovery phase that can last from two weeks to months and includes susceptibility to other respiratory illnesses. Hilary had the complication of pneumonia in mid-to-late March 1904, during what would have been his recovery phase (*Bio* 29). This means that Hilary, and, presumably, Ronald's illness, as siblings can be expected to share most germs, lasted from approximately February 27, until mid-to-late March.

This timeframe contrasts with Carpenter's complete absence of any information on when the boys became sick and for how long. Carpenter's statement that "The New Year did not begin well. Ronald and Hilary were confined to bed with measles followed by whooping cough" is now seen as misleading because the New Year generally only includes January and not the end of February. In fact, Hilary's and Ronald measles began on approximately February 27 because "[a]t the time Hilary was ill with measles, uncle William Suffield had passed away suddenly [on February 27, 1904]" (Gardner/Holford 270).

Carpenter reports that the "additional strain of nursing" her sons "proved too much" for Mabel Tolkien (*Bio* 29). If she was in the hospital "[b]y April," then this would dovetail with both boys being sick for most of March 1904.

Mabel's Hospitalization

By April 1904, thirty-four year old Mabel was in the hospital in Birmingham and diagnosed with the then-incurable disease of diabetes (*Bio* 29). Victorian and Edwardian hospitals were organized and funded differently than they are today. All hospitals, from a workhouse infirmary to a superior voluntary hospital, were created and funded by the middle and upper classes to serve the medical welfare needs of the working-class population without charge.[29]

A patient entering a hospital was not only greeted by nurses wearing white caps, announcing their status as professionals and keeping their long hair out of the way, but also by a "lady almoner." The almoner, almost always a woman, interviewed each patient and decided what would be an appropriate rate for the patient to pay. Hospitals did not use financial clerks or debt collectors. Patients paid hospital fees in Britain for only three decades beginning around World War I and lasting until 1948 when the National Health Service began providing medical coverage for all.

The almoners took into account an individual's social background and family resources when deciding the amount to charge.[30] The almoners also maintained the separation of the social classes by placing middle-class patients in a few private rooms on a different floor or perhaps in a different hospital building away from working-class or indigent patients.[31] Mabel Tolkien was likely to have been placed in such a separate room given her middle-class background.

In 1904, Mabel Tolkien probably arrived at the hospital as an emergency patient. The majority of emergency patients at that time would have come to the hospital in a horse-drawn ambulance. A major hospital, like Birmingham's, would have had its own specialized stables where the horses' harnesses hung from the ceilings. The harness could then be quickly lowered onto the team in seconds when an emergency call came.[32]

Mabel's presenting physical symptoms were likely to have been the classic ones for late-stage diabetes: serious weight loss, thirst, excessive urination, and the pathognomonic "hay breath" characteristic of diabetes. In formal case histories and in the general medical literature in the nineteenth century, only measurable, objective, physical symptoms would be reviewed and discussed. Symptoms of irritability and rage were not amenable to that bedrock—the gold standard of modern medicine—of repeatable quantification, and those symptoms would have been ignored. The psychosis, identity confusion, and/or disorientation, which can develop in diabetes, would have been of interest only to early twentieth-century psychiatry (Jefferson/Marshall 167, Kaplan/Sadock 199). The rapid resolution of these problems with adequate diet indicated their physical cause. Although the American National Institutes of Health (NIH) now list irritability among its top five symptoms of diabetes, no mention of this symptom would have appeared in the medical literature on diabetes at the turn of the twentieth century.[33]

In 1900, doctors treated patients for free because acute and general treatment in voluntary hospitals was underwritten by upper and middle-class philanthropists.[34] Doctors used the prestige of their hospital work as advertising to build their lucrative private practices.[35] Mabel was treated by the respected physician Dr. Robert Saundby (*C&G* 1.11), who would have seen in Mabel's case confirmation of the then prevailing belief and "well known fact that the disease [diabetes] is much more common among the educated than the uneducated classes" (Tattersall 36). Dr. Saundby, like most physicians of his day, advocated a controlled diet for diabetics (*C&G* 1.11), but getting patients to cooperate with the extreme limits and changes in their diet required by the physicians was a serious problem (Tattersall 22-23). The medical literature contained much controversy and debate about exactly what kind of diet would benefit diabetics, given the limited understanding of the disease's process.

While Mabel stayed in the hospital for more than two months (McIlwaine 135), possibly eleven weeks from late March to late June (*Bio* 29), her parents took care of the much debilitated Hilary. Probably, after a brief stay at his Suffield grandparents, Ronald was sent away to Hove to live with Edwin Neave, who was the fiancé of Ronald's Aunt Jane Suffield and was well-known to Ronald. Sending Ronald to Hove was probably done partly to minimize Ronald's continued exposure to Hilary's pneumonia and partly to let his grandparents focus their nursing on the seriously sick Hilary. Hove is about 177 miles or 285 km southeast of Birmingham. Ronald was most likely to have gone to Hove by train. If the train followed a similar route to the tracks today, the trip would have taken around five hours.[36]

Mabel's Puzzling and Unusual Convalescence in Rednal

In late June 1904, when the Birmingham hospital released Mabel, Fr. Francis Morgan of the Birmingham Oratory arranged for Mabel's convalescence in Rednal, accompanied by only her sons. However, this situation is anomalous. At the turn of the century, families took care of their own. The medical community extolled the "constant close unwearying waiting" on and "untiring thoughtfulness" for the sick and dying, who were tended at home by wives, mothers, spinster daughters, and other female nurses (Jalland 98). During the Victorian era and into the Edwardian era, "[a]ll sick people in these families were nursed at home" (Jalland 98, Flanders 302). That is what happened when Mabel's parents took in the two Tolkien brothers while Mabel was in the hospital and before Ronald was later sent to Hove to live with Edwin Neave.

The fact Mabel's Suffield family did not take Mabel in after her discharge from the hospital, when she was in such need, is remarkable. Previously, when Mabel was in need after becoming a widow, the extended Suffield and

Tolkien families rallied to support her with Walter Incledon supplementing her income and Laurence Tolkien paying Ronald Tolkien's school fees in 1900 (McIlwaine 13).

By December 1903, Mabel and the Suffield family would have known she was seriously ill if her sister Jane had had to take off work and pay for a substitute teacher in order to help Mabel. Mabel's parents appear to have had the room, possibly the optimal environment, and the ability to care for their very sick daughter. By 1901, Mabel's parents were living at 9 Ashfield Road in King's Heath. One servant and a boarder, Edwin Neave, an insurance inspector who was there by 1894, were also residents. Of the Suffield children, only Jane was still at home working as a school teacher. If the Suffields were still at the Ashfield address in 1904, they had an empty bedroom because Edwin Neave was now in Hove. Mabel's parents moved to the more affluent 15 Cotton Lane address in Moseley sometime in 1904 (Burns, "An unlettered peasant" 17). In the 1911 census, the Cotton Lane address had seven rooms, and the Suffields lived there with one live-in servant (Morton/Hayes 11, Morton 2, 1911 census). Cotton Lane was in Moseley which had the countryside ambiance recommended for Mabel's recovery.

As discussed above, Mabel's Unitarian father, John Suffield, and his wife were not likely to have objected to Mabel's Catholicism, especially given her terminal diagnosis. The Suffields were the kind of people one would have expected to harbor and tend to a dying child. The Suffields' willingness to take in Hilary shows that Mabel and her sons' Catholicism was not an insurmountable obstacle. Mabel's seeming exile from her family in Rednal points to an exceptional estrangement. The Suffields had presumably overcome the initial shock at Mabel's deceptive conduct and her placing her sister May and May's marriage at risk in June 1900, so there seems to be no good explanation for why they should turn their back on their dying child.

If the Suffield grandparents took in and nursed Hilary, and probably made arrangements for Ronald to stay with Edwin Neave, then it is a puzzle why they did not take in their daughter, dying from diabetes and not expected to live long, when she came out of the hospital. All Mabel had at the 'Woodside' cottage in Rednal was a bedroom and a sitting room (*Bio* 29). This level of accommodation would not have been difficult for the Suffields to provide. However, it is possible Mabel had rejected any offers of her parents to help her—if she believed they were opposed to her Catholic conversion. Given the report that Mabel Tolkien's "one further great dread [was] that her own [Suffield] and Tolkien families might seek to force the boys to abjure their Roman Catholic faith," Mabel, in her late stages of chronic illness, may not have been thinking clearly and believed that her parents were not going to follow their Unitarian principles.[37] Her fears may have been overwhelming her thinking. Because the Guardianship of Infants Act 1886, stating that a mother had the right to be her children's sole guardian on the death of her husband, was a relatively recent legal innovation (Flanders 196), Mabel may have been defensive about her rights. However, her father's beliefs should have forestalled Mabel's worry that her family would pressure her and/or the boys about their Catholicism hoping they might still enter a Protestant heaven.

The Suffield family's violation of expected Victorian, middle-class social norms and mores has previously been overlooked. Their unwillingness to welcome and care for Mabel, when she was known to be dying, points to serious implications. This lacuna in the chronology of Ronald's life should be considered in light of the Carpenter biography's vague and misleading dating of the Tolkien brothers' illnesses: "The New Year did not begin well. Ronald and Hilary were confined to bed with measles followed by whooping cough" (*Bio* 29). Carpenter consulted, corresponded and checked information with Hilary Tolkien when he was writing the official biography (Gardner/Holford 285). He would have been aware that the boys became ill in late February when Mabel's younger brother William died on February 27, 1904 (Gardner/Holford 270).[38]

Carpenter's omission of any dating of the events of early 1904 until the unspecified terminus "by April," and his admission that "several difficult issues" ("Review: Cover Book") were redacted from the first draft of the official biography suggest that the events of 1904 surrounding the illnesses of Mabel and her sons were part of his cutting "out everything which was likely to be contentious" when he "castrated" the first draft of the biography at the request of the Estate/Tolkien family ("Learning about Ourselves" 270, 271). In other words, in Carpenter's view, the published, "castrated" biography is seriously compromised by the excision of important, and possibly unflattering, information. This is analogous to a similar pattern of Carpenter's withholding and/or concealing facts about Edith Bratt, Ronald Tolkien's fiancée and later wife, in the official biography (Bunting/Hamill-Keays, *Edith* 60-62, 217-218, 220-22). One is left to wonder what facts about Mabel and her sons' illnesses were seen as so unacceptable or deleterious that they were removed or obscured.

The Unstated Complications of Mabel Tolkien's Diabetes

Diabetes would have disabled Mabel Tolkien from carrying out the laborious tasks of bringing in water from the pump, scouring the stove, hauling coal, doing laundry, and running errands. This illness would have also changed Mabel Tolkien's functioning in ways that are now rarely seen with today's well-controlled insulin treatment. Presently, most people with diabetes run the risk of high blood sugar levels due to the overabundance of sugary calories in the modern diet. In 1904, blood sugar swings with hypoglycemia (low blood sugar) were a frequent part of diabetes and created scenes which have almost disappeared. Something as simple and seemingly innocuous as skipping or delaying a meal could be enough to induce hypoglycemia. Old case records, like this one from the early 1920s, document what it was like: a patient

> during a meal, pressed his friends, to help themselves to more pepper. Then in a loud voice, he insulted his wife, who, realising he was hypoglycemic, asked him to take some sugar. He replied that, of course, she wanted him to take sugar, so that she could get rid of him and marry someone else. Eventually he was forced to take sugar, became normal within a few minutes, and had no recollection of what had happened (Tattersall 69).

This pattern of sudden irritability followed by very rapid recovery of a normal mood and thinking is quite distinctive and easily differentiated from superficially similar episodes. Intoxication, induced by drugs, alcohol, or even an "adrenaline high," can create irritability and irrational thinking, but mood and cognition do not improve until the state of intoxication has been resolved by the body over a period of time. An intense surge of adrenaline underlies most states of anger and the concomitant faulty thinking that accompanies anger. This emotional state will pass, but the usual safe margin is enshrined in guidelines like "go take a twenty-minute walk" or count backward from one hundred slowly. That is, the recovery from adrenaline is a slower process than the very rapid turnaround in emotional and cognitive states that accompany a change in blood sugar. The pattern created by the drop and then correction of blood sugar is also different and distinguishable from the extreme emotional states that Tolkien might have witnessed in battle or in the hospital (i.e. "shell shock" or the World War I variant of Post-Traumatic Stress Disorder). The rapid recovery seen in the stabilization of blood sugar levels is completely different from the typical course of a psychotic process in states of schizophrenia, manic-depression, or even dementia (typically senile). The distinguishing characteristic, the very rapid recovery of normal emotional and cognitive processing, differentiates low blood sugar swings from other pathological states.

Ronald Tolkien appears familiar with this phenomenon of unjustified, angry, or paranoid accusation coupled with a brief forgetting of reality, because he repeatedly depicts examples of a "passing madness" in relation to the Ring. When Bilbo asks to see the Ring in Rivendell, Frodo, "feeling a strange reluctance," finds suddenly "to his distress and amazement [...] that he was no longer looking at Bilbo, a shadow seemed to have fallen between them and through it he found himself eyeing a little wrinkled creature with a hungry face and bony groping hands. He felt a desire to strike him" (*FR* II i 225-26). Similarly, Boromir levels paranoid accusations at Frodo: "Miserable trickster! [...] You will take the Ring to Sauron and sell us all. You have only waited your chance to leave us in the lurch. Curse you and all halflings to death and darkness!" (*FR* II x 390). He then "passed his hand over his eyes, dashing away the tears. 'What have I said? He cried. 'What have I done? [...] A madness took me, but it has passed.'" (*FR* II x 390). This occurs again when Sam returns the Ring to Frodo in the Tower of Cirith Ungol: "Sam had changed before his [Frodo's] very eyes into an orc again, leering and pawing at his treasure, a foul little creature with greedy eyes and slobbering mouth. But now the vision had passed [...] The hideous vision had seemed so real to him [Frodo]" (*RK* VI I 891).

The most likely source of Ronald's familiarity with this unusual phenomenon of abrupt irritability and possible memory lapses would appear to be the hypoglycemic episodes that his mother almost certainly experienced, given that her diabetes was undiagnosed and untreated. Mabel died in November 1904, so especially during her last year uncontrolled fluctuations in blood sugar were expectable. Mabel's illness was following the predictable course of increasing dysfunction as her disease gained a greater and greater grip on her life. She was likely to have exhibited the intermittent, brief losses of contact with reality found in the clinical literature on the observed progress of the diabetes from the time when diabetes was untreated or poorly managed. Episodes featuring this specific combination of anger, irrational thinking, and forgetting would not be common for other people Ronald knew. This abrupt irritability and memory lapses may have contributed to her Suffield family forgoing close contact and the care of Mabel after her hospitalization.

These symptoms were likely to be accompanied by another serious complication of diabetes, namely that

> the fluctuating blood glucose levels that characterize uncontrolled diabetes can contribute to mood swings and lead to unpredictable or even aggressive behavior. [...] What's sometimes called "diabetic rage" can be dangerous, because it may involve behaviors a person isn't consciously aware of. Physiologically, when someone's blood sugar fluctuates, spikes, or drops, it can produce feelings of anger, anxiety, or depression that are out of the control of the person experiencing them. More seriously, extremes of both hypoglycemia or hyperglycemia can lead to cognitive impairment, confusion, loss of self-control, or hallucinations. These conditions should be considered a medical emergency.[39]

The medical practice of Mabel Tolkien's time did not have the above level of sophistication about the possible escalating risks of uncontrolled diabetes. However, once the state of hypoglycemia was understood in the 1920s, clinicians documented the range of effects that could begin with "nervousness or tremulousness," escalate to "definite anxiety, excitement or even emotional upset," and with continued lowering of blood sugar: "marked excitement, emotional instability, sensory and motor aphasia, dysarthria, delirium, disorientation, [and] confusion" (Tattersall 68-69). The standard response to Mabel's medical emergency, hospitalization, only occurred sometime before April 1904.

For early 1904, a partial timeline can be inferred for the Tolkien family. On Tuesday, January 19, 1904, Ronald Tolkien probably began Hilary term at King Edward's School, given that Hilary's measles occurred in late February 1904 (Gardner/Holford 45). If whooping cough "swiftly followed" Hilary's late February measles (Gardner/Holford 45), Hilary's whooping cough would have occurred in early March 1904.

Once young Ronald Tolkien came down with the measles and whooping cough which his brother had, he could no longer go to the store as he had since approximately late November 1903 when his mother became too ill to leave the house due to her undiagnosed diabetes (*Bio* 28-9). By mid-March 1904, Ronald, Hilary and Mabel were all likely to have begun suffering from the effects of irregular meals and the neglect of general housekeeping due to illness. Once young Ronald fell ill, he would have been only able to carry out his task of placing a bucket to catch water when it was running through the tap intermittently, at best. His weakened physical condition would have left him without the strength to dump the buckets of water into the storage tank and then cart any needed water into the house. Moreover, if, as was probable, due to the expected and predictable deterioration in Mabel's level of functioning as a result of the uncontrolled nature of her diabetes, their mother was unable to deal with the effort and strain necessary to resume meal preparation, the Tolkien brothers would have been forced to attempt to prepare meals as best they could. In addition, the more effort Mabel made, the more likely she was to lower her blood sugar level because physical activity decreases blood sugar level just as skipping a meal does.[40] Given their ages, lack of skill, and the poor-quality staples dictated by their limited budget, the boys' attempts at meal preparation would have been predictably inadequate in terms on complete nutrition.

If Mabel's daily calorie intake dropped below 1200 calories, the minimal required level in the medical literature to preserve bodily and mental functioning, she would have fallen into an ongoing protracted state of diabetic hypoglycemia (or low blood sugar).[41] "When severe diabetes is allowed to progress without proper treatment, [...] weakness and sweet odor of breathe; nausea, headache vomiting, dyspnea, sense of intoxication, delirium, [follow] and deep coma resulting in death" (Thomas D-28). On less than 1200 calories, she would have been at risk for slipping into a coma or death, but this did not happen. The clinical literature on diabetes also reports that diabetic hypoglycemia can result in mental disturbances, including unexplained outbursts of anger, periods of detachment, bizarre fugue-like states as well as episodic confusion (Jefferson/Marshall 167).[42] In a fugue state, or a state of dissociative amnesia as it would be now labeled, a patient would not have known who she was, but rather would have believed that she was someone else and would not have recognized her own children. "Tremor, irritability, increasing confusion, delirium, or frank psychosis may follow" in this state (Kaplan/Sadock 199). These are clinical findings presented in today's standard medical-school textbooks, and a consultation with a competent, experienced internist will confirm the likely, dangerous, and uncontrolled progression of this disease that occurs when there is no treatment.

It is worth noting that Ronald Tolkien depicts this distinctive scenario with a dramatic recovery of identity after an altered state of consciousness twice in *The Lord of the Rings*. The first instance of this reorientation occurs when Merry awakens in the tomb of the Barrow wight saying, "The men of Carn Dum came on us at night, and we were worsted. Ah! The spear in my heart! [...] What am I saying? I have been dreaming" (*FR* I viii 140). Here Merry regains consciousness of his own identity. This scene is parallel to the scene in the tombs of Minas Tirith when Denethor, emerging from his "trance" of "madness," recognizes his son Faramir, and "the flame died in his eyes" (*RK* V vii 834). Denethor's recollection fulfills Gandalf's promise: "Your father loves you, Faramir, and will remember it ere the end" (*RK* V iv 799). Both of these scenes feature a confusion of identity in bare settings, which mirror each other.

The human body has certain requirements and limits and in many ways functions like a machine. For example, when Harvey discovered that the heart works like a pump, medicine was revolutionized. Medicine is about predicting what will happen given the condition of the structure and functioning of the body (i.e. the anatomy and physiology), and the known behavior of the disease or trauma process that is disrupting the body's normal level of functioning. Just as one can predict that not maintaining the level of oil in a vehicle will cause the vehicle's engine to burn up, one can predict that a late-stage, untreated diabetic patient with inadequate calorie intake will develop low-blood sugar. If the disease process of hypoglycemia continues unchecked, past the stage where the patient is weak, shaky, drowsy, or irritable, then there are only a very limited number of possible outcomes including: death, coma, or psychosis.

Certainly, other complications are possible, for example, stroke, but that would destabilize the acidosis created by diabetes, resulting in death (Nuland 68). We know of no other complications of this kind for Mabel. Given the intermittent water supplies and the demands of diabetes for frequent urination, Mabel may easily have suffered from dehydration which can lead to electrolyte imbalances that can also fuel a psychotic process.[43]

The modern management of diabetes is based on clinical studies. In late-stage diabetes, a drop in food intake will have predictable consequences, with a serious risk of coma or death. Ronald Tolkien's perception—both in 1904, as seen in his postcards to his mother (as discussed below), and later—of the true gravity of this situation is underscored by his apparent familiarity with the distinctive pattern of emotional and cognitive changes due to blood sugar fluctuations: the intermittent pattern of anger, paranoid thinking, and memory lapse, and the distinctive fugue state with loss of identity found in diabetic psychosis. This knowledge of rather arcane psychiatric symptoms is reflected in the effects of the Ring on Bilbo and Frodo, the identity confusion of Merry in the barrow, and Denethor in the Tombs of Minas Tirith.

Mabel's judgment and comprehension may have already begun to fail. By December 1903, Mabel would have known she was seriously ill if her sister Jane Suffield had to take off work and pay for an alternate teacher in order to help Mabel. Mabel may have dismissed the seriousness and consequences of her incapacity and/or was too proud or stubborn to get help. In a similar way, Mabel denied the seriousness of her diagnosis of diabetes and the need to have a will drawn up, as is seen in her dictating a will only two days before she lapsed into a coma.

At the turn of the twentieth century, doctors were more likely to inform patients of terminal diagnoses if there was no hope of any improvement. Information was withheld if it was believed that the patient's efforts could turn the tide. Doctors and family wanted hope to do all it could. They were afraid the patient would become depressed and give up if told there was nothing that could be done and no improvement was expected (Flanders 327).[44] However, Victorians believed strongly in being warned about their likely death; not only so that they could be properly prepared to meet their Judge and Maker, but also to tie up loose ends and settle all the business of this earthly life (Flanders 330, 328). The fact that Mabel Tolkien had two children, ages twelve and ten, would have weighed heavily in any doctor's decision to reveal the terminal nature of her diagnosis. There was no hope for her or any other diabetic, and the future of her children was at stake.

Further, if Jane Suffield had been confronted with the sudden irritability, paranoid thinking, and possibly a memory lapse, like the one cited above for the patient with hypoglycemia, this experience may have contributed to Jane's not returning to help with the Tolkien household in late January 1904. As a result of Mabel's illness following the course of the clinical example given above, the Suffield family may have decided to discontinue their offers of household help. This loss of family contact would have prevented them from knowing about any worsening of Mabel's home situation.

This would have been especially true if Mabel had made accusations of poisoning similar to the ones in the case study or accusations that the Suffields were determined to oppose her and her children's Catholicism. As a result of this likely aspect of Mabel's diabetes, the Suffield family would not have been likely to have been checking to see if Mabel needed groceries or other aid.

Mabel repeatedly displayed an independent and willful disposition. She had conducted an unorthodox courtship with Arthur Tolkien, flouting Victorian proprieties. She had little respect for the conventional, racist views prevalent among her husband's Boer clientele in South Africa. Consequently, when it was discovered that she had allowed a native servant the English custom of giving servants permission to take young children in their charge to visit the servants' families, she appears to have created an elaborate cover story that Ronald had been "kidnapped" (Bunting, "Zanzibar" 32). Mabel let Ronald and Hilary wander unsupervised in Sarehole, much like working-class children, as opposed to the usual constraints imposed on middle-class children, who were not yet of school age (Bunting, "Zanzibar" 34-35). Her embrace of and continued adherence to Catholicism in the face of family and cultural disapproval indicate that she was intransigent and not likely to take criticism or correction well.

With the increasing severity of chronic diabetes, Mabel's judgment and comprehension may have begun to falter and lapse. The Suffields may have thought they could trust Mabel to tell them if she needed help, but they were evidently not correct. Given the seriousness of her sons' illnesses, perhaps she should have asked for help, but did not. Mental impairment, brought on by her diabetes, may have prevented her from recognizing the escalating risks to her children.

With whooping cough, in particular, the standard recommendation of the time was to give warm milk or a cream soup to stop the vomiting brought on by the intense bursts of coughing because milk was seen as preventing weight loss and the undernourishment that prolonged the whooping cough (Peters 223). The impoverished Tolkien household would have been hard pressed to afford enough food to avoid malnutrition, which can have major health consequences.

Modern readers have difficulty appreciating the relative cost of food at the turn of the twentieth century: "At the start of the First World War, food purchases consumed half the average paycheck; today the figure is six percent. According to the federal statistics, an American in 1919 had to work for two and a half hours to earn enough money to buy a chicken; these days it would take less than fifteen minutes of labour."[45] These figures are for Americans, but the figures should be comparable in England. There are figures from the 1860s and 1870s in Britain, when a lower middle-class family with an income of £140 yearly spent £30 on rent, property taxes and water. Nearly £80 or more than half of the yearly income was spent on food (Flanders 224). Many middle-class households had milk delivered twice daily, and other perishables, that require refrigeration to prevent spoilage, like meat, fish, and green groceries, were delivered daily or every other day (Sitwell 223). Only iceboxes were available in middle-class homes so frequent deliveries were needed to have fresh products. However, the indigent Tolkien household could not afford the middle-class lifestyle of having groceries delivered.

If Mabel or one of the boys attempted to the recommended treatment of warm milk or a cream soup for whooping cough, there were a series of problems. No one in the Tolkien household could go to the store for milk, assuming they could afford it. It is not clear if anyone had the strength and competence to handle all the required work to warm the milk or make soup including: having stored water from the intermittently running tap in the water tank, bringing the water into the house from the scullery, hauling in the coal needed to have the stove heat the milk or soup, or tending the fire in the stove to cook the soup or warm the milk. Malnutrition and hunger appear to be an unspoken context for the boys' serious illness and slow recovery as well as the deterioration of Mabel's diabetes.

Mabel evidently did not let her family know how desperate her situation was. She may have been afraid to tell them given her fixed idea that they rejected her and the boys' conversion to Catholicism. Whatever the circumstances, events appear to have spun out of her control and worsened, compounding the seriousness of her and her sons' illnesses.

When Mabel Tolkien went to the hospital in late March 1904, we can infer that not only was she ill, but both of the Tolkien brothers were still quite ill from their bout with measles and whooping cough, compounded by pneumonia for Hilary. In late July, approximately a month after Mabel left the hospital and was reunited with her sons, Mabel wrote about her impressions, stating that her sons are so: "*ridiculously* well compared to the weak white ghosts that met me on train 4 weeks ago" with Hilary now looking "*immense*" (*Bio* 29; all italics are in the original). In an age without antibiotics, Hilary would have still been recovering from pneumonia and Ronald would have been in the recovery phase for whooping cough—which could last for months. In 1910 to 1912, "most cases," of whooping cough continued for ten weeks, but it readily lasted longer "if neglected or not properly treated."[46] Whooping cough/pertussis was known to lead to weight loss due to dehydration and an inability to keep food down.

If in late June 1904, the brothers were "weak white ghosts" and Hilary at age eleven now looks "*immense*," then one wonders what they looked like in April when Mabel entered the hospital. The boys had spent almost three months with other caregivers: Hilary with his Suffield grandparents and Ronald with Edwin Neave in Hove (*Bio* 29). The Suffields and Edwin Neave can be assumed to have taken the best possible care of the boys.

From Mabel's description that the brothers were now "*ridiculously* well," we can infer that when she went to the hospital, her sons were quite sick and thin. It seems only natural that Hilary's grandparents would have done everything they could to "fatten up" a sick child who had had a bout of pneumonia on top of whooping cough. Presumably in the four weeks since arriving in Rednal, Mrs. Till, the postman's wife, who "gave them good meals," continued the generous servings that the boys received previously (*Bio* 29). In the photograph from May 1905, in the Carpenter biography, almost one year later, Hilary appears clearly of average weight, certainly not chubby or plump or *immense* (Priestman 16). Consequently, we can conclude that in April 1904 Hilary must have been quite underweight, if not emaciated.

The seriousness of the situation when both brothers were ill seems reflected in Ronald Tolkien independently indicating that he believed that both he and/or his brother Hilary might die. While Ronald stayed with Edwin Neave in Hove (*Bio* 29), on April 27, 1904, he mailed a sketch to his mother of himself and his soon-to-be uncle, Edwin Neave, sleeping in a shared bed in Edwin's home (*A&I* 10). The picture is titled *They Slept in Beauty Side by Side*. This title probably comes from the first line "They grew in beauty, side by side" of the poem, "The Graves of a Household" by Felicia Hemans, a very popular and well-known poet of that time (*A&I* 12).

The poem is about three brothers and a sister who grow up happily in a home where their "smiles lit up the hall" and "cheered with song the hearth." Perhaps most importantly for Ronald Tolkien, the poem's line, about the children's "voices mingled as they prayed/Around one parent knee," reflects the religious fervor of his mother. Much of Catholic education of the young occurs in the 'domestic church' of the family (Ordway *Tolkien's Faith* 37), and Ronald Tolkien emphasized how his mother "hand[ed]" on the Catholic faith when he was a small boy (*Letters* 354). Ronald probably kept his mother's book on prayer—*The Lord's Prayer and the Angelical Salutation* by Fr. Jerome Savonarola OP (Ordway, *Tolkien's Faith* 38).

The poem continues by acknowledging that now the children's graves are "severed far and wide" in America, at sea, in Spain, and in Italy. This would parallel Ronald and Hilary now sleeping apart and being separated by a five-hour train ride.

In this drawing, Ronald may also be recalling sleeping in the same bed with Hilary, which is almost certainly a fact, while thinking about brothers who may lie separated in their graves. Ronald Tolkien appears to refer to himself and his brother sleeping in the same bed in "You and Me and the Cottage of

Lost Play", written April 27-28, 1915 (*C&G* 1.71; see Bunting/Hamill-Keays, *Edith* 125-26; Bunting "Reply"). Alternatively, it could be a joke—as who would consider Ronald Tolkien and Edwin Neave beauties, and Tolkien was known for his humor (Burns, "They Slept" 11; *Bio* 130), though that does not fit well with the somber implications of the poem and the mournful allusions found in the other titles of drawings of 1904 discussed below. Further, clean sheets in a clean room with predictable, regular hours enforced by a trusted, familiar adult, after the probable disarray of Oliver Road earlier in 1904 resulting from their mother's incapacitation by her diabetes, may have felt like sleeping "in Beauty." Tolkien was certainly capable of this kind of play with concepts and words as evidenced by his "precocious" rebus letter of August 8, 1904, just a few months later, to Fr. Francis Morgan (Bridoux, "Letting Images Speak" 1; Hooker "Rebus Letter" 2).

The other picture postcards carry more allusions to death, underlining Ronald's perception of the near death of his brother and mother. Tolkien's title for his drawing *What Is Home Without A Mother* echoes an adage that was sometimes inscribed on Victorian gravestones.[47] Maggie Burns also notes that Tolkien's title—*For Men Must Work*—for what looks to be an innocuous picture of Ronald and Edwin Neave walking to work, is also part of the refrain in Charles Kingsley's poem "The Three Fishers".[48] Kingsley (1819-1875) was a Church of England clergyman, a university professor, and a writer who was known for his children's book *The Water Babies, A Fairy Tale for a Land Baby* (1863)—a forerunner of fantasy books for children. In Kingsley's bleak, hopeless poem, the fishermen go out to work and drown, leaving the women to mourn:

> For men must work, and women must weep,—
> And the sooner it's over, the sooner to sleep.

The contrast between the dark and devastating allusions found in the titles to the drawings and the almost jaunty subject matter of darning socks in *What Is Home Without A Mother* and parading to the office in *For Men Must Work* points to Ronald Tolkien struggling to come to terms with what seems to have been a catastrophic experience with the near-death of his mother, his brother, and perhaps himself. The twelve year old Ronald would have spent six months watching the collapse of his mother's health while he lived across from the

Catholic boys' orphanage where he might soon be residing. This scenario is worthy of Charles Dickens.

Given the seriousness of the illnesses of both the Tolkien brothers in the first quarter of 1904 and Mabel Tolkien's choosing to not involve her family and to not ask for help, the Suffield family may have judged Mabel's actions irresponsible, especially if she and the boys were suffering from hunger and malnutrition. This neglect of parental care would have been judged even more harshly in the Victorian era, when Motherhood was elevated to a sentimentally charged, sacred calling (Douglas 74-75; Dijkstra 13, 85, 173). A mother, an "Angel in the House," was expected to protect, guard, and nurture her innocent children at whatever cost to herself. If, in her diabetic confusion and likely psychosis, Mabel had neglected and/or endangered her children or left them hungry and thirsty, this would have been likely to be difficult for the Suffields to understand.

The unstated complications of Mabel's diabetes include her likely episodes of anger and irritability as well as the now rarely seen diabetic psychosis with a fugue state as documented in medical textbooks. These likely complications are now considered 'surprising' today, not only because the improvements in management and treatment of diabetes have completely changed what is typically seen, but also because the vast majority of complications today are caused by hyperglycemia and not hypoglycemia, which was much more common in 1904. In the clinical literature of the time, hypoglycemia was known to cause "marked excitement, emotional instability, sensory and motor aphasia, dysarthria, delirium, disorientation, [and] confusion," along with irritable outbursts with memory lapses and paranoia (Tattersall 68-69). Given this well-documented progression of diabetes from her time, there is no reason to believe Mabel was spared these problems in the last year of her life as her illness progressively worsened over the months leading up to her death in November 1904.

Furthermore, in 1904, it was assumed most cases of mental illness with its accompanying disordered behavior were due to hereditary causes. Although the dynamics of hypoglycemia were only elucidated in the 1920s, Mabel's doctor could have explained to the Suffield family that a loss of self-control, angry outbursts, and psychosis could occur in late-stage diabetes, although in 1904 the medical profession had no understanding of the underlying physiological mechanism. Physicians of that time would have been quite familiar with the clinical presentation of this diabetic complication. If Mabel's attending physician, Dr. Saundby, had explained clearly that diabetes was the physical source of Mabel's actions, then the family would have been reassured that if Mabel had acted in a seemingly senseless manner, this behavior had no hereditary component that would reflect on the family or affect her children.

Part of the popularity of Freud and others' talking therapy at the end of the nineteenth century was that it created an alternative explanation for mental and psychological disorders and held hope for the patient's improvement without the stigma of heritability as primary (Sulloway 92-93). This fear of hereditary "taint" is an entirely different cultural and historical context than the one of the twenty-first century. Henrik Ibsen's play, *Ghosts*, first staged in 1882, deals with the unspoken fears of the hereditary transmission of insanity.

If Mabel betrayed the expected Victorian standard of trust in caring for her sons, the shocked and ashamed Suffield grandparents' first reaction may have been only to retreat from Mabel and care for their grandsons, gladly letting Fr. Francis Morgan step in and arrange alternative lodging. The Suffields may have been relieved to have Mabel exit the hospital and proceed directly to Rednal. Fearing gossip and scandal, the family would have prioritized making sure no one knew that anything untoward or unusual had been involved in Mabel's medical crisis leading to a diagnosis of diabetes, thereby preserving the family's reputation. Previously, John Suffield had probably acted to preserve the family's reputation when he was likely to have sent Mabel away from Birmingham when he discovered her defiant and scandalous behavior with Arthur Tolkien in 1888. At that time, a likely refuge could have been with her brother Roland in Manchester.

The concern to eliminate any possible slander may explain the odd episode of Mabel's widowed sister-in-law, Beatrice Suffield, burning "all [Ronald's] mother's personal papers and letters" (*Bio* 33).

Aunt Beatrice had been married to Mabel's younger brother William, who died on February 27, 1904, at the age of 30—not quite nine months before Mabel's death and at the start of the Tolkien brothers' repeated illnesses. For Beatrice

Suffield, being a young widow would have meant suffering a loss of social status, income, and the reason for her existence which would have centered on the socially sanctioned activities of creating a home and catering to her husband (Flanders 348). Carpenter reports the childless Aunt Beatrice was "deficient in affection" to the two Tolkien brothers. However, her attitude is quite typical for the early 1900s. Before the twentieth century and psychoanalytic validation of the importance of childhood memories and experiences, orphans went where they were told to go "with the admonition that they should be grateful to be fed, clothed, and sheltered" (Simpson 148). If sympathy was expressed at the death of a parent, it was not offered to the children, but was "offered to the surviving relatives who would be burdened with raising someone else's child" (Simpson 148). But as someone recently bereaved herself, it would seem likely that she would understand that the boys would want to save any keepsakes from their mother. The episode is puzzling unless, like Carpenter's other deletions and omissions, family secrets were being protected.

The Tolkien boys occupied Aunt Beatrice's top-floor bedroom beginning in January 1905, after Fr. Francis Morgan officially became their guardian. Presumably, the boys deposited all their meager possessions in that bedroom. It seems they had some sort of keepsake box which held Mabel's papers and letters and other *momento mori* of their mother. Aunt Beatrice would have had to go out of her way to find and then burn these documents. This action cannot have been motivated by any antipathy toward Catholics as the widow Aunt Beatrice had "no particular religious views" (*Bio* 32).

Such an odd action suggests a wish to erase or expunge evidence of any possible malfeasance from Mabel's life. The incineration of Mabel's letters and papers may indicate the Suffield family had reason to be concerned about what any diaries or "papers" might reveal. The Victorians set great store by "respectability," the safeguard against scandal and being led astray. Respectability was based on church and prayer, family, and prompt bill-paying; conformity and conventionality were morality (Flanders xxxiii-xxxiv). The concern that led to the destruction of Mabel's papers might well have also been the basis of the Suffield family's apparent ostracism of Mabel in the summer of 1904.

Whatever the cause, the Suffields would have wanted to go to the greatest possible lengths to restrict who might know about any conduct that might be perceived as failing to maintain the high moral calling of Victorian Motherhood. Although Mabel wrote to her mother-in-law, Mary Tolkien, chattering as if nothing was wrong, this was possible because Mary Tolkien was far away in Newcastle. The Suffields would be eager to contain the spread of any rumors in the Birmingham area. Mabel's family's response, like Beatrice's purging of Mabel's papers and letters, was to lock the unspoken past in silence and keep their distance from Mabel during what was left of her short life. Carpenter, who was allowed unhindered access to all papers and letters, alludes to a possible "family secret" ("Learning about Ourselves" 271), and wrote that he left out "*several* difficult issues" in the Tolkien biography ("Review: Cover Book," italics added). Mabel's uncontrolled conduct during episodes of hypoglycemia and probable diabetic psychosis with its distinctive fugue state as well as its effects on her children may be a "difficult issue" kept secret.

After the summer in Rednal when the Tolkien family lived at the postman's cottage, Ronald returned to school. Diabetes slowly finished its work on Mabel Tolkien's body. Mabel died on November 14, 1904 and was buried three days later.

Ronald Tolkien could only speak of his mother in the most positive and idealized terms (Rosegrant, "Mother Music" 121-122): "a gifted lady of great beauty and wit" whose "sole tuition" (except in geometry) "gained [Ronald] a scholarship to King Edward VI School in Birmingham" and whose death was due to "persecution, poverty, and largely consequent, disease, in the effort to hand on to us small boys the Faith" (*Letters* 54, 377, 354). In Tolkien's 1968 BBC interview, he was at pains to portray his mother in a positive light, stressing he was "very well brought up" and would not think of disobeying or even feeling frustrated by his mother's expectations or requirements (Lee, "Tolkien in Oxford" 139). Tolkien observed that his mother "obviously had philological talents which had not been developed by education" (Lee, "Tolkien in Oxford" 134).[49] He praised his mother's teaching, emphasizing his academic success was due to "luck," as opposed to "merit," and specifically the luck of having had a "good education [...] particularly in having an extremely attractive, beautiful and extremely able mother" (Lee, "Tolkien in Oxford" 134, 172). Having an "extremely attractive, beautiful" mother is not a requirement for a good education and serves to highlight Tolkien's emphasis on his mother's best qualities.

If Ronald Tolkien's mother had done anything that engendered censure in the Suffield family, Ronald would be expected to avoid any mention of such a falling out. Stressing his debt to his mother, he wrote: "I am Suffield by tastes, talents, and upbringing" (*Letters* 54, see also 218). But Ronald Tolkien also wrote he endured "dreadful sufferings" in "childhood" which "records do not record" (*Letters* 421). We can infer that the time of the Tolkien brothers' illnesses was marked by hunger and their mother's deterioration from diabetes—with the last entailing significant cognitive changes and distortions. These experiences appear to only surface in "mythical and legendary dress" in Tolkien's writings (*Letters* 211). During his mother's last stage of illness, Ronald Tolkien also would have been his mother's "ceaseless companion, the silent witness" who "breathed the atmosphere of [her] pain [...] physical suffering and weariness" (Flanders 313).[50] Is it any wonder that in Ronald's mythical world, the Elves experience no chronic pain, helpless suffering, and the disabling indignities of age, though they could die of grief or wounds in war? If Ronald Tolkien experienced "dreadful sufferings" in early 1904, that might be a reason for the Suffield family's seeming detachment and distance from Mabel and the destruction of her "papers." Their attitude would, of course, foster reciprocal distancing by Mabel.

The adult Ronald Tolkien and his literary executor and son, Christopher Tolkien, continued the Suffield family's policy of an abundance of discretion when revealing family history to the general public, leaving out any information that did not display Mabel Tolkien in the best possible light. Tolkien's praise of his mother and her family suggests not only a wish to bury the painful parts of the past and retain only the good, but also an understanding of his mother that must have slowly evolved and been fostered by the Suffield family and their forgiveness toward Mabel. The indelible experience of watching his mother deteriorate and crumble under the onslaught of "hunger, thirst, poverty, pain, sorrow, injustice, death" (OFS 151) may have fueled his fairy tale creation of the seemingly ageless, never infirm Elves.

End Notes

1 Personal email from Nhia Huynh, Temporary Project Officer, Archives, The Schools of King Edward VI in Birmingham Foundation Office, Edgbaston Park Rd Birmingham, 11/3/2020.

2 "Royal Automobile Club route planner, walking." https://www.rac.co.uk/route-planner/, accessed on 1/24/2023. In the fall of 1900 when Ronald started at King Edward's School, the Tolkiens had moved in late September to 214 Alcester Road, Moseley, near a tram route (*C&G* 1.8).

3 Distance is calculated from 86 Westfield Road to King Edward House at 135a New Street. King Edward House was built on the site of the Old King Edward's School. The RAC [Royal Automobile Club] route planner gives 3.68 miles, https://www.rac.co.uk/route-planner/, accessed on 12/30/2002.

4 *The Official Catholic Directory and Clergy List*, Volume 22, M. H. Wiltzius Company, 1905 names Rev. Haskew at St. Peter's (13). St Peter's Catholic school in Bromsgrove is listed under "Aid Grants to Voluntary School Associations 1903-1904' in Parliaments *Accounts and Papers* (140). Nuns usually lived in the school complex and consequently would have given the associated church as their address.

5 In a New York City traffic study undertaken in 1907, horse-drawn vehicles moved at an average speed of 11.5 mph." "Fast Facts." https://parkcityhistory.org/wp-content/uploads/2012/04/Teacher-Background-Information.pdf, accessed on 12/8/2020. One expects a pony on a country road between two small English towns to be trotting.

6 "Treating diabetes, 1921 to the present." Understanding diabetes. History of diabetes. Diabetes Québec. https://www.diabete.qc.ca/en/understand-diabetes/all-about-diabetes/history-of-diabetes/treating-diabetes-1921-to-the-present-day/, accessed on 8/26/2020.

7 At that time, Mary Tolkien (1833-1915) was living in Sydenham Terrace, Newcastle so she would probably not have any other information on Mabel and the boys' condition (See "Tea in Hay" this volume).

8 "Inflation Calculator." Bank of England. https://www.bankofengland.co.uk/monetary-policy/inflation/inflation-calculator and "XE Currency Converter." https://www.xe.com/currencyconverter/convert/, both accessed on 12/2/2020.

9 ."Viaticum" here refers to "Holy Communion given to those in danger of death" (New Advent, the Catholic Encyclopedia). This is different and separate from extreme unction or Last Rites. Even the most conservative Catholic opinion would not see a need for viaticum in Mabel Tolkien's case given that she had gone to Mass on Sunday, November 6 and received Last Rites ("Viaticum," Catholic Encyclopedia. New Advent. https://www.newadvent.org/cathen/15397c.htm, accessed on 12/10/2020).

10 "Apostolic Pardon Brings Total Forgiveness Before Death." National Catholic Register, accessed 9/25/2023. https://www.ncregister.com/features/apostolic-pardon-brings-total-forgiveness-before-death.

11 Compare this to Gollum, who has been consumed by the Ring: "No name, no business, no Precious. Nothing. Only empty" (*TT* IV vi 673).

12 It is unclear who or what was the source for Carpenter's statement.

13 "Sue Young Histories." https://www.sueyounghistories.com/2009-11-21-john-suffield-1802-1891/, accessed on 12/5/2020.

14 "Jane Neave was granted a leave of absence due to ill health on the condition that she paid the salary of a temporary mistress to replace her." Personal email from Alison Wheatley, Schools of King Edward VI in Birmingham Resources Centre, dated August 27, 2008.

15 "Diabetic Neuropathy." Mayo Clinic. https://www.mayoclinic.org/diseases-conditions/diabetic-neuropathy/symptoms-causes/syc-20371580, accessed on 1/24/2023.

16 "Foot Problems Caused by Diabetes," posted January 12, 2017.Orthodpaedic and Spine Center, Newport News VA. https://www.osc-ortho.com/blog/foot-problems-caused-by-diabetes/, accessed on 1/24/2023.
17 The Birmingham Oratory website's "Tolkien and the Oratory" states the fees for Kings Edward's "were proving a great financial burden" and imply this was part of the reason Mabel chose to place Ronald at St. Philip's (http://www.birmingha-oratory.org.uk/TheOratory/Tolkien/tabid/76/Default.aspx, downloaded 1/2/2010).
18 A copy of *Poetical Works of Keats* has the dedication "To E.J. Suffield on her departure for the Scilly Islands 1.i.04." (personal email from Neil Holford).
19 The Mayo Clinic lists symptoms of diabetes as including: increased thirst, frequent urination, extreme hunger, unexplained weight loss, fatigue, and irritability. https://www.mayoclinic.org/diseasesconditions/diabetes/symptoms-causes/syc-20371444, accessed on 12/6/2020.
20 "Inflation Calculator." Bank of England. .https://www.bankofengland.co.uk/monetary-policy/inflation/inflation-calculator and "XE Currency Converter," https://www.xe.com/currencyconverter both accessed on 9/17/2022.
21 In 1908 Old Age Pension law recipients received 5 shillings a week.
22 Personal email from Nhia Huynh, Temporary Project Officer, Archives, The Schools of King Edward VI in
Birmingham Foundation Office, Edgbaston Park Rd Birmingham, 11/3 /2020.
23 On July 21, 1904, this situation completely changed when King Edward VII and Queen Alexandra opened the dams and inaugurated a state-of-the-art water system for Birmingham. "How Victorian Birmingham created the best clean water supply in the country." By Fionnuala Bourke, 15 Nov. 2015. https://www.business-live.co.uk/economic-development/how-victorian-birmingham-created-best-10439853, accessed on 12/3/2022.
24 "[W]eights of bituminous (common soft) coals vary even more than those of anthracite, according to the locality from which the coal comes. Such weights range from 47 to 55 pounds per cubic foot." "U.S. Department of Commerce Bureau of Standards: Weights of Coal," accessed on 11/28/23. https://www.govinfo.gov/content/pkg/GOVPUB-C13-52d96cacae47984029d4eef719f028e3/pdf/GOVPUB-C13-52d96cacae47984029d4eef719f028e3.pdf
25 From "a reminiscence from one of the letters" which cannot be presently quoted in full (email from Neil Holford).
26 *Birmingham Post*, March 1, 1904.
27 "Measles." U.S. Center for Disease Control. https://www.cdc.gov/vaccines/pubs/pinkbook/downloads/meas.pdf, accessed on 1/24/2023.
28 ."Signs and Symptoms: of Pertussis (Whooping Cough): Centers for Disease Control and Prevention," https://www.cdc.gov/pertussis/about/signs-symptoms.html, accessed on 9/30/2023.
29 "Paying for healthcare: life in Britain before the 'free' NHS." HistoryExtra, official website of the BBC Magazine. https://www.historyextra.com/period/20th-century/nhs-history-pay-healthcare-free/, accessed on 12/3/2020.
30 "Paying for healthcare: life in Britain before the 'free' NHS." HistoryExtra, accessed on 12/3/2020. https://www.historyextra.com/period/20th-century/nhs-history-pay-healthcare-free/.
31 "Paying for healthcare: life in Britain before the 'free' NHS." HistoryExtra, accessed on 12/3/2020. https://www.historyextra.com/period/20th-century/nhs-history-pay-healthcare-free/.
32 "9 Strange Things You'd See in a Hospital in 1900." mentalfloss. https://www.mentalfloss.com/article/57987/9-unfamiliar-things-youd-see-hospital-1900, accessed on 12/3/2020.
33 "What are the symptoms of diabetes." National Institutes of Health, https://www.nichd.nih.gov/health/topics/diabetes, accessed on 12/13/2020.
34 "What was healthcare like before the NHS?" Doyle, Barry and Rosemary Cresswell, July 3, 2018. https://theconversation.com/what-was-healthcare-like-before-the-nhs-99055, accessed on 94-/2023.

35 Paying for healthcare: life in Britain before the 'free' NHS." HistoryExtra, accessed on 12/3/2020. https://www.historyextra.com/period/20th-century/nhs-history-pay-healthcare-free/.

36 "At the beginning of the twentieth-century railroads had an average speed of 40 mph." "The development of the railway network in Britain 1825-1911." Dan Bogart, Leigh Shaw-Taylor and Xuesheng You, accessed on 6/4/2020.https://pdfs.semanticscholar.org/beca/ae2e1cf76dca3ecc5a252d529e583806ecec.pdf.

37 "Tolkien and the Oratory." http://www.birmingham-oratory.org.uk/TheOratory/Tolkien/tabid/76/Default.aspx, downloaded 1/2/2010.

38 From "a reminiscence from one of the letters" which cannot be presently quoted in full (email from Neil Holford).

39 "Domestic Violence, Anger, and Diabetes." verywellhealth. https://www.verywellhealth.com/is-anger-at-a-spouse-normal-with-diabetes-1087327, accessed on 12/6/2020.

40 "U.S. Department of Health and Human Services:National Insititute of Diabetes and Digestive and Kidney Disease: Diabetes Diet, Eating &Physical Activity," accessed 12/1/23. https://www.niddk.nih.gov/health-information/diabetes/overview/diet-eating-physical-activity#howMuch.

41 The widely quoted statement that adults require at least 1,200 calories per day for basic bodily functions and to stay out of starvation mode, is a low amount. It is not necessarily healthy. (See "emedicinehealth: Is it Safe to only Eat 1200 Calories a Day," https://www.emedicinehealth.com/is_it_safe_to_only_eat_1200_calories_a_day/article_em.htm, accessed on 12/1/23).

42 A "fugue state," in recent terminology, has been redefined to include only "purposeful travel or bewildered wandering that is associated with amnesia for identity or for other important autobiographical information" (DSM-5 298). In this new nomenclature, the effect of the diabetic psychosis would now be a "dissociative amnesia" to highlight the inability to recall important autobiographical information, inconsistent with ordinary forgetting. This amnesia can be "localized" for forgetting events of a circumscribed period of time or "generalized" when a person forgets their own identity. With the establishment of a normal level of blood sugar, the amnesia of a diabetic psychosis, resolves.

43 See Webb, William L. Jr and Mohan Gehi. "Electrolyte and fluid imbalance: Neuropsychiatric manifestation." *Pscyhosomatics*. Vol. 22, iss. 3, March 1981, pp. 199-203. Storing the amount of water necessary to maintain adequate drinking water as well as water for cooking and bathing with an intermittent water supply would have been beyond the physical capabilities of Mabel and her sons, given their poor health and diminished strength. (https://www.sciencedirect.com/science/article/pii/S0033318281735321, accessed on 10/25/2023).

44 National Library of Medicine: Journal of the Royal Medical Society 2006 Dec; 99(12): 632–636: "How the doctor's nose has shortened over time; a historical overview of the truth-telling debate in the doctor-patient relationship." https://www.ncbi.nlm.nih.gov/pmc/articles/PMC1676322/, accessed on 12/1/23.

45 "Freedom from Fries." *The New Yorker*. November 2, 2015, p. 58.

46 "Whooping Cough." *Every Woman's Encyclopædia*, volume 8, London, [1910-1912], p. 5331

47 "Further Corrigenda and Addenda." https://www.hammondandscull.com/addenda/artist.html, accessed on 12/10/2022. *What is Home Without A Mother?* was also an 1854 popular song by Alice Hawthorne.

48 "Further Corrigenda and Addenda." https://www.hammondandscull.com/addenda/artist.html, accessed on 12/10/2022.

49 See Smith "Book Review" 175.

50 This is approximately what eight year old Edmund Gosse recalled watching his mother die of cancer in 1856-57.

Chapter Seven

The Interlace of Autobiography and Faërian Imagery in *Smith of Wootton Major*

Nancy Bunting

Smith of Wootton Major is generally acknowledged as Ronald Tolkien's charming, but "perplexing" last story (Flieger, *GS* 167). Although, in the official biography, Humphrey Carpenter wrote *Smith of Wootton Major* "was related closely and even consciously to himself [Tolkien]" (*Bio* 243), biographical considerations have been discounted and undervalued. Verlyn Flieger inveighs against the "hidden trap of autobiography" (*QT* 232) and states "Tolkien's purpose in writing this story [... is] to capture, like a butterfly in a net, the atmosphere, the essential nature of the Perilous Realm" or Fairyland (*GS* 66). Consequently, the story lacks a plot and the traditional happy ending (*GS* 66, also *QT* 235). Flieger's approach, however, leaves the reader no "key with which to unlock its [the story's] secrets" (*GS* 68), its "particular and unexplainable magic" (*GS* 170), or its "gossamer appeal" (*QT* 231).

This paper builds on earlier works to argue that this story is indeed autobiographical in important ways.[1] A close reading of the text of *Smith of Wootton Major* provides compelling evidence. Ronald Tolkien admits his writing method is one of hints, rather than explicit statements: "I feel it is better not to state everything" (*Letters* 354). Looking at *Smith of Wootton Major* through a biographical perspective may offer a way to understand Ronald Tolkien's hints concerning this fairy-tale's secrets.

I. Tolkien's Life as the Frame of Reference for *Smith of Wootton Major*

Context of the Impetus to Tolkien's Writing *Smith of Wootton Major*

A request to write a preface for George MacDonald's "The Golden Key" was the stimulus for Tolkien's creation of *Smith of Wootton Major* in November

1964. A broader survey of Tolkien's life circumstances, when writing *Smith of Wootton Major*, as well as the debt Tolkien owed to MacDonald, seems to clarify what fueled Tolkien's writing *Smith of Wootton Major* as an answer to MacDonald (Long, "Clinamen").

Beginning in 1959, Tolkien underwent a series of changes when he retired from Oxford University, five years before the writing of *Smith of Wootton Major*. Although he saw this "compulsory retirement" as "distressing" (*C&G* 1.580), Ronald Tolkien now had the time to tie up loose ends and address his own interests. In 1959 and 1960, Tolkien wrote almost a dozen essays or stories in the legendarium as well as an attempted revision of *The Hobbit* which he abandoned after two chapters (*C&G* 1.584).[2] Various drawings on Elvish themes complemented these writings (*C&G* 1.589-90, 1.594-96). Then in October 1961, in response to a letter from his Aunt Jane Neave, Tolkien began collecting poems for *The Adventures of Tom Bombadil* which was published in November 1962. Tolkien spent a good part of 1961 completing his work on *Ancrene Wisse* which was published in December 1962. On December 5, 1962, at a small dinner party at Merton College for Ronald and Edith, Norman Davis presented Ronald with a specially bound *Festschrift* on Tolkien's work containing twenty-two contributions (*C&G* 1.633). In Michaelmas term of 1962, Ronald filled in for his friend and colleague Charles Wrenn during Wrenn's sabbatical leave, teaching *Beowulf* and in Hilary term 1963 lecturing on *The Freswæl* ('Frisian Slaughter' Episode and Fragments) (*C&G* 1.630, 636). In 1963, both Tolkien and his wife Edith suffered episodes of poor health, and the year drew to a close with the death of Ronald Tolkien's friend and fellow Inkling, C.S. Lewis, on November 22, 1963. In response, on November 30, 1963, Ronald Tolkien began once again to keep a diary written in a modified alphabet (*C&G* 1.645).

Carpenter highlights how Ronald Tolkien's active social life of the University academic circles dwindled to contact with his children and visits from Oxford faculty. Alistair Campbell, the professor of Anglo-Saxon, came to see him, and Norman Davis, the new Merton Professor of English Language and Literature, and his wife went to lunch with Ronald and Edith (*Bio* 238-39). Retirement left Tolkien vulnerable to "gloom" and "despair" (*Bio* 236).

Despite the successful appearance of *Tree and Leaf* in May 1964, Tolkien appeared to remain "a very complex and depressed man," as noted by his longtime friend Fr. Murray (West, "Letter" 135). In his diary, Tolkien wrote: "Life is grey and grim […] I can get nothing done, between staleness and boredom (confined to quarters), and anxiety and distraction. What am I going to do? Be sucked down into residence in a hotel or old-people's home or club" (*Bio* 242). Ronald Tolkien was ready to write "an old man's book, already weighted with the presage of bereavement" (*Letters* 389). By 1971, Tolkien described himself as a "prisoner starving in a tower" (*Letters* 415).

In the middle of these changes, on November 19, 1964, Tolkien's new secretary, Mary E. Hares, sent a letter to the editor, Michael di Capua, replying that Tolkien was willing to do a preface to "The Golden Key" (*C&G* 1.658). As recently as the 1964 preface to *Tree and Leaf*, Ronald Tolkien had called "The Golden Key" one of MacDonald's "stories of power and beauty" (28, OFS 125). However, in a note on a copy of another letter of November 19, Tolkien wrote "the project fizzled out" "after re-reading that ['The Golden Key'] (and much also of G[eorge] MacDonald's)" (*C&G* 1.658). Instead of a preface, Tolkien's sketch of an alternative to "The Golden Key" led to the birth of *Smith of Wootton Major*.

The phrase, "and much also of G[eorge] MacDonald's," may explain some of Ronald Tolkien's negative assessment and reaction to MacDonald whom he characterized elsewhere as "a horrible old grandmother" (Resnik 41; see also Kilby, *Tolkien & the Silmarillion* 31). Tolkien objected to MacDonald's implicitly condescending asides and the tone of the story's narrator toward MacDonald's intended audience, children (Long, "Clinamen" 129; *SWM* 85).[3] Ronald also complained that MacDonald's allegories are "overly didactic:" Tolkien warned the reader in the abandoned preface that MacDonald "is a preacher […] in all his many books" (Long "Clinamen" 129; *SWM* 90).[4] This is unsurprising because George MacDonald was, in fact, a Protestant minister and wrote books on theology as well as fairy tales.

Long can cite only a brief episode at the beginning of "The Golden Key" as an example of MacDonald's "preaching" in this story. The neglected and "ill-used" [read abused] girl Tangle is told to be "clean and tidy" by the Grandmother with the additional comment that one should not focus on how one looks but on how other people look. The story's fairies' dislike of untidiness and persecution of slovenly people serves as a plot device to drive Tangle to the Grandmother's house. MacDonald's Fairyland and Grandmother seem quite in tune with popular ideas of Fairyland, as found in the "Frau Holle" fairy tale, which advocated conscientious hard work. The Grandmother's act of taking care of Tangle and making her "clean and tidy" is an act of kindness, not just propriety. Consequently, Ronald Tolkien's complaints about MacDonald seem to be beside the point for "The Golden Key" and may refer rather to the "and much also of G[eorge] MacDonald's."

A review of MacDonald's writings may have reminded Ronald Tolkien of his use of MacDonald's essay, "The Fantastic Imagination."

> Many of MacDonald's ideas in this essay read as if they form an initial outline of points Tolkien addresses in 'OFS': [...] Imagination versus fancy, Law and laws of the spirit (which corresponds to Tolkien's Moral Law), the meaning of fairy tales, children and such tales, allegory and significance, beauty, and its destruction by intellectual greed (Wickham-Crowley 22).

The origin of Ronald Tolkien's term for the concept 'sub-creation' could also easily derive from MacDonald's discussion of creation in that essay (Wickham-Crowley 1).

Besides "On Fairy-stories," Ronald Tolkien may have had other debts to MacDonald. *There and Back Again*, Tolkien's subtitle for *The Hobbit*, could be taken as a reference to or a comment on MacDonald's 1891 book, *There and Back*. Bilbo Baggins chooses *There and Back Again* as one of the titles for his memoirs (*RK* VI ix 1004).

MacDonald's *There and Back* has elements that would be congenial for Ronald Tolkien in *The Hobbit* and elsewhere in his writings. The story has what might have been an attractive protagonist for Tolkien: Richard Tuke, a bookbinder who loves old books and who cites John Gower's *Confessio Amantis* (1389). Richard is also the story's unknown heir, Richard LeStrange. His maternal grandfather is Simon Armour, an honest smith, with a "true old heart", known for making fine gates. The story presents the hero's love interest, Barbara, in terms of being a fairy, a star, and having radiance. Richard Tuke marries the fairy-like

Barbara, and in *The Hobbit,* Tolkien states a Took, one of the many variant spellings of the name 'Tuke', "married into a fairy family" (*Tolkien and Welsh* 127-28, *H* 12). If the "Again," in *The Hobbit*'s subtitle, *There and Back Again,* is taken to indicate a sequel, then MacDonald's *There and Back* could be read as the establishing background of a Took/Tuke married to a fairy.

MacDonald's *There and Back* is choc-a-block stuffed with so much religious commentary, intermissions, interludes, allegories, digressions, explanations, meditations, and a mini-sermon, that it is a credit to MacDonald's art how seldom these interruptions drag on the story or render it tedious. Here Tolkien's complaint about "preaching" seems quite apt. The remarkable correlation of the two titles and a Tuke/Took married to a fairy seem too close to be accidental for a man who, according to C.S. Lewis, was "soaked" in MacDonald and "grew up on William Morris and George MacDonald" (quoted in Ordway, *Modern Reading* 89, 163).[5]

Previously, Ronald Tolkien not only praised "The Golden Key," but also readily cited MacDonald as the source of the goblins in *The Hobbit* (*Letters* 178, *TOFS* 250). Tolkien's later change of attitude toward "The Golden Key" and George MacDonald seems based not only on his criticism of "The Golden Key," but also on other unacknowledged debts to MacDonald. Consistent with this reading, Holly Ordway interprets Tolkien's reaction to George MacDonald as an example of influence-by-opposition (102-03; see also Bowers 256-67; Hooker, *Tolkienothēca* vi-vii).

The Permutations of Tolkien and Biography

Carpenter's comment, as quoted at the beginning, implies that Tolkien's biography is relevant. In contrast, Verlyn Flieger indicates there is a "hidden trap of autobiography" (*QT* 232). Her protest against the use of biography would be congenial to Tolkien, whose enthusiasm for a biography of himself during his life led him to compare it to "vivisection" (*C&G* 1.622). In a January 1973 letter, Ronald Tolkien's intense dislike for "biographical tunneling and scavenging" was so painful that he begins writing in the third person: "I cannot of course, foresee, forestall, nor forbid the activities of those ghoulish creatures that after his [*sic*] death seek to exhume him [*sic*] and disinter what is buried" (*Revised Letters* 600).

Ronald Tolkien made repeated and well-known strong protests denying the importance of biography in appreciating his writings. For example, in 1957, Tolkien wrote, "I doubt its relevance to criticism. Certainly in any form less than a complete biography, interior and exterior, which I alone could write, and which I do not intend to write" (*Letters* 257). However, this would not biography, but autobiography, which would still not be of use to an appreciation of Tolkien's writings because

> only one's Guardian Angel, or indeed God Himself, could unravel the real relationship between personal facts and an author's works. Not the author himself (though he knows more than any investigator) [...]
>
> I do not like giving 'facts' about myself other than 'dry' ones (which anyway are quite as relevant to my books as any other more juicy details). Not simply for personal reasons; but also because I object to the contemporary trend in criticism, with its excessive interest in the details of the lives of authors and artists. They only distract attention from an author's works (if the works are in fact worthy of attention) [...] Then there are more significant facts, which *have* some relation to an author's works; though knowledge of them does not really explain the works, even if examined at length (*Letters* 288).

Tolkien's prestige as an Oxford professor, holding first the Rawlinson and Bosworth chair of Anglo-Saxon, and then the Merton Professorship of English Literature, certainly lends weight to this declaration.

Ronald Tolkien, in fact, appears to have routinely drawn on incidents and details from his life in his writings.

1) Beginning in 1912 at the age of twenty, his anticipated reunion with his soon-to-be fiancée, Edith Bratt, was the source of his play, *The Bloodhound, the Chef, and the Suffragette* (*Bio* 59).

2) Ronald drew on his personal life in his story of Lúthien and Beren from *The Silmarillion* (*Letters* 420).

3-5) The models for the Valar include: Edith Bratt "almost certainly" because in Elvish *Erinti* means 'Little one' (QL 36), Ronald's nickname for Edith; *Amillo* for Hilary Tolkien (QL 30); and *Lirillo* for Ronald Tolkien (QL 65, Garth 128).

6-8) Ronald's early Elvish vocabulary included references to his wife's blue eyes in the word 'Helinyetille' (Bunting/Hamill-Keays, *Edith* 164-65), to the realities of World War I including the words 'gas-bag balloon', 'noise of drums', 'louse', etc. (Garth, *Great War* 128, *Edith* 209), and to Tolkien's Catholic faith—such as 'nuns', 'monks', 'the gospel', and 'crucifix', including his guardian Fr. Francis Morgan listed as *Faidron* or *Faithron* (Hooker, *Glossology* 223-31; GL 33).

9) Ronald's nightmare of the Great Wave appeared in notes in late 1914 (*LT2* 274, 264), became material for the Fall of Númenor, an episode in *Roverandom*, the dream of Faramir (*RK* VI v 941), and the image of the destruction of Sauron (*RK* VI iii 926) in *The Lord of the Rings.*

10) *Leaf by Niggle* was based on a dream Tolkien had around the fall of 1938 (*Letters* 113, 320).

11) The two millers from his childhood in Sarehole "went straight into *Farmer Giles of Ham*" (W. Foster "An Early History").

12-16) Belladonna Took, her sisters, and the Old Took in *The Hobbit* were all characters based on Mabel Tolkien and her family of origin (*Bio* 175).

17) "The Shire [...] is in fact more or less a Warwickshire village of about the period of the Diamond Jubilee" (*Letters* 230, also 235).

18) The name 'Bag End' came from the farm of Ronald's Aunt Jane (*Bio* 106).

19) Tolkien told Clyde Kilby that the Sarehole mill was "the Shire mill" (*Tolkien & The Silmarilion* 51).

20) The "thunder-battle" in *The Hobbit*'s Misty Mountains, and the background for the crossing of the Misty Mountains and the peaks of Moria in *The Lord of the Rings* came from Ronald's experiences during his 1911 Swiss walking tour (*Letters* 309, 391).

21-23) The "Lost Road," is "clearly a kind of idealized autobiography" (*Bio* 171), and "Alboin's biography [...] is in many respects closely modeled" on Ronald's life (*LR* 58). In the "Lost Road," the father Oswin Errol, a widowed schoolmaster, whose name means 'God-friend', appears to stand in for the celibate

Fr. Francis Morgan, Ronald's guardian, who had also tutored him (Bridoux, "Letting Images" 1).

24-26) Various characters in "The Notion Club Papers" were based on members of the Inklings, including Tolkien as 'Rashbold', the English calque of his Germanic surname 'Tolkien' (*SD* 150).

27) In his writings about *The Lord of the Rings*, Tolkien wrote, "I am in fact a *Hobbit* (in all but size)" (*Letters* 288, also *Letters* 170, 315), and he apparently wanted to show that this was true by naming his home or family estate, 'Dwaling' on the map of the Shire (Hooker *Mathomium* 50-51).

28) because 'Dwaling' marks the ancestral home of Dwalakonis, the Gothic calque of the name 'Tolkien' (*Letters* 357).

29) the name 'Gamgee' came from a family joke (*Bio* 188).

30) The 'glittering caves' in *The Lord of the Rings* are based on the caves of Cheddar Gorge (*Letters* 407).

31) The character Lobelia in *The Lord of the Rings* was based on someone Tolkien knew (*Letters* 229).

32). In *Rovernamdom*, the mother and three little boys are identified as Tolkien's family in 1925 (*R* 92). There are references to a "Tinker, a large black cat" (*R* 4, also 89). Ronald Tolkien's Aunt Mabel Mitton had a large black cat named Tinker which was "ancient" in 1933 when Priscilla Tolkien visited the Mittons.[6]

It appears Ronald Tolkien mined his own experiences for plots, characters, motives, and settings, even though he repeatedly belittled "excessive interest in the details of the lives of authors [... that] only distract[s] attention from the author's works" (*Letters* 288). Given the pervasive presence of components of Tolkien's biography in his works, as documented above, Tolkien's wish to have the events and experiences from his life ignored, simply cannot be honored by serious researchers.

By the age of twenty in 1912, Tolkien was already using autobiography in his play, *The Bloodhound, the Chef, and the Suffragette*, which was based on his anticipated reunion with his soon-to-be fiancée, Edith Bratt (*Bio* 59).

Tolkien wrote that after attempting a "diary with portraits," he "took to 'escapism': or really transforming [my] experience into another form and symbol with [...] the Eldalie (representing beauty and grace of life and artefact)" (*Letters* 85). Tolkien's method, as indicated in "The Notion Club Papers," was to take selected aspects from a person. Although members of the Inklings were the starting point or models for characters in "The Notion Club Papers," "the mirror is cracked, and at the best you will only see your countenances distorted, and adorned maybe with noses (and other features) that are not your own" (*SD* 148-49). Ronald Tolkien was not a copyist, but rather revised his own experiences in his writings.

Ronald Tolkien mined his own experiences for his writings, yet he belittled "excessive interest in the details of the lives of authors [... that] only distract attention from the author's works" (*Letters* 288). His view of biography becomes even more complicated, if not contradictory, when it came to authors that interested him such as Chaucer (Bowers 49, 100, 140, 217). In these cases, Tolkien was willing to ignore his own maxim. He commented on the *Parlement of Foules*:

> It is actually in accordance with the ways of literary composition that accidental exterior things such as the battered book in need of binding, and the glimpse of star through his window, should be genuine and personal and embedded in references to feigned personal feelings and experiences (Bowers 141).

Again, commenting on Chaucer's "The Reeve's Tale", Tolkien wrote: "The chance events of the actual lives of authors get caught up into their books, but usually they are strangely changed and intricately woven anew one with another, or with other contents of the mind" (Bowers 217). Such "accidental exterior" details in the personal life of Ronald Tolkien became embedded in his invented language and the world of Middle-earth. In Tolkien's "Qenya Lexicon," "*Erinti* [Edith] = *helinyetille*," with *helin* meaning 'pansy' (QL 39). *Helinyetille* is also glossed as "Eyes of Heartsease", a common name for pansy (W.P. Wright 270). Tolkien's definition of *helin* or 'pansy' in his lexicon emphasizes that this is a blue violet pansy (QL 39). Although pansies come in many colors, it is one of the rare blue flowers. Consequently, the "Eyes of Heartsease" gloss is very likely to refer to Edith's eyes which were "bright blue" (Martsch, "Tolkien Reading Day" 9). Tolkien evidently was extrapolating from his own experience when writing about what other authors do.

Tolkien's tendency to identify with Chaucer and to "know" what that poet was trying to convey also encompassed other poetry, such as *Beowulf* and *Sir Gawain and the Green Knight*, which he had studied for years (Shippey, "Tolkien and the *Beowulf* poet," "Tolkien and the *Gawain*-Poet"). Ronald Tolkien's publication of "Chaucer as a Philologist" indicates Tolkien's confidence that he understood Chaucer was much like himself (Bowers 241). Tolkien did not think "excessive attention to detail" was unwarranted when studying poets and poetry that interested him.

Ronald Tolkien's manifest attention to the biographical details of various authors' lives, which can illuminate his/her writings, collides with his dictum: "excessive interest in the details of the lives of authors and artists [...] only distract attention from an author's works." Despite Tolkien's strong and seemingly irrefutable statements on the unimportance or irrelevance of biography in general and his biography in particular, the numerous examples in his own writing undercut and belie his stated position and personal preference. This untenable contradiction seems to have evolved into a dogma when Tolkien's heirs faced the task of presenting a biography of Ronald Tolkien. On careful examination, Tolkien's official biography is, unsurprisingly, less a biography and more a biographical legend—a "romanticized, distorted image of [Tolkien's] biography, controlled by the author [or his heirs and later the Tolkien Estate] and used as the basis of literary criticism" (Fimi 7). The lack of "truth" in the biographical legend about Tolkien is the result of the perennial issues of both access and control, well-known conundrums of biographies (Bair ix-xiii, 585; Remnick).

Rayner Unwin, Tolkien's publisher, had long worried that without an authorized biography: "neither he [Tolkien] nor we [his publishers], would have any *control*. [... and] after [Tolkien's] death it was one of the first matters that I raised with the [Tolkien] family. They [...] were doubtful about [...] what *control* there might be over what was written" (17, italics added). Unwin probably counseled the literary executor, Christopher Tolkien, in his legal rights, namely that he could have the final decision on what to include in the biography (i.e. the "control"). It seems the naïve, inexperienced, ambitious Carpenter was so elated over his good fortune in landing the contract for the biography, he evidently did not correctly interpret the contract's fine print about final control of the book, because otherwise he would not have been so taken aback by the required revision of the original draft that was "unacceptable" to Christopher Tolkien: "I went away and rewrote it [...] What I'd actually done was castrated the book, cut out everything which was likely to be contentious. I've therefore always been displeased with it ever since" ("Learning About Ourselves" 270). The revised book was approved by Christopher Tolkien (Unwin 249).[7]

Carpenter repeatedly tried to advertise the limitations and unreliability of the official biography ("Review: Cover book," *Bio* 260). Carpenter could not make any explicit statements about problems with accuracy or reliability because he was almost certainly bound by a Nondisclosure Agreement like everyone who has access to the Tolkien Archives (Testi 97). Consequently, the difficulty of obtaining accurate biographical information on Tolkien, as well as the gaps in the information now available, create obstacles.

Is the Ball's Bounce a Useful Metaphor?

Both Ronald Tolkien (*Letters* 388) and Verlyn Flieger cite with approval (*SWM* 80) Roger Lancelyn Green's review of *Smith of Wootton Major*: "To seek for the meaning is to cut open the ball in search of its bounce: those who read will certainly enjoy the cake, probably find the charms and possibly glimpse the star. But if one caught the star with a telescope it would not be there" (*C&G* 2.1222).

Green, the author of the review, was Ronald Tolkien's "old friend" (*Letters* 388). Tolkien supervised Green's thesis on Andrew Lang in 1943-44, and from 1945 to 1950 Green met with Tolkien "frequently" while Roger Green was Deputy Librarian of Merton College (Green, "Recollections" *C&G* 2.471). When Green published the review of *Smith of Wootton Major*, he had already published four positive reviews of Tolkien's work (J. Johnson 22, 47, 59, 65). In addition, Green socialized with C.S. Lewis and other Inklings—all friends of Tolkien. Green last met with Tolkien in March 1972 (*C&G* 2.472), so he had an ongoing relationship with Ronald Tolkien at the time of the review and quite possibly had some idea of what kind of review would please his friend and former professor.

Green's thesis in the review of *Smith of Wootton Major* seems to be of the school that believes the close analysis of a Shakespearean sonnet leads to a loss of appreciation for its art and/or of the experience of its beauty. Critical thinking by the reader is seen as possibly ill-advised, because that would go beyond the simple superficial enjoyment of the cake, charms, and star. Green's metaphor seems to have discouraged discussions about *Smith of Wootton Major*.

Green's view does not seem equivalent to Tolkien's often repeated position that he wanted the reader "to read with literary pleasure" (*Letters* 414; italics in original). Tolkien wanted readers to "*first* read it [*The Lord of the Rings*] with attention throughout," and only then analyze and criticize, though Tolkien had less sympathy for those activities (italics in original).[8]

The science-fiction community seems to have best appreciated the focus on the unmediated experience of Tolkien's writings.

> Tolkien, like most storytellers in most societies throughout history, values stories *as stories*, not as essays in disguise. Tolkien does not want you to read his stories, decoding as you go. He wants you to immerse yourself in the tale, and care about what the characters do and why they do it (Card 156, italics in original)

In contrast, postmodern methods—feminism, multiculturalism, deconstructionism—look for and/or at the author's unconscious encoded messages and then judge the author for what (s)he is found to have "revealed about himself in his text," again treating the text as something to be decoded, like an allegory (Card 155). Writers in the modern tradition comply with this convention of decoding the text by inserting symbols "in ways that careful readers cannot miss," and these objects/symbols, even when vague, are "fraught with meaning and attention must be paid" (Card 155).

"Escapist" literature, like science fiction and *The Lord of the Rings*, demands that "readers leave their present reality, and dwell, for the duration of the story, within the world the writer creates" (Card 158). This would be consistent with Tolkien's goal to go beyond a mere literary "suspension of disbelief" by creating a "Secondary World which your mind can enter—a special form of sub-creation, fantasy (OFS 132, 139). For Ronald Tolkien, successful sub-creation produced "an *involuntary* suspension of disbelief" (Phelpstead, "Myth-making" 87, italics in the original). In contrast, the serious literary reader, who rejects "Naïve Identification," remains "in their present reality, perpetually detached from the story, examining it from the outside" until they find the symbols and extract a meaning that they can detach (Card 158). Consequently, "'serious' literature is so simple that it can be decoded, its meaning laid out in essay form, while 'escapist' literature is so complex and deep that it cannot be mediated, but must be experienced; and no two readers experience it the same" (Card 159). To summarize, the

> point is that Joyce's *Ulysses* can be taught. But The Lord of the Rings [*sic*, not in italics] can only be read. When someone takes you through *Ulysses* and discusses it in serious literary terms, you constantly get the pleasures of a cryptic crossword puzzle: Ah, so *that's* why this chapter was so unintelligible! But when you discuss LOTR, each explanation takes you, not farther into the text, but farther out of the story (Card 160).

However, to create the time, place, and characters in *The Lord of the Rings*, "that rang true as chimes" (Hobb 90) in which the reader could experience an immediate immersion, it seems logical that Ronald Tolkien would have needed to live through these, or similar, experiences himself before he could describe or convey them to the reader. Orhan Pamuk, the Nobel prize-winning Laureate, stresses how an author must use his own sensory experiences and project his experiences in writing a novel. As an author, he can summon up:

> How I feel when I inhale the scent of rain-soaked earth, when I get drunk in a noisy restaurant, when I touch my father's false teeth after his death, when I regret that I am in love, when I get away with a small lie I have told, when I stand in line in a government office holding a document moist with sweat in my hand, [...] when I feel sad after everyone has left the resort at the end of summer, [...] when I run into an old friend from military service (50-51).

Ronald Tolkien did not write according to literary theory but out of "what you might call the heart, the emotional side, and what I should call the leaf-mould of the mind, and say all the things you think you've forgotten" (*Bio* 126; Lee, "Tolkien" 158-59). He thought literary theory and "criticism" "tends to get in the way of a writer [i.e. Tolkien] who has anything personal to say" (*Letters* 126). This "leaf mould" brings the discussion back to the contribution of Tolkien's biography with its stores of personal experience.

Douglas Anderson's discussion of what relevant background materials Flieger chose to withhold in her edition of *Smith of Wootton Major* may point to an omission of biographical references that inform the story ("Smith" 3). Verlyn Flieger does not print the draft of the remarks that Tolkien made at Blackfriars,

October 26, 1966, when he read the story publicly, nor the correspondence about the story with Eileen Elgar, his cousin Marjorie Incledon and John Ezard "which provide a wider context to Tolkien's concerns about this work" (Anderson, "Smith" 3). Without notifying the reader, Flieger published only ten and three-quarters of the fourteen typewritten pages of the "Smith of Wootton Major Essay" (Anderson, "Smith" 5). The deleted ending "directly continues Tolkien's argument; he obviously intended these pages to be part of his essay, though they do not discuss his story" (Anderson, "Smith" 5). The essay contains Tolkien's thoughts on the recently completed story allowing it to be dated to around February 22, 1965 (Anderson, "Smith" 6).[9]

Autobiography in *Smith of Wootton Major*

The evidence of Tolkien's use of his own biographical experiences in his work is consistent with Carpenter's statement that *Smith of Wootton Major* "was related closely and even consciously to himself [Tolkien]" (*Bio* 243). Ronald Tolkien may not have deliberately drawn on all the biographical counterparts found in *Smith of Wootton Major* because "the creative imagination did not always and only depend on conscious memory" (Ordway, *Modern Reading* 274, also 34). The fact that Ronald Tolkien first shared this story with family—his wife Edith (*Bio* 158), and then by mid-February 1965, his cousin, Marjorie Incledon (*C&G* 2.1216)—suggests that there may be biographical elements in *Smith of Wootton Major*. Tolkien could have shared the new *Smith of Wootton Major* with any number of Oxford colleagues with whom he was still in touch—for example, Roger Lancelyn Green. Viewing *Smith of Wootton Major* within the context of Tolkien's life promises to make this "perplexing" work more transparent and meaningful.

In addition to Carpenter's assertion of Tolkien's close connection to Smith, an examination of Tolkien's biography and the characters in *Smith of Wootton Major* suggests that Smith is the most logical candidate for an avatar of Tolkien. The Smith in *Smith of Wootton Major* is known for his singing. The attribute of singing would seem to fit well with the generic, rustic village with its working-class artisans in *Smith of Wootton Major*. In the 1890s, the Sparks brothers ran a blacksmith's forge with a cart and wagon workshop at the end of Webb Lane in Hall Green, not far from 5 Gracewell in Sarehole where Ronald Tolkien lived (Blackham 44). In the nineteenth century and early twentieth century, it was common for working-class people to sing as they worked. Ronald probably heard some of this when he was growing up in Sarehole and Birmingham. These work songs, like the American "Erie Canal," "What Will We Do with a Drunken Sailor?," and "Pick a Bale of Cotton," or the British "The Wark of the Weavers," "Moses of the Mail," and "Cosher's Bailey's Engine" were characteristic of various trades.

In the "Qenya Lexicon" of 1915/1916, Tolkien lists himself as Lirillo "Valu of song" or Noldorin (65). It is hard to believe Tolkien would have chosen a name for himself that was somehow uncharacteristic. Only snippets about Tolkien's singing appear in primary sources. When Fr. Francis Morgan became Tolkien's guardian in 1905, Ronald served and would have been expected to sing at daily Masses before school (*Letters* 395). The congregational singing at the Birmingham Oratory was exceptional because Cardinal Newman had a particular interest in music and had created a hymnal (Ordway, *Tolkien's Faith* 50). Ronald sang marching songs when training for the military (McIlwaine 155). Later, he contributed verses to be sung in *Songs for the Philologists* 1922-25 (*C&G* 2.1244). Some of these songs were part of the activities of the Viking Club, sponsored by Ronald Tolkien and E.V. Gordon, which featured beer drinking, reading sagas, and singing comic songs (*Bio* 105). In July 1924, Ronald Tolkien joined in an impromptu singing session with George S. Gordon playing the piano (*C&G* 1.135). Tolkien was recorded chanting his elven verses (*Poems and Songs of Middle Earth*), and Christopher Tolkien recalled his father chanting *Beowulf* to him in the early 1930s (Tolkien, *Beowulf* xiii). The character Arry Lowdham in "The Notion Club Papers", though initially identified with Hugo Dyson (*SD* 150), evolved to have a number of Ronald Tolkien's interests, including "Anglo-Saxon, Icelandic, and Comparative Philology. Occasionally writes comic or satirical verse" (*SD* 159). Lowdham sings a silly song (*SD* 224) which would be consistent with Tolkien's affinity for Lewis Carroll's nonsense verse which Lowdham, in fact, draws on (Ordway, *Modern Reading* 52-53, *SD* x-xi). After Tolkien's retirement to Merton College in Oxford in 1972, Charles Carr, his scout or servant, could recall Tolkien sometimes sitting in his room "occasionally whistling and singing to himself," signaling a lifelong pattern (Grotta-Kurska 145).

Tolkien's chanting his own verses qualified him as a bard, or a poet—one who sang or recited his own verses. This bard-like singing could recall the *Kalevala*'s Väinämöinen, whose singing is the source and expression of his creativity and power. Ronald Tolkien would have known the Old Norse epithet, "song smith," as another name for a poet (Long, "*Smith*" 111). Tolkien knew the *Kalevala* would have been sung or chanted to its original audience. Singing, therefore, appears to be an appropriate descriptor for Ronald Tolkien and his likely avatar, Smith.

The Finnish epic, the *Kalevala*, had a significant impact on Ronald Tolkien. He found the *Kalevala*'s Finnish language "intoxicating," because he had "the most overwhelming pleasure" from the sound of Finnish (*Monsters* 192). He adapted his new Elvish language to reflect its phonetic structure (*Letters* 214). Ronald gave a lecture on the *Kalevala* in the fall of 1914 at Oxford and rewrote part of the *Kalevala* as his Kullervo story (*C&G* 1.64). The *Kalevala* also was the source for Ronald's intricate watercolor, *The Land of Pohja*, painted on December 27, 1914, when he was almost twenty-three years old (*C&G* 1.65; *A&I* 44, 45; McIlwaine 44).

In the character of the singing Smith of *Smith of Wootton Major*, Tolkien may be looking back on his youth—the creative Lirillo—and the burst of creativity that began in 1915-1916 before Ronald's active participation in World War I, and continued when he returned from the front in 1916 in order to recuperate from trench fever. While Ronald was healing, he created the epic of the Silmarillion with its stories of Beren and Lúthien based on his new Elvish languages, a word and/or song smith creating new worlds which his invented languages could inhabit (R. Evans 25). The stories "arose in my mind as 'given' things [...] so the *links* grew [...] in continually interrupted *labour*" (*Letters* 145, italics added). Tolkien, the word smith, begins with the humble, but magical, adjective:

> The incarnate mind, the tongue, and the tale in our world are coeval. The human mind endowed with the powers of generalization and abstraction, sees not only *green-grass*, discriminating it from other things (and finding it fair to look upon), but sees that it is *green* as well as *grass*. But how powerful, how stimulating [...] was the invention of the adjective: no spell or incantation in

> Faerie is more potent [...] The mind that thought of *light, heavy, grey, yellow, still, swift*, also conceived of magic that would make heavy things light and able to fly, turn grey lead into yellow gold, and the still rock into swift water (OFS 122).

This poetic alchemy leads to a green sun which requires a Secondary World to make it credible (OFS 140). A Secondary World is the locus where words can evoke the magical, true names revealed by Tom Bombadil or preserved by the Ents or hidden, like the Dwarves' names, or that can even open the doors of Moria "governed by words." The name can reveal the essence, just as proclaimed by St. John: "In the beginning was the Word, and the Word was God" (1:1, R. Evans 55).

The suggested retrospective picture of Tolkien's opening burst of creativity points to the possible significance in the names of the story's villages: Wootton Major and Wootton Minor. The names, Wootton Major and Wootton Minor, seem to echo the names of the villages, Great Haywood and Little Haywood, which were close to the camps where the Army stationed Tolkien in 1915-16 and again in 1918 during World War I. 'Wootton', found in many English place-names, means 'farmsted in or near a wood': OE *wudu+tun* (Mills 509).

In that area of Staffordshire where Tolkien was stationed, there is a nearby village called 'Weston'. This is a common English place name and recalls the smith being known from "Far Easton" to "the Westwood" (*SWM* 17). Although 'Easton' is also a common British place name with namesakes in Hampshire, Dorset, and Cambridgeshire, Ronald Tolkien appears to have reversed the directional portion ('West-tun' OE *tun* = settlement) of the name 'Weston', that he knew in his youth, changing it to 'Easton' ('East-tun'). He then continued playing with reversal of directions by completing the image with the addition of 'Westwood'. 'Westwood' is again another actual place name with an example in Wiltshire. Reversing the directional part of the place names masks the biographical association of Weston in Tolkien's life and demonstrates the linguistic playfulness of a man who could indulge in "a low philological jest" in the name of Smaug the dragon in *The Hobbit* (*Letters* 31).[10]

Returning to Tolkien's biography and the place of Great Haywood in his life, the newly married Edith Tolkien and her cousin Jennie Grove arrived to stay in Great Haywood by Friday, May 26, 1916. Later, in 1918, Edith, their young son John, and Edith's cousin, Jennie Grove, moved to a house not far from Great Haywood in Gipsy Green on the Teddesley Park estate in Staffordshire in order to be near Ronald Tolkien at his new posting (McIlwaine 260-1). Gipsy Green was the name of a small hamlet with four dwellings, not the name of a house (1911 census), near 'Little Haywood'—a name meaning 'little wood of the hay or hedge'. 'Farmsted in or near a wood' is a good description of the hamlet of Gipsy Green. As seen in his drawings of *Gipsy Green* and *High Life at Gipsy Green* from May-June 1918 (McIlwaine 260-1, *A&I* 26-27, *C&G* 1.112), Ronald Tolkien was apparently quite happy to be able to live with his family and know they all were safe from the unpredictable bombing runs of Zeppelins in Yorkshire where they had been previously living (Bunting/Hamill-Keays, *Edith* 195). He would have also greatly enjoyed the trees around Gipsy Green which were such a contrast to the bare, treeless plain where the barracks for Rugeley and Brocton Camps were located.

The figure of Smith not only seems to call on the persona of Lirillo, a bard, but it also appears to echo Ronald Tolkien's description of himself as "Mercian," a "West-midlander at home only in the counties upon the Welsh Marches" (*Letters* 108, 218, see also *MC* 162). For Tolkien, the English and Welsh languages are "coinhabitants of Britain" and, like Faery, Welsh is "[d]angerous, and yet desirable" (*MC* 167,163). Smith, living on the edge of the Forest and Faery, can be seen as the linguistically Mercian or Hwiccian Ronald Tolkien with a "cradle-tongue," "a first-learned language, a language of custom" of English, but with a "*native language*" of his "inherent linguistic predilections" of Welsh, which "stirs deep harp-strings in our linguistic nature [...] to which in unexplored desire we would still *go home*" (*MC* 190, 194, italics added).[11] Tolkien emphatically rejected having his linguistic roots in the later-arriving Anglo-Saxons (*Letters* 136).

Tolkien's Western Elves, in *The Lord of the Rings*, have a language "very like (though not identical with) British-Welsh [...] because it seems to fit the rather 'Celtic' type of legends and stories told of its speakers" (*Letters* 176). While Ronald Tolkien may have wondered at the Welsh names on railroad cars or trucks around early 1901, his formal interaction with Welsh started with an 1877 edition of Salesbury's *Dictionary* inscribed "9 May 1907" (i.e. when Ronald was fifteen years old) (Phelpstead, *Tolkien and Wales* in Lyman-Thomas 284). In his essay on the *Kalevala*, Tolkien compares the Welsh *Mabinogion* favorably with the Finnish *Kalevala* (Lyman-Thomas 274). Ronald Tolkien, in the figure of Smith, on the linguistic frontier of English and Welsh, crosses the border to sample British Welsh, his linguistic home of "inherited memory" with its "'Celtic' type of legends and stories," just as Smith explores the Forest admiring and wondering at its beauty.

Tolkien's detailed and carefully worked out chronologies for *Smith of Wootton Major* appear to reveal other autobiographical references. Shippey states that the forty-eight years that Smith wanders in Faery should be accounted for ("Allegory" 177). Ronald Tolkien wrote that *The Lord of the Rings* was "primarily linguistic in inspiration" or "*fundamentally* linguistic in inspiration" (*Letters* 409, 219 italics in original). Published in 1955, *The Return of the King* was the final flowering of Tolkien's linguistically inspired work. Forty-eight years earlier, in 1907, Ronald created his first fully fledged, independent language *Naffarin*, after earlier attempts and collaboration with his cousins (*C&G* 1.15; see also Lee, "Tolkien" 136). This match suggests an autobiographical source for this number. Again, Smith is fifty-seven when he makes his last journey into Faery, and Ronald Tolkien was fifty-seven when he finished writing the main draft of *The Lord of the Rings*, in October 1949 (*SWM* 104, Chance Nitzsche 140). Both of these seemingly arbitrary numbers correspond to important and relevant events in Ronald Tolkien's life.

One other feature of *Smith of Wootton Major* points to a personal connection with Ronald Tolkien. Tolkien, in his major published works, *The Hobbit* and *The Lord of the Rings*, maintained for his readers the fiction that he was only a translator or redactor of material from other sources for those books. Tolkien acknowledged *Leaf by Niggle* (1945) and *Famer Giles of Ham* (1949) as his own original writings. He did not use a translation/editorial conceit for the former and the Foreword to *Farmer Giles of Ham* is obviously meant as a joke, so both escaped the reach of the legendarium (*Letters* 145). Tolkien's transparently fictitious dodging of authorship follows in many ways the popular literary device used by a long line of predecessors, including Rider Haggard, Daniel Defoe, Sir Walter Scott, Charles Dickens, Horace Walpole, Jonathan Swift, Sir Arthur Conan Doyle, Miguel de Cervantes, and John Buchan (Brljak 3; Hooker, *A*

Tolkienian Mathomium 153-177). In a similar way, Umberto Eco draws on this medieval tradition of fictional attribution of authorship. Part of purpose of the lost-manuscript conceit is to affect the reader's perception of the work by giving it an aura of historical authenticity.

Tolkien's use of this literary trick was not a function of trying to attract readers because the title page of *The Hobbit* and *The Lord of the Rings* always declared his authorship. He had long acceded his authorship of these two books in interviews and in responses to letters. Ronald Tolkien's willingness to forego the editor convention in *Smith of Wootton Major* may have multiple sources, including the fact the story is no longer set in Middle-earth and/or he no longer needed to construct a framework for his stories and/or he did not need the depth of history, etc. However, perhaps, a personal motive maybe present here, namely Ronald Tolkien no longer needed the psychological distance of being the mere reporter of someone else's stories of "far away and long ago" places, times and people. In a valedictory reflection on his life and writings, Tolkien may now be willing to take some "ownership" of this work, by conceding his authorship.

The many autobiographical parallels uncovered so far validate Carpenter's comment that *Smith* "was related closely and even consciously to himself [Tolkien]" (*Bio* 243). These autobiographical elements suggest that the themes in *Smith of Wootton Major* were likely to be personally meaningful to Tolkien.

II. The Faërian Setting and Ingredients of *Smith of Wootton Major*

The Implications of the Great Hall/Church Allegory

Ronald Tolkien places his biographical main character, Smith, in the context of a village on the edge of Faery. In the oldest draft, some inhabitants "were a bit elvish" (*SWM* 147). The defining feature of this village is immediately presented as the Village-Hall, later called the Great Hall in the published story. The Great Hall is the domain of the Master Cook.

Ronald Tolkien's efforts to clarify the meaning of this setting have led to an extended discussion of what Tolkien might have intended, given his reference to allegory in his letter to Clyde Kilby. In the "Genesis of the story, Tolkien's note to Clyde Kilby," Ronald wrote: "As usual there is no 'religion' in the story; but plainly enough the Master Cook and the Great Hall etc. are a (somewhat satirical) allegory of the village-church and village parson" (*SWM* 86-87).[12]

Specifically, in relation to *Smith of Wootton Major*, Tolkien stated:

> But it [*SWM*] is *not* allegory—properly so-called. Its primary purpose is itself, and any applications it or parts of it may have for individual hearers are incidental. I dislike real allegory in which the application is the author's own and is meant to dominate you—I prefer the freedom of the hearer or reader (*C&G* 2.1227; italics in source).[13]

Based on the two quotes above, Tolkien leaves the reader free to interpret or understand *Smith of Wootton Major*, including the setting of the Great Hall with its Master Cook, in whatever way they wish, but Ronald Tolkien also wrote the story with a certain meaning in mind and expressed in an allegory. Readers, however, left to their own resources have been mostly uncertain about the story's meaning. Flieger comments on the "opacity of this story" (*GS* 167). Christopher Derrick's review can only assume children are its "primary readership," as the "elders will grope" among various hints (*C&G* 2.1221). Because of comments like these, an analysis of Tolkien's "somewhat satirical" allegory seems worthwhile because that investigation might clarify and make the story more understandable.

In *Green Suns*, Verlyn Flieger downplays Tolkien's statement that the allegory of the Great Hall is the village church, and the Master Cook is the Parson (*SWM* 86-87, 141-43). Disputing Shippey's allegorical reading of *Smith of Wootton Major*, she states, the

> heart of *Smith of Wootton Major* lies not so much in the village machinery of Great Hall, Cook, and Parson, as in Smith's wanderings in Faery and in the reader's participation in his enchantment, bewilderment, and acceptance of that which he cannot understand (*GS* 168).

Flieger believes that "the story began as allegory" about "the cake, the Cook, the Great Hall" (*GS* 168) and "the remnants still lurk on the edges," but "the allegorical leftovers add nothing to the reader's understanding of its particular and unexplainable magic" (*GS* 170) or its "gossamer appeal" (*QT* 231). She also writes that we cannot assume "Tolkien intended the Faery of the story to stand for something outside of itself" (i.e. as allegorical). However, this last statement seems confused as Tolkien explicitly states, "There is no allegory in the Faery which is conceived as having a real extramental existence" (*SWM* 86).

Flieger takes a similar approach in minimizing Tolkien's statements about the Great Hall and Master Cook in *A Question of Time*. She allows "that Tolkien's original allegorical impulse left its ghost in the narrative [...] tempting readers to see in it a variety of specific correlations from its author's view on art [Kocher, Kilby] or religion [Jane Chance Nitzsche] or scholarship [Shippey, *Road* 230-31]."

She then refers to Tolkien's at-the-time unpublished essay on *Smith of Wootton Major*. Because of its dating, the essay appears to be Tolkien's meditation on the finished story. Flieger cites various of Tolkien's statements in the essay including its beginning: "This short tale is not an 'allegory', though it is capable of course of allegorical interpretations at certain points. It is a 'Fairy Story'" (*QT* 232, *SWM* 111).

Tolkien defined 'Fairy-stories' as

> about Fairy, that is *Faërie*, the realm or state in which fairies have their being. *Faërie* contains many things [...] dwarfs, witches, trolls, giants, or dragons [...] seas, the sun, the moon, the sky; and the earth, and all things that are in it: tree and bird, water and stone, wine and bread, and ourselves, mortal men when we are enchanted. [...] Most good 'fairy-stories' are about the *aventures* of men in the Perilous Realm or upon its shadowy marches (OFS 113, italics in original).

He elaborated on this definition in *Smith of Wootton Major* writing Faery "meant enchantment or magic, and the enchanted world or country in which marvelous people lived, great and small, with strange powers of mind and will for good and evil," as well as "earth, water, air, and fire, and all living and growing things." Fairy "means powerful, magical, belonging to Faery or coming from that strange world" (*SWM* 95).

Ronald Tolkien then writes, "The Great Hall is evidently in a way an 'allegory' of the village church; the Master Cook [...] is plainly the Parson [...] 'Cooking' [... is] personal religion and prayer" (*SWM* 142). Tolkien's phrase, "evidently in a way an 'allegory,'" should alert the reader that what follows is not "properly so-called or a real allegory," given Tolkien's well-documented dislike of strict allegory. Tolkien's comments on his story *Leaf by Niggle* elaborate on the distinction Tolkien was trying to make: "It is not really or properly an 'allegory' so much as 'mythical'. For Niggle is meant to be a mixed-quality *person* and not an 'allegory' of any single vice or virtue" (*Letters* 320-21, italics in the original).

After stating *Smith of Wootton Major* is a 'Fairy Story', Tolkien adds much later in the essay:

> There is no need to hunt for allegory. Such teaching as this slender story contains is implicit, and would be no less present if it were a plain narrative of historical events (*QT* 232). But (as in my stories generally) it will be observed that there is no religion. [...] In a story written by a religious man this is a plain indication that religion is not absent but subsumed [...] It [religion] does not therefore appear as such (*SWM* 141-42, underlining in original).

Based on Ronald Tolkien's various statements about allegory in *Smith of Wootton Major*, Flieger concludes, "Tolkien conducted a running argument with himself on the question of whether the story is or is not an allegory," and implies that he vacillates like a pendulum (*QT* 232). She attributes this to Tolkien "never wholly abandon[ing] the allegory of the cake in the original preface" (*QT* 233), but Flieger "doubts 'whether a reading on that level comes closest to Tolkien's final intent and best serves the story as a work of art'" (*C&G* 2.1222).

Shippey's interpretation that all parts of the *Smith of Wootton Major* are part of an extended allegory (*Road* 272-280) does not seem in accord with Tolkien's stated intentions. David Doughan notes that it has led to difficulties like the expectation that a Smith should produce a Great Cake (17).

Contrary to Flieger's assertions (*QT* 232), Tolkien never indicates he saw the whole story as an allegory, but rather states the opposite (*SWM* 111). He specifies the "trace of allegory" only applies to the "Human part" (*SWM* 86). Ronald Tolkien called the original preface "an illustration of 'Faery,'" not an allegory, and Tolkien's precision in his use of language is well-known (*SWM* 86). Tolkien's "allegorical interpretations at certain points" seem to refer to his allegory of the Great Hall as stated both in the undated note to Kilby (*SWM* 86-87) and in the essay, written shortly after the completion of the story (*SWM* 142). Only an exploration of Tolkien's imagery can decide if it serves the story.

The Master Cooks, Faery, and the Return of Biography

In specifying that the Great Hall is the village-church and the Master Cook is the Parson, Ronald Tolkien is most likely to be identifying a Church of England church and vicar, who could carry the specific title of Parson. The church has been "reformed" (*SWM* 143)—pointing to a Protestant church—a product of the Reformation, where a minister would be known as a Parson (Shippey, *Road* 275; *SWM* 206). In a Catholic church, the contrasting title would be Priest. For Tolkien, the despised Church of England was "a pathetic and shadowy medley of half-remembered traditions and mutilated beliefs" (*Bio* 65) and "hatred of our church [Catholicism] is after all the real only final foundation of the C[hurch] o[f] E[ngland]" (*Letters* 96). It would be consistent with Tolkien's attitude toward the Church of England that an allegory about a Protestant village-church and its parson should be "somewhat satirical," if not more so (*SWM* 86).

Nokes seems to be a representative of the stereotype of a Protestant Parson: "a solid sort of man with a wife and children, and careful with money" (*SWM* 7). The vulgarization of Wootton means the "festivals are mere public assemblies, for talk assisted by eating and drinking" (*SWM* 143, also 129, 87) because the Protestant churches rejected the literal Bread of Christ. Tolkien foresees the logical conclusion of Wootton's esteeming of profit and money and ignoring the spiritual realm as leading to the abolition of "the office of MC," the evolution of the Great Hall into "a mere place of business," and any Cooks "will become traders" (*SWM* 143).

Tolkien states Nokes's name is a "deliberate exception" to his use of crafts as surnames (*SWM* 117). Tolkien knew the name 'Nokes' was "a type-name for a fool or a ninny, an ignorant person," as in Old Noakes of Bywater in *The Lord of the Rings* (*SWM* 199, Chance Nitzsche 70, *FR* I i 22). The name, 'Nokes', defined by a location, "by the oak(s)," indicates a lack of any grounding in the mastery of a skill. Tolkien shows Nokes's disregard for competence and skill in Nokes learning slowly, his not liking being corrected, giving up quickly, and discounting any unmastered task as "just a fal-lal" (*SWM* 124).

Tolkien presents rumors that Nokes, an opportunist, proposed marriage to Rider's daughter, Ella, in an attempt to become an apprentice, implying his willingness to use others for his own ends (*SWM* 125). Tolkien states, "The vulgarization of Wootton is indicated by Nokes [...] an extreme case" (*SWM* 128). The "vulgarity and smugness" of Wootton finds a model in the "vain" Nokes—admiring himself in a "polished frying pan" and saying that "[the white Master Cook's] hat suits you properly" (*SWM* 7)—and being "shrewd or sly" in learning from Alf without admitting it (*SWM* 136).

Nokes also seems to be an exemplar of Tolkien's concept of 'grownupishness'. Nokes was fond of children in a "facetious and patronizing way," so that "Faery" was something permitted to amuse children, "children's stuff" (*SWM* 137, 138, 129). When Alf, the apprentice, tells Nokes the star is *fay* or from Faery, Nokes's response is to tell him "you'll grow up someday" and to think "he [Alf] had a lot to learn yet" (*SWM* 10). Tolkien presents his concept of grownupishness in his drawing, *Grownupishness*. This picture has the descriptors "'Sightless: Blind: Well-Wrapped-Up'," "suggesting an adult's narrow vision" (*A&I* 38). Tolkien's comment on rejecting the "shallow vulgarity" of Browning in relation to "the general grownuppishness of things I was expected to like" (*Letters* 311) gives the reader another instance of this concept. Tolkien appears to include Hans Christian Andersen's rather patent, and perhaps commercial, moralizing in this distasteful "grownuppishness" or "(even bogus) form" *C&G* 2.611). Perhaps these writers are "sly" "old fraud[s]," like Nokes (*SWM* 50), who "smirks" at Alf when he mocks Alf in front of the children saying a magical star that vanishes is "not a nice trick to play" (*SWM* 15).

Nokes intends to cast doubt on Faery, and it is doubt about Faery that kills, as seen in the modern case of the near-death of Tinker Bell when people do not believe in fairies in J.M. Barrie's *Peter Pan, or the Boy Who Wouldn't Grow Up* (1904) The approved-of growing up, which Nokes advocates to Alf (*SWM* 10), could be associated with industry and hard work for profit (*SWM* 143), which Tolkien linked to "vulgar self-satisfaction" (*SWM* 112) rather than to the love and imagination that allows delight, wonder, and creativity (*SWM* 144).

In contrast to the Protestant Parson, whose cake was "no bigger than was needed," leaving no second helpings, Tolkien sees the occupation of the Master Cook as one, that provides "plentiful and rich" nourishment (*SWM* 14, 4). This conception fits well with the role of a Catholic priest because of the injunction, repeated three times, from the Risen Christ to Peter to "Feed my sheep" (John 21:15-17). Tolkien wrote: this instruction [in John 21] was "His [Christ's] last charge to St. Peter; and since His words are always first to be understood literally, I suppose them to refer to the Bread of Life. It was against this that the [...] Reformation was really launched—'the blasphemous fable of the Mass'" (*Letters* 339). The ritual of Holy Communion or Eucharist is strongly suggested in the first draft of *Smith of Wootton Major* because "once a week the villagers had a meal together, and most came regularly, except the very old, or the very young, or any that might be ill"—the typical pattern of weekly gathering by the faithful (*SWM* 147).

The priest brought the Bread of Life, Christ's Body (John 6:35), but the Protestant churches rejected this. Perhaps this is why Alf arranges to place the star of Faery, seemingly a sign of grace, in a cake because the Protestants do not want the Bread that has been offered, so "let them eat cake." The King of Faery, with his various interventions in Wootton Major, appears to be instituting a "faerian [*sic*] counter-reformation" (Sternberg 317), consistent with Tolkien's negative view that the Protestant Church of England.[14]

These duties of the Master Cook also fit well with the role of a priest who was to spread the message that Christ is "come that they might have life and they might have it more abundantly" (John 10:10). The Master Cook apparently provides meals for the Inn, marked by the three trees—the crosses of Calvary (*SWM* 118). As only travelers use the Inn, it recalls the early Christian practice of providing hospitality for others (Acts 21: 4-8). As early as the 11th century, religious orders created hospices for the ill and weary to house pilgrims and travelers, particularly those going to the Holy Land.

In *Smith of Wootton Major*, the first named Master Cook is Rider, who is later revealed to be Smith's maternal grandfather. Autobiography may be the source of this character "Grandfather Rider" (*SWM* 97). This Master Cook seems to have been inspired by the maternal grandfather of Ronald Tolkien, John Suffield. Rider is a "great traveler" (*SWM* 39, 121), and the 1891 census lists John Suffield, as a "commercial traveller" for Jeyes Fluid (*Bio* 18). John Suffield enjoyed travel and worked as a commercial traveller until he was eighty-six years old (Burns "John Suffield"). Consequently, Ronald Tolkien would have known his Suffield grandfather as a "traveller" for years. John Suffield was married for approximately fifty-five years, because his oldest son was born in 1859 and his wife died in 1914. After the death of his "kind and understanding" wife, Emily Jane (*Bio* 16), John Suffield probably became "grave and taciturn," just as Grandfather Rider is described as "sad and taciturn" after the death of his wife (*SWM* 100, 121).

In *Smith of Wootton Major*, Grandfather Rider had had contact with Faery as a young man until he married (*SWM* 134). The year after Rider's wife's death, he began to revisit Faery and also became the Apprentice to the Master Cook. As a result of his contact with Faery, Rider reintroduced singing and dancing as part of the festivities at the Twenty-four Feast (*SWM* 100, 123). After eight years of holding the post of Master Cook, Grandfather Rider went on an "unprecedented holiday," which included visiting Faery (*SWM* 100, 134). When he returned, he brought an apprentice, Alf. Grandfather Rider returned "merrier," "did most laughable things," and sang "gay songs" (*SWM* 5, 101).

Smith of Wootton Major's description of Grandfather Rider is a good match for the 1928 interview of John Suffield on his ninety-fifth birthday by R.J. Buckley of *The Evening Despatch*. The journalist wrote of Suffield's "insuppressible vivacity, his merry humour, his geniality and his boyish playfulness, his exuberant vitality [...] with his varied gifts as tenor singer, expert reciter, inexhaustible and dramatic raconteur"—so reminiscent of Grandfather Rider in *SWM* (Burns "John Suffield"). Like the Master Cook Rider, John Suffield took an extensive holiday, a cruise around the British Isles (*Bio* 106). Although there is very little information in the official biography about Ronald Tolkien's relationship with his grandfather, the fact that Tolkien had his grandfather's picture over the mantel in his last residence indicates that John Suffield was a significant person in his grandson's life (S. Tolkien).

In *Smith of Wootton Major*, Smith's Grandfather Rider left when Smith was two, because with his daughter having married, Rider "felt free" (*SWM* 140). This description of the grandfather/grandson relationship may replicate a situation in Ronald Tolkien's own life. Like Smith's Grandfather Rider, Tolkien's grandfather was likely to been absent at important times in Tolkien's early years because of his business travels.

Grandfather Rider, the Master Cook, presents Alf as his apprentice and gives him the name Alf (Old English for 'elf') (*SWM* 118). Alf forms a sharp contrast to Nokes. Rider knew Alf was an elf, but he did not know Alf's "identity" as King of Faery (*SWM* 126). As Tolkien notes, "the trouble with the real folk of Faërie is that they do not always look like what they are" (OFS 113). Alf chooses to appear as a mere teenager because he planned to make "at least two Great Cakes" and leave "a tradition of a long 'reign' of light coulour and mirth, as well as culinary excellence" along with a "rumour that this was due to a beneficent intrusion from Faery" (*SWM* 136).

Grandfather Rider, whose reintroduction of singing and dancing under the influence of Faery has Tolkien's approval, is a widower when he apprentices and then becomes a Master Cook. Both he and Alf are apparently celibate. Both of these celibate characters could be seen as Catholic priests whose marital status contrasts them with the Protestant parsons, like Nokes, who are married, have children, and are "parsimonious" (e.g. leaving no second helpings at the Feast for Good Children) (*SWM* 14).

Although the basis for the character of Rider appears to be Tolkien's maternal grandfather John Suffield, the model for Alf seems to be the Catholic priest Fr. Francis X. Morgan, who became Tolkien's guardian in 1905. Tolkien wrote: "In 1904 [*sic*] we (H[ilary] & I) had the sudden miraculous experience of Fr. Francis' love and care and humour" (*Letters* 417). Ronald Tolkien referred to him as "my beloved Father Francis" (Priestman 53). Even as early as the summer of 1904, when Ronald sent Fr. Francis Morgan a rebus letter with a dazzling display of language and visual play (Priestman 13, 17, *TFA* 33, Bridoux 11-12), Fr. Francis was addressed as "M-eye deer owl-d Frances-hiss." The feeling was returned as seen in Fr. Francis having a professional photograph taken of the two Tolkien brothers in May 1905, six months after their mother's death. The priest hung the framed photograph in his room until he died in 1935 (McIlwaine 135, 136, *Bio*). Fr. Francis, whose father was Welsh and whose mother was Spanish, encouraged Ronald's "interests in these languages (Priestman 13).

Fr. Francis met the ten year old Ronald Tolkien in early 1902, when the Tolkien family moved from King's Heath to Edgbaston (*Bio* 26-27). In *Smith of Wootton Major*, on Smith's tenth birthday, the "dawn-song of the birds," combined with a rising sun, precipitates Smith's thinking of Faery (*SWM* 16). This imagery draws on the equation of the Son of God, Christ, with the Sun of Righteousness made in Catholic litany and theology.[15] Smith begins singing and this allows the silver Faery star to fall out of his mouth. He catches it, and when he claps it to his forehead the star stays. Ronald Tolkien's meeting the deeply religious Fr. Francis, a conduit for the Sun of Righteousness, shortly after turning ten in 1902, forms a parallel with the awakening at the age of ten of Smith's sensitivity to the rising sun/Son and bird song that leads to an experience of Faery. Tolkien's deep faith and "the language and imagery of the Catholic Church" were indebted to Fr. Francis (Carpenter, *Souvenir Booklet* in Long, "*Smith*" 100).

Alf's "tradition of a long 'reign' of light coulour and mirth" (*SWM* 136) fits well with the model of Fr. Francis. Fr. Francis was someone with "an immense fund of kindness and humour and a flamboyance" (*Bio* 27; Ferrández Bru 59, 65). The Oratory Fathers recall Fr. Francis as having "ebullience."[16] Appropriately, when accompanied by Alf, Smith is able to see the newly painted Hall "in wonder" (*SWM* 40). Tolkien wrote, "The King dwells in Wootton for 58 years" (*SWM* 115). Fr. Francis entered the novitiate at the Oratory in Birmingham on September 18, 1877 (Ferrández Bru 53), and he died on June 11, 1935. Fr. Francis served God for almost a full fifty-eight years. The careful chronology of *Smith of Wootton Major* finds another parallel with Ronald Tolkien's life.

Alf is "generous" (*SWM* 138) and even kind to Nokes in shielding his "injured pride" (*SWM* 139). Alf even foresees and facilitates the appointment of Nokes as Master Cook in hopes of fostering a possible change in Nokes's heart (*SWM* 137). Analogously, Fr. Francis was "generous" not only by being self-effacing and humble, but also by not seeking recognition, and never becoming Provost like many senior Oratory members (Ferrández Bru 58-59). Fr. Francis was also "generous" with his own money. Although Fr. Francis was a priest, the Oratory of Saint Philip Neri did not require its members to take a vow of poverty. Instead, Fr. Francis, as "a man of considerable private means," gave his funds generously; not only paying for Hilary's education at King Edward's (Gardner/Holford 52), seaside holidays for the Tolkien brothers, and helping fund Tolkien's Oxford education, but also continuing to support the Tolkien brothers' widowed Aunt Beatrice Suffield (Ferrández Bru 59, 65; www.Birminghamoratory.org.uk).

Tolkien implies Alf has a special interest and care for children because the children at the final Twenty-four Feast are "more beautiful and lively" than previously. This leads Smith to wonder "what Alf might have been doing in his spare time" (*SWM* 53). Fr. Francis was known for his work with children in the parochial school and was "devoted" "to these little ones," recalling Christ's instructions to "Let the little children come to me [...] for the kingdom of heaven belongs to such as these" (Ferrández Bru 59, Matthew 19:14).

Elvenfolk are "beneficent" with regard to Men (*SWM* 130) "since the Elves [...] realize that this love of Faery is essential to the full and proper human development."[17] "The love of Faery is a love of love" (*SWM* 131). In *Smith of Wootton Major*, Alf "always greeted Smith kindly and had looked at him with friendly eyes" (*SWM* 35-36). Similarly, Oratory members remembered Fr. Francis for cheering others "with his hearty laugh and witty remarks [...] and words of encouragement" (Ferrández Bru 59).

Many of Fr. Francis's characteristics find an echo in the character of Alf, because they are both types of Christ. As the Faërian envoy of the timeless Otherworld, Alf ages, experiences change, and submits to Time. Alf, when he first arrives at the village, is "a mere boy," "barely in his teens" (*SWM* 5-6), and he allowed "time [...] to appear to age in human fashion" (*SWM* 136). Alf, of timeless Faery, as a type of Christ, humbles himself in relation to Time and to the changes it entails. However, Alf shows no obvious signs of age: "there was no grey in his hair, nor line in his face" (*SWM* 35).

Dickerson and Evans see Alf as a Christ figure (181). Jane Chance Nitzche's *Tolkien's Art* identifies Alf as both a Christ figure (71) and as an Augustinian New Man (68). As a medieval "type" of Christ, Alf, "the King of Faery," fulfills the scripture and "comes and serves as an apprentice:" "The Son of Man [the Christ] came not to be served but to serve" (*SWM* 131, Matthew 20:38).[18]

Alf is not only a type of Christ, but also an imitator of Christ. In René Girard's theory of 'mimesis', the imitation of Christ is the only path that does not involve rivalry and the ensuing envy of the rival, thereby allowing an escape from this destructive cycle.[19] In Girard's theory, the desire to imitate Christ leads to Being, as contrasted with the escalation of the mimetic cycle of rivalry which leads to

Satan and the absence of Being (Girard, *I See* 69). Girard's theory focuses on myths and particularly the difference of and contrast of the Christian myth with all other myths. The mimesis of Christ is the desire to resemble God the Father: "be perfect, therefore, as your heavenly Father is perfect" (Matt. 5:48).

Fr. Francis would be a suitable prototype for Alf because Ronald Tolkien has a long history in his writings of combining his Catholic faith and fairies: he wrote *The Lord of the Rings* is "a 'fairy-story', but one written [...] for adults" (*Letters* 232); and the "Gospels contain a fairy-story [. . .] which embraces the essence of fairy-stories" with God being "the Lord, of angels, and of men—and of elves" (OFS 155, 156; also *Letters* 100). As early as Ronald's "Gnomish Lexicon" dating from 1917, the entry, 'Francis', clearly referring to Fr. Francis Morgan, is listed in Gnomish as *Faidron* or *Faithron*—evoking the word 'faith'. Further, Fr. Morgan's typically Welsh surname offered Tolkien plenty of room to elaborate a network of Faërian, mythical, legendary, and Christian allusions (Bunting, "Bombadil" 236-37, 239-41).

Alf, the King of Mystical Faery

Although Faery can express a mystical "unpossessive love" toward all other things leading to delight in beauty, wonder, and even Imagination (*SWM* 144), Ronald Tolkien, a careful Catholic, is emphatic: "Faery is not religious. It is fairly evident that it is not Heaven or Paradise" (*SWM* 143).[20] Tolkien's presentation of the land of Faery in *Smith of Wootton Major* recalls Frodo's dream or vision in the house of Tom Bombadil which is seemingly of Paradise and foretells his exit from Middle-earth: "and a far green country opened before him under a swift sunrise" (*FR* I viii 132). Tolkien, however, when later writing about this passage, clarifies that Frodo's eventual stay in Aman is "a 'purgatory', but one of peace and healing" (*Letters* 411; see also *Letters* 328). Tolkien's purgatory certainly is more beautiful and pleasant than Dante's and more like the Celtic Earthly Paradise.[21] A more detailed discussion of the status of Faery appears in a later section.

Tolkien conceived of Faery as having "three faces: the Mystical toward the Supernatural; the Magical towards Nature; and the Mirror of scorn and pity towards Man" (OFS 125). The presence of Alf, the King of Faery, who brings back tradition, suggests a Mystical, specifically Catholic, revival of the "True" church in Wootton. Tolkien believed the "Gospels contain a fairy-story [...] which embraces the essence of fairy-stories" (OFS 155, 156; see also *Letters* 100).

As the embodiment of Mystical Faery, Alf comes and goes as "the wind blows where it will" (John 3:8, Ruud 419).[22] The Mystical King of Faery's gift of the star, that Smith finds on the morning of his tenth birthday, opens to Smith the world of Faery and its creativity, transforming him into a "Starbrow" or a Taliesin (Welsh *tal* = 'forehead', *iesin* = 'radiant, shining') who, like the famous Welsh bard, suddenly sings "in strange words that he seemed to know by heart" (*SWM* 16). When Smith places the Faery star on his forehead, he becomes a pale copy of Alf, the true "Starbrow" with "a great jewel like a radiant star" on his forehead (*SWM* 51).

Tolkien seems to focus on the Mystical aspect of Faery in Alf, who arranges for Smith to receive the Faery star. Consequently, the King's Tree could also be part of the Mystical face of Faery (*SWM* 24).[23] Smith finds the King's Tree when he searches toward the mountains for "the heart of the kingdom." Lost in a grey mist, he sees a great hill of shadow rising from a wide plain. Rising from the shadow, the King's Tree grew "tower on tower" and radiated light "like the sun at noon" (*SWM* 24). Its innumerable leaves, flowers, and fruits were all unique (*SWM* 24). The magic mist surrounding the King's Tree is one of the traditional signs that mortals have encountered the Otherworld or Faery (Rhŷs, *Celtic Folklore* 233; Haliday 83). The vision of the King's Tree seems to be a gift of the grace of the Faery star because Smith, although he tries, never finds the tree again.

This tree seems to be kin to Tolkien's *Tree of Amalion* ('Blessing') (*A&I* 64, McIlwaine 183), which Tolkien drew repeatedly, or the "Tree of Tales," found in "On Fairy-stories" (145). Its variously shaped leaves and flowers represent "poems and major legends," possibly including the Trees of Valinor—Laurelin and Silpion/Telperion (*A&I* 64; Long, "*Smith*" 113). Hammond and Scull elaborate on this remark seeing a network of images in the *Tree of Amalion*, which include "the oldest images in Indo-European art and literature, a symbol of immortality," as well as the Tree in *Leaf by Niggle* (McIlwaine 80).

The "oldest images in Indo-European art and literature, a symbol of immortality" could refer to the Indian and Persian myths and images of a "Tree of Life and Wisdom"—found in Hindu, Muslim, Jain, and Buddhist temples and writings (Hooker, *Tolkienotēca* 32). This would also be the basis of the Tree of Life in the book of Revelation 22:2: "On either side of the river was the tree of life, bearing twelve kinds of fruit, yielding its fruit every month; and the leaves of the tree were for the healing of the nations." The famous *Tree of Life Jali* bears a strong visual resemblance to Tolkien's *Tree of Amalion* (*Tolkienotēca* 33). In Vedic writings, the Soma Tree or the *Kalpadruma*, *Kalpataru*, or *Kalpavriksha*, known as the world-tree, becomes in Indian mysticism a tree of Paradise, which gives off light and is sometimes hidden in clouds (*Tolkienotēca* 18). The Soma Tree was immense and bore "fruit and seed of every kind" (*Tolkienotēca* 20) and, with its radiance and multiple fruits, was known as "the king of all trees and vegetation," that is, a "King Tree," supplying both spiritual and physical sustenance (*Tolkienotēca* 22). The ancient and mystical sources for the *Tree of Amalion* mesh with the imagery of the King's Tree in *Smith of Wootton Major.*

This ancient imagery appears in Hosea who wrote during a period of invasions and repeated exposures to foreign religious imagery in the eighth century BC: "I [the Lord God] am like an evergreen cypress; your fruit comes from me" (14:8b). This is the only place in the Bible where God is compared to a tree. However, this evergreen with fruits is clearly an ideal, perfect, imaginary tree and like the tree of life in the Garden of Eden (Genesis 3:24, Eidenvall 230).

The Great Cake and the Faery Star

Tolkien specifies that the Great Cake was part of the only winter festival, which lasted one week, ending on the last day at sundown with "The Feast of Good Children" (*SWM* 4). A wintertime festival, the merrymaking by children, and the name 'The Feast of Good Children' all parallel the Roman Catholic celebration 'The Feast of the Holy Innocents' also called Childermas or [Holy] Innocents' Day.

'The Feast of the Holy Innocents' is in remembrance of the massacre of children under the age of two in Bethlehem, as commanded by King Herod the Great in an attempt to kill the infant Jesus (Matthew 2:16–18). The feast, along with the commemoration of Stephen, the first martyr, and the feast of John, the Disciple of Love, is kept within the octave of Christmas because the Holy Innocents gave their lives for the newborn Savior. The Roman Catholic Church "venerates these children as martyrs (*flores martyrum*); they are the first buds of the Church killed by the frost of persecution; they died not only for Christ, but in his stead" (St. August, "Sermo 10us de sanctis")."[24] In Roman Catholic communities, this feast is also a day of merrymaking for children.

The Great Cake of "The Feast of Good Children" appears to draw on the once popular, United Kingdom tradition of a cake on the last day of the Christmas season or Twelfth Night (Davidson 814). It was known as the Twelfth-night cake, the Twelfth Cake, or Twelfth-tide cake. Traditionally, a bean and a pea were hidden inside the cake. The man who found the bean became King for the night, and the woman who found the pea became the Queen.[25] Ronald Tolkien apparently knew that historically "a great cake" with its bean and pea was part of the Christmas festivities in "Roman Catholic countries" where the only mass said at night was on Christmas Eve (Wa. Scott 312). With the limitation of the celebration of the Christmas season in the nineteenth century, due to the Scrooge-like demands of capitalist efficiency, the Twelfth cake migrated from Epiphany to Christmas (Long, "*Smith*" 101).

Twelfth Night is the eve of Epiphany when the three Kings, Magi, or Wise Men traditionally found the Christ child, so this cake is also known as a king's cake or the three kings's cake in other countries. The king's cake tradition included a figure, presumed to represent the Christ child, hidden in the cake.

In addition to the tradition of a "great cake" or a Christmas cake, descended from the Twelfth Cake with its hidden tokens, the Victorians created the Christmas pudding in which it was the common practice to include small silver coins to foretell wealth as well as a tiny wishbone or 'merrythought' for good luck, a silver bell or ring to indicate a betrothal or wedding, a thimble or button portending being unmarried and the thrift it would entail, or an anchor to promise a safe harbor (Broomfield 149-150, F.A. 458-9). A Christmas pudding with trinkets, which Ronald Tolkien was likely to have had during his growing up, either at home or at his Suffield grandparents' house or at his Aunt May Incledon's Christmas gatherings, is a likely model for the Great Cake with its trinkets.

In *Smith of Wootton Major*, the Great Cake was the highlight of the Twenty-four Feast. This celebration's name came from the fact the feast was only held every twenty-four years and only twenty-four children were invited (*SWM* 4). The Great Cake was inside a ring of twenty-four red candles (*SWM* 11).[26] Although twenty-four is the number of blackbirds baked in a pie in the traditional English nursery rhyme "Sing a Song of Sixpence," there is also a religious context for the number twenty-four. Twelve implies maturity or totality as there were Twelve Apostles in the New Testament and this corresponded to the Twelve Tribes of Israel in the Old Testament, yielding a sum of twenty-four. The book of Revelation has imagery built around the important number twelve and its multiples:[27] "Surrounding the throne were twenty-four other thrones, and seated on them were twenty-four elders. They were dressed in white and had crowns of gold on their heads" (Rev 4:4, also Rev 5:8).[28] After the Reformation, the Catholic Church regulated all iconography so it would be consistent with doctrine. At the Sanctuary of Oropa near Biella, Italy, the statuary for the Coronation of the Virgin includes forty-six angels, twenty-six cherubs, fifty-six saints, and twenty-four innocents (Butler 133).

As was typical for Tolkien, he appears to have combined a number of elements including the merrymaking of the Feast of the Holy Innocents and the tradition of hiding "trinkets" in a cake or pudding associated with the Christmas season to create a festival fraught with recognizably meaningful customs. A king's cake, created with the help of the King of Faery, could contain a trinket, like a figure representing the Christ child, a Mystical token. The Great Cake, as the culmination of the Twenty-four Feast, becomes a fitting vessel in which to bake the Faery star.

The Faery star, placed in the Great Cake, was a token of the Faery King's emblem, a "brilliant star on his forehead" (*SWM* 133). The Faery King created a silver star, hidden in the Great Cake, as a way to have all Elves protect the bearer of the star.[29] The star was first given to Grandfather Rider (*SWM* 133) and found by the young Smith, his grandson, in Nokes's Great Cake of 1062. Although Tolkien is quite definite *Smith of Wootton Major* is not part of Middle-earth (*Letters* 355), stars are a sign of elves in *Smith of Wootton Major*, just as they are in Middle-earth. In Middle-earth, *Eldar*, the name of the Elves or Elf, comes from the root ELED- meaning 'Starfolk' ("The Etymologies" 395).

Long points out the etymological association of *fay* not only to 'fairy'/'faery', but also to 'faith' so that the faery star also points to the star that led the Three Wise Men to their epiphany ("*Smith*" 103). This would fit with the star being placed in a king's cake. Long notes that Nokes calls the star a "trinket" (*SWM* 10). Under 'trinket', the OED lists an obsolete meaning: "decorations of worship, and to the religious rites, beliefs etc., which the speaker thinks vain or trivial" (Long, "*Smith*" 104). Long then sees this as further evidence that Nokes is irreverent or disrespectful toward Faery.

However, there is a turn-of-the-twentieth century context that Tolkien experienced in relation to vain religious rites or trinkets, as a number of his Tolkien relatives were Baptists or Evangelical Church of England members (*Bio* 24):

> Evangelical Protestants saw adoration of bread and wine as gross idolatry [...] Frequently Protestants saw the adoration of the Eucharistic elements as evidence that Catholicism was, in fact, a pagan religion. [...] For Protestant critics, the use of choral music, bright colors, and (sometimes) incense revealed Catholic worship to be essentially pagan [...] Some even seemed to believe that Catholics worshipped pagan gods,

based on suspicions that the IHS monogram stood for "Isis, Horus, and Serapis" (Kilcrease 39). Evangelicals here refers not only to denominations like the Methodists, but also the Evangelical wing of the Church of England which was quite vocal and politically active in the nineteenth century.

Tolkien seems willing to embrace "pagan" Faery as a valid path to the true religion of Catholicism, which was also maligned as "pagan." In an Open Debate at King Edward's School on April 2, 1912, Ronald Tolkien spoke on the topic "That it is better to be eccentric than orthodox." He said that there is no "true opposition between the orthodox and the eccentric, and [he] maintained the possibility of a man's being both at the same time" (*C&G* 1.39). As a result, Ronald could be both orthodox and eccentric because for him there was no "true opposition" between the two. For him, Christian "truth" and Faery could mutually illuminate each other.

The religious connotations of the Twenty-four Feast, The Feast of Good Children, and a king's cake create an expectation that the Faery star might have a divine dimension. Although Long focuses on the star associated with the Feast of the

Epiphany—a star that provides safety and suggests the Virgin Mary.[30] The Catechism of the Catholic Church states: "From the most ancient times" the Blessed Virgin extended her protection to the faithful "in all their dangers and needs."[31] In September 1916, having arrived in France, seen action in the trenches on the Western Front, and learned of the death of his friend and fellow T.C.B.S. member Rob Gilson, Tolkien wrote a poem beginning, "O Lady Mother throned amid the stars" (*C&G* 1.97). He titled this "Consolatrix Afflictorum" (Comforter of the Afflicted) or "Stella Vespertina", showing his familiarity with and use of the Virgin's protection and her association with stars.

Stella Maris, Latin for the 'Star of the sea', or the North Star, was a title or name for the Virgin Mary. This aspect of Mary sees her as a guide. The Morning Star or *Stella Matutina* was another name of the Virgin Mary because Mary—like the Morning Star rising in the east—heralds the coming of her Son, who is the light of the world and the Sun of righteousness.[32] As the Morning Star, Mary is a sign of hope.[33] In the pre-Christian world of Middle-earth, the star of Eärendil also functions as a sign of hope, and specifically the "Hope without guarantees" of the pre-Christian or pagan setting of Middle-earth (*Letters* 237). The "hope without guarantees" contrasts with the "sure and certain hope of the resurrection to eternal life through Our Lord Jesus Christ" of Catholic doctrine found in the funeral mass with which Ronald Tolkien was familiar.

Catholics would easily recognize the titles, *Stella Maris* and *Stella Matutina*, as references to the Virgin Mary. Tolkien seems to imply that the Faery star of Alf alludes to being under the protection of the Blessed Virgin Mary. This emblem of the star, an instantiation of the *Stella Maris* or *Stella Matutina*, would be fitting for Alf, who recalls the Catholic priest Fr. Francis. The Faery star with its allusions to the Virgin Mary links both Alf and Fr. Francis. The Oratory website states that Fr. Francis had a special veneration for Mary because, when he was not "on a public Mass, he always celebrated at Our Lady's Altar." On Fr. Morgan's death, Tolkien inherited "a miniature of the Virgin Mary" which Fr. Francis had kept on his mantelpiece (Priestman 53). Fr. Morgan appears to have wished for his ward to continue to be aware the Virgin was watching over him and guarding him. Further support for the reading of the Faery star as an allusion to the Virgin Mary's protection comes from Tolkien's comments about Mary that indicate a deep reverence for the Virgin Mary (*Letters* 172) and his poem "Stella Vespertina", written in France during a rest period in the Somme. Smith, as Tolkien's avatar in *Smith of Wootton Major*, is literally protected by the Faery star on his forehead—the source of his name 'Starbrow' and the token that protects him during his journeys in Faery.

The Faery star appears to signal an unmerited, unforeseeable grace that comes to young Smith in a way he is unaware of, because he "swallowed it [the Faery star] without ever noticing it" (*SWM* 15). It is a pure gift, just as in *Leaf by Niggle* the painting of a tree which becomes a living tree, is a gift (157). Ironically, Christopher Williams' review of *Smith of Wootton Major* complains that the star is a "gift" "and not the right and possible prerogative of every child, as modern children expect to be" (*QT* 234). Ronald Tolkien, I think, would have agreed with Williams' insight, but held a different view that grace is a gift, given freely but also constrained by divine providence; that is, "many are called, but few are chosen" (Matthew 22:14).

The Faery star, like the sudden and miraculous grace of the *eucatastrophe*, that can "never be counted on to recur" (OFS 153), appears to apply to Ronald Tolkien. Tolkien, speaking of the publication of *The Hobbit*, wrote, "I have always been undeservedly lucky at major points" (*Letters* 374). His "luck," from what we know, was quite remarkable. After his mother's death, he and his brother, in a time of indifference to and ignorance of the needs of children, had the "miraculous experience" of coming under the loving care of Fr. Francis (*Letters* 417). In 1909, he fell in love with the one and only love of his life, Edith Bratt (Grotta-Kurska 23), who was willing to not only accept the destitute Ronald's proposal in 1913 but also to break her engagement to another man. She then waited for him to graduate from Oxford in 1915 and married him on the eve of his departure for World War I in 1916. Despite being sent to the trenches of France in the Somme offensive where the survival rate for junior officers was six weeks (Lewis-Stempel 6), Ronald Tolkien returned home alive and in one piece due to trench fever. He remained in England for the rest of the war due to recurrences of this illness. Tolkien became the Rawlinson and Bosworth Professor of Anglo-Saxon at Oxford University in July 1925 at the startling age of thirty-three. After the enthusiastic reception of *The Hobbit*, he then had the runaway success of *The Lord of the Rings*. Given Tolkien's Catholic faith, he was likely to see being "undeservedly lucky" as the result of the providence and mercy of God. Tolkien, like his avatar Smith with the Faery star on his forehead, had been the recipient of grace.

Returning to the image of the "Great Cake," Flieger notes, Tolkien kept the original title, "The Great Cake," until late in the revision process (*SWM* 72). Given that the Great Cake is the vehicle to convey the Faery star, which grants protection in a way analogous to the compassion of the Virgin Mary, the cake and its star function as a Sacrament—"an outward sign instituted by Christ to give grace."[34] The twenty-four red candles recall the red candle traditionally lit beside the tabernacle which contains the consecrated Bread and Wine, the Body and Blood of Christ, again signaling the Sacrament. The Sacrament of Holy Communion comes from the gift and sacrifice of Christ's life—his body and blood in the Bread and Wine (John 6:32-35, 48-51, 58). The Faery star could be a token of a Mystical grace, just as the king's cake held a figure to represent the Christ who brings grace. Consequently, it is understandable that Tolkien would retain the title, "The Great Cake," and focus on it because he "fell in love with the Blessed Sacrament [in the form of a Communion wafer] from the beginning" (*Letters* 340). For him:

> Out of the darkness of my life, so much frustrated, I put before you the one great thing to love on earth: the Blessed Sacrament [...] There you will find [...] the true way of all your loves upon earth, and more than that: Death: by the divine paradox, that which ends life, and demands the surrender of all, and yet by the taste (or foretaste) of which alone can what you seek in your earthly relationships (love, faithfulness, joy) be maintained, or take on that earthly complexion of reality, of eternal endurance, which every man's heart *desires* (*Letters* 53-54, italics added).[35]

Desire, Art, and Language

Desire is the heart of Faërie because: "Fairy-stories were plainly not primarily concerned with possibility, but with desirability. If they awakened *desire*, satisfying it while often whetting it unbearably, they succeeded" (OFS 134, italics in original). The "magic of Faërie [...] is in [...] the satisfaction of certain primordial human desires" (OFS 116). What satisfies in fairy-stories or fantasy is: Recovery, Escape, and most of all the Consolation of the Happy Ending or joy (OFS 145, 155). Further, this desire includes "the peculiar quality of the 'joy' in successful Fantasy" which is due to "a sudden glimpse of the underlying reality or truth [...] a satisfaction, and an answer to that question, 'Is it true'?" (OFS 156).

Desire, for Ronald Tolkien, is at the heart of the pursuit of artistic beauty. Art and creative or "sub-creative" desire "seem to have no biological function, and [are] apart from the satisfactions of plain ordinary biological life, with which, in our world, it is indeed usually at strife" (*Letters* 145). This artistic desire loves "the real primary world," but is not satisfied by it. Desired artistic beauty sounds like it could be an outgrowth of the admonition: "Take delight in the Lord, and he will give you the desires of your heart" (Psalm 37:4). In *Smith of Wootton Major*, the Mystical King's tree, kin of Tolkien's *Tree of Amalion* ('Blessing') or the "Tree of Tales," a descendent of the Indian tree of Paradise, supplies both spiritual and physical sustenance, fulfilling the heart's desire.

Desire leads to "opportunities of 'Fall'" by clinging or possessiveness or by "the desire for Power, for making the will more quickly effective—and so to the Machine (or Magic)" (*Letters* 145). The fall of the Elves is because of the Kinslaying, the result, not of a typical war for territory or more power or revenge for the kidnapping of a beautiful wife, but rather to reclaim "primeval Jewels"—precious objects of beauty. Temptation is aesthetic, implying a moral or spiritual transgression, and can be found in the conception of powers of sublime darkness in Burke's *Philosophical Enquiry into the Origin of our Ideas of the Sublime and Beautiful* (Sly 112). An obsession with, if not a lust for, "precious," beautiful objects permeates Tolkien's created world: Fëanor, his sons, and Thingol with the Silmarils in *The Silmarillion*; Thorin Oakenshield with the Arkenstone in *The Hobbit*; Sauron, Gollum, and Frodo with the "precious" One Ring in *The Lord of the Rings*; and even the narrator of the "precious" *Pearl*, the Middle English poem which Tolkien studied and translated (Koubenec 127, 125). The *Oxford English Dictionary* states "precious" means something "Of great moral, spiritual, or other non-material value; beloved, held in high esteem." In *Smith of Wootton Major*, the precious Faery star, which can become a vehicle like the Ring for the satisfaction of Desire, is a gift and a temptation.

The pursuit of a precious Faërian object suggests a parallel to Ronald Tolkien's own experience. He is quoted as saying that "[I] invented several languages when I was only about eight or nine, [...] but I destroyed them. My mother disapproved. She thought of my language as a useless frivolity taking up time that could be better spent in studying" (Grotta-Kurska 18). At that time, "I was always inventing languages. But that was naughty. Poor boys must concentrate on getting scholarships" (Plimmer/Plimmer). Tolkien knew only too well that this 'art' "is also—like poetry—contrary to conscience, and duty; its pursuit is snatched from hours due to self-advancement, or to bread, or to employers" ("Secret Vice" 207). Tolkien's "precious" invented languages, his unique experience of beauty and aliveness, may be equivalent to Fëanor's Silmarils, but they are at the same time an art "contrary to conscience, and duty."

As Krishnan Venkatesh comments, Tolkien is sympathetic to the Romantics' yearning for transcendent beauty (230). Tolkien expresses this amid the terrors and exhaustion of Mordor, when Sam is like the "hardened warrior [...] brought to tears by a glimpse of the moon" in Japanese literature (146):

> Sam saw a white star twinkle for a while. The beauty of it smote his heart, as he looked up out of the forsaken land, and hope returned to him. For like a shaft, clear and cold, the thought pierced him that in the end the Shadow was only a small and passing thing: there was light and high beauty for ever beyond its reach (*RK* VI ii 901).

Again, Gimli expresses this "shock of transcendent beauty" that renders all else, the rest of life, not worth living for—weeping openingly after receiving Galadriel's parting gift:

> why did I come on this quest? Little did I know where the chief peril lay! [...] I would not have come, had I known the danger of light and joy. Now I have taken my worst wound in this parting (*FR* II viii 369).

Part of the beauty and impact of Galadriel's gift is the result of Gimli's unanticipated experience of meeting Galadriel's eyes and feeling that "he looked suddenly into the heart of an enemy and saw there love and understanding" (*FR* II vii 347).

The "strife" or clash of beauty and the demands of putting food on the table, the "ordinary biological life," crystalizes in *Smith of Wootton Major* when the community with its increased prosperity and financial success has become "vulgarly self-satisfied" (*SWM* 112). This is why in *Smith of Wootton Major* the artistic activities of "dancing, singing and tale-telling were little thought of." The trades of the musicians, painters, and carvers declined as the community focused on "marketable and exportable crafts" and the beauty, that came from contact with Faery, faded in both the "taste and skills" of the local artisans (*SWM* 128). This spirit of mercantile utilitarianism will not miss Alf when he leaves (*SWM* 54). As a, perhaps, indirect emissary from Faery who has the Great Hall repainted and re-glazed following "old custom," Alf offers intangible riches, like love and imagination, that the bottom-line, practical, and seemingly Protestant mentality of Wootton Major has little use for (*SWM* 144). Protected by the precious Faery star, Smith can explore Faery, seek its wonders, and deepen his experience of beauty, released from the demands of practical, everyday life, but tempted by Faërian possibilities.

The almost guilty desire for Faery with its enchanting beauty and nourishment for the imagination drove Tolkien's storytelling to create "a world in which a form of language agreeable to my personal aesthetic might seem real" (*Letters* 264). For Tolkien, when a fairy-story is successful and achieves *eucatastrophe*, it produces a "sudden glimpse of Truth, [and] your whole nature chained in material cause and effect, the chain of death, [i.e. "ordinary biological life"] feels a sudden relief" (*Letters* 100).

This desire for Faery informs Ronald Tolkien's creation of the quandary of his avatar Smith in *Smith of Wootton Major*. The Smith of *Smith of Wootton Major* creates beautiful objects inspired by his visits to Faery, but yearns for more—a forbidden meeting with the Faery Queen.

III. The Drama of Faery

Living in Exile

Returning to the attractive, yet fearsome, Faery in *Smith of Wootton Major*, Flieger states:

> distilled out of Tolkien's deepest memories of his own adventures in the perilous realm [i.e. his imagination based on the "leaf mould" of his mind] [...] At the heart of the story [*SWM*] is the figure that Tolkien returned to again and again in his fiction—the wanderer, the restless, unquiet human traveler.

This "suggests Tolkien felt himself to be such a one" (*QT* 236). In relation to the wanderers that fled the drowning of Númenor, recounted in Arry Lowdham's papers (*SD* 258), Flieger cites Tolkien's variation on the poem *The Seafarer* (*LR* 84, *SD* 243-44): "Now we sit in the land of exile" and "longing is on us" (*QT* 162). She states Ronald Tolkien sees himself as an exile, like Eriol/Aelfwine and Eärendil (*QT* 163). Tolkien, a man who builds his stories around names, seems to support Flieger's view because he writes at one point that Smith in *Smith of Wootton Major* was "probably Ned" (*SWM* 98)—a name that could be the nunnated Elvish *edlen*(*n*) meaning 'exiled' ("Words" 51). Flieger then includes the longings of Bilbo and Frodo, but overlooks the fact that so many of the chief characters and peoples of Middle-earth are exiles.

Exile is everywhere in Tolkien's stories of Faery. "The Fall of Gondolin," the first story of the legendarium that Tolkien wrote, is full of images reflecting Tolkien's war experiences and his reading of the classics, especially the fall of Troy and the *Aeneid* (Bruce; Lewis/Currie, *The Forsaken Realm*). The story ends with the exile of the survivors. In the *Aeneid*, the outcasts are "survivors of a terrible persecution," and their leader Aeneas is "so fractured by the horrors of the past [...] that the only thing that gets him through the present is a numbed sense of duty to a barely discernible future that can justify every deprivation." Aeneas's psychological trauma leaves him swinging from cold fatalism to sentimental violence (Mendelsohn 99).[36]

Tolkien's first narrator, Eriol, "the one who dreams alone," is a wanderer, an orphan, an enslaved refugee, and a likely trauma survivor—both physically and psychologically—given that both of his parents died in the war and he presumably endures the physical abuse of subjugation (*LT1* 2, *LT2* 4). Eriol hears the tales of the elves who leave their home in Middle-earth to travel to Aman, becoming exiles. In later stories, the Valar expel the High Elves to Middle-earth after the Kinslaying, which Fëanor leads. In the Second Age, the Valar reward the men who aided the Elves in the war with Morgoth by giving them a refuge on the island of Númenor, making them refugees. Later, with the Downfall, an Atlantis-like drowning of Númenórean civilization, a remnant of Númenóreans will escape to return to Middle-earth and set up the Kingdoms of Anor and Gondor, meeting the requirements for being refugees and exiles, again.

In *The Hobbit*, Thorin and company are refugees, exiled by the dragon Smaug. Smaug's reign of destruction also expels Bard and the Dale men to Lake-town.

In *The Lord of the Rings*, we learn the hobbits were migrants when they settled the Shire, and the Rangers or Dúnedain are men in exile. The Istari, like Gandalf, qualify more as emissaries, whose home is not Middle-earth. The dwarves feel exiled from Moria. The High Elves feel like exiles and are returning across the sea.

For the High Elves, Legolas, and perhaps Frodo, the "sea longing" is a longing for home, Elven Home. After learning from Gandalf the power of the Ring, Frodo knows that instead of a holiday with adventures, like Bilbo, he will have "exile, a flight from danger into danger [...] I feel very small, and very uprooted, and well—desperate" (*FR* I ii 61). Eventually, Frodo, a casualty of history, out of place in the peaceful Shire, journeys to Valinor "where time loses its meaning" (Hiley 135). Bilbo, Frodo, and eventually Sam choose to leave their home in Middle-earth as do the friends, Gimli and Legolas. After the death of their wives, Pippin and Merry go to live out their days as honored emigrés in Minas Tirith, the stage for the most exciting adventures of their lives. The Ents have lost the Ent-wives due to war and have retreated deep into a small area of Fangorn in a self-imposed banishment. Even Gollum—who has lost home, friends, family, and comfort—is an outcast, but one who does not mourn his losses except for the Ring which has now supplanted all of those previous links to real life (*TT* IV i 602). The state and experience of exile are everywhere in the legendarium.[37]

The reality and pain of exile find expression in two elegiac Old English poems, *The Seafarer* and *The Wanderer*, which Ronald Tolkien studied: "the sorrows of the lonely seafarer [...] a symbol of desolation of spirit" (Lee, "Wanderer" 194). *The Wanderer* addresses issues of exile, loss, lonely wandering, suffering, and the "transitory nature of existence." *The Wanderer*'s conclusion that suffering can lead to wisdom appeals to all lonely wanderers in life "—which to a Christian is everyone;" that is, "we are all exiled from Eden and temporarily from Heaven" (Lee, "Wanderer" 190). *The Seafarer*, too, has a long history of textual discussion in which exile is seen as analogous to the pilgrimage, on earth, of the soul whose home is Heaven (Wilcox 134-37). Ronald Tolkien agreed, writing that we are exiles from the Eden, our ancient home, which "certainly" was "on this very unhappy earth" (*Letters* 110). In Tolkien's Christian context, Fallen Man is an exile (*Letters* 48, 51, 194).

Tolkien debated what the best title for *The Wanderer* should be and considered "an exile," "alone a banished man," and the "survivor" (Lee, "Wanderer" 197). Tolkien's reflections on the poem note that the survivor, "a man who dwells alone" who has a "solitary abode," has a purpose to "reach a land where he had some hope of being allowed to live unmolested [...] and equally important he was trying to find people in whom he could confide" (Lee, "Wanderer" 199).

The Wanderer, along with *The Seafarer*, "captured the 'horror and allurement of the sea'" and the interconnected working of fate/*wyrd* and God (Lee, "Wanderer" 201). Tolkien contrasts this Christian poem with the regret and despair of paganism (Lee, "Wanderer" 201). Lee notes how appropriate it is for Aragorn, an exile known as Strider, a wanderer (*eardstapa* or 'earth-stepper' in the poem), to recite Tolkien's variation of *The Wanderer* in *The Lord of the Rings* (*TT* III vi 112; Lee, "Wanderer" 203). Regarding his poem "Where now the horse and the rider," Tolkien wrote:

> I never attempted to "recreate" anything. My aim has been the basically more modest, and certainly more laborious one of trying to make* something new [...] the sentiment is different: it laments the ineluctable ending and passing back into oblivion of the fortunate, the full-lives, the unblemished and the beautiful. To me that is more poignant than any particular disaster, from the cruelty of men or the hostility of the world (Lee, "Wanderer" 204).

Ronald Tolkien saw *The Wanderer* in the context of the evangelium which denies the "universal final defeat" and foresees the *eucatastrophe*. The *eucatastrophe* is the sudden joyous turn, the ultimate form of consolation, that Tolkien saw in the "happy ending" in fairy tales (OFS 153). *The Wanderer* gave a glimpse of light: "I at least find more sustenance and support in 'The Wanderer,' amid the present catastrophe (which seems likely to leave Europe in ruins[...]) than in all the pretty prattle" (Lee, "Wanderer" 205).[38]

Another experience of exile appears in Ronald Tolkien's poem "Looney", written in 1932 or 1933 and later rewritten by 1962 as "The Sea-Bell" for *The Adventures of Tom Bombadil* (*ATB* 252, 17). Tolkien's narrator presents the pain of not being able to communicate to others what he has experienced. This is the experience of an exile because the one who is exiled has not only been cut off from both his own previous life and experiences, but also may not even have the command of a language that will allow him to express himself in a new land. He fails to "find people in whom he could confide" (Lee, "Wanderer" 199). Flieger comments that Looney of "The Sea-Bell" and also Eriol are "baffled and alienated" by their experiences in Faery (*QT* 237), but the narrator in "The Sea-Bell" finds no response from others either in Faery or in the primary world.

In "The Sea-Bell", the narrator finds "a white shell like a sea-bell". The narrator hears "a ding within [...] a calling ringing" (i.e. the sound of a bell). Bells mark time, and realizing "It is later than late!" the narrator sets off on his voyage that is "wrapped in mist, wound in a sleep," with both the mist and the dream as signs of Faery (Hiley 136). In the original version of "Looney", the phrase, "I journeyed away for a year and a day," also marks that the narrator has been enchanted (*ATB* 254). He is at first delighted with the beauty of Faery and the hidden promise of dancing feet, pipes, and voices that always flee in the new/Otherworld he has found. Seemingly being the sole and proud inhabitant, a "king of this land," he demands words and a face but finds he is impotent and helpless, "wandering in wit" (*ATB* 106). The narrator has a terrible realization: "I have lost myself, and I know not the way." He is a "stranger in a strange land" (Ex 2:22). Looney echoes Frodo's "I do not know the way," when he accepts the Ring (*FR* II ii 264). The speaker, under a shadow and feeling the cold of winter, returns to find himself excluded from connection with other people by "shuttered" houses in a "sad" lane, a "blind alley." He continues to talk only to himself. The seashell, that came "as a star-beam" and called him to the promise of Faery, is now "silent and dead" (*ATB* 106, 108). He has not escaped Time and cannot return to Faery.

Klinger notes that the attribution of "The Sea-Bell" to Frodo makes little sense because the poem is from the Fourth Age and Frodo departed at the end of the Third Age ("Strange Powers" 98). Further, the 'buoys' and the 'harbours' cited in the poem are not features of the Shire, and Frodo only heard the sound of the sea in his dreams (*FR* I v 106).[39] She cites Shippey's view that this poem has many biographical features (*Road* 283-85), and Flieger comments that Shippey's speculation is "persuasive" (*QT* 210). In *Splintered Light*, she states the speaker in the poem "is certainly Tolkien," though she sees Ronald Tolkien calling his statements into question by the odd and questionable attribution to Frodo (148-150).

The reader can compare Tolkien's focus and description of the various experiences of exile with a description of the experience of the exile of the Sephardic Jews:

> A violent uprooting, which takes away all normal props, breaks up our world, snatches us forever from places that are saturated in memories crucial to our identity, and plunges us permanently in an alien environment, can make us feel that our very existence has been jeopardized (Armstrong 8 in Brothers 45).

Exile can be a metaphor for psychological trauma because exile is almost always traumatic. Like an exile, many who experience trauma have their familiar world shattered and fall into an unknown realm, leading to feelings of estrangement from one's self ("I have lost myself") and isolation from others ("shuttered" houses and talks only to himself) (Brothers 45). Since the experience of the unfamiliar lacks meaning, the traumatized person, like an exile, now lives in an unrecognizable world. The comforting, predictable certainties of 'home', that regulate and manage life, no longer exist.

> With their memories on overload, exiles see double, feel double, are double. When exiles see one place they're also seeing—looking for—another behind it [...] they are addicted to a lost past [...] an exile is continuously prospecting for a future home (André Aciman *Letters* 13 in Wilcox).

Psychological trauma opens a person to feelings of terror and dread along with accompanying feelings of helplessness, vulnerability, and inadequacy. With safety, meaning, and stability gone, painful shame hides this turmoil (Brothers 47). The conditions of trauma can both interfere with memory, as possibly represented in *Smith of Wootton Major* by Smith's difficulty remembering or reporting to friends what he had seen, and at the same time burning certain memories into the brain which can have both voluntary and involuntary recall: Smith "often recalled" "wonders and mysteries" that he had experienced in Faery (*SWM* 22).

In trauma, as in exile, there is a "before" and "after" because the person experiences not only their environment as different from the past, but also themselves with a 'past self' and a 'present self'. The traumatic event creates a threshold.

Tolkien expresses this threshold in an evocative set of drawings labeled *Before* and *Afterwards* (*A&I* 34, 36; McIlwaine 45). Here the suffering of "a terrible chaos which darkened my youth and early manhood" (McIlwaine 170, *Bio* 31) indicates a traumatic event or threshold that could create a mind that was "receptive when presented with an opportunity for a transformative experience" (Croft, "Tolkien's Faërian Drama" 33).

Because Tolkien drew on his personal experiences repeatedly, the "terror" that Smith experiences in the Faery of *Smith of Wootton Major*, a dangerous and unpredictable place, as well as the long roster of displaced and homeless characters in Tolkien's fiction, suggests exile is a compelling metaphor for Tolkien's own experience. However, there are no explicit or overt monsters in the Faery of *Smith of Wootton Major*, although Tolkien knows "the monsters do not depart, whether the gods come or go" (OFS 22).

The undefined "terror" in the "perilous land" of Faery points to one very ironic detail in *Smith of Wootton Major*. Because of his work, Smith inhabits a world of iron at his forge: farm and carpenters' tools, "kitchen tools and pots and pans, bars and bolts and hinges, pot-hooks, fire-dogs, and horseshoes," as well as gates and lattices (*SWM* 17). Iron, first mastered around 3,000 years ago, changed the ability of men to deal with their environment, including stone. Many cultures, including those of India, Africa, and Europe, considered iron—an unnatural, manmade material—to be a deterrent and a protection against spirits, ghosts, and witches (Elworthy 221). Professor Rhŷs, with whom Tolkien studied at Oxford, reported a Welsh story of a young man who was warned that his fairy wife would disappear if iron struck her (Elworthy 222). Smith's prosaic workday world seems to be a parallel for Tolkien's daily round of classes, lectures, and committee meetings that had little use for beguiling flights of creative imagination.

Iron repels Faery as seen in the way Smith's brightly shining star dims when he crosses the threshold of his house (*SWM* 29; see Flieger, "The Trees" 121).[40] Smith's being surrounded by iron probably contributed to the fact the star "did not usually shine," so that people were not likely to notice it (*SWM* 16). Although Smith's craft is "enriched" by the "blessing of [his] acquaintance with the fairy folk and a real, if limited, understanding of their world and its ways" (*QT* 237), it is almost as if Smith has exiled himself in an everyday world of work and family, clearly separated from Faery, by means of an iron barrier he controls. If Smith's first name was in one version Ned (*SWM* 98), then the nunnated diminutive of Ed or Edward could recall Sindarin: *edlon* meaning 'outsider', 'stranger', 'foreigner' ("Words" 141) and *edlen*(*n*) meaning 'exiled' ("Words" 51). Exile provides the backdrop to Smith's excursions in Faery. Like Smith, Tolkien's writings and art, works of his leisure, were "enriched" by Faery, but Ronald Tolkien sees himself as an observer, not an inhabitant, of this other dimension.

Tolkien stresses that Smith never "forged a sword or a spear or an arrow-head" (*SWM* 20). Nevertheless, from his visits to Faery, Smith knew how to forge weapons powerful enough "to become the matter of great tales and be worth a king's ransom" (*SWM* 20). Tolkien knew that in the lore of ancient northern Europe, as in the stories of the powerful Waylund or the Welsh Gofannen, the smith's skill was at least partly magical. In the Völsung saga, the smith inscribed magical runes on the sword Gram to aid the warrior who used it (Huttar 185). Tolkien drew on these legends for the swords from Gondolin that Thorin and company find in the troll cave in *The Hobbit* (II) and for Andúril, Aragorn's sword that was broken and reforged in *The Lord of the Rings*. This knowledge comes from Faery, but weapons are easily part of the lust-like desire for Power and therefore readily part of Magic (*Letters* 145). Smith's rejection of manufacturing weapons in *Smith of Wootton Major* would be in harmony with Tolkien's particular view of Faery which embraces beauty, delight, and enchantment and rejects power.[41]

Tolkien redefines Faery as a source of "special skill and 'artistic quality'" (*SWM* 127). He states that Faery rejects "the spirit of possession and domination"—the "ruthlessness" that leads to "mere power" and destructiveness (*SWM* 131). The distinction between elvish Enchantment that is "artistic in desire and purpose" and Magic, as a technique for obtaining power to dominate things and wills, emerged in "On Fairy-stories" (143, see Huttar 176-80). The Faery star that Smith finds on the morning of his tenth birthday opens to the world of Faery and its creativity to Smith, transforming him into a "Starbrow" or a Taliesin (Welsh *tal*='forehead', *iesin*=radiant, shining') who, like the Welsh bard, suddenly sings "in strange words" (*SWM* 16). Like the young boy Gwion Bach, who swallows the three drops from the cauldron of poetic Inspiration, prophetic vision, and knowledge or wisdom, Smith is transformed and now has almost a mystical relationship with nature, like Taliesin. This bardic inspiration will be channeled into his singing while he works.

Smith's Exile from Faery

In Tolkien's first draft of *Smith of Wootton Major*, written in response to "The Golden Key", there are only two sentences about Smith's travels in Faery (*SWM* 159, 161). Most of the first sentence was published on page 18 of the 2015 edition of *Smith of Wootton Major*. The second sentence, containing "seldom in danger there: for the evil things avoided the star," was placed on the published page 20. This initial neglect of Smith's journeys seems to be a function of the first draft's focus on the Mystical Faery found in the Great Cake, the ring found in the cake, and the drama of Alf and Nokes.[42] Consequently, Tolkien's draft introduction to "The Golden Key", that began the *Smith of Wootton Major* story, featured the Mystical face of Faery but almost none of the Magical face of Faërie, as Tolkien specified in his lecture (OFS 125). In subsequent drafts, Tolkien added the scenes in Faery, including the Mariners, the dancing Elven maids, the King's Tree, the Lake of Tears, and the final meeting with the Queen of Faerie. In other words, Tolkien added what he believed: "most good 'fairy-stories' contain the *aventures* of men in the Perilous Realm or upon its shadowy marches" (OFS 113).

Tolkien's Faery world of *Smith of Wootton Major* follows the popular view of the Middle Ages that seemed to accept fairies/elves as another race of beings who were wholly themselves and inherently magical (Hutton 184, Flieger *GS* 67, OFS 110). Catholic doctrine never successfully interfered with the belief of most medieval people, including theologians, that the borders between this world and the Otherworld were permeable, not only in dreams or in visions, but also at various places where the lands of the dead and the living touch. For example, St. Patrick's Island in Ireland reputedly gave access to purgatory.[43]

Wishing to follow this medieval view of fairies, Tolkien is at pains to explain how people can visit Faery (*SWM* 112-13). Humans can enter Faery at certain points, "if fitted to do so or permitted to do so" (*SWM* 116). Tolkien notes that

Rider's wife, Rose, may have visited 'Outer Faery' (*SWM* 135). Smith's wife, Nell, and his daughter, Nan, "were probably themselves elf-friends and even walkers in Outer Faery" (*SWM* 141). Tolkien describes Rider as having found an entrance to Faery "by 'accident'" (*SWM* 132) and experienced "grave perils" (*SWM* 133), but ones less dangerous than Smith's (*SWM* 141). This statement probably means he had been under the protection of the Faery King because he received the star prior to his marriage with the understanding the star was on loan (*SWM* 134) and later was "unstarred" (*SWM* 140).

The relationship of Faery and the everyday world in *Smith of Wootton Major* may represent Tolkien's new synthesis which would allow for magic and Faery on a round world. Tolkien explored the possibility of reformulating his view of a "flat earth" Arda in the late 1950s and in early 1960s, as found in *Morgoth's Ring*, published in 1993. In this reconceptualization, Arda becomes the name of the whole planetary system, not just a single world, and the Round Arda has always had a sun (*MR* 370; Leśniewski, "Round Arda" 353). Tolkien's new cosmology would be compatible with *Smith of Wootton Major*.

In *Smith of Wootton Major*, Tolkien followed the fairytale tradition of using common or generic names. This naming tradition is part of what distinguishes fairytales from myth. Myths have a unique, often awe-inspiring hero, whose well-known, individual name sets him or her apart, like Theseus, Beowulf, or Hercules. Further, unlike the often-tragic endings of many myths, fairy tales are known for their happy endings here on earth (Bettelheim 39).

Ronald Tolkien was not only an expert on English names and place-names (Shippey, *Road* 272), but he enjoyed the myriad potentialities embedded in names: "it gives me great pleasure, a good name. I always in writing start with a name; give me a name and it produces a story, not the other way about normally" (Gueroult BBC Interview). 'Smith' is a common name—as anyone can see by consulting a phone book from an English-speaking village or town—suggesting the protagonist is an "everyman" or someone ordinary. Tolkien's use of craft names for many of his characters in *Smith of Wootton Major* fits this model (*SWM* 117). The relatively modern trade name of 'Smith' fits Gregory Pepetone's reading of *Smith of Wootton Major* in the Romantic tradition, as having the "heroic theme, The Spiritual Quest of Everyman" (143). However, Pepetone's conclusion that Smith is an "archetypal romantic hero—a courageous but lonely sojourner through spiritual terrain hidden from others," an inspired artist seeking fresh and new imaginative experiences in Faery, trades on mythical sources that assume smiths commanded semi-magical powers (144).

Fairy tales typically use either very common names: 'Jack' or 'Hansel and Gretel', or identify characters only as "the youngest brother," "the stepmother," "Little Red Cap," or "a poor fisherman" (Bettelheim 40). Smith's family has common names that have been nunnated (Shippey, *Road* 273): Nell, Nan, and Ned for Ellen (Ella or Helen or Eleanor), Ann, and Edward or Edmund.[44] In addition, Tolkien specifies that Ned is a name that denotes not only an individual but also a type, one of "the practical and plain normal men and workers" (*SWM* 141). Tolkien wavered in his name for Smith. He is called "Joe Smith of West-side" in the Essay (*SWM* 125) and Alfred (Old English *Ælfræd* or 'elf-counsel' from *ælf* ('elf')+*ræd* 'counsel') in an early draft (*SWM* 161) but "probably Ned like his son's" in "Characters" (*SWM* 98).

Fairy tales portray their unusual and improbable events in an everyday manner, as occurrences which are possible on a walk in the woods. Tolkien's slightly generic setting of the village, the Great Hall, the common place-names or Easton and Weston, and Smith's occupation creates the proper fairytale backdrop for *Smith of Wootton Major*.

Tolkien presents Faery as an alluring and attractive land of "marvels" with "fair valleys" and "bright waters in which at night strange stars shone" (*SWM* 20).[45] The Vale of Evermorn is of a green unsurpassed elsewhere in Outer Faery with "bubbling waterfalls" which cause "delight" (26).[46] Faery, as illustrated in *Smith of Wootton Major*, is a "land of Wonder" (*TOFS* 256), like Nokes's pretty cake—covered in white sugar-icing glittering like frost (*SWM* 11). Flieger writes that although Smith's journeys into Faery occupy only fifteen of fifty-five pages, they are "the heart and purpose of the story" (*GS* 66). Flieger adds that Smith "does not fully understand" the "dangers, the wonders, and mysteries he finds there" (*GS* 66). Smith's journeys recall Tolkien's statement about himself that he was "hardly more than a wandering explorer (or trespasser) in the land [of Faërie], full of wonder, but not of information" (OFS 109).

Smith's *aventures* in Faery are all narrated in the third person and with the barest descriptions of feelings or thoughts.[47] On "longer journeys [in Faery], he [Smith] had seen things of both beauty and terror that he could not clearly remember or report to his friends, though [...] he did not forget." He "often recalled" "wonders and mysteries" that he had experienced there (*SWM* 22). Smith experiences wonders and transitory perils in the scenes of the elven mariners and the Lake of Tears, but there are no monsters or wars among the Lesser and Greater Evils, both of which Tolkien knew how to portray. Smith does not suffer or struggle except when saying good-bye to the Faery Queen. The phrasing, Smith's "heart was shaken with fear" by the elven mariners and his "heart was saddened" by the birch's tears, results in keeping the reader at a distance from Smith and his thoughts and feelings, which seem remote and almost muted. Although the lack of nuance for interior, psychological states is typical of medieval literature and fairy tales, Tolkien is certainly able to delineate psychological states elsewhere, for example in "Aldarion and Erendis."

In contrast to *Smith of Wootton Major*, *The Lord of the Rings* has a secondary world that makes the characters' sufferings compelling and intense. Traditional fairy tales often address the pressing issues and suffering of children, like the threat of desertion by parents in "Hansel and Gretel;" the jealousy and envy on the part of parents in "Snow White" or of siblings in "Cinderella;" or the devouring anger of the giant in "Jack and the Beanstalk" (Bettelheim 147). In a similar way, *The Lord of the Rings* addresses a related but different problem, the "slings and arrows of outrageous fortune" in the form of the suffering of vulnerable, if not helpless, and persecuted innocents from betrayals, attacks, thirst, hunger, despair, fear, and horror.

The never-named perils of Faery in *Smith of Wootton Major*, although potentially terrifying in their lack of definition, have little impact on Smith in *Smith of Wootton Major*. Implicitly, the "terror" of *Smith of Wootton Major*'s Faery recalls Tolkien's dictum that Faery's is a "perilous country," but the habitation of the Lesser and Greater Evils has no dreadful or frightening manifestations (*SWM* 20). Flieger tries to reply to this lack of danger by stating that Tolkien's "repeated use of the word 'perilous' is the marker of how seriously Tolkien took the concept" (*SWM* 69). Elsewhere, Flieger states Tolkien called Faery the perilous realm because the word 'Faery' derives etymologically from the Latin *fàta* (the Fates), plural of *fàtum* (Fate) (*There Would Always* 60, 205). Given that a writer wants to portray what he/she wants to convey to the reader, as opposed to simply presenting concepts, only giving the label 'perilous' suggests a possible weakness in Tolkien's writing. However, surely *The Lord of the Rings* contains adequate evidence of Tolkien's ability to invoke terror in a concise and economical fashion as opposed to the much less potent presentation in *Smith of Wootton Major.*

Another attempt to understand the lack of portrayed terror makes the assumption that Faery is 'numinous', a term Tolkien was familiar with (*Letters* 151, 361). If Faery is 'numinous', then the "peril" could be from the conjunction of both the "sacred" and the "cursed" or "impure" (Sternberg 312). However, there is no evidence that Tolkien is using the concept of the "numinous" here.

Tolkien does not resolve the tensions between the unstated and unseen "terror" of Faery's "perilous country" with its Lesser and Greater Evils, (*SWM* 20) and the beckoning beauty of the landscape, which he dwells on and praises (*SWM* 20, 24, 26). Contact with Faery fosters creativity or "'artistic' quality" (*SWM* 127), as seen in Smith's iron work and singing (*SWM* 17). "Faerie resembles the other world of Heaven, literally or figuratively" (Chance Nitzsche 50) or "a transcendent dimension of reality that parallels the Christian Kingdom of God" (Pepetone 151). Eden might also be an appropriate description of Faery in *Smith of Wootton Major*, as Tolkien affirmed his belief in Eden and that we all long for this "home" that is free of time and its decay (*Letters* 110).

Smith may have begun visiting Faery for recovery (OFS 146), as Faery is in the Forest—areas "not dominated" by man (*SWM* 116). Recovery is "regaining a clear view [...] I might venture to say 'seeing things as we are (or were) meant to see them'" (OFS 146); that is, "the perception of the created order as it was meant to be, i.e. a perception of God's 'intentional will'" (Pepetone 148). In Faery, perception can break "free of the iron ring of the familiar, still more from the adamantine ring of belief that it is known, possessed, controlled" (*SWM* 144). "At first," Smith walks "among the lesser folk and the gentler creatures" and he could spend a brief visit "looking at one tree or one flower" (*SWM* 21-22), suggesting how things in fantasy/Faery are "made luminous by their setting" (OFS 147). Although Smith does not have a guide, he does have a reason, a goal, or a purpose, and is not simply wandering in Faery to marvel as Flieger proposes (*GS* 68). Smith has "business of its own kind in Faery" (*SWM* 20). This appears to be his wish, "desired in his heart," to see the Faery Queen, which began when he first saw the doll with a wand on the Great Cake (*SWM* 32). Smith, then, is analogous to Orfeo who longed with an unselfish, pure desire, to be with his beloved, his Queen, and spent years in a seeming wasteland.

The Faërian Otherworld of the Dead

Following medieval tradition, Ronald Tolkien's Faery or Otherworld is accessible to some people. A consensus views the source of Faery of *Smith of Wootton Major* in the fourteenth-century, Middle English Breton lai/poem *Sir Orfeo* (Honegger; Rateliff, *History* 309, 401, 425; Shippey, *Road* 62-63). Tolkien's involvement with this poem spanned his academic career. Ronald formally studied this poem with Kenneth Sisam as part of his degree studies at Oxford, and it was part of his final examination in 1915 (Ryan 16). Tolkien gave extensive help to A.J. Bliss who acknowledged Tolkien's mentoring when Bliss published an edition of *Sir Orfeo* in 1954.

In *Smith of Wootton Major*, the tableaux of the elven mariners and the dancing elves derive from corresponding scenes in *Sir Orfeo* (Honegger 117-18, lines 289-302; *A Tolkien Miscellany* 348). Replacing Pluto/Hades with the King of Faery, the *Sir Orfeo* poet moves the Orpheus myth to Britain and resets the myth in the context of a Celtic tradition of Faerie and its Otherworld. Geoffrey Chaucer, who was writing during this same period, also exploits the poetic equivalence of Pluto and the King of Faery in "The Merchant's Tale" in *The Canterbury Tales* (*The Riverside Chaucer* lines 2225-2229, 2038-2041). The *Orfeo* poet stresses Orfeo's suffering in the wilderness as he has left behind all traces of normal life to share in the suffering of his wife (Honegger 122). The Magical face of Faery in *Smith of Wootton Major* corresponds to the enchanted Celtic Otherworld—the land of the dead or those on the point of death.[48]

In the brief scene of meeting with the elven mariners, Smith is frightened, but protected by his star. The mariners are not one of "evils" of Faery. If *Smith of Wootton Major* represents a retrospective summary of Tolkien's life and writing, only the elven mariners present a warlike theme. Although Tolkien endured the "animal horror" of the Western Front's trench warfare and saw the effects of war on many, this appears as a passing terror (*Letters* 72). The lack of military conflict in *Smith of Wootton Major* is a departure from previous writings in the legendarium, *The Hobbit*, and *The Lord of the Rings* (Pepetone 144). The main result of this experience seems to be to turn Smith's wanderings away from the sea to the mountains.

The next tableau from Smith's journeys in Faery is the late addition of the Lake of Tears scene (*SWM* 74). Flieger writes that the Lake of Tears is the third face of Faery, one of the scorn and pity toward Smith as he is "unwary and overbold" and suffers the "pitfalls and dungeons" reserved for such in Faery (OFS 109, *GS* 71). Flieger does not discuss Smith's seeming defiance of the resulting prohibition from the birch, "Go away and never return!" in light of Tolkien's previous respect for this type of limit (OFS 129, 152; *TOFS* 229). Flieger states, the "encounter with the birch and the wind are the most powerful experience in Faery and is far and away the most compelling, most daunting scene in the story" and the "most direct and most forbidding of his adventures in Faery" (*QT* 241). "The scene both invites and defeats attempts to interpret it, for no interpretation can match the power of the scene itself." "It demands attention but it defies exegesis" which would contribute "little or nothing to the value of the scene, whose impact is all the more powerful for being inexplicable" (*QT* 245).

Perhaps this scene of the Lake of Tears could be seen as one that Tolkien needed to add because he wrote: "There cannot be any 'story' without a fall—all stories are ultimately about the fall—at least not for human minds as we know them and have them" (*Letters* 147). This would include: the fall of Melkor and his host, "a fall of Angels" (Letters 147); the fall of the Elves in the war for the Silmarils, led by Fëanor who is consumed by his need to possess the Silmarils to the point of instigating the Kinslaying; and the Downfall of Númenor. Frodo, claiming the Ring in the heart of Orodruin, succumbs to temptation, is maimed by Gollum, and literally falls to his knees. In the episode at the Lake of Tears, Smith also enacts the fall.

Smith is surprised to find the Lake of Tears is not filled with the expected fluid water, but rather the lake's surface is hard and "sleeker than glass" (*SWM* 25). A lake of glass recalls the "sea of green glass" that was "clear and transparent" in the Celtic *Imram Maelduin* (or Mailduin) (Colum 41). The lake of glass also resembles the "sea of glass, like crystal" when the heavens are revealed at the end of time (Rev 4:5). Smith falls on this slippery surface and reveals himself to be a truly fallen man in the Otherworld of Faery. In Tolkien's Christian context, Fallen Man is an exile (*Letters* 48, 51, 194).

The lake is also remarkable because light like "a red sunset" "came up from the lake" (*SWM* 24). In the lake are "strange shapes of flame" and "fiery creatures" (*SWM* 24-25). The fire of the lake recalls the fate of Tolkien's fallen characters, whose desire for the possession of precious objects consumes them. Fëanor, who "laughed as one who was fey," set fire to the white ships of the Teleri, which were "as the gems of the Noldor: the work of our hearts, whose like we shall not make again" (*S* 101, 97). The laughing and "fey" Fëanor attacks the host of Morgoth, is "wrapped in fire and wounded," and was then "consumed by the flame of his own wrath" (*S* 124-25). When he dies, "so fiery was his spirit that as it sped his body fell to ash, and was borne away like smoke" (*S* 125). This image recalls Saruman's spirit rising "like smoke from a fire," though he left a shriveled body (*RK* VI xviii 997). Fëanor's refusal, "This thing I will not do of free will," (*S* 87) is echoed by Frodo, who having become possessed by the Ring: "I will not do this deed" (*RK* VI iii 924). The "broken" Frodo falls to his knees at the edge of the Crack of Doom, but it is Gollum, consumed by his desire for the Ring, who falls into the fire with the Ring (*RK* VI iii 925).

A fiery death awaits those who lust after precious objects and the power they confer. When Maedhros finally obtains a Silmaril, it burns his hand and he throws himself "into a gaping chasm filled with fire" (*S* 314). Maglor, too, is burned by a Silmaril, which he casts into the Sea. In *The Lord of the Rings*, Denethor, clinging to the power, pride, and the honor of the past, symbolized in the palantír, is immolated on his pyre (*RK* V vii 836). In contrast, Beren, who loves Lúthien and not the jewel, can hold up the Silmaril, as a "shining lamp" (*S* 219-20), while its fire consumes the wolf, Carcharoth, an agent of the covetous Morgoth. Thingol also is not burned by the Silmaril. This may be because originally Thingol's demand for a Silmaril is only a way of getting rid of Beren, and the treasure the two both wanted is Lúthien. However, Thingol's obsession with the jewel grows with time.

Smith, protected by the star of Faery and by the fact that he has not yet become attached to or possessive of any precious object, does not fall into the chasm, the abyss, and the Faërian hellfire. Instead, the wild wind of Faery, like the mystical wind of the Bible in the primeval image of "the Spirit [or Wind] of God swept over the face of the waters" (Gen 1:2) "swept him [Smith] up" because Smith is standing on the solid surface, a face, of the lake waters (*SWM* 25). The wild wind also recalls the wind Ezekiel experiences when he becomes a prophet (Ez 1:4) or the wind of the Pentecost (Acts 2:2). The wild Wind would be a mystical force under the control of the Faery King (*SWM* 177).

The Wind attacks Smith because a fallen man does "not belong" in Faery. Like the mark of the cross made on the forehead on Ash Wednesday, Smith's star can invoke: "Remember that you are dust, and to dust you shall return" (Gen 3:19), the words spoken by God after Adam and Eve have fallen into sin by eating from the Tree of Good and Evil.[49] Smith, who is not from Middle-earth, is a fallen man due to the sin of Adam and Eve. The fall on the lake of glass is only a reminder of his status, and being fallen does not require his having done something wrong. Rather it is simply part of being human. Like the rest of humankind, Ned or Joe Smith is an exile from Eden (*SWM* 98, "Words" 51, *Letters* 110).[50]

Blown by the wild Wind, Smith clings to a birch tree whose leaves are torn away by the Wind. Flieger acknowledges the parallel between the stripping of the birch tree in *Smith of Wootton Major* and the stripping of the birch tree in Runo 44 of the *Kalevala* ("The Forests" 120-21). The birch, however, played an important role not only in Scandinavian myth, but also in Celtic folklore, which informs this scene in *Smith of Wootton Major*.

Celtic folklore presents the birch both as a symbol and as a provider of needs. Birch supplied the charcoal that gave off the greatest heat, so it was the preferred wood for smiths in Irish lore (Joyce 234). Birch was also a symbol of purity and granted protection from evil (Coitir 48). The earliest known use of Ogham writing contained a caution to Lugh that the fairies would take his wife unless "birch guarded her." In the Scottish Hebrides, birch was put over cradles, and in Wales, cradles were made from birch to protect children from fairies. At the winter solstice, when the bounds were beaten to expel evil spirits, birch twigs or brooms were used.

Beith or 'birch' was the name of the month that began with Samhain or the Celtic New Year. Samhain began at sundown on October 31st as the Celtic day began and ended at sundown (Dáithí 402). At the beginning of the Samhain, birch twigs were used to drive out the spirits of the old year as part of an important purification. Samhain was seen as a liminal time, when both men and the *Sídhe* or *Aes Sí*, the Celtic deities of pre-Christian Britain, could more easily cross the boundary between this world and the Otherworld (Koch 1557). *Sídhe* or *Aes Sí* is usually translated as the 'spirits' or 'fairies'. In Old Irish, *sídhe* means a 'blast' or 'gust' of wind (Hooker, *Tolkienotēca* 209). A *sídhe* appears sweeping the fallen Smith on the "face of the waters" so that he clings to a birch (*SWM* 25, Gen 1:2).

Consequently, when a 'blast' or 'gust' of wind or a *sídhe* in the Celtic Otherworld of Faery, attacks Smith, clinging to a birch for protection would be exactly what Smith needed to do. Although the birch in the *Kalevala* laments how people used and stripped it for various purposes, Smith's apparently Celtic birch does not complain because it is being used appropriately. Instead, it continues to try to protect Smith telling him, "Go away! The Wind [the *sídhe*] is hunting you" (*SWM* 25).

Smith ignores the birch's message to "Go away and never return!" because his desire to find the Faery Queen is "stronger" (*SWM* 25). This is what a fallen man would do because he wants the power to have his desire come true. Smith has now crossed the line and is using the star for Magic, and not Enchantment or Recovery. Smith pays for the breaking of a Faërian prohibition by gaining and then losing the thing he sought.

Smith continues searching until he eventually finds the Vale of Evermorn with its odd optical quality that things far away can be seen very clearly (*SWM* 26). Elven maidens are singing and dancing there, and Smith is "enchanted" by their movements (*SWM* 26).

Tolkien gives the reader ample clues that the maiden in the Vale of Evermorn with flowing hair is the Queen of Faery because she knows Smith's Elvish name of Starbrow and reads his mind (*SWM* 28). In *The Lord of the Rings*, the Elves converse by reading minds (*RK* VI vi 963) and Galadriel reads the minds of the surviving Fellowship in Lórien (*FR* II vii 348-49). Smith's intoxication with "the joy" of dancing with her recalls the devotion of the very unlikely Gimli, who experiences the "shock of transcendent beauty" and "the danger of light and joy" that renders all else, the rest of life, not worth living (*FR* II viii 369).

Tolkien knew the "fear of the beautiful fay that ran through the elder ages eludes our grasp" (OFS 151), and this implies that "[b]eauty itself is dangerous" (Shippey, *Road* 59). The Faery Queen is "the Queen of Faery, a great and dangerous person, however beautiful" (*SWM* 95). Like Galadriel, who has the potential of a dark side but rejected it, the Faery Queen in *SWM* seems to mock Smith with: "Have you no fear about what the Queen might say [...]? Unless you have her leave" and "Maybe we shall meet again, by the Queen's leave" (*SWM* 28). This attitude is completely different from the humble, gentle King of Faery, Alf, and his source, Fr. Francis, who is willing to submit to Time and change while he ages and serves others.

The Faery Queen toys with Smith, playing on the fact that she both knows more than Smith (i.e. both her identity and his), and that she has the power to arrange another meeting if she wishes as she does later (*SWM* 31). She could even merit Nokes's description of her as a "tricky little creature" who may or may not play fair (*SWM* 14).[51] Smith is "abashed" because he is now in a sense naked if she knows his history and that he has broken a Faërian prohibition. Previously, he made an innocent assumption of what the Faery star allowed, consistent with his repeated testing of where he could go. Her parting comment, "Maybe we shall meet again, by the Queen's leave," repeats a previous reference to "her [the Queen's] leave," meaning permission, and foreshadows the Queen's leaving (i.e. parting), when they meet again.

Her parting gift is a Magical white flower which does not wither and gives off light, like the vial of Galadriel. Her placement of the flower in Smith's hair is an intimate, almost flirtatious, gesture which Smith's wife ignores (*SWM* 28-29). The flower retains the odd visual quality of the Vale of Evermorn as it seems to be seen "from a great distance" (*SWM* 29). Perhaps this represents the enchantment of time and space in Faery (OFS 116). The Living Flower comes from the Celtic Otherworld, the land of the dead. Consequently, the light from the flower, which casts a shadow, is literally and metaphorically "the shadow of the valley of death" or of the dead of the Otherworld in the Valley of Evermorn (SWM 29). Tolkien wrote:

> it is one of the lessons of fairy-stories (if we can speak of the lessons of things that do not lecture) that on callow, lumpish, and selfish youth peril, sorrow, and the shadow of death can bestow dignity, and even sometimes wisdom (OFS 137).

Smith places the flower in a casket where it is repeatedly viewed as if it were a dead body at a wake. The casket with the *momento mori*, a warning or reminder of death, from the Faery Queen parallels Gimli's placing Galadriel's golden strands in "imperishable crystal" (*FR* II viii 367).

Tolkien gave many female characters flower names in his writings (e.g. Belladonna Took, Lobelia Sackville-Baggins, and Rose Cotton) (See *RK* Appendix F "On Translation" 1109). Belladonna Took was a character based on Mabel Tolkien (*Bio* 175). A "flower" in a casket suggests a seemingly dead woman in a casket, almost like the fairytale Snow White.

The Living Flower is saved as a "secret" and a "treasure" in a casket (*SWM* 29). Like Bilbo's hood and cloak set aside in a drawer in Bag End, it seems to be a "fraught memory object" "kept to preserve memory," but also "stored away so as 'to prevent recollection of past experience entering immediate consciousness'," warding off involuntary intrusion of emotionally charged memories (Marcoux in Loughlin 48).[52] The Living Flower recalls the Silmarils of Fëanor, "living things" (*S* 72), "guarded close, locked in the deep chambers of his [Fëanor's] hoard," seen only by Fëanor's father and his sons (*S* 74). As Smith made this casket, it is likely to be bound in iron, containing the Faërian object. At this point, Smith, the fallen man, has violated the enchantment of Faery as he used the forbidden encounter with the enchanting Faery Queen to gain possession of and hoard a souvenir, literally a memory. At this point, Smith is using the Faery star as a mechanism, like the Ring, to obtain his desire which might be characterized as having turned to lust.

When Smith enters his house with the flower shining in his hair, it casts a large shadow on the wall. Smith's son comments, "You look like a giant" (*SWM* 29).

Later, when Smith returns from his last journey when he sees the Faery Queen, the son says, "The shadow was the truth" (*SWM* 46). This statement is not a simple one. The impetus for *SWM* was George MacDonald's story, "The Golden Key". Tolkien's best memory of this story was the valley of the shadows (*SWM* 91), an offspring of the shadows of Plato's cave. In both the MacDonald story and in Plato's, shadows are misleading distortions of truth. In Middle-earth, Mordor is "the land where the shadows lie," the land of the deceiving Sauron and his lies. In Tolkien's writings, shadows deceive and are dangerous.

If the shadow represents the shadow of death from the Otherworld, recalling both the Living Flower and the Faery Queen, then the shadow can be "truth." In the Otherworld of the Dead, the Vale of Evermorn could also be the Vale of Evermourn. By violating the Faërian prohibition to capture the experience he desired, Smith has transformed something of beauty into something unnatural and even "monstrous." When we understand that Tolkien, like the Ents, pays attention to every detail, then the richness of *Smith of Wootton Major*'s imagery becomes apparent (*TT* III xi 574).

Meeting the Faery Queen

The turning point of *Smith of Wootton Major* is Smith's meeting with the undisguised Faery Queen. Smith cannot be satisfied with the gift of the Living Flower, because he "desired in [his] heart to see" the Faery Queen (*SWM* 32). Because the Faery Queen is the "fair maid of the Green Vale," we can assume this is still part of the Magical Faery of the Otherworld, the land of the dead.

Previously, in *Smith of Wootton Major*, the forest of Faery was "not dominated" by human activities and was separate from "a familiar or anthropocentric world" (*SWM* 116). Smith appeared to experience freedom in that forest. Smith actively explored Faery on his own as when he found the elven mariners, the dancing maidens, the King's Tree, and the Lake of Tears. Now Smith is "dominated" and is subject to the power of the Faery Queen, being summoned and "guided, and guarded" —the price for the granting of his wish (*SWM* 31). Contact between humans and Faerie was traditionally accidental or initiated by denizens of Faerie, that is, involuntary on the part of humans. However, Smith, like Orfeo waiting and wanting to see his beloved Queen, submits willingly, as he "desired in his heart" to see the Faery Queen for forty-eight years according to Tolkien's chronology (*SWM* 32, 104).[53]

Smith is "blindfolded by mist or by shadows" on his way (*SWM* 31). This recalls the way Wood Elves in *The Hobbit* conduct their captives to meet the ElvenKing: they place "a spell" on Thorin, blindfold the rest of the dwarves, and Mr. Baggins is as good as blindfolded because he "could not see where they were going" (*Hobbit* VIII). The Elves of Lothlórien blindfold the fellowship when they enter the heart of Lothlórien on their way to meet Galadriel and Celeborn, the lady and lord of the Galadhrim (*FR* II vi 338). Similarly, Gwendeling's (later Melian), "magics" and "spells" hid the dwellings and paths of Tinwelint (later Thingol) in Artanor, in what was later called the "girdle of Melian" (*LT2* 7, 63). Blindfolds serve the same function as the magic mist, which was one of the signs that mortals had encountered the Otherworld (Rhŷs, *Celtic Folklore* 223; Haliday 83). Like many who were "pixy-led," this suggests a potentially dangerous situation (Crossing 67).

Smith's anticipated goal, the Faery Queen, has multiple and contrasting qualities associated with her beauty. Tolkien wrote much earlier, "We find it difficult to conceive of evil and beauty together" (OFS 151). He showed the danger of and/ or the ambivalence toward a Fairy or Elven Queen's beauty in *The Lord of the Rings* when Boromir complains, "I do not feel too sure of this Elvish Lady and her purpose" (Shippey, *Road* 59; FR II vii 349). Éomer echoes these suspicions about Galadriel, saying "Few escape her nets" (*TT* III ii 422). Faramir confirms this, calling her "perilously fair" (*TT* IV v 664). When the Faery Queen in *Smith of Wootton Major* reveals herself in the midst of a "great host" with "great spears" "in her majesty and her glory," she is the "great and dangerous person, however beautiful" (*SWM* 95).

Although both the narrator of *Smith of Wootton Major* and Alf, the King of Faery (*SWM* 42), refer to the Faery Queen as "Queen," Smith refers to her as "lady of Faery" (*SWM* 33), "a Great Lady" (*SWM* 34), and "The Lady" (*SWM* 35). Smith's calling the Queen "The Lady" may be part of the careful address of powerful and dangerous fairy figures.[54] This is similar to the way the greatly dreaded Fairies or *Shídhe* [*sic*] of Ireland were called 'the good people', not because they were good, "but in order to propitiate them" (Lewis in *SWM*

190). Alternatively, perhaps it is a marker of Smith's ignorance that he calls her "lady of Faery."

Or perhaps it is a play on True Thomas, the Rhymer, who greets the beautiful lady with "All hail, thou mighty Queen of Heaven!" only to be told "I am but the queen of fair Elfland." The confusion of the Queen of Heaven and a Faery ruler can be seen in Galadriel who has several attributes associated with the Virgin Mary (Fisher, Mahler). She is called the Lady of the Galadhrim or the Lady of the Wood. "Our Lady" is a common epithet for the Virgin Mary.

In *Smith of Wootton Major*, the Faery Queen has a "white flame" burning on her head (31-32). The Queen's white flame seems to be the analogue of the Faery King's Mystical star. Like the Poets in Paradise in Tolkien's poem "Mythopoeia", who "shall have flames upon their heads," the white flame appears to be a sign or symbol of her ability to engender artistic creativity, especially with language.[55] This view of language and a female Faërian presence are also seen in Tolkien's poem "The Nameless Land". This Faërian power over language is seen when Smith first sings, "in strange words that he seemed to know by heart," when the star falls out of his mouth (*SWM* 16).

Tolkien's "Mythopoeia" places pagan myths as forerunners or incomplete foreshadowings of the true myth of Christianity, including the story of the Pentecost. The poem's theory of knowledge or epistemology follows the Platonic or Neoplatonic model which believed recovery (*anamnesis*) of a mythic truth revealed the true meaning of the perceived world (Phelpstead, "Myth-making" 84, 89). The Faery Queen appears to grant this mythic language. She becomes like a patron saint or muse of languages whose origins are in myth. Ronald Tolkien uses Owen Barfield's theory of names and language where words are mythical vehicles referring to phenomena both spiritual and physical (Phelpstead, "Myth-making" 84). In the Faërian world of the Queen, language and myth and nature are one. There "is no weariness in the eyes" (i.e. no loss of delight in the mythic world) (*MR* 316).

Perhaps the most alarming aspect of the meeting with the Faery Queen is her ability to read Smith's mind. This is how the Queen can state she has granted Smith's wish to see her, which began the day he saw the doll on the Great Cake

(*SWM* 33). Later, Smith tries to read Alf's thoughts when Smith asks Alf who will receive the star (*SWM* 40).

The Faery Queen's use of mind reading in *Smith of Wootton Major* should be set in the context of how Tolkien presents this elsewhere in his writings. The Faery Queen in *Smith of Wootton Major*, "the Queen of Faery, a great and dangerous person, however beautiful" shares this ability with Galadriel in *The Lord of the Rings* (*SWM* 95, *FR* II vii 348-49). The Elves communicate this way with each other (*RK* VI vi 963). However, in many ways, the Ring, or rather perhaps Sauron via the Ring, also appears to read minds, offering the bearer of the Ring what he/she want most: Sam's turning Mordor into a garden (*RK* VI i 880-81) and Lord Sméagol or Gollum the Great having fish every day (*TT* IV ii 619). When a Ring bearer understands the Ring/Sauron's strategy of undermining the bearer's will by fulfilling desires, the bearer's own desires (i.e. part of the interior or subjective self) can remain separate, and the Ring bearer's will can oppose the will of the Ring (Klinger, "Fallacies" 361-2). The power of mind reading is ambiguous and can be perverted depending on how it is used.

If the Faery Queen in *Smith of Wootton Major* has a dark, powerful subtext suggested in the mind reading of Sauron/the Ring/Galadriel, Tolkien is clear this is Smith's fault as he broke the Faërian prohibition and ignored the fact he was a fallen man. Tolkien implies that the Faery Queen is only fulfilling Smith's long-held wish, granting him the experience that he can treasure in his memory and so "arrest change and keep things [here the encounter with the Queen] always fresh and fair" (*Letters* 236). Smith colludes with the Elvish/Faery Queen because he is "unwilling to face change" (*Letters* 236).

The decisive moment in Smith's meeting with the Faery Queen comes when the Queen asks Smith to kneel. Because she is tall, she stoops to put her hand on his head. The tone of the writing shifts abruptly from dialogue to philosophical reflection: "a great stillness came upon him; and he seemed to be both in the World and in Faery, and also outside them and surveying them, so that he was at once in bereavement, and in ownership, and in peace" (*SWM* 33). Smith, standing in a "silent and empty" field, that seems to exteriorize his internal state, anticipates "that his way led back to bereavement" (Pepetone 152). Smith states to Alf, whom he meets shortly, "I do not think I shall ever return [to Faery]" (*SWM* 34), although he later hopes he could enter Faery to deliver the star (*SWM* 39).

In Tolkien's early draft of *Smith of Wootton Major*, Smith is at first "grieved" because he believes giving up the star means he cannot enter Faery again. However, Smith learns the star left a mark on his brow so that he could return to Faery, but he would not see new things nor visit new regions (*SWM* 165). Identifying bereavement with the loss of Faery makes sense (*QT* 225), but only in the early draft of *Smith of Wootton Major*. By the time of the "Essay," written when the story was completed, Tolkien decided Smith could return to Faery if he wanted to, but Smith could not be content with visiting only 'Outer Faery' (*SWM* 140-41). Smith, knowing he must abstain or be unprotected if he went on other journeys, stopped because he had his wife and son, as well as a grandson, to consider: "he was not free" (*SWM* 141).

The meaning of Smith's bereavement or grief is unclear. Anna Slack argues that the "true bereavement" in *Smith of Wootton Major* is the "echo of the Great Escape." Smith's knowing he "cannot keep the [Faery] star" (i.e. return to Faery), means this renunciation is equivalent to Bilbo's giving up the Ring (Slack 184). Slack's view focuses on "bereavement" as an abstract, impersonal Death. She also ignores Tolkien's explanation and his use in the story of "bereavement" only in relation to persons or relationships.

In the published version of *Smith of Wootton Major*, Tolkien identifies the loss of visiting Faery as a "deprivation," not a bereavement. This indicates that there was sorrow or sadness in this loss, but not the loneliness, despair, hopelessness, or depression often seen in grief. That is what Smith's Grandfather Rider experienced when he could not visit Faery (*SWM* 134). When Rider goes on his holiday, he is "refreshed by his visit to Faery" (*SWM* 140). In contrast, "bereavement" is a word used in relation to the loss of an important person or relationship, and this term seems best applied to Smith's loss of the Faery Queen—the person he has longed to see for years—who says farewell (*SWM* 33). Consequently, Smith's "bereavement," that is stated twice, is not the result of Smith's loss of traveling in Faery—which Smith anticipates and then chooses—but due to the loss of a person, the Faery Queen (*SWM* 140-41).

IV. Mabel Tolkien as Faery Queen and the Return of Biography

From various memories of his mother, Tolkien could construct a Faery Queen, like the one in *Smith of Wootton Major*, or like any of his characters who are described in terms befitting a Faery Queen: Meril-i-Turinqi, "the Lady of the Isle;" Galadriel, the lady of the Galadhrim; Queen Guinever in *The Fall of Arthur*; and even in the ElvenKing in *The Hobbit*. There are a number of parallels between Mabel Tolkien and Faery Queens. Mabel Tolkien called herself, and was also called by others, Mab, as in Mab, Queen of the Fairies, found in Shakespeare's *The Most Excellent and Lamentable Tragedy of Romeo and Juliet* (*Bio* 12, 29). Carpenter draws an explicit parallel between Belladonna Took and Mabel Suffield (*Bio* 175). Belladonna has a Took ancestor who is purported to have fairy blood (*Hobbit* I). Belladonna is not only the name of a flower, which literally means "beautiful lady," like Mabel Tolkien, but was also the name of the queen of the fairies in the story, "Rosanie or the Inconstant Prince," with which Tolkien was familiar (*A&I* 57).[56]

Mabel Suffield Tolkien's self-identification with this role as a Faery Queen is further highlighted by her describing the infant Ronald Tolkien as looking "such a fairy" and undressed "looks more of an elf still" (*Bio* 29, 14).[57] In a letter of July 16, 1894, Mabel wrote to her brother Roland: "*He's* (Ronald) the Fairy now-a-days, but Hilary will be the handsome one in about 15 years" (Gardner/Holford 20, emphasis in original). Victorian babies, both boys and girls, with their long curly hair were expected to be 'pretty' "to gladden their parents' eyes and hearts" (Goodman 226). In the photograph of September 1895 of the two brothers (McIlwaine 120), Ronald holds a toy elf (H. Tolkien 62, McIlwaine 120), evidence of the continued prevalence of elves/fairies in the Tolkien household.

Like Tolkien's Elves who are exiled, Tolkien, writing about his mother, believed that Englishwomen in South Africa could only be "in exile" there (*Letters* 90). In Tolkien's earliest writings in *The Book of Lost Tales*, England, the Lonely Isle, is a home for the Elves, an Elvenhome (*LT*1 15). The real-life parallel to this mythology could be Mabel Tolkien going home to England in 1895—the home of Mab of the Elves/fairies or an Elven home. Tolkien wrote in the manner of a *roman à clef* in his 1912 play, *The Bloodhound, the Chef, and the Suffragette*, (*Bio* 59) and the seminal scene of Beren's meeting Lúthien (*Letters* 420). In Tolkien's writings, "[l]egend and History have met and fused" (OFS 156).

Ronald Tolkien would have cherished happy memories of his mother. In the summer of 1904, when the Tolkien brothers were reunited with their mother in Rednal, after her hospitalization and diagnosis and their own lengthy illnesses, the reconstructed family appears to have enjoyed unexpected pleasant and enjoyable times. Tolkien appears to have maintained a reminder of this last special summer when his family was intact at Rednal with his pipe smoking. Only at Rednal did Fr. Francis smoke a pipe. Tolkien allowed, "Possibly my own later addiction to the Pipe derives from this" (*Bio* 30). Mabel Tolkien could have become idealized during a last, happy summer marked by tall trees, and her memory treasured and preserved in smoke.[58]

Mabel Tolkien's delight in the recovery of her two sons, after their serious illnesses in the spring of 1904, is quite evident in her letter of July, 1904: "Tea in Hay–Kite flying with Fr. Francis–sketching–Tree Climbing–they've never enjoyed a holiday so much" (*Bio* 29). "Tree Climbing" was important to Ronald as well as his brother Hilary (*Bio* 22). Hilary, skipping over a gap of approximately four years in his recall of important memories, wrote "we used to live a big part of the summer [in Rednal] up trees, particularly a certain sycamore" (28). Sycamores are very tall trees and can be described as having "storeys." Tolkien's memories of the happy time with his mother in the summer of 1904 would have included tall trees. Faint echoes of these tall trees may be found in the Mallorn trees associated with the Lady Galadriel (see also "Tea in Hay" in this volume).

Tolkien seems to have drawn on his memories of his mother, using bits and aspects which he elaborated and wove into *Smith of Wootton Major* and into his legendarium with his depiction of Elven Ladies. Some of these elements are inferred as there is no specific description of Mabel Tolkien beyond stating she was "beautiful." However, the number of parallels seems more than suggestive and beyond the level achieved by pure chance. Tolkien's method of writing appears to involve taking distinctive elements from various models and combining them into something new. He worked in this way when he used particular, chosen elements from the various members of the Inklings as the basis of characters in "The Notion Club Papers" (*SD* 148-49). He did this when recalling books: "I [Tolkien] found certain elements in books that I liked and stored in memory" (Byrne and Penzler 43).

The lack of detailed information on Mabel Tolkien is not surprising or likely to be accidental. Tolkien's literary executor and editor, his son, Christopher Tolkien, required Humphrey Carpenter to rewrite his original draft of the official biography. Carpenter's first draft of the biography was "unacceptable," and Carpenter then "castrated the book, cut out everything which was likely to be contentious" ("Learning about Ourselves" 270). The official biography contains substantial omissions, misleading statements, and unsubstantiated assertions that devalue the important role that Ronald Tolkien's wife, Edith Bratt, played in his life and art (Bunting/Hamill-Keays *Edith*). This means Carpenter's work was used as the basis of a "biographical legend," a "romanticized, distorted image of [Tolkien's] biography, controlled by the author [or his heirs] and used as the basis of literary criticism" (Fimi 7).

Although some of the distortions concerning Edith Bratt Tolkien have been documented, Carpenter wrote that he left out "*several* difficult issues" in the Tolkien biography ("Cover book," italics added). Carpenter's presentation of Mabel Tolkien, the other powerful woman in Tolkien's life, has a lack of detail similar to what is found in the official biography for Edith Bratt, suggesting Mabel's role has also been excised as far as possible. For example, Carpenter's presentation and explanation of the exclusion of Mabel Tolkien from her parents' home after her terminal diagnosis of diabetes in April 1904 does not make sense given the very strong cultural and moral mandates for Victorian and Edwardian families to care for dying members and the fact that her father, the Unitarian John Suffield, would not have objected to Mabel's Catholicism (see "1904: Mabel Tolkien" this volume).

Tolkien's writings contain a sequence of variations on the image of a Faery Queen. Meril-i-Turinqi, the earliest figure in this series, lives among her maidens in a ceremonial circle of tall elm trees that rise in "three lessening storeys" found in one of Tolkien's earliest stories, the February 1917 version of the "Cottage of Lost Play" (*LT*1 101). Tolkien was very fond of trees (*Bio*

22), and trees have a special significance in his stories. Like Meril-i-Turinqi, Galadriel, the Lady of the Galadhrim, lives within a great circle hedge or korin of tall golden Mallorn trees, "many-tiered" "living towers" (*FR* II vii 344). The tall Sycamores at Rednal could be described as having "storeys." Both Meril-i-Turinqi and Galadriel are descendants of Inwë and full of ancient knowledge and sources of vitality: Meril with her *limpe* drink and Galadriel with her gift of the phial of starlight and of lembas (Garth, *Great War* 228). In Tolkien's childhood, Mabel Suffield encouraged an "'almost idolatrous' love of trees, flowers, nature, classical mythology," (Grotta-Kurska 19), and could easily be seen in connection with the beauty and vitality of nature.

In *Smith of Wootton Major*, Tolkien shifts his focus from Faërian trees and elixirs to a new image. The imagery, expressing the power of the Faery Queen in *Smith of Wootton Major*, shifts to a "white flame" on the Faery Queen's head (*SWM* 32) which appears to express a mythical power to foster language. Mabel Tolkien appears to be a good model for this aspect of the Faery Queen. Tolkien wrote, "My interest in languages was derived solely from my mother" who taught German, Latin, and French to Ronald (*Letters* 377, *Bio* 22). Further, "[m]y mother obviously had philological talents" (Lee, "Tolkien" 135-36). The continuity of nature, myth, and language, found in the image of the Faery Queen with a white flame on her head, could flow from the source in Mabel Tolkien's teaching.

There are other similarities between Galadriel, the Lady of the Wood, and the Great Lady or the Faery Queen of *Smith of Wootton Major* that may derive from Mabel Tolkien. Like the Faery Queen, Galadriel is tall: "Very tall they were, and the Lady no less tall than the Lord" (*FR* II vii 345). In *Smith of Wootton Major*, the "Lady of Faery" is "taller than the points of [the host's] great spears" (31). We do not know how tall Mabel Tolkien was, and all adults tend to look tall to children as seen in the transparent presentation of the giants as the parental couple in "Jack and the Beanstalk." However, photographs of Mabel's sister, Jane Neave, show Jane to be exceptionally tall (Morton/Hayes 23). In Morton and Hayes' plate X from 1911, she appears possibly taller than Tolkien who was "5'8½" (*Letters* 373). In 1912, the average twenty-one-year-old American female was 5 feet, 3.75 inches, and this agrees with typical historic British dresses, which, in 1912, fit women 5 feet 3 to 4 inches.[59] Consequently, Jane would have loomed over most women and many men in 1911. Their father, John Suffield, was tall (*Bio* 106) so part of her beauty was her statuesque height, like that of Lady Diana Spencer, the well-remembered Princess of Wales.

Galadriel is also like Mabel Tolkien as both are mothers. They may also have been alike as Tolkien wrote that "in her youth," Galadriel was of "Amazon disposition and bound up her hair as a crown when taking part in athletic feats" (*Letters* 428). Mabel Tolkien was athletic as she played both golf and tennis (*Bio* 12). Her enthusiasm for athletics appears in her letter of July 16 1894 writing that both she and her husband have both "taken to Golf [...] *madly*" with a long description of his having a broken club cut short for her and the "jolly hazards" on the links, ending with: "We've quite deserted 'Tennis'" (Gardner/Holford 20, italics in original). It certainly would have been practical and unremarkable for Mabel to wear her hair up on her head when taking part in sports.

Both Galadriel and the Faery Queen of *Smith of Wootton Major* read minds as discussed above. Mindreading is something that preschool children between the ages of three and five often assume their parents do as is shown in a number of studies.[60] Tolkien, with his excellent memory, may have been able to recall when this seemed like an ability his mother had. This is suggested when Tolkien reports, "I was buried in the same lunatic beliefs as my children at the time," though the context is unspecified (Castell, "Talking to a Maker of Modern Myths").[61]

Tolkien was an avid reader (*Bio* 28), and a beautiful, "enchanting" character—who styled herself as Mab, queen of the fairies—like Tolkien's mother, would have immediately focused Tolkien's attention in S.R. Crockett's *The Black Douglas*. To deal with the loss of his mother, Tolkien may have turned to images found from his reading. Tolkien wrote that *The Black Douglas* "deeply impressed me in school-days [i.e. at King Edward's when he would have been nineteen years old at the most], though I have never looked at it again" (*Letters* 391). The pivotal character of this story is a Lady Sybilla, a "beautiful and queenly," charming young woman, who appears in the second chapter dressed in white on a white palfrey and "fair to look upon as an angel from heaven" (*The Black Douglas* [*BD*] 18). She introduces herself as "Queen Mab" (*BD* 23). Lady Sybilla, a victim of a family pledge of revenge on the house of Douglas (*BD* XXVI), arranges the death of the young Earl of Douglas, but the Earl and Sybilla fall in love. After his death, Sybilla is described as having "the face of an angel cast out of heaven, or perhaps, rather, of a martyr who has who has passed through the torture chamber on her way to the place of burning" (*BD* XXXVII). Her remorse fuels her embrace of Catholicism and she redeems herself by delivering the child-murderer, de Retz, to justice and death.

Tolkien's list of the memorable qualities of his mother—beauty, wit, youth, martyr, died of suffering—match to a striking degree the lady in white, the conjuror of faery, Mab or Lady Sybilla. At the age of twenty-one, nine years after his mother's death, Tolkien wrote: "My own dear mother was a martyr indeed [...] a mother who killed herself with labour and trouble to ensure us keeping the faith" (*Bio* 31). In another of Tolkien's descriptions of his mother she is: "a gifted lady of great beauty and wit, greatly stricken by God with grief and suffering, who died in youth (at 34) of a disease hastened by persecution of her faith" (*Letters* 54). A penitent Faery Queen, like Galadriel (*Letters* 407), could carry the dangerous undertones of a repentant martyr like Lady Sybilla, leaving Tolkien to focus on only the positive outcomes of his mother's bringing him to the true religion of Catholicism and to a love of languages. Mabel Tolkien is the model for Belladonna Took, who has the name of another fairy queen (*Bio* 175; Bunting, "Fairies"). The image of a powerful, beautiful, and ambivalent female figure is suggested by Belladonna Took's rumored Took ancestor, who had a wife from "a fairy family (goblin family said severer critics)" (Rateliff, *History* 29).

Loss and Exile in Faery and Tolkien's Sarehole

In *Smith of Wootton Major*, Tolkien's preoccupation with loss and bereavement centers on the Faery Queen. However, the theme of loss is pervasive in Tolkien's writings. Tolkien refused to call *Beowulf* an 'epic', a 'lay', or even 'a narrative poem', but rather an 'elegy' with "the inevitable victory of death" ("Beowulf" 31, 28). Both *The Seafarer* and *The Wanderer*, as discussed above, highlight loss. *Pearl*, a Middle English poem which Tolkien translated, features a father grieving for his dead daughter Pearl. *Sir Orfeo*, which Tolkien also translated and used as the starting point for the Faery of *Smith of Wootton Major*, retells the story of the grief-stricken king Orfeo who successfully translates his beloved wife back from the Otherworld.

Tolkien's elegiac invocation of the cycles and the decline of civilizations may also show the wide-spread influence of Oswald Spengler's *The Decline of the West* (*Der Untergang des Abendlandes* 1918, 1922) which used organic metaphors to frame the growth and decline of cultures (Potts 150). Spengler's cyclical view of civilizations asserted that the late-stage imperialistic nations' "expansive tendency is a doom, something daemonic and immense" (Spengler 28 in Potts 152).[62] In this framework, the Rohirrim are like "the youth of men" (*TT* IV v 663) and the hobbits fill Spengler's role of the humble "eternal peasants," close to the earth and fertile. They are contrasted to the people of Gondor who are a "failing people, a springless autumn" (*TT* IV v 662), "Middle Men of the Twilight" (*TT* IV v 663), with "Minas Tirith falling in ruin" (*TT* IV v 656) and depopulated (*RK* V i 736, 747). For Spengler, Faustian Western civilization leveraged its appetite for knowledge into a controlling and utilitarian machine that destroys the "concept of nature as something whole and sacred," as did Saruman, Sauron, and the Númenórean empire (Potts 165). Against this theme of doom is set the renewal of the return of the King seen in the reestablishment of the White Tree so that "Spring and Summer joined and made revel in the fields of Gondor" (*RK* VI v 942).

In *The Lord of the Rings*, Middle-earth's cultures and songs, except for the scattered fragments dispersed throughout the book, are extinct, fallen into the loss and silence—the Doom of Men (Hiley 150). The hope is that the creation of a story or a song will hold in memory the struggles and pains of the past, giving survivors meaning and perhaps preventing the repetition of history (Hiley 133), but this expectation seems to be fading. Only the siren song of the mythical time of Faery, found in *Smith of Wootton Major* and in Lothlórien and Rivendell in *The Lord of the Rings*, allows respite from time's rapacious destruction.

Smith of Wootton Major seems to present another image of loss in a Faery: a recreation of the "paradise" which Ronald Tolkien knew in childhood in Sarehole (*Bio* 23, 124-5, Ezard). In an early draft of OFS, Tolkien, writing about time and the change it brings, recalls, "I lived in childhood in a cottage at the edge of a really rural country," that is, in Sarehole (*TOFS* 282). Ronald's childhood in Sarehole created a sensitivity to the "nostalgia" found in fairy-stories "the aching desire to go home" (*TOFS* 282, underlining in original). Sarehole was the home of a secure and comfortable childhood with his mother and with the freedom of the countryside, where the Forest was "not dominated" by man (*SWM* 116). Sarehole was the time and place where Ronald began his invented languages and discovered the artistic or "sub-creative desire," which was "wedded to a passionate love of the real primary world" (*Letters* 145), presumably the delight of Sarehole countryside. Faery's mythical timelessness in *Smith of Wootton Major*, as in Lórien, was "a vision of the lost paradise and the longing to return to it" (*QT* 19). In *Smith of Wootton Major*, Smith "cannot recover the past, a lost country that now only exists in the imagination" (Flieger, "The Forests" 120). A "lost country that now only exists in the imagination" could be the long-gone Sarehole of Ronald Tolkien's childhood (*Bio* 124-25).

In *Smith of Wootton Major*, the Otherworld of Faery, the timeless land of the dead of *Sir Orfeo*, fits well with this nostalgic yearning for a mythic past. *Smith of Wootton Major*'s Faery could represent an image of Sarehole, the place and time, the "home" "before" his mother became sick with diabetes, which killed her in 1904, and "before" the demands of earning a scholarship that ended the enjoyment of linguistic games, an 'art' which "like poetry—[is] contrary to conscience, and duty; its pursuit is snatched from hours due to self-advancement" ("Secret Vice" 207). The "nostalgia" and "the aching desire to go home" were for a time and place "before" his trauma that reverberates in the dream of the Great Wave, a nightmare that expresses exile and psychological trauma, which began while Tolkien was living in Sarehole (*Bio* 23). Bereavement and the trauma of exile are intertwined.

Tolkien's vanished haven of Sarehole was full of memories of the "extremely attractive, beautiful and extremely able" Mabel Tolkien (Lee, "Tolkien" 134). Like the Elves, Tolkien seems to have "hoarded memory [...] regretted the past [... and] was unwilling to face change" (*QT* 111). This reluctance was probably particularly true of Tolkien's memories of Sarehole and of his mother. These hoarded memories of his mother could indeed entwine with "nostalgia," "the aching desire to go home."

In *Smith of Wootton Major*, like Smith hoarding a casket with a Faërian Living Flower, Ronald Tolkien could keep Mab, the Faery Queen, embalmed and unchanged in memory and in his writings. The casket is also like a martyr's reliquary, containing a precious object of the sufferer and recalling how Ronald Tolkien considered his mother a martyr who suffered for her faith. The inviting, artful enchantment of Faery, where time stands still, is perhaps best seen in Tolkien's presentation of Lórien with its timeless beauty where there is no death, decay, sickness, stain, or change (*FR* II vi 341). It is both "Eden before the Fall" and a fly in amber (*QT* 109). Lórien's perfection of beauty, engineered by Elves, is its flaw because it leads to the desire to possess and keep, to "arrest change and keep things always fresh and fair" (*Letters* 236).

In having Smith create the "secret" "treasure" of the casket of the Living Flower, Ronald Tolkien, like the exalted and admired Elves has become one of the "embalmers," who "tried to stop change and history, stop its growth." Their deep "hoarding memory" resulted in their being "overburdened with sadness and nostalgic regret" (*Letters* 197). Tolkien wrote that the Elves' attitude of clinging was a "second fall or at least 'error' of the Elves," resulting in their becoming "obsessed with 'fading'" or the changes of time (*Letters* 151).

The Nightmare of the Ineluctable Wave

Ronald Tolkien's intertwined losses of his mother and the "paradise" of Sarehole are embedded in a feeling of bereavement and being torn from the past. This is the experience of a person exiled from their familiar routines and comforts of home. The exile is now a "stranger in a strange land," vulnerable and afraid, a pilgrim in an alien land seeking a home. Exile is traumatic and is a metaphor for psychological trauma. Trauma leads to feelings of estrangement from one's self (e.g. "I have lost myself") and isolation from others (e.g. "shuttered" houses and talks only to himself) (Brothers 45).

By the age of eight in Sarehole, Ronald Tolkien began to have a repetitive dream, a recurrent nightmare, of being overwhelmed by a "Great Wave," which he called his Atlantis dream (*Bio* 23).[63] A terrifying repetitive dream, especially in children, is not likely to be the usual combination of fantasy/wish/defense, but rather are likely to be the result of traumatic real-life event(s) (Terr 209-10).

This "dream" was a nightmare. The Great Wave brings the annihilation of Ronald's familiar green world. The Great Wave is overwhelming—"towering up," "stupendous and ineluctable"—and Ronald Tolkien is helpless because it seems to come without warning from a "quiet sea," (*Letters* 213, 361, 347). Ronald survives "gasping out of deep water," as an exile from his obliterated past (*Letters* 347). The Great Wave appears to be a metaphor for Ronald Tolkien's psychological trauma.

Several traumatic events in young Ronald Tolkien's life could be described as "ineluctable" and might have fed this nightmare of the Great Wave. First, Mabel Tolkien disapproved of young Ronald Tolkien's invented languages as "a useless frivolity taking up time that could be better spent in studying" for his November 1899 entrance examination for King Edward VI High School at the age of seven (Grotta-Kurska 18, Plimmer/Plimmer). Ronald passed the examination on his second attempt in June 1900, but the price of his initial failure was his mother's displeasure and "after repeated remonstrances" his mother's insistence he destroy his first notebook containing his earliest attempts at inventing languages (Grotta-Kurska 18). Tolkien's gratification in an esthetically pleasing invented language may be like "the thirst that is in every child of Men for the flawless loveliness they seek" (*LT*2 327). Like Fëanor, young Tolkien, faced with the loss of his invented language, might have felt that he lacked now a "joyous heart without which works of loveliness and magic cannot be" (*LT*1 165) and that "never again shall I make their like" (*S* 87).

Another personal near-tragedy, Hilary's near-drowning in a local millpond, during the time the family was living in Sarehole, probably contributed the image of awakening "gasping out of deep water" (*Letters* 347). Carpenter's biography reports the pool was a hazard: "At the foot of the pool the dark water suddenly plunged over the sluice to the great wheel below: a dangerous and exciting place" (20).

Tolkien may have experienced yet another loss and unspoken grief while living in Sarehole. William Ready reports Tolkien wrote the

> Niggle story, he says, because of a relationship that grew between him and a tree, the branches and foliage of which he could see from his bed when he was young, living in Sarehole. When the tree was cut down, nobody remembered

> it, it seemed to Tolkien, save himself, so the story is in memory of the long-gone tree. That is all he has to say about the story (141).

The writing of *Leaf by Niggle*—from about 1938 or approximately thirty-four years after the death of the Sarehole willow—in memory of this tree, points to a serious ungrieved loss from Tolkien's time in Sarehole.[64]

According to Tolkien, the time in Sarehole was "the longest seeming and most formative part of my life" (*Bio* 24), and it coincided with Ronald Tolkien's "'nursery' days, and [...] the years, few but long-seeming, between learning to read and going to school. In that (I nearly wrote 'happy' or 'golden', it was really a sad and troublous) time" (OFS 135).[65] No explanation has ever been given for why Tolkien would consider this time in a seeming paradise "sad and troublous."

The omitted context and facts of Hilary's near-drowning, the slaughter of the willow, and Mabel Tolkien's iron-willed discipline that led to the destruction of Tolkien's first invented languages could be factors underlying the traumatic dream of the Great Wave which he survived as an exile from his own earlier life.

Tolkien's desolation and despair over the annihilation of his invented languages, sacrificed to his future success at school; a death of a tree; and his brother's near-drowning can be understood only by comprehending the larger context of Tolkien's early life. The nightmare of the Great Wave seems to be a witness to the impact of these experiences. Ronald Tolkien would now seem to be in the position of Gollum: "Poor, poor Sméagol, he went away long ago. They took his Precious, and he's lost now" (*TT* IV i 602). Gergely Nagy writes that Gollum is marginal, meaning without power, and that "he demonstrates what happens to the subject when it cannot exert any control over the forces and processes that determine it, when it cannot partake in interpretation" (59).

This would have been true of young Ronald Tolkien. Stripped of his "precious" invented languages that were uniquely part of his identity, Ronald Tolkien could have felt that only the demands of school and success "had meaning and all other subjects are erased in their subjection" (Nagy 63). Power "means *physical* power over subjects" (Nagy 64, italics in original), and this would be true of the public school whippings at King Edward's and probable discipline at home from his mother who had been a governess.[66] The temptation is to lose oneself, to give in to "a desire to *submit*," (Chance, *The Mythology of Power* 23 in Nagy 67, italics in original) to authority, seduced by the power authority wields and wanting to share in it or at least survive in subjection, complying, performing as the powers choose, and thereby betraying the self and its feelings of aliveness (Gruen 28).

"In an adult-made world, the child is treated as an intruder, an alien, who has to conform to the external requirements of his socializers, instead of the internal requirements of his own system of values" (Gruen vii). The powerless child "comes to feel toward adults much as the inhabitants of an occupied country feel toward the occupiers" (Gruen viii). The image of an alien or a survivor in an occupied land is already kin to, or close to, imagery of the exile or refugee, both metaphors seeking to express and encompass a range of emotional experiences. Adaptation to the demands of parents and society, meaning obedience and submission to those with power and control, leads the child to reject his/her own feelings and experiences—the foundation of an autonomous self—because these feelings put him/her in conflict with the success demanded by authority (Gruen 1). The ignoring of one's own needs and motives leads to a state of "emptiness" with accompanying feelings of helplessness, dismay, and rage that can change to apathy and depression (Gruen 6). "Smeagol [*sic*, no accent] is the desperation within us, the lack of an imagined self—as opposed to the threat from without" (Evans 163). Consequently, there would be a need to reconstruct the "lost" subject, the "damaged good in the corrupt" (*Letters* 329) after such an experience.

Layered on top of the psychological trauma represented by the nightmare of the Great Wave, after his mother's death in November 1904, Ronald Tolkien began to suffer "a terrible chaos which darkened my youth and early manhood" (McIlwaine 170, *Bio* 31).

It appears that the unnamed perils of Faery are psychological pain and turmoil left in the rubble of loss and trauma, seen in the nightmare of the Great Wave and a "terrible chaos." Loss and trauma, like exile, make hope painful or intolerable due to uncertainty (Brothers 46). This kind of complicated loss is likely to create a longing and clinging to a predictable, if imaginary, certainty of a cherished past that enshrines a happy paradise—a Faery—and a yearning for a carefully imagined relationship with the beautiful, witty Faery Queen, a Mab, whose insignia are a white flame of philology and languages and a white flower. White is the color of Faery and the Celtic Otherworld of the dead, an omen of bereavement.

V. Bereavement in *Smith of Wootton Major*

Tolkien's description of Smith's encounter with the undisguised Faery Queen as being "at once in bereavement, and in ownership, and in peace" (*SWM* 33) leaves the reader with an enigma. The climactic phrase requires an examination of each of its elements to elucidate Tolkien's possible intentions.

"In bereavement" could be read as deriving from the complicated losses that Ronald Tolkien experienced that occurred with his mother's death, as discussed below in detail. Bereavement is a survivor's initial sense of loss and exile from the companionship of the dear departed.

The word "ownership" here cannot refer to mere physical possession, as in 'having ownership', because "possessiveness" became a "major sin" in Tolkien's writings, beginning in *The Silmarillion* with Fëanor's possessiveness of the Silmarils (*C&G* 2.1007-09). Tolkien notes that in a sub-creator, "[b]oth these [possessiveness and rebellion against mortality] (alone or together) will lead to the desire for Power, for making the will more quickly effective" (*Letters* 145). Rather, 'ownership' would seem to express a mental state in the sense of 'belonging' or being in relationship with the beloved other or possibly the ownership of the feelings of grief, a mental state, just as "in bereavement" and "in peace" are mental states. If Tolkien had meant to convey a sense of physical ownership, he could have used the phrase "having ownership," instead of "in ownership."

Peace could follow from this sense of owning the grieving process and belonging in a continuing relationship in memory, despite the physical absence of the loved one. As discussed below, Smith's remaining in exile from Faery in Wootton Major suggests that there are other feelings that he has, in fact, not yet owned.

Pepetone takes the view that peace comes to Smith from this process of bereavement and owning. Hearing the story of his father's last journey to Faery and of his parting with the Faery Queen and the star, Ned states the "shadow was the truth" (*SWM* 46). Smith is now in the "Evening" of his earthly stay and the "shadow of the valley of death" is now a "shadow of his own approaching death" (Pepetone 154). However, by "faithfully, courageously, and sometimes recklessly following his guiding star, namely his spiritual and aesthetic gifts, deep into the *terra incognita* of the Perilous Realm" and by his willing abnegation of the star, Smith has acquired an authenticity that elicits respect in his family, community (except for Nokes), and Faery (Pepetone 153-54). This is a very positive and straightforward view of Smith's bereavement.

The word 'bereavement' can be paradoxical. In Tolkien's "Essay" of February 1965 on the completed *Smith of Wootton Major*, the loss of visiting Faery is a "deprivation," not a bereavement (*SWM* 134). Deprivation can refer to the loss of things we are accustomed to so that one is left with feelings of sadness or sorrow. In contrast, Tolkien uses "bereavement" in relation to the loss of an important person or relationship. Tolkien's *Smith of Wootton Major* occurs in the Otherworld, a land of the dead, where Smith has been seeking a beautiful woman, the Faery Queen. This plot parallels the central quest of *Sir Orfeo*, Orfeo's search to rescue and reclaim his wife, the Queen, who has been abducted by the Faery King/Pluto. Orfeo, and analogously Ronald Tolkien with his mother, is literally bereaved of his Queen because 'bereaved' comes from the Old Germanic *beroven* meaning 'to steal, take away'. In the poem, Orfeo strikingly goes into the wasteland because he cannot enjoy his life while his beloved Queen suffers in captivity. He may also have some hope of being reunited with her. Like Orfeo, Smith, has been waiting and seeking what he "desired in his heart," the Faery Queen.

Smith's reunion follows the lines of the original legend of Orpheus, in which the reunion is only temporary, and not the happy ending of *Sir Orfeo*. When viewed through the lens of Tolkien's biography, the important figure, whose loss would cause the "bereavement" Smith/Tolkien experiences when the Faery Queen says "farewell," would be Tolkien's mother. Smith's being "in bereavement" and knowing "his way now led back to bereavement" (*SWM* 33) point to the loss of the relationship in the everyday world outside of Faery, in the world of time and change.

Time

Tolkien's statement in *Smith of Wootton Major* that Smith "seemed to be both in the World and in Faery, and also outside them [...] in bereavement, and in ownership, and in peace" recalls his comment about Jacob and Wilhelm Grimm's "The Juniper Tree:"

> Such stories have now a mythical or total (unanalysable) effect [...] they open a door on Other Time, and if we pass through, though only for a moment, we stand outside our own time, outside Time itself, maybe (OFS 128-29).

For Tolkien, "the distance and a great abyss of time" was what "linger[ed] in the memory" more than the beauty and horror of "The Juniper Tree," the story of the murder of a child and its consequences (OFS 128). A journey to Other Time or Faërie is an escape from time, the linear clock time of past, present, and future; the accidents of history; and death (134 Hiley).

In the Celtic Otherworld of *Smith of Wootton Major*, the Faery Queen raises the issue of time by saying: "The time has come." This statement does not necessarily apply to the next sentence—"Let him choose"—which seems to refer to the fate of the Faery star, either giving it up or not or picking a successor or not (*SWM* 33).[67] Flieger notes that "The time has come" stood alone without "let him choose" until late in the writing of the story suggesting "the message came to be as much for the author of the story as for its hero" (*QT* 236). "The time has come" could also apply to the farewell of parting forever, the probable cause of Smith's bereavement.

Tolkien's phrase, "The time has come," is likely to draw on antecedents that illuminate the meaning of this phrase in *Smith of Wootton Major*. This expression appears in several important places in the Knox translation of the Catholic Bible: "And Jesus answered them thus. The time has come now for the Son of Man to achieve his glory" (John 12:23) and "Jesus answered her [...] My time has not come yet" (John 2:4).[68] The New Testament section of the Knox Bible was published in 1945. In a New Testament context, "The time has come" refers to Christ's time of suffering and spiritual salvation, his choice to submit to his torture and crucifixion in order to save the souls of many. This foreordained time and event finally arrives in the New Testament. In the New Testament, this appointed or right, critical, or opportune moment is expressed in Greek with the word *kairos* (κάιρός) as opposed to the other Greek word for time, *chronos* (χρόνος) which refers to chronological, sequential, or quantitative time; for example, a day or an hour. The Faery Queen's echo of this phrase suggests both her foreknowledge in Faërian time of an expected event, and the suffering of bereavement Smith will undergo (*SWM* 107, 108).

Tolkien did wrestle with Time and its relation to Faery as seen in his use of the work of J.W. Dunne, a military officer and engineer, who wrote *An Experiment with Time* (*QT* 39). By keeping a record of his own dreams, and later those of friends, Dunne noticed how elements in dreams appear in real life, sometimes days, weeks, or years later (*QT* 40). In Dunne's view of dreams, the observation of a particular time or dream entails standing outside of that time at a second observation point, that is, one could be said to be outside of Time. Flieger asserts that Tolkien used Dunne's diagrams of Field of Time 1 or 2 in his efforts to resolve the flow of time in Lórien (figure 3 *QT* 105 and figure 4 *QT* 106).

The name 'Lothlórien' comes partly from *lórien* meaning 'dream', so it would be an attractive place for Tolkien to try out Dunne's scheme based on dreams and time. In Lórien, one "stepped over a bridge of time into a corner of the Elder Days [...] a world that was no more" (*FR* II vi 340). In the Naith at Cerin Amroth, Frodo is "lost in wonder" as it seemed he "looked on a vanished world." Sam thinks he is "inside a song if you take my meaning," presumably a song that recorded the history of the Elder Days (*FR* II vii 342).

> In winter here no heart could mourn for summer or spring. No blemish or sickness or deformity could be seen in anything that grew upon the earth. On the land of Lórien there was no stain (*FR* II vi 341).

The mythical timeless world has "no stain." The Nimrodel, the boundary of Lórien, brings "sleep and forgetfulness of grief" as it washes away "the stain of travel and all weariness" that are part of the accidents of history and continually changing linear time (*FR* II vi 330). In the same vein, Gandalf sings in Théoden's hall: "Unmarred, unstained is leaf and land/ In Dwimordene, in Lórien/ More fair than thoughts of Mortal Men" (*TT* III vi 503). Like the Earthly Paradise found in *Pearl*, in Lórien, grief for Gandalf is forgotten and beauty mesmerizes (Shippey, *Author* 197-99, see also Green's *Elf Queens and Holy Friars*). The stain of grief is what Smith is facing in his bereavement.

To "stand outside our own time" "represents a desire to escape from it [time] and its burdens" (Hiley 133). In the modern view, time, history, and Myth are seen as artificial constructs (Hiley 109), even though Myth can be seen as embodying truth and timelessness (Hiley 107). In Tolkien's world, myth is paradoxically history: *The Silmarillion* is both a history of the First Age and a mythology (Hiley 114). In *The Lord of the Rings*, characters like Elrond and the High Elves, Galadriel, Saruman and Gandalf, the Ents, and the balrog are all survivors of the First Age and are historical figures. Myth and history are not only conflated in Tolkien's writings on Middle-earth, but since Middle-earth is our real world (*Letters* 220), and not purely imaginary (*Letters* 298), Tolkien has created a cosmic model for our mythology and world (Hiley 115). Tolkien's claim in the Prologue "Concerning Hobbits," that "Even in the *ancient days* they were as a rule, shy of 'the Big Folk'; as they call *us*, and *now* they avoid *us* with dismay" (*FR* 1 italics added), implies that characters and happenings in *The Lord of the Rings* are "actually real in the primary world [... so that] in the primary world, too, myth and history converge" (Hiley 116). The desire to overcome *Indifferenz der Zeit* [the indifference of time] guides both Myth and history (Blumenberg in Hiley 109) creating a possible escape from grief and loss.

What Hiley would call the mythical time of Faery allows the reader (and Tolkien) to escape the primary world and its familiar linear time. In the dreamlike, "timeless land" of Lórien "that did not fade or change or fall into forgetfulness," Frodo "walked and breathed" and believed that when he "had gone and passed into the outer world," he "would walk there" again (*FR* II vi 342). In other words, time encompasses not only the present, but also the future. On Cerin Amroth, Frodo hears the sea on beaches that no longer exist because they have "long ago been washed away" as well as sea-birds, "whose race had perished from the earth" (*FR* II vi 342). Both Time and Place seem to warp as Frodo experiences the past of a place that no longer exists. Frodo perceives Aragorn "wrapped in some fair memory" and "Frodo knew he beheld things as they once had been in the same place," meaning Frodo perceives Aragorn in the present and also Aragorn's memory of a time in the past (*FR* II vi 343). The chapter's last line has Aragorn leaving Cerin Amroth in the present and with an ambiguous promise of a possible future return with the phrase: "came there never again as living man" (*FR* II vi 343).

Hiley's reading of mythical time in Tolkien's writings is somewhat different from Flieger's. Flieger sees Tolkien as exploring the relationship between exterior or real-world time (i.e. primary world) and "interior, illimitable time and space of the imagining, remembering, dreaming mind" without resolution (*QT* 19). For Flieger, neither the conceptualization of mythical timelessness, as in Lórien, nor "The Lost Road" metaphor of Time as a road "between the worlds of past and present, of everyday and Faerie, of waking and dream," seem to be a satisfactory solution to Tolkien's problem: "a vision of the lost paradise and the longing to return to it" (*QT* 19).

The world of Faery and the Faery Queen in *Smith of Wootton Major* present the magical face of Faery which is timeless, allowing the possibility of eluding or forgetting loss and bereavement. Faery seemingly allows time to bend or blur the distinctions between the past and the future. In a mythical, timeless world, the exiled wanderer can avoid the "before" and "after" of psychological trauma. Mythical time is colored by the vision of a paradisiacal "before," namely before the catastrophe. In such an interpretation, a person would then no longer experience the alienation from their environment and their self that the trauma engendered.

Abnegation

Following this encounter with the Faery Queen, Smith meets Alf who tells Smith the star has only been lent and "Time is pressing" (*SWM* 38). Smith's immediate, unquestioning acceptance of this news shows Smith's complete trust in Alf. Alf then reveals that the star connects Smith with his Grandfather Rider, who left when Smith was two. Smith then decides to give up the star, which he recalls with gratitude (*SWM* 39).[69] When Smith takes off the star, which "came away readily," he "felt a stab of pain, and tears ran down his face" (*SWM* 41). This pain could be emotional, and not only physical.

After relinquishing the star, Smith leaves and sees the "Even-star [...] shining in a luminous sky close to the Moon" from the threshold of the Hall (*SWM* 41). The reader should recall that the Evening Star is Venus, which is also the Morning Star. The Morning Star, a sign of hope, heralding the coming of the Son/Sun is a title of the Virgin Mary. "Consolatrix Afflictorum" (Comforter of the Afflicted) or "Stella Vespertina" (Evening Star) was the title of Tolkien's poem written in September 1916 in France during the extended engagement of the Battle of the Somme. The Virgin's protection and her association with the Morning and Evening stars were personal for Tolkien. The Evening Star rises in the west and would be consonant with Tolkien's valorization of the West and its association with elves and Alf, the Elven King.

While Smith is looking at "the beauty" of the Even-star and the Moon, Alf touches Smith's shoulder and lets Smith know that he can tell him who will receive the star. Smith, to his surprise, is allowed to choose. Then, under the influence of the Even-star, a sign of the Blessed Virgin Mary, Smith realizes Alf is the Mystical King of Faery, a type of Christ (*SWM* 42).[70] Alf, the Faery King of the Mystical or perhaps mythical face of Faery, in contrast to Magical Faery and its Queen, has allowed himself to age and change in the linear Time of the real world. Alf's benediction, "Go home now in peace," fits easily with the last phrase of the Catholic Mass: "The Mass is ended, go in peace," as would be appropriate for a priest, which seems to be the role of the Master Cook in this story.[71]

Tolkien presents the Mystical King as willing to accept the "wish" of the Queen of the Magical face of Faery that Smith may choose his successor. That agreement does not necessarily mean that she controls or commands the King. Tolkien arranges for Smith's free choice to coincide with the seemingly preordained "fate" that the King of Faery has chosen (*SWM* 42). This free concordance of wills forms a *voluntas communis*, a sharing in the will of God or finding a common will (Sternberg 312).

When Smith/Tolkien then surrenders the Faery star, Smith's experience of timelessness stops, the past becomes unchangeable, and only a reminder of the Faery Queen, The Living Flower, remains as a consolation. Since Faery has three faces, Smith appears to be renouncing the Magical face towards Nature (OFS 125), the Otherworld with access to a timeless past and the dead. The lament of "the ineluctable ending and passing back into oblivion of the fortunate, the full-lives, the unblemished and the beautiful," which kept Tolkien's mother present, may be released in "bereavement" in his writings in *The Lord of the Rings*, and yield some peace.[72]

The giving up of the star is an example of *abnegation* which presents "[t]he greatest examples of the action of the spirit and of reason" (*Letters* 246, italics in original).[73] The peace, resulting from the passing on of the star of Faery, "includes sacrifice, and the handing on, with trust and without keeping a hand on things, of power and vision to the next generation," as well as the understanding that "the visions of imagination are not enough; they are only pictures and intimations" (*SWM* 106). Wisdom, "though enriched by imagination," knows death leaves behind both Men and [Magical] Faery. Like the challenge Bilbo faced when letting go of the magic Ring in *The Lord of the Rings* with its perfection of power, Smith yields the star of Faery—briefly a ring in the first draft (*SWM* 153f., 161)—a passport to a timeless world. Smith releases control so that he is left in a world where things die, decay, fade, and are lost to time in the real world of limitations. Though Smith no longer visits Magical Faery, he can hand on to his son Ned and others his knowledge of Faery through the artistry of his craft work. Ned is an 'outsider, 'stranger,' or 'foreigner' to Faery as indicated by his name.

Returning home, Smith meets his son Ned. Smith feels "weariness"—as if he had walked "All the way from Daybreak to Evening"—and "bereavement" (*SWM* 43). Tolkien writes Smith needs to help his son Ned set up his business (*SWM* 141), but the relationship with a grandson is also important.

Smith's Grandfather Rider left when Smith was two, as Rider "felt free" because his daughter was married (*SWM* 140). In contrast, Smith will use his final souvenir of Faery, a silver flower with three flower bells on a stem, to connect with his two-year-old grandson, Tomling (*SWM* 44). Thinking about his grandson, Smith becomes mindful of the passage of time—"the counting of days […] and of weeks, and of months, and of years"—which is irrelevant for his grandson, but marks Smith's life now, and even more so without the escape of timeless Faery.

Smith's silver flower resembles a harebell or a bluebell, and folklore said the ringing of the harebells or bluebells summons the fairy folk to their gatherings. Folk songs recall how coral bells and lilies of the valley ring when the fairies sing. Calling the fairies goes back to Tolkien's poem, "The Lonely Harebell", dating from November 1916 when he was in the hospital in Birmingham with trench fever (*C&G* 1.103). Tolkien's separations from his fiancée Edith, who ultimately became his wife, appear to have precipitated his creation of "The Lonely Harebell". Ronald Tolkien seems to have invoked a hopeful future with the harebells summoning the "holy fairies and the immortal elves" of Kortirion/ Warwick upon his reunion with Edith when Ronald returned from the front lines on the Western Front in World War I in France (Bunting/Hamill-Keays, *Edith* 163).

Tolkien never states where this artifact of silver bells comes from. Smith has just seen the Faery Queen, but he has also been with Alf, the Faery King. However, this time, instead of a Living Flower, the gift is a fabrication, a simulacrum of nature. Echoing Nokes, Smith calls it "a trinket" (*SWM* 44). Recall 'trinket' has an obsolete meaning: "decorations of worship, and to the religious rites, beliefs etc., which the speaker thinks vain or trivial" (Long, "*Smith*" 104). The power of the bells to make the candles flicker when they are rung (*SWM* 44) suggests a faint copy or shadow of the powerful Mystical wild Wind, the 'blast' or 'gust' of wind or a *sídhe* of the Celtic Otherworld of Faery. This may be why Smith calls the bells a "trinket": not only because it will indeed be a toy for his grandson, but also because they too are from the Faery King and express his power, just as the Faery star was and did. Smith's willingness to give the silver bells to his grandson suggests that these silver flowers are not charged with the emotional significance that a gift from the Faery Queen would have had.

The silver bells, not by their music, but by their fragrance, remind Ned "of something I've forgotten" (*SWM* 44).[74] The music of the bells recalls the music of birdsong at sunrise on the morning of Smith's tenth birthday when he first found the Faery star (*SWM* 16). If the Faery bells, like the doll with the wand on top of the cake, are just an image of Faery, then the silver bells again supply "[f]or some the only glimpse. For some the awakening" (*SWM* 32). This would be true for Ned, whom Tolkien states is an exemplar of a type, one of "the practical and plain normal men and workers whose enlightenment and vivification was one of the objects" of the Faery King (*SWM* 141).

Smith requests that his nephew, Tim, receive the star associated with creativity and Faery (*SWM* 42). Smith's choice recalls the way Bilbo picks Frodo, a distant relative, to be his heir in *The Hobbit*. Tim is not a blood relation to

Smith, although Tim's mother is a sister to Smith's wife, Nell. Tim is Nokes's great-grandson, but Smith can state he has "kinship" with Tim. Kinship can denote not only a blood relationship, but also one of affinity, sympathy, or rapport. Tolkien writes that Elves and Men have a "kinship" (*SWM* 129, 130). The name 'Tim' is also linguistically an appropriate choice. *Tim* is found in the "Gnomish Lexicon" meaning 'spark', 'gleam', and 'star' (70). A star is the sign of the Elves of Faery. In "Suggestions for the ending of the story," Tolkien is still debating if the recipient of the star should be named (*SWM* 110). Only in a late draft did Tolkien include the name Tim.

Smith's attitude toward the star's recipient is quite different from his son's. Ned says he hopes the star "may go to someone worthy" and the "child should be grateful" (*SWM* 46). Smith replies, "The child won't know" (*SWM* 46), perhaps recalling how he did not know. Previously, Smith called his great-nephew, Tim, "not an obvious choice," and later at the Twenty-four Feast Smith remarks, "any one of them [the children] seemed fit to find the star" (*SWM* 42, 53). Like Smith, who was kind to the disappointed Nell and gave her the coin he found in his slice (*SWM* 15), Tim is kind and asks for only "a small slice," foregoing any greed for sweets or for possible treasures (*SWM* 53). Smith can only wonder where "the star will lead" Tim and how Nokes's implied disapproval of this shocking artistic bent will unfold (*SWM* 54).

VI. Resolution in *Smith of Wootton Major* and Tolkien's Biography

In 1964 when Tolkien began writing *Smith of Wootton Major*, it had been sixty years since his mother's death. This anniversary dating suggests Tolkien was looking back, trying to create a new narrative of the past and his experience with his mother, Mab, the Faery Queen. Freud called this kind of reflection, *Nachträglichkeit* ('afterwardness' sometimes translated as 'deferred action'), a reinterpretation or a revised, belated understanding of an earlier event in light of later experience. Looking back in his seventies from the vantage of having raised children and having had a successful career, Ronald Tolkien emphasizes his mother's good intentions for his future success at King Edward's School because he must comply and become a respectable cog in the great iron machine of late nineteenth-century prosperous, bourgeois, Birmingham capitalism. Her gift of Catholicism also might compensate and outweigh any pain caused by any past behavior, especially once the disease of diabetes began to take its toll.

Ronald Tolkien appears to have used earlier anniversaries of his mother's death to reconsider and understand his mother and her impact on his life. In January 1914, he painted the watercolor *Eeriness*, almost ten years after his mother's death and the hypothesized trauma of 1904. This painting seems to intimate Mabel Tolkien's need for salvation, as indicated by a praying guardian angel behind her and the three trees of Calvary. In May 1924, Tolkien wrote the poem "The Nameless Land" on the twentieth anniversary after the hypothesized traumatic events of 1904 (Bunting "1904" 64-66, 76-78). In the mid-1930s, Tolkien wrote "The New Lay of Gudrún" or "*Guðrúnarkviða en nýja*", along with "The New Lay of the Völsungs", an "untold tale" that might be the result of a thirty-year anniversary. Tolkien completed a polished manuscript for which there would have been an eager audience among the Inklings, but he destroyed the drafts, did not refer to it as he did much of his unpublished work, and put away the idiosyncratic version of a legendary and heathen queen who kills her two sons out of grief for her brothers' death (*S&G* 5, 40). Corresponding to Tolkien's novel reading of Gudrún's situation, Mabel's thirty-year-old brother, William, died on February 27, 1904 and Tolkien elevates the motif of 'heathen' or 'heretic' found implicitly in the painting *Eeriness* and in *The Lord of the Rings*.[75] The care and attention that Tolkien gave to this story, which he apparently wrote only for himself, suggests a meditation on analogous past events. The narrative of "Shelob's Lair" and "The Choices of Master Samwise" was written in the spring of 1944 on the fortieth anniversary of the hypothesized events of 1904. As a result, *Smith of Wootton Major* can be seen as one in a series of Tolkien's reckonings with his mother and all she meant to him.[76]

Tolkien's description of his mother as "extremely attractive, beautiful and extremely able" (Lee, "Tolkien" 134) takes on a new meaning when considered in relation to what he wrote about his variant of *The Wanderer*, in which Tolkien "laments the *ineluctable* ending and passing back into oblivion of the fortunate, the full-lives, the unblemished and the beautiful. To me that is more poignant than any particular disaster, from the cruelty of men or the hostility of the world" (Lee, "Wanderer" 204, italics added). Like the "ineluctable Great Wave," which casts Ronald Tolkien out of his Eden of Sarehole into exile, the disease of diabetes, the ineluctable ending, wiped out the full-life, the unblemished and the beautiful Mabel Tolkien, seemingly before her time.

When Tolkien began writing *Smith of Wootton Major* on the sixtieth anniversary of his mother's death, he appears to have reached a new synthesis and resolution. First, Tolkien's ambiguous "in bereavement and in ownership and in peace" in *Smith of Wootton Major* is perhaps partly an acknowledgment of having had a full life in the primary world with a family and work he loved (*Letters* 336-37), a life that was denied to his mother. Ronald Tolkien married his "first—and only—love" (Grotta-Kurska 23). He was a poor, orphaned boy who managed to graduate from Oxford in 1915, to return against all odds from World War I physically intact, and to raise a family. Ronald Tolkien not only taught the languages and stories he loved, but also had the time to create languages, paintings, poems, and stories—all the fruits he associated with Faery. He developed his talents and did his best not to injure or interfere with the development of others while praising God (*Letters* 399-400).

Smith's dichotomy of experience in *Smith of Wootton Major* could represent one that Tolkien experienced: busy with family, and his artistry protected by the iron in his smithy from the power of Faery. Like his avatar, Ronald Tolkien had an everyday life that he enjoyed while he held the past of his mother Mab, the Faery Queen, at bay. In *Smith of Wootton Major*, Smith is not left with only disappointment and an impoverished life without the star (Shippey, *Author* 300-01). He has a full life of family, work, and community in the Great Hall. Tolkien/Smith seem to have an unspoken basis, like Sam Gamgee in *The Lord of the Rings*, in

> the simple 'rustic' love of Sam and his Rosie (nowhere elaborated) [which] is absolutely essential to the study of his (the chief hero's) character, and to the theme of the relation of ordinary life (breathing, eating, working, begetting) and quests, sacrifice, causes and the 'longing for Elves', and sheer beauty (*Letters* 161).

Second, in coming to terms with the impact of his mother on his life, Ronald Tolkien had to reckon with his experience that she was his initiator into this special pleasure of languages. Tolkien's exuberant delight, sensitivity, and receptivity to languages were exceptional and unusual, but he credits his mother as his source: "My interest in languages was derived solely from my mother" (*Letters* 377) and "[m]y mother obviously had philological talents" (Lee, "Tolkien" 136). This last would have been particularly true for Tolkien if, in fact, his mother was the source of the invented language Fonwegian (Smith, "Book Review" 175).

In addition, Mabel Tolkien was also her son's initiator into the wonders of nature. As the ecologist, Rachel Carson noted:

> If a child is to keep alive his inborn sense of wonder without any such gift [an indestructible sense of wonder, an unfailing antidote against the boredom and disenchantments of later years, the sterile preoccupation with artificial things, the alienation from the sources of our strength] from the fairies, he needs the companionship of at least one adult who can share it, rediscovering with him the joy, excitement and mystery of the world we live in (*The Sense of Wonder* 45).

Mabel Tolkien, with her "'almost idolatrous' love of trees, flowers, nature, classical mythology," appears to have provided this experience to her son.

The desire for languages, invented languages, the joy of a living nature filled with Faery, and a lost past engenders a "desire, which seeks that which is experienced as absence and loss" (Jackson 3, in Hiley 213). This complex can perhaps be best addressed through the framework of René Girard's theory of mimesis.

In *Deceit, Desire, and the Novel*, Girard argues it is an illusion that we desire things, objects, people, etc. for themselves. Instead objects of desire receive their value and emotional charge because they are possessed and/or valued/desired by another. Desire is not a transaction between the desiring person and the desired object, but rather a three-way situation in which the desire is mediated or modeled by a third-party, a rival and/or the possessor of the desired object. Except for simple, biological desires, like hunger and thirst, all desire is born of imitating the desire of another (Girard's acquisitive mimesis).

In Girard's view, Ronald Tolkien's desire for languages becomes an imitative, mimetic, or a mediated desire. On the one hand, the mediator of desire, here Mabel Tolkien, would be seen as superior. On the other hand, the one who feels the desire would see himself as inadequate in relation to the model, and this leads to feelings of both "submissive reverence" and envy toward the model

(Girard, *Deceit* 10). The desiring subject, Ronald Tolkien, perceives himself as inferior, feeling as if he is an imitative "nothing" as compared with the self-sufficient, powerful model of his mother, whose "Being," essence, or mastery of languages, the aspiring imitator desires (Girard, *Things Hidden* 296).

In *Smith of Wootton Major*, when Smith takes "ownership" of the Living Flower, which he has obtained by breaking a Faërian prohibition, he enshrines this "precious" magical object. Smith builds a casket that protects the flower. Smith may be the guardian of the Living Flower, but the casket has the power to choose the time of its shutting, retaining control and demonstrating the flower's Faërian power (*SWM* 29). In Smith's devotion to the Faery Queen's token, Ronald Tolkien seemingly avows his inferiority to the power of Faery Queen, the source of his knowledge and appreciation of languages. He relinquishes any attempt at being superior and therefore, any envy. This is equivalent to the abnegation seen in Smith's relinquishing of the Faery Star. Smith, and presumably Tolkien, is at peace because he is willing to accept his limited being and talents. He is content with his invented languages—the fruit of his own creativity. He abandons imitative desire which always entails envy, "a desire to be Another," a desire for the other's being (Girard, *Deceit* 83).

The "secret" "treasure" of the Living Flower, restricted to immediate family, seems to repeat the pattern of Fëanor who "locked" the radiant and "living" Silmarils in his "hoard" (*S* 74), but the meaning is different in *Smith of Wootton Major*. The shrine of the Living Flower has almost the opposite implication. Fëanor restricts access out of pride and possessiveness. In contrast, Smith pays reverential tribute at the sanctuary of the Faery Queen's flower, and by his craftsmanship with iron, he shields the "precious" Faërian qualities that he values and desires so much from the materialistic, commercial setting of Wootton Major. These precious, artistic qualities are like those found in Tolkien's art languages created for the personal satisfaction of his own linguistic aesthetic and pleasure.

Because of Smith's "secret" "treasure" of the Living Flower, *Smith of Wootton Major* falls short of Tolkien's prerequisite of Recovery for a fairy tale. The Recovery function of Fantasy releases things that we have "locked in our hoard" because "all you had (or knew) was dangerous and potent, not really effectively chained, free and wild; no more yours than they were you" (OFS 146, 147). Although Smith's surrender of Faery star appears to be a releasing of the star's ownership with a resulting sense of peace, Smith continues to own a "secret" treasure, a Faërian souvenir—obtained after a Prohibition to not return to Faery—kept in a strongbox locked with a key. Although Smith does not display the pride and possessiveness of Fëanor, the use of "hoarding memory" of the encounter with the Faery Queen is an attempt to escape time and/or death (*Letters* 284) and leads to the penalty for "hoarding:" Smith remains trapped in illusion, nostalgia, and out of touch with his own experience of freedom. There is, as a result, no *eucatastrophe.*

If *SWM* is part of Tolkien's reconsideration of his mother and her gifts, Tolkien preserves the fiction or illusion of the Faery Queen's/his mother's power and perfection. The illicitly-obtained, "precious," preserved token of the meeting with the Faery Queen, the Living Flower, may free Tolkien from rivalry and its accompanying envy of imitative desire or mimesis, leaving him "in peace." However, Tolkien appears to be still be burdened by old feelings of helplessness, despair, fear, guilt, and the betrayal and sacrifice of his first invented languages, which were his unique experience of beauty and aliveness (Gruen 1-2). Tolkien said, "I hold the key" to understanding his writings (Resnick 38). That would seem to include the key to the casket of the Living Flower. The perils of Faery for Smith/Ronald Tolkien appear to be not only bereavement or loss of the "dangerous" Faery Queen, but also an inability to deal with the pain of guilt and the losses to his self.

Tolkien invokes the concept of the "happy ending" in *Smith of Wootton Major* with Smith taking "ownership" of a full life of family and work after releasing the star. However, Smith's need to hoard or own a creation of Faery limits Recovery with its attendant freedom, peace, and joy. Consequently, Smith, in his workshop filled with faery-repelling iron, is still living in exile, and that is very likely for Ronald Tolkien, too. Preserving the beauty of the Magical Living Flower of Faery in an iron-bound casket serves as an homage to Faery and its powerful Queen, to whom Smith cedes superiority and power. This renunciation may give some Consolation. However, attached to "hoarding memory," edited to see only preferred perfections, the Elves and Ronald Tolkien seem "overburdened with sadness and nostalgic regret" (*Letters* 197). Like Looney in "The Sea-Bell" from both 1932/3 and 1962, Tolkien may "hear still the spell," and he apparently cannot bring himself to share his experience of distress, guilt, and loss to uncomprehending others (*ATB* 255).

Faërian drama in *Smith of Wootton Major*

There have been several attempts at elucidating Faërian drama in *Smith of Wootton Major*. Flieger states Smith of Wootton Major is Tolkien's "best example yet of Faërian drama" and "his strongest statement about Faërian drama" (Flieger, "The Forests" 118, 122). "For the entirety of his excursions into Faery, Smith is in a Faërian drama, a dream that some other mind is weaving." But, Flieger says no character in the story is the mind that is weaving the dream, and Smith's experiences are simply a demonstration of "the power of imagination." So it is Tolkien's mind that is weaving the dream and creating Faery. This would be consistent with Tolkien writing that the author is the reader's guide in "Fairy" (*SWM* 95-96). Flieger's definition of "Faërian drama" is different from and deprecates Tolkien's statement that in Faërian drama "you are in a dream that some other mind is weaving"; that is, Flieger has shifted the meaning of "Faërian drama" (OFS 142). For Flieger, the newly defined Faërian drama is due to "altered state of consciousness created by *faerie*" which allows "acceptance as real of what is imagined" because it is "so convincing that it seems to be really happening" (Flieger, "The Forests" 111). Flieger's reformulation seems to be a restating of the well-known "suspension of disbelief" that writers, including Tolkien, ask of their readers. Flieger also proposes that Faerie is a "literary construct, an imaginal exercise, a make believe world, a place to go, and an altered state of being" (*GS* 67).

Janet Croft also proposes that *Smith of Wootton Major* is a Faërian drama. For Croft, "Faërian drama is a useful tool for thinking about the profound work the subconscious does, in cases where the mind is deeply conflicted or in need of major change or growth and thus receptive when presented with an opportunity for a transformative experience" ("Tolkien's Faërian Drama" 33). Faërian drama has a moral element, a "meeting of the aesthetic and the ethical" (Garbowski 45 in Croft 37). Taking her model of Faërian drama from *Pearl*, Croft hypothesizes that the "'dreamer' must be troubled in mind [...] or in need of an intervention," as otherwise, "a dream of the fantastic is just Enchantment and nothing more" (Croft, "Tolkien's Faërian Drama" 38). She then wants to apply these criteria to *Smith of Wootton Major*, but it is the "Village and society" that needs intervention, not Smith who is "not troubled in mind or in need of an intervention" (Croft, "Tolkien's Faërian Drama" 41).

But Croft's newly-created, defining criteria for Faërian drama does not fit Tolkien's writings. For example, she cites the classic case of Aragorn, who wonders, when he sees Arwen for the first time, if he "strayed into a dream" or "received the gift of Elf-minstrels, who can make the things of which they sing appear before the eyes of those that listen" (*RK* Appendix A 1033, 40). Though a new destiny may result from this meeting, there is no deep conflict or need for major change at the outset of this scene as specified by Croft. In another paradigmatic scene of Faërian drama, set in the Hall of Fire in Rivendell when the chanting of poetry is a "spell" with a "dreamlike" enchantment (*FR* II i 227), Croft's required conflict or need for change is not evident. Her new criteria for Faërian drama, like Flieger's, ignores Tolkien's distinctive specification that "you are in a dream that some other mind is weaving and the knowledge of that alarming fact may slip from your grasp" (OFS 142).

Smith of Wootton Major does contain a true Faërian drama. It occurs when Alf, the King of Faery, confronts old Nokes. Alf reveals himself as the true "Starbrow" with "a great jewel like a radiant star" on his forehead (*SWM* 51). According to Flieger, Alf seemingly shows the face of scorn and pity toward Man (*GS* 71, OFS 125).

Alf's disdain would then contrast with Nokes's contempt. Nokes previously was the scornful one who leered at Alf (*SWM* 49) and sneered at him (*SWM* 51). Nokes accused Alf of "making [things] up" as Alf was "always a tricky fellow" (*SWM* 48, 50), just as Nokes describes the Fairy Queen as "a tricky creature" doubting that she "plays fair" (*SWM* 14). Having denounced Alf, Nokes closes his eyes in satisfaction and blindness (*SWM* 50; Long, "*Smith*" 110). This pose recalls Tolkien's *Grownupishness*: "'Sightless: Blind: Well-Wrapped-Up'." Like Tolkien's comment that "Satan's just a toad" (Lee, "Tolkien" 164), Nokes comes across as small and mean. At the end of *SWM*, Nokes loudly proclaims that he is "glad" Alf is gone because he was "artful" [*sic*] (*SWM* 55), as if Alf was the Artful Dodger instead of the source of 'artistic' quality, skill, and creativity (*SWM* 127).

However, in contrast to the conceptual framework of "On Fairy-stories," Tolkien stresses Alf does not bait or gloat over Nokes (*SWM* 139). The generous Alf, rather shows "pity and kindness," in return for a "confession," even easing Nokes's "injured pride" by arranging for him to fall asleep and believe he had only a dream, while granting his wish "to make me thin again" (*SWM* 139). Pity is what saved both Bilbo and Frodo from the slavery of the Ring and befits the King of Faery. As a result, Nokes experiences a beneficent "Faërian drama" which occurs "when you yourself are, or think that you are, bodily inside its Secondary World. The experience may be very similar to dreaming [...] But in Faërian drama you are in a dream some other mind is weaving, and the knowledge of that alarming fact may slip from your grasp" (OFS 142). Nokes's language of denial—"Why, he hadn't no wand"—reveals, through double negation, the true situation (*SWM* 52; Long, "*Smith*" 110). In a similar way, Nokes's earlier, persistent dreams of the Great Cake may have been a pleading, merciful call from Faery (*SWM* 47).

Alf's apprentice and successor is Harper, whose marital status is unknown. Tolkien writes that the name 'Harper' is "significant" (*SWM* 112). Tolkien used the harp as a metonymic for ancient poetry, from the use of the harp as an emblem for the Old Testament *Psalms* (Holmes 360). In addition, a harper was a bard, and in that role he would contribute as a Master Cook to the "Cauldron" of soup or story (OFS 120, 125, 128, Smol 273). The Master Cook, Harper, could transmit the old stories as "History and legend and above all tales touching on 'faery', have become regarded as children's stuff, patronizingly tolerated for the amusement of the very young" (*SWM* 129). This transmission echoes the alignment of Faery and the divine: "God is the Lord, of angels, and of men—and of elves. Legend and History have met and fused" (OFS 156). Tolkien joins pagan myth and Christian poetry noting how the minstrel of Heorot in *Beowulf*, singing of the Creation of the earth and the lights of Heaven, maddens Grendel who lurks in the dark ("Beowulf" 26, 33).

Like Väinämöinen, the bard of the *Kalevala* with his harp, Harper will create beauty in tales and legends. The Elvish word for 'harp', *kantl* or *kantil* (QL 45), appears to derive from the Finnish word for harp, *kantele*, given in Kirby's translation of the *Kalevala* which Tolkien read (Hooker, Glossology 105-108). The power of the harp in *Sir Orfeo*, the legend that suffuses the background of Faery in *Smith of Wootton Major*, allows the title character to release his wife from the Faery King/death (Shippey, *Road* 64). Harper and Smith, who sings like the bard, Taliesin, or the 'shining brow', "grieved" at Alf's leaving. They keep the Hall gilded and painted in Alf's memory, maintaining and passing on a tradition of beauty and imagination (*SWM* 54).

VII. Conclusion: Tolkien on Death, the Doom of Men

The Otherworld of *Sir Orfeo* and of *Smith of Wootton Major* is consistent with Tolkien's dictum that the "magic of Faërie [...] is in [...] the satisfaction of certain primordial human desires [e.g.] [to] survey the depth of space and time, [... to] hold communion with other living things, [...] the realisation, independent of the conceiving mind, of imagined wonder" (OFS 116), and "the Great Escape, the Escape from Death" (OFS 153). If Faerie holds the "Great Escape, the Escape from Death," it still "is not the road to Heaven; nor even to Hell, I believe" (OFS 110). When Tolkien introduces "the oldest and deepest desire, the Great Escape: the Escape from Death," he, in fact, does not give any specifics in the "many examples" he claims, but rather switches topics to the Escape from endless or unceasing Life (Manlove 112).

None of Tolkien's writings that consider the question of death seem to resolve this question of the Escape from Death. For example, although the medieval poem and dream-vision, *Pearl*, which Tolkien translated, uses the Faërian imagery of the sleeper on the mound, the sleeper's dream of his dead daughter, Pearl, is a homily about Christian doctrine, including grace and salvation, and the need to resign one's self to patience and God's will (Slack 178). Tolkien's story, *Leaf by Niggle*, offers almost an allegory of death and purgatory with a glimpse of Paradise in Faërian imagery, but it does not confront the issue of grief and bereavement. In Bilbo's *Last Song*, the ship to Valinor is guided by the "Lonely Star," a star of Faery leading to Faery, seemingly an Earthly Paradise, not Heaven.

On the one hand, "The oldest and deepest desire, the Great Escape: the Escape from Death," violates the reality of the primary world. On the other hand, Tolkien writes that fairy-stories teach "the burden of [...] immortality, or rather endless serial living to which the 'fugitive' [of death] would fly" (OFS 153). In a letter from November 1957, discussing his fairy tale, *The Lord of the Rings*, Tolkien writes that it "is not really about Power and Dominion [...] it is about Death and the desire for deathlessness. Which is hardly more than to say it is a tale written by a Man!" (*Letters* 262). To acknowledge death and its finality, Tolkien created the surprising and perplexing principle that the Men of Middle-earth are blessed because "Death is their fate, the gift of Iluvatar, which as Time wears even the Powers shall envy" (*S* 38). In contrast, the "Elves die not till the world dies, unless they are slain or waste in grief [...] and dying they are gathered to the halls of Mandos in Valinor, whence they may in time return" (*S* 38).

This idea is difficult to accept, not only for Tolkien's readers, but also for Tolkien's characters. Faced with the Doom of Men, the "loss and the silence," Arwen admits, "As wicked fools I scorned [Men], but I pity them at last. For if this is indeed, as the Eldar say, the gift of the One to Men, it is bitter to receive" (*RK* App. A 1037-38). Andreth states, "All passing and dying is a grief to [the heart of Man]" (*MR* 307).

The "Escape" function of the fairy tale and fantasy, the source of Middle-earth and its characters, creates a fictional space that real life does not have, where a rejection of death is possible. But without acceptance of reality, the imagination and its possibilities would trap the reader in the "permanent misery of resisting what cannot be resisted—such as sickness, old age, and death. In the face of the inexorable fact of death, Tolkien, even in his created world, offers the final benefit of fantasy literature, 'Consolation'" (Venkatesh 244). Tolkien's third blessing of fairy tales, Consolation, replaces and supersedes Recovery and Escape. The *evangelium*, "the Joy beyond the walls of the world" (OFS 153), as found in the Gospel fairy-story of the birth of Christ and his Resurrection, the eucatastrophes of Man's history and the Incarnation (OFS 156), is not available to the characters of Middle-earth. However, Aragorn adumbrates this, saying: "we are not bound for ever to the circles of the world, and beyond them is more than memory" (*RK*, Appendix A 1038).

Smith's farewell to the Magical Faery Queen in *Smith of Wootton Major*, being "at once in bereavement, and in ownership, and in peace," seems to be Tolkien's attempt to have his fairy-story teach "the burden of [...] immortality." To let go of Magical timeless Faery, with the memories it may invoke for Ronald Tolkien, may bring grief, but there may be peace for him, too. Alf's statement, "Go home now in peace," echoing the end of the Mass, appears to be a comment on Smith's willingness to give up the star—Smith's passport into Magical Faery (*SWM* 42). Moreover, "go home" recalls "the aching desire to go home" (*TOFS* 282, underlining in original) to the lost paradise of Sarehole and Tolkien's belief about his "native language" of Welsh, to which "in unexplored desire we would still go home" (*MC* 190, 194). Going home is what Tolkien, an exile, like Eriol/ Aelfwine and Eärendil (*QT* 163), or Ned Smith whose first name recalls Elvish Sindarin *edlen*(*n*) meaning 'exiled' ("Words" 51), would long for.

Since Faery has three faces, Smith appears to be renouncing the Magical face towards Nature (OFS 125), and the Otherworld with access to a timeless past and the dead. This leaves Smith with the Mystical face of Faery which is turned toward the Supernatural. Tolkien's conception of a Mystical Faery is not religious, but rather a "breaking out (at least in mind) from the iron ring of the familiar [... and] of belief that it is known, possessed, controlled [...] it represents [...] a love and respect for all things [...] an unpossessive love of them as 'other.'" Mystical Faery appears to still be available to Smith, even after the renunciation of the star (*SWM* 143-44). In *SWM*, Mystical Faery continues in the beauty of the traditions of singing, dancing, and stories in the painted Great Hall (*SWM* 53). The new Master Cook, Harper, a literary descendant of the harper Orfeo and of the legendary harper Väinämöinen in the *Kalevala*, will transmit in song the old stories including "History and legend[s]."

When we view *Smith of Wootton Major* as Tolkien readdressing his complicated past by playing with representations of himself as Smith, Fr. Francis as Alf, his maternal grandfather Suffield as Grandfather Rider, and his mother as the Faery Queen, then the richness of *Smith of Wootton Major*'s imagery becomes apparent. The allegory of the Village church and its Parson sets up the tension that the arrival of Alf, the King of Faery, precipitates with the trinkets of the Great Cake, which include the Faery star. Smith's journeys in Faery, protected by the Faery star, can be understood by acknowledging their groundings in Celtic folklore. A 'blast' or 'gust' of wind becomes a *sídhe* of the Celtic Otherworld of Faery, moving on the face of the waters and leading Smith, a fallen man, to cling to a birch for protection. In contrast, Smith's everyday life in his workshop is filled with faery-repelling iron, creating a balance that Smith controls. Preserving the beauty of the Magical Living Flower—from the then-unknown Faery Queen—in an iron-bound casket, becomes a "hoarding memory," as Smith has already fallen and broken a Faërian prohibition. When Smith says farewell to the Faery Queen in a meeting he had desired in his heart, and then renounces the Faery star, he loses magical Faërian Time and acknowledges death. Written on the sixtieth anniversary of his mother's death, *Smith of Wootton Major* is "an old man's book, already weighted with the presage of bereavement" (Letters 389). Written just before his assessment of 1965—"I find it difficult to work—beginning to feel old and the fire dying down," Smith of Wootton Major shows the tying up of many themes and loose ends in the winter of Tolkien's life. The vehicle for "the burden of [...] immortality," Tolkien's fairy-story, expresses resignation and a longing to "go home." In the face of inexorable death, Tolkien chooses consolation in "hoarding memory."

End Notes

1 Flieger, *GS* and *QT*; Shippey, "Allegory Versus Bounce;" and Long, "Two Views of Faerie" and "Anxiety of Influence."
2 These included: "The Converse of Manwë and Eru," "Athrabeth Finrod ah Andreth," "Tale of Adanel," "Reincarnation of Elves" (*C&G* 1.578), "Quendi and Eldar," "Communication of Thought," "Orcs," "Cuivienyarna," Elvish genealogies," "Concerning Galadriel and Celeborn," and "The Elessar" (*C&G* 1.582-83)
3 See *Letters* 215, 218, 297, 310.
4 See Manlove's presentation of MacDonald's very different views, especially on the function of allegory in fairytales (111) as well as the differences in style (113-14).
5 The books of George MacDonald and Andrew Lang "most affected the background of my imagination since childhood" (*TOFS* 207).
6 "[A]nother member of the household was a big, ancient black cat called Tinker, [...]." "Lieutenant Thomas Ewart Mitton: The Moseley Society." http://moseley-society.org.uk/wp content/uploads/2018/03/29.-Lieutenant-T-Ewart-Mitton-2.pdf, accessed on 1/19/2024.
7 Carpenter denied he was "censored" (Ross in Anderson, "Obituary" 220) because to fulfill one's contract is not technically censorship, though the result may be as misleading and inaccurate.
8 See Tolkien's reaction to allegorical interpretations of *The Lord of the Rings* ("*Smith*" 118-19).
9 Crane qualifies Anderson's claims about errors but does not dispute Flieger's withholding of information.
10 See "Ambidexter" in this volume for other linguistic, pictorial, and narrative reversals.
11 Notice how Tolkien writes that he is rejecting his "mother tongue," English, in favor of his language of his "individual nature," Welsh, which would have been associated with his half-Welsh guardian, Fr. Francis Morgan.
12 "Myth and fairy-story must, as all art, reflect and contain in solution elements of moral and religious truth (or error), but not explicit" (See *Letters* 144).
13 See Geier on varieties of allegory in *Smith of Wootton Major* (217-218). See Tolkien's difficulty with allegory (*Letters* 145, 297-98, 351). Bowers highlights Tolkien's narrow definition of allegory in *Pearl* (xii) and Tolkien's 1965 Foreword to *The Lord of the Rings*.
14 This does seem to contradict "Elves are not busy with a plan to reawaken religious devotion in Wootton" (*SWM* 144).
15 The music passing into the "West" suggests Valinor. The birds recall the birds in the Celtic *The Voyage of St. Brendan*, who are angels who did not remain faithful to God (i.e. they are of Faery) (Colum 73).
16 "Tolkien and the Oratory: The Oratory Birmingham." www.birmingham-oratory.org.uk/TheOratory/Tolkien/tabid/76/Default.aspx, downloaded 1/2/2010.
17 See Tolkien's earlier view: "elves are not primarily concerned with us, nor we with them. Our fates are sundered" (OFS 113).
18 Typology was based on "figural interpretation" which "establishes a connection between two events or persons, in such a way that the first signifies not only itself but also the second, while the second involves or fulfills the first" (Auerbach 73).
19 See how H. Head uses Girard's theory of mimesis for Tolkien's characters: Melkor, Sauron, and Saruman. Tom Bombadil is the exemplar of Being, the character who escapes the cycle of mimetic rivalry. (Bunting, "Reconsidering Tom Bombadil").
20 See the explicit presence of Christian religion in myths as "fatal:" (*Letters* 144, 193-4, 206, 282).

21 Tolkien calls it a 'purgatory', but Aman seems modeled on the folklore of the Earthly Paradise, found throughout Europe in Celtic and Germanic stories. (See Green 182-83, 147-54). Thomas the Rhymer's "Elfland" was an offshoot of this Earthly Paradise (OFS 110).

22 This recalls the Celtic *Sídhe* or *Aes Sí*, the Celtic deities of pre-Christian Britain, translated as the 'spirits' or 'fairies'. In Old Irish, *sídhe* means a 'blast' or 'gust' of wind (Hooker, *Tolkienotēca* 209). The Hebrew word *ruach* is translated as 'wind', 'breath', or 'spirit', and is used to convey God's presence. The corresponding words in Greek *pneuma* and in Latin *spiritus* have the same three translations.

23 Flieger places the scenes of the Sea of Windless Storm [later Lake of Tears], of the dancing elven maidens and the Living Flower, and of the King's Tree in the Magical face of Faery (*GS* 70).

24 Catholic Answers." "Catholic Encyclopedia: Holy Innocents." https://www.catholic.com/encyclopedia/holy-innocents from unabridged entry from the original Catholic Encyclopedia, published between 1907 and 1912. Accessed on 10/02/2023.
Chaucer's "the Prioress's Tale" in *The Canterbury Tales* has a number of liturgical allusions to Childermas or the feast of the Holy Innocents (Correale 589).

25 MacClain, Alexia (4 January 2013). "Twelfth Night Traditions: A Cake, a Bean, and a King." *Unbound: Smithsonian Librarie and Archives*. https://blog.library.si.edu/blog/2013/01/04/twelfth-night-traditions-a-cake-a-bean-and-a-king/#.Ysc6uoTMLcc, retrieved 10 January 2018, accessed on 10/02/2023.

26 Red candles recall the votive candle or the sanctuary lamp, traditionally lit beside the tabernacle which contains the consecrated Bread and Wine, the Body and Blood of Christ. The red candle means the Christ is present in the tabernacle. "Classroom: The Meaning of the Red Candle on the Altar of a Catholic Church." https://classroom.synonym.com/meaning-red-candle-altar-catholic-church-5591.html, accessed on 10/02/2023.

27 "Catholic Culture," "Catholic dictionary: religious numbers," https://www.catholicculture.org/culture/library/dictionary/index.cfm?id=35179, accessed on 10/02/2023.

28 "About Catholics." "Catholic Beliefs and Catholic Teachings." "Revelation: Symbols and Numbers." https://www.aboutcatholics.com/beliefs/revelation-symbols-and-numbers/, accessed on 10/02/2023.

29 Consequently, the star on the forehead of Smith, a man, has an entirely different meaning and function than the star-like Silmaril on the brow of Eärendil, a half-elven in the world of Middle-earth.

30 The standard prayer, the "Hail, Mary," ends with "Holy Mary, Mother of God, pray for us sinners now, and at the hour of death."

31 *Catechism of the Catholic Church* (2nd ed.). Libreria Editrice Vaticana. 2019. Paragraph 971.

32 "Catholic Straight Answers." "Why do we call Mary by all these titles." https://catholicstraightanswers.com/why-do-we-call-mary-by-all-these-titles/, accessed on 10/3/2023.

33 Christ is also metaphorically referred to as a morning star in 2 Peter 1:19 and Christ describes himself as the morning star in Rev. 22:16. This imagery is separate from its use with Mary. In the Holy Saturday liturgy, the ancient hymn, the *Exsultet*, refers to Christ as "the morning star."

34 There are seven sacraments for Catholics: Baptism, Confirmation, Holy Eucharist, Penance, Extreme Unction, Holy Orders, and Marriage. "Catholic News Agency." "Lesson 13: On the Sacraments in General." https://www.catholicnewsagency.com/resource/55451/lesson-13-on-the-sacraments-in-general, accessed on 10/3/23.

35 Recall *The Lord of the Rings* "is about Death and the desire for deathlessness" (*Letters* 262, see draft 246, 284). "In *The Lord of the Rings* the conflict is [...] about God, and His Sole right to divine honour" (*Letters* 243).

36 See Shay for the *Iliad* as a story of post-traumatic stress disorder.
37 Hiley discusses issues of language and exile in James Joyce and C.S. Lewis's writings (208-219), but only considers Tolkien's characters in exile (212-13).
38 This undated note refers to World War II, so it could have been written from 1939 to 1945.
39 The preface of *The Adventures of Tom Bombadil* asserts that the various poems are from *The Red Book*, so Tolkien needed to offer a link to *The Red Book* by supposing Frodo was the author of this rewritten poem (29).
40 In Middle-earth, the Elves appear to avoid working with iron by employing dwarves (*H* XIII). Elves are known as silver smiths (*Letters* 426) and, like Fëanor, creators of jewels.
41 This pattern recalls the Smith, Ilmarinen, in the *Kalevala*, who rejects a crossbow, a ship, a cow, and a plow as they are all destructive.
42 The specifying of the draft introduction of "The Golden Key" follows Anderson ("Smith" 4).
43 "Walewein in the Otherworld and the Land of Prester John." https://www.medievalists.net/2011/02/walewein-in-the-otherworld-and-the-land-of-prester-john/, accessed on 10/3/2023; (Anonymous, *Fasciculus Morum* 578-79; see also Watkins 65-66).
44 Tolkien appears to have exploited the possibilities of nunnation in order to indulge his linguistic predilections. Ann could be a pun on *anna* meaning 'gift' (*S* 356; "Etymologies" ANA– 386; "Words" 90, 125; GL 62; QL 31). Tolkien was also likely to know that the name of the queen of the fairies in Celtic mythology was *Aine*, meaning 'radiance', which is the Irish form of the name 'Ann' (Hanks).
45 "The enchanting garden of the Otherworld is at once the most definitely marked and the vaguest of the Otherworld features. We always find the lovely meadows, the beautiful flowers with their subtly strange perfumes, the sparkling fountains and streams, and the tree of life" (Patch 619).
46 Like Aman, "the far green country" in *The Lord of the Rings* (*RK* VI ix 1007, *FR* I viii 132).
47 The perilous encounters called *avantures* in courtly romance are not the modern accidental, disordered, peripheral experiences that stand outside the real meaning of existence, but rather a trial through adventure which calls forth the very essence of the knight's ideal of manhood, the real meaning of his ideal existence (Auerbach 135). Tolkien owned a copy of Auerbach's *Mimesis* (Cilli 10).
48 Tolkien, who refers to himself as a Celtophile, disparages the "fundamental unreason" of "Celtic things" which are "mad" (*Letters* 26) as a rebuke of the professional philologist to the popular, romantic stereotypes (Lyman-Thomas 273-74).
49 The placement of the Faery star on Smith's forehead recalls the marking of the cross on the forehead on Ash Wednesday as a sign of repentance.
50 The "fantasies of fallen man" "has stained the elves" (OFS 122).
51 Pepetone sees an invocation of the unpredictable Dame Fortune of medieval literature in Nokes's comments about the "tricky" Fairy Queen (*SWM* 14). Long sees 'trick' in relation to the earlier 'trinket' ("*Smith*" 108).
52 The Living Flower may also recall the "ineffable blue flower" of the early Romantic fantasist Novalis or Friedrich von Hardenburg. Novalis was well-known and admired by C.S. Lewis, who cites Novalis' concept of *Sehnsucht* in his autobiographical *Surprised by Joy* (7). It may have precisely the same emotional resonance as the emotional state that accompanies *eucatastrophe*: "Joy beyond the walls of the world, poignant as grief" (OFS 153, Pepetone 150). Tolkien uses the term *sehnsucht* to describe a "happy childhood" which seems to refer specifically to the time in Sarehole, despite Tolkien's broader time-frame of events before the loss of his mother (Plimmer/Plimmer).
53 Smith wanders forty-eight years in Faery just as Tolkien's invented languages, beginning with Naffarin in 1907 and ending in 1955 with the publication of *The Return of the King* (with *The Lord of the Rings* being "primarily linguistic in

inspiration" (*Letters* 409, 219)), spanned forty-eight years.

54 Galadriel is not an elven queen although she has the compelling combination of beauty and dangerous power (*Letters* 274).

55 Tolkien said the story "contains elements that are relevant to the consideration of Poetry, with a capital P or that some may find so" (*C&G* 2.1216-17).

56 This is found in *In Powder and Crinoline* (*A&I* 57).

57 'Fairy' and 'elf' were interchangeable terms for Ronald Tolkien in his early writings (Fimi 22-23, *B&L* 33).

58 Théoden, Aragorn, and Bilbo, all recommend smoking as a way to remember (*RK* V vi 824, *RK* V viii 851, *RK* VI vi 965).

59 Their father, John Suffield, was "tall" (*Bio* 106). "A Hundred Years Ago: Average Height for Males and Females." accessed 3/17/2021. https://ahundredyearsago.com/2012/02/06/average-height-for-males-and-females-in-1912-and-2012/ and "Titanica: 1912 Height and Weight." https://www.encyclopedia-titanica.org/community/threads/1912-height-and-weight.4362/, accessed 3/17/2021.

60 "How children come to understand false beliefs: A shared intentionality account." Michael Tomasello. July 11, 2018. Proceedings of the National Academy of Sciences of the United States of America. https://www.pnas.org/content/115/34/8491. PNAS August 21, 2018 115 (34) 8491-8498; first published August 13, 2018; https://doi.org/10.1073/pnas.1804761115, accessed on 10/3/2023.

61 A number of factors, including brain maturation with an attendant ability to coordinate multiple perspectives and realizing they can refer to something that a parent does not know about—for example, what happened with their teacher at school—bring about the receding of this egocentric point of view.

62 In response to growing modernization and imperialism, there was a call starting after the Boer War for a renewal in England of "its ancient traditions [...] restoring the moral and material health of English Society [...] undermined by [...] urbanism, industrialism, and cosmopolitanism" (Weiner 59-60. in Potts 156). This coincides well with the 1915 consensus that the purpose of the T.C.B.S., Tolkien's early literary group, was to "reestablish sanity, cleanliness and the love of real and true beauty in everybody's breast" (*C&G* 2.1285).

63 Tolkien did call this a "dream." That label should be seen as a function of Tolkien's characteristically English self-deprecation and understatement (Ordway, *Modern Reading* 44, 285-86).

64 Tolkien dates *Leaf by Niggle* and "On Fairy-stories" to the same period (1938-9). See Bunting's "Reply to Noad" for a discussion of alternate dating.

65 Flieger and Anderson date this to when he was twelve years old (*TOFS* 108). See Bunting "Reply to Noad" and "Checking the Facts."

66 See Bunting's "1904" for a discussion of the cultural context of the late nineteenth century's view of corporeal punishment as appropriate and normal (71), as well as the expectation that mothers would have complete control of their children and therefore would have been judged on the basis of their children's behavior (75).

67 In the section, "Suggestions for the Ending of the Story," Tolkien's phrase, "The time has come," seems to mean the Queen believes it is now time for the Smith "to relinquish the star" (*SWM* 107). However, this is not necessarily Tolkien's final thoughts on this phrase because he is still considering the timing of the message, how the King will persuade Smith, and if the recipient of the star should be revealed (*SWM* 108, 110).

68 Tolkien was familiar with the Knox Bible, as it is called, because it was one of the approved vernacular versions of the Bible used in the lectionary readings for the Mass from 1965 to the early 1970s. The Inkling, Robert E. Havard was received into the Catholic Church at the age of thirty-one by Ronald Knox (Ordway, *Tolkien's Faith* 232), and the two became such good friends that Knox dedicating his 1934 detective novel *Still Dead* "To Dr. Robert Havard".

69 In Tolkien's "Suggestions," Alf's line—"I understand. Go home now in

peace"—which precedes the scene of the Hall in the sunset, appears to be a comment on Smith's willingness to give up the star (*SWM* 109).

70 In "Suggestions for the Ending of the Story," Tolkien writes that Smith's recognition of the Faery King would mean that "the time has come" (*SWM* 108).

71 "Vatican prepares three alternative endings for dismissal at Mass." John Thavis. *National Catholic Reporter*. Oct 20, 2008. https://www.ncronline.org/news/vatican-prepares-three-alternative-endings-dismissal-mass, accessed on 10/03/2023.

72 Sternberg believes *Smith of Wootton Major* does not deal with death (315).

73 "To practice self abnegation is a greater thing than to raise the dead" (McGovern 267).

74 The fragrance recalls the enchanting garden of the Otherworld (Patch 619).

75 *Birmingham* Post, March 1, 1904. See Bunting's "Finding Tolkien in His Stories" for more detail.

76 The fiftieth anniversary fell in the very busy year of 1954 when Tolkien was preparing *The Lord of the Rings* for publication. C. Tolkien comments the surprising amount of time is father spent on "Tal Elmar" in late 1954 (*Peoples* 422).

Future:

New Directions

Chapter Eight

Tolkien as Forgotten Utopian

Toby Widdicombe

I will not, in this essay, be arguing Tolkien was a utopian thinker. It is very clear that the motivation for the legendarium was his desire to create a mythology for England rather than a wish to create another world according to More. However, in this process of developing his mythology, Tolkien created a remarkable number of pocket eutopias and dystopias—communities of betterment or deterioration within a larger, even epic, landscape. Such a creation is hardly surprising since Tolkien was so fecund a fantasist. Then, too, Tolkien's Catholicism meant that he saw the world very much as a struggle between the desire for good (eutopia) and the desire for evil (dystopia) with neither permanently victorious. So, I shall concern myself here only with elaborating on Tolkien's creation of pocket utopias and, in the conclusion, speculate on what such a creation says about how to read the legendarium. In doing so, I shall briefly stray beyond the formal legendarium to pay some attention to two rather neglected works: *Leaf by Niggle* and *Smith of Wootton Major*. The former is useful in understanding Tolkien's work habits as they relate to the particular qualities of his legendarium; the latter in interpreting his sense of the motivation behind fairy stories (or fantasy) as a genre. My claim is simply this: Tolkien had a vision of utopia, and it was vital to how the legendarium (the work of almost *sixty* years) was worked out by him throughout his long life.[1] In this respect, I know I must argue against Tolkien's own view—expressed in a letter to Naomi Mitchison in 1954—that his is "not a Utopian vision" or an "ideal." However, the fact that he connects "Utopian "and "ideal" in the same sentence indicates his misunderstanding (derived from the standard dictionary definition) of what More meant by Utopia (*Letters* 197). And now I will indirectly explain the reasons for that misunderstanding.

The Meaning of Utopia

The word "utopia" was coined by Thomas More in his 1516 eponymous book. It was, for More, a pun as, in Classical Greek, *topos* means "place" and *u* means "no." That prefix is identical in sound, however, to *eu*, which means "good." So, *utopia* may mean a fictive nonexistent place or it may mean a fictive good place. The *Oxford English Dictionary* defines "utopia" as "An imagined or hypothetical place, system, or state of existence in which everything is perfect, esp. in respect of social structure, laws, and politics." As far as common usage goes, that definition is entirely accurate, but it represents a serious misreading of More's originary work. More never intended *Utopia* to be read as presenting perfection, merely a markedly better state of being for those living in Tudor Britain and early Renaissance Europe in the early sixteenth century. He only mentions the word "best" once (in the subtitle to the work), and that is heavily ironized in its hyperbolic use. The best short definition of the key term and the one I am using here is Lyman Tower Sargent's 1994 definition: "the broad, general definition of utopianism" is "social dreaming—the dreams and nightmares that concern the ways in which groups of people arrange their lives and which usually envision a radically different society than the one in which the dreamers live" (Sargent 3). Along with this, I have internalized in my thinking Sargent's *Introduction to Utopianism, A Very Short Introduction* (2010), which renders this simple definition more subtly in its historical and cultural contexts. The antonymic word "dystopia" was coined by Henry Lewis Younge in 1747 and means a place where, as the *Oxford English Dictionary* puts it, "everything is as bad as possible." Once again, as with "utopia," exaggerated but nonetheless useful. So, for the purposes of this argument I am using "utopia" as the umbrella term, "eutopia" as an imagined and markedly better condition of society, and "dystopia" as markedly worse. This semantic strategy has been the habit in the discipline of utopian studies for some time now.

The Shire

The land of the hobbits was by no means Tolkien's first effort to create a pocket utopia. Its creation dates from the early 1930s—a score of years after he began his legendarium. It is, however, by far his best-known effort, so I shall begin there and then go back in the legendarium to the beginning and move forward from there. The Shire is, of course, the land in which the hobbits dwell. Curiously, however, the geographic label is not used at all in *The Hobbit* itself, which was first published in 1937. The label first appears in a crudely drawn map of the Shire dating, probably, from early 1938 with its creation wrapped up in some very early work on *The Lord of the Rings* (see McIlwaine 390-391). On this map, it is simply referred to as "Shire," without, that is, the definite article. Next, the term shows up in a letter from Tolkien to his son Christopher dated 29 November 1944 (*Letters* 103-104). There Tolkien talks of the putative end of *The Lord of the Rings*: "the final scene will be the passage of Bilbo and Elrond and Galadriel through the woods of the Shire on their way to the Grey Havens" (*Letters* 104). In the first volume of *The Lord of the Rings* itself (which was published in 1954), the term appears early (in the Prologue) with a simple reference to "the Hobbits of the Shire" (*FR* 2). So, we can say that in 1938 Tolkien first gives the land of the hobbits a name—and a generic one at that. By 1944, the Shire had become familiar enough in Tolkien's own mind to need no further explanation for his son. By 1954, his readers are finally let in on the nomenclature. He had, after all, been living with this part of Middle-earth creatively for more than 20 years by the time his famous trilogy was published. It was about time.

Enough on the origins of the term. What matters is how the Shire qualifies as pocket eutopia. First, any such utopia needs a history and a location and a definable community. The Shire has all three. As Tolkien remarks in "Concerning Hobbits" (the sole topic of the Prologue to *The Fellowship of the Ring*), the hobbits are a "very ancient people" (*FR* 1). At one time they lived near the Anduin between Greenwood the Great and the Misty Mountains before—for unknown reasons—moving into Eriador. Then Argleb II, the high king of the Northern (Arnorian) line of the Dúnedain, ceded to the hobbits the land between the Baranduin river and the Far Downs—that land which became known as the Shire. That was in the year 1601 of the Third Age. As to being a community, well, the hobbits themselves were divided into three friendly groups: the Harfoots, the Stoors, and the Fallohides. Each was somewhat different in appearance and habits but all were dedicated to the same harmonizing eutopian principles: "peace and quiet and good tilled earth" and "a well-ordered and well-farmed countryside" (*FR* 1). They disliked machines because of their complexity and tendency to disrupt their "close friendship with the earth" (*FR* 1). They loved simple, joyful, generous living: "laugh they did, and eat, and drink, often and heartily, being fond of simple jests at all times, and of six meals a day (when they could get them)." And Tolkien continues his portrait of them as refugees from the Land of Cockaigne: "They were hospitable and delighted in parties, and in presents, which they gave away freely and eagerly accepted" (*FR* 2). As the first hobbit Tolkien created, Bilbo best represents the principles of the Shire as pocket eutopia, and does so right from the beginning of *The Hobbit*. His house in Bag End is well-ordered and comfortable and convenient. The Hill on which Bag End is located is trim and artistically laid out. Tolkien's sketches for the novel, which were broadly contemporaneous with the creation of the narrative, bear this out.

However, *The Hobbit* (and, for that matter, the broader legendarium) is not a philosophical treatise in the same sense that More's *Utopia* or Plato's antecedent *Republic* is. For some sense of what the pocket eutopia of the Shire is meant to represent or to recall beyond a generic sense of eutopia, we need to look at Tolkien's letters for guidance. In a letter to Milton Waldman (undated but written, probably, in late 1951), Tolkien explicitly says that the hobbits were not modelled after Swiftian satire (*Gulliver's Travels*), but were meant to be read as a branch of the human race in order for their characteristics to contrast favourably with humanity in the twentieth century. So, they are "more in touch with 'nature' (the soil and other living things, plants and animals), and, abnormally, for humans, free from ambition or greed of wealth" (*Letters* 158, note †). So, they represent "an ordered, civilised, if simple and rural life," one which is not accidental but deliberate and "maintained" (*Letters* 158). In January or February 1956 (shortly after the publication of all three volumes of *The Lord of the Rings*), Tolkien wrote to Michael Straight (the editor of the *New Republic*) that the Shire was a nostalgic representation by "an Englishman brought up in an 'almost rural' village of Warwickshire on the edge of the bourgeoisie of Birmingham" (*Letters* 235). In that same year in a letter to W. H. Auden, Tolkien remarks that the Shire is "half republic half aristocracy" and symbolizes "the liberation from an evil tyranny" of all other human political systems (*Letters* 241). In the draft of an incomplete letter to C. A. Nunn from late 1958 or early 1959, Tolkien views the political organization of the Shire as remarkably egalitarian. It is based on the family and the clan with the former being founded on "dyarchy": a system "in which master and mistress had equal status, if different functions" (*Letters* 293).

Rivendell

I have spent some time discussing the Shire (and hobbits) as both represent Tolkien's most sustained effort to create a pocket utopia (in the sense we now understand that term), but I should move on to other pocket eutopias and dystopias to sketch out the full range of Tolkien's view of social betterment and social decay from his twentieth-century perspective. As *The Hobbit* was Tolkien's first published account of Middle-earth, I shall follow that narrative for what it says of pocket utopias. After a chapter spent in the Shire and a chapter spent dealing with the three trolls, Bilbo and Gandalf and Thorin and the rest of the dwarves make it safely to Rivendell—also known as Imladris, "The Last Homely House" "west of the Mountains" (*Hobbit* 44) and "The Last Homely House east of the Sea" (*FR* 219). They stay there for more than a fortnight. As with the Shire, Rivendell has a location, and history, and a definable community. It is located in the foothills of the Misty Mountains in eastern Eriador between two rivers: Mitheithel and Bruinen. It was founded in Second Age 1697 by Elrond Half-elven. It serves as a refuge for any and all enemies of Morgoth and Sauron (respectively "Dark Enemy" in Sindarin and "Abominable" in Quenyan). It is, perhaps, utopian even in the dictionary's misguided sense of the word: "perfect, whether you liked food, or sleep, or work, or story-telling, or singing, or just sitting and thinking best, or a pleasant mixture of them all. Evil things did not come into that valley" (*Hobbit* 48). Rivendell and Elrond aid Thorin and company in their journey to the Lonely Mountain to eradicate the Desolation of Smaug. Eutopia fighting dystopia.

To this sketch in a children's story, Tolkien added much almost two decades later in *The Lord of the Rings*. Now, Rivendell as an elven pocket eutopia represents a "cure for weariness, fear, and sadness" (*FR* 219). It is a place where, as Pippin puts it, it "seems impossible, somehow, to feel gloomy or depressed" (*FR* 220). It is an inaccessible "fortress" against the "dark" (*FR* 220). It is, as

Bilbo puts it, "a remarkable place altogether," and one outside of time ("Time doesn't seem to pass here: it just is") (*FR* 225). It is, as Frodo senses when he hears Bilbo sing or chant of Eärendil the Mariner, a place in which "visions of far lands and bright things" beyond imagination appear "like a golden mist above seas of foam that sighed upon the margins of the world" (*FR* 227). It is, above all things, a place of learning and lore and memory: the perfect place for the Council of Elrond at which the Fellowship decides to destroy the One Ring. Rivendell is so because just as the Shire is protected as a eutopian site by the watchful Rangers (most particularly Strider) and the ignorance of the rest of the world as to its existence, so Imladris is protected by Elrond, a half-elf who possesses great wisdom. This wisdom is founded on his having "seen three ages in the West of the world, and many defeats, and many fruitless victories" (*FR* 237) and on possessing the most powerful of the three elven rings: Vilya. That ring was a gift to Elrond from Gil-galad, the only elven king to defeat Sauron. It is Elrond in his wisdom who knows that Imladris cannot stand alone against Sauron: "I have not the strength" (*FR* 259), and Elrond in his wisdom who knows the One Ring must be destroyed: "We must send the Ring to the Fire" (*FR* 260). And just as Tolkien sketched the ordered beauty of the Shire, so he sketched the natural, hidden beauty of Rivendell, as inaccessible in its own way as another site of learning and wisdom against the decline of the world: Shangri-La in James Hilton's utopian classic *Lost Horizon* (1933).

Beorn

After their sojourn in the Last Homely House in Chapter III of *The Hobbit*, Bilbo and the dwarves encounter another pocket eutopia only four chapters later: Beorn's house. Beorn (along with Tom Bombadil) is one of Tolkien's stranger creations. Not without reason does he title the part of the narrative involving Beorn "Queer Lodgings." Like the earlier pocket utopias, Beorn's domain has a definite history and a definite location near the Carrock (a boulder in the Great River of Wilderland some miles north of the Old Ford). It also has a definite set of peculiar qualities. Beorn himself is ancient but likely came down from the Misty Mountains to dwell in an oak wood near the Anduin. He is a shape changer, a "Somebody" or "*somebody*," "a very great person" (*Hobbit* 105):

sometimes man, sometimes bear, part magician. He has a "great wooden house" (*Hobbit* 106) that (as illustrated in *The Hobbit*) looks like nothing so much as a Viking or Anglo-Saxon mead hall. He keeps horses and cattle and dogs and sheep and bees. All but the last can apparently talk with him and work for him and are "wonderful animals" "nearly as marvelous as himself" (*Hobbit* 115, 106); the last are huge, bigger than hornets. He eats mainly honey and cream (as would befit a bear). And as with the other pocket utopias, Beorn's realm is protected—not just by his stature or powers (he is instrumental at the end of *The Hobbit* in the victory over the orcs) but by nature. For his land is fenced and the hall is screened by "A belt of tall and very ancient oaks" and a "high thorn-hedge through which you could neither see nor scramble" (*Hobbit* 107). It is further protected by a "wooden gate, high and broad" (*Hobbit* 108). The principle of this eutopia is a certain gruff kindness to strangers, that kindness including food of course, "a supper, or a dinner, such as they had not had since they left the Last Homely House in the West and said good-bye to Elrond" (*Hobbit* 115). When Beorn discovers that Gandalf's story about their dire journey is true he promises them aid: "I have hurried home as fast as I could to see you were safe, and to offer you any help that I can" (*Hobbit* 121). That aid is horses, ample food, advice about the dangers of Mirkwood, and an open invitation to them to stay with him again. Yes, the Beorn episode is slight as pocket utopias go (it seems to derive in part from the story of three bears in Tolkien's *Mr. Bliss*), but it matters precisely because it does little to drive the narrative. It matters because Tolkien wanted to show the reader a character utterly one with nature.

There are no more pocket utopias in *The Hobbit* (it is, after all, a slight children's story and not an epic), but it is interesting that it ends in a manner that suggests Tolkien sees the world as one which oscillates between eutopia and dystopia. Bilbo returns to his beloved home to find Bag End put on the auction block by the loathsome Sackville-Bagginses, but he discovers from Gandalf years after his return from his adventure that Smaug's mischief has been righted by Bard. The valley in which Dale sits "had become tilled again and rich, and the desolation was now filled with birds and blossoms in spring and fruit and feasting in autumn" (*Hobbit* 272). And Lake-town had been "re-founded and was more prosperous than ever, and much wealth went up and down the Running

River" (*Hobbit* 272). And most eutopian of all "there was friendship in those parts between elves and dwarves and men" (*Hobbit* 272).

Doriath

As I began by saying in this chapter, when *The Hobbit* was published in 1937 Tolkien had been at work on his legendarium for more than a score of years. That work we now know well because his late son Christopher published *The Silmarillion* in 1977 (a few years after his father died) and because he also published an exhaustive account of the earlier versions of the legendarium as *Unfinished Tales of Númenor and Middle-earth* (1980), The History of Middle-earth series in twelve volumes (1983-1996), and *The Children of Húrin* (2007), *Beren and Lúthien* (2017), and *The Fall of Gondolin* (2018). The legendarium includes three hidden elvish kingdoms of the First Age that I want to examine in chronological order as pocket eutopias: Doriath; Nargothrond; and Gondolin.

Doriath (earlier Artanor), which means "Land of the Fence" in Sindarin, is the forested realm of Elu Thingol in the First Age of Middle-earth. It is protected (as all eutopias must be). In this case, it is so by the Girdle of Melian. (Melian is a Maia—or servant of the Valar—and Thingol's wife.) The kingdom gets swept up in Tolkien's greatest love story, that of Beren and Lúthien, as Lúthien is Thingol and Melian's daughter and the most beautiful being in all the long history of Middle-earth. The principal claims of Doriath as pocket utopia are, as before, that it has a definite location, point of origin, and philosophy antagonistic to evil. The location is Beleriand (between the regions of Dimbar and East Beleriand) with the kingdom including the forests or woods of Neldoreth, Nivrim, and Arthórien. The kingdom is founded early in the First Age after Thingol (the king of the Sindarin elves) falls in love with Melian in Valar Year 1152 and turns aside from the Valar's summons to the elves to return and be protected from the depredations of Morgoth. Doriath's philosophy is aesthetic and ideological and moral. The first part of that philosophy, the aesthetic, blossoms into Menegroth (the hidden halls of a thousand caves built by the dwarves of Belegost on the river Esgalduin). It is worth quoting in full from the description in "The Grey Annals," for these caves are wondrous. Built in Valar Year 1300, they constitute

> images of the wonder and beauty of Valinor beyond the Sea. The pillars of Menegroth were hewn in the likeness of the beeches of Oromë, stock, bough, and leaf, and they were lit with lanterns of gold. The nightingales sang there as in the gardens of Lórien; and there were fountains of silver, and basins of marble, and floors of many-coloured stones. Carven figures of beasts and of birds there ran upon the walls, or climbed upon the pillars, or peered among the branches entwined with many flowers. And as the years passed Melian and her maidens filled the halls with webs of many hues, wherein could be read the deeds of the Valar, and many things that had befallen in Arda since its beginning, and shadows of things that were yet to be. That was the fairest dwelling of any king that hath ever been east of the Sea (*WJ* 11).

Part living art installation then, and part chronicle. The second part, the ideological, reinforces, through Doriath's forests and woods, Tolkien's delight in trees for their own sake and as bastions against the rise of the machine age. The third, the moral, substantiates the elves' desire to overthrow Morgoth at any cost. And as with so many pocket utopias, it has a definite end—in this case with Thingol being murdered by the dwarves of Nogrod and the destruction of Doriath by dwarves intent on capturing one of the silmarils. (See chapters 4 and 22 of *The Silmarillion.*)

Nargothrond

Nargothrond, which means "fortress on the river Narog" in Sindarin, is unusual in the legendarium for being created in imitation of another realm—in this case, Doriath. After the Noldor return to Middle-earth, the Valar Ulmo advises Finrod to construct a refuge for the Noldorin. He does so, and deliberately models the refuge on Doriath's Menegroth. There he builds "deep halls and armouries, after the manner of Menegroth" ("The Grey Annals", *WJ* 35). It has a specific location on the river Narog in West Beleriand. As a pocket utopia, it has both a definite beginning and a definite ending. The latter occurs when the ill-fated Túrin Turambar persuades the Noldor of Nargothrond (the largest of the Noldorin kingdoms) to move from stealthy harassment of the forces of Morgoth to open battle. The strategy initially works and large areas in West Beleriand are freed from the malign influence of Morgoth. In First Age 496, however, Morgoth sends a massive army against Nargothrond led by the dragon Glaurung. Túrin and Finrod's successor and brother Orodreth are defeated at the battle of Tumhalad, and Glaurung sacks Nargothrond. The city is then left utterly deserted. In the absence of a defensive shield like that provided to Doriath by Melian's Girdle, Nargothrond depends upon secrecy to survive. Its eutopian beliefs are those of Doriath on which it was modelled: aesthetic caves and an implacable hatred of the evil Morgoth represents. Beauty and implacable hatred are not, however, enough. As with Doriath and, later, Gondolin, eutopia falls in battle to dystopia. (See chapter 21 of *The Silmarillion.*)

Gondolin

Gondolin ("Hidden by Rocks" in Sindarin) is unique in the legendarium as the only story of Tolkien's about something other than characters (such as Túrin Turambar or Beren and Lúthien) worthy of being separately published as a book by Tolkien's son Christopher. It is fitting that it should also have been his son's last edited work (published in 2018) before his death in January 2020. The city was founded by Turgon, son of Fingolfin, and built on Amon Gwareth on the plain of Tumladen surrounded by the Echoriath mountains. Unlike Doriath and Nargothrond, Gondolin is both a city and a kingdom, and not a kingdom distinguished by its glorious underground caves. Like Doriath and Nargothrond, Gondolin is protected. Where Doriath had Melian's Girdle and Nargothrond, until late in its existence, a policy of stealth resistance to Morgoth, Gondolin has Ulmo's blessing and the vigilance of the eagles led by Thorondor. It is the eagles which constantly drive away any and all of Morgoth's spies. The secrecy of this pocket eutopia is grounded, however, not just in Ulmo and eagles but also in a strict aversion to visitors. For many long years, only four outsiders ever visited the city: Eöl, Huor, Húrin, and Maeglin. It is in this city that Eärendil (the savior of Middle-earth) is born. The general location of the city is ultimately but unintentionally revealed to Morgoth by Húrin, and the passes to its entrance maliciously and deliberately betrayed to Morgoth by Maeglin. The city is sacked in First Age 511 by a terrible onslaught from balrogs, dragons, orcs, and wolves, but, crucially, Eärendil escapes. It is the last of the elven kingdoms in Beleriand to fall to Morgoth. Its credentials as a pocket eutopia are founded (as with Doriath and Nargothrond) on aesthetics and an implacable opposition to evil. The first is shown by the city being the fairest elven city in all of Middle-earth, for it is modelled on the city of Tirion, the principal city in Eldamar (also Elvenhome). As *The Silmarillion* put it:

> High and white were its [Gondolin's] walls, and smooth its stairs, and tall and strong was the Tower of the King. There shining fountains played, and in the courts of Turgon stood images of the Trees of old, which Turgon himself wrought with elven-craft; and the Tree which he made of gold was named Glingal, and the Tree whose flowers he made of silver was named Belthil (*Silmarillion* 126).

The latter (an implacable opposition to evil) by Turgon's wise decision not to fight in the Dagor Bragollach (or "Battle of Sudden Flame"), the fourth battle of the elves against Morgoth, but to contribute 10,000 men to the Nirnaeth Arnoediad ("Battle of Unnumbered Tears"). In the latter conflict, the location of Gondolin remains hidden to Morgoth through the brave rearguard action of Huor and Húrin. (See chapter 23 of *The Silmarillion* and *The Fall of Gondolin.*)

Númenor

The Second Age is the least developed of all the Ages in the legendarium. The story of Númenor (also Númenórë) is best developed in the "Akallabêth" (*Silmarillion* 257-282), and also constitutes the first part of *The Lost Road and Other Writings* (7-38) and the first section in part two of *Unfinished Tales of Númenor and Middle-earth* (165-172). There are reasons for Tolkien's brevity. He came late to the story in the development of the legendarium; he may have felt the myth hewed from its beginning too closely to the story of Atlantis; and its inspiration, unusually, was a competition with C. S. Lewis begun in about 1936. Lewis would produce a "space-travel" story; Tolkien, a "time-travel" one. Lewis, as usual, got a book from his efforts, *Out of the Silent Planet.* Tolkien (as so often) did not, for his "effort, after a few promising chapters, ran dry" (*Letters* 378). Nevertheless, despite its relative slightness, the history of Númenor is the most interesting account of Tolkien' s many pocket eutopias besides, of course, the Shire. Above all, it is a cautionary tale about what happens when a race is given a eutopia without having to work for it.

Númenor as the kingdom of the Dúnedain in the Second Age is everything that realms such as Doriath and Nargothrond and Gondolin could only aspire to be. It's almost as if the first is the apotheosis of all the rest. It is founded in year 32 of the Second Age on an island raised from the sea by Ossë, "established by Aulë, and enriched by Yavanna" (*Lost Road* 14). It was situated to the west of the Great Sea of Belegaer. It is a reward to the Edain (or the Three Houses of Elf-friends: Bëor, Hador, and Haladin) for their loyal support in the War of the Jewels and the eventual overthrow of Morgoth in the War of Wrath. By Eönwë, the Númenóreans are also granted "wisdom and power and life more enduring than any others of mortal race have possessed" (*Silmarillion* 260). They are a "great people" who become "mariners whose like shall never be again, since the world was diminished" (*Lost Road* 15). Indeed, ordinary men of Middle-earth considered them to be "Gods or sons of Gods out of the West" (*Lost Road* 15). On this island, there is much beauty in the capital of Anadúnië and the city of Armenelos the Golden, "fairest of cities" (*Silmarillion* 261). The land as a whole is "fair and fruitful" (*Silmarillion* 261), and by the Eldar the Númenóreans are given "birds of song, and fragrant flowers, and herbs of great virtue" and the tree Nimloth, a direct descendant of Galathilion, the tree in which the memory of Telperion, the elder of the Two Trees of Valinor, lives (*Silmarillion* 263). As if to emphasize the eutopian potential Númenor represents, Tolkien has the Valar term the island Andor or "the Land of Gift" (*Silmarillion* 260).

So, what goes wrong? Well, the Valar properly forbid the Númenóreans from sailing to Valinor and they deny them immortality. The Númenóreans come to envy the Eldar their deathlessness, and are unpersuaded that, in death, Men's purpose is fulfilled just as in life without end the Eldar fulfill theirs. They want to visit Valinor when they wish and return to Númenor as they desire. They are unpersuaded by the eloquence of the messengers of Manwë, who essentially make Tolkien's argument that eutopia (any pocket utopia, too) must be an expression of potential in this sublunary world and in no other. The messengers state: the Eldar (or elves)

> cannot escape, and are bound to this world, never to leave it so long as it lasts, for its life is theirs. And you [the Númenóreans] are punished for the rebellion of Men, you say, in which you had small part, and so it is that you die. But that was not at first appointed for a punishment. Thus you escape, and leave the world, and are not bound to it, in hope or in weariness. Which of us therefore should envy the others? (*Silmarillion* 264-265).

The Númenóreans become proud, troubled by the thought of death, and decadent ("they drank and they feasted and they clad themselves in silver and gold") (*Silmarillion* 267). In truth, Sauron comes among them and corrupts them. Morgoth has been banished for ever from the world, but not his servants. Like Satan or like Wormtongue, Sauron learns to ingratiate himself through "flattery sweet as honey" that "was ever on his tongue" (*Silmarillion* 271). Three of the Númenorian lords become ensnared by Sauron's offer of rings and become Ringwraiths.

From such eutopian beginnings, the Númenorian kings decline to "worship of the Dark" (*Silmarillion* 272). The last king of Númenor, Ar-Pharazôn, becomes so deluded that he fells the tree Nimloth and worships in a great temple constructed by Sauron for the adoration of Morgoth. In that temple, there is "spilling of blood and torment and great wickedness"—all in an effort to avoid death (*Silmarillion* 273). In an act of extraordinary arrogance, Ar-Pharazôn sails at the last with a mighty fleet to try to overthrow the Valar and succeed thereby, he thinks, in achieving immortality. There can only be one result from such eutopian beginnings gone so horribly wrong: utter destruction. Yes, Ar-Pharazôn's "heart misgave him when he looked upon the soundless shores [of Valinor] and saw Taniquetil shining, whiter than snow, colder than death, silent, immutable, terrible as the shadow of the light of Ilúvatar," but that is not enough for "pride was now his master" (*Silmarillion* 278). Númenor sinks beneath the waves; Sauron perishes only to return in a new guise; and all the Númenóreans who dared to challenge the Valar are imprisoned in "the Caves of the Forgotten, until the Last Battle and the Day of Doom." And everything eutopian perishes too:

> all its [Númenor's] gardens and its halls and its towers, its tombs and its riches, and its jewels and its webs and its things painted and carven, and its laughter and its mirth and its music, its wisdom and its lore: they vanished for ever (*Silmarillion* 279).

Sic transit gloria mundi. Only three Númenóreans—Elendil, Isildur and Anárion—and nine ships survive. These three found kingdoms in Middle-earth, and it is their descendant, Aragorn, who defeats Sauron yet again at the end of the Third Age.

After the fall of Númenor, the Third Age begins, but, given limitations of space, I will not talk here of all its several pocket eutopias. I have talked already of the Shire and of Rivendell. I will not mention Minas Tirith (as a pale image of Armenelos the Golden) or Fangorn before Saruman's depredations. I shall only talk of one remarkable person and one remarkable realm: Tom Bombadil and Lothlórien ("Blossom Dreamland" in Sindarin).

Tom Bombadil

Of all the many beings in Tolkien's legendarium, Tom Bombadil is, perhaps, the strangest. Part of the reason may be that the character was based on a Dutch doll Tolkien's son Michael had when a child. However, rather than appearing in a children's story, that is, in *The Hobbit*, he shows up fully created in the epic tale of *The Lord of the Rings*. (It may be that in *The Hobbit* there was not room enough for Beorn *and* Bombadil.) He is fascinating, but in some ways an awkward fit in the epic, awkward enough that Peter Jackson excised him entirely from his cinematic version of *The Lord of the Rings*. Tolkien himself was aware of this problem, for in a letter dated 12 April 1962 to Rayner Unwin (one of the sons of his publisher), he comments that the character was "inserted" into *The Lord of the Rings* and not with enough elegance (*Letters* 315). He had known almost a decade earlier, indeed, that "many [readers] have found him an odd or discordant ingredient" (*Letters* 192). Bombadil wears big yellow boots, a blue coat, and an old hat much the worse for wear with a long blue feather in its band. Bombadil's name derives from the Middle English "bobadil," that is "braggart," but in other languages what is emphasized is his age. He himself says, and others suggest the same, that he is the oldest being in Middle-earth, older than Galadriel, older, perhaps, than even Treebeard. The elves call him *Iarwain Ben-adar* ("oldest and fatherless" in Sindarin); the Rohirrim, *Orald* ("very ancient" in Anglo-Saxon); the dwarves, *Forn* ("of ancient times" in Old Norse). He has a small kingdom along the Withywindle river between the edge of the Old Forest and the Barrow-downs. There he lives an ideal life with Goldberry, the River-woman's daughter, and there he is absolute master. The One Ring, uniquely, has no influence over him. He is generous and kind to the hobbits: Frodo, Merry, Pippin, and Sam. He rescues them from the dangerous and cunning Old Man Willow in the Old Forest and from the even deadlier barrow-wights on the Barrow-downs. He was popular enough with readers for him to feature in a 1962 collection of poems titled *The Adventures of Tom Bombadil and Other Verses from the Red Book* (a sequel of sorts to his appearance in *The Fellowship of the Ring*) and a slight, one-off poem, "Once upon a Time," published in 1965 in a collection edited by Caroline Hillier (*Winter's Tales for Children 1*). However, it is important to note that the idea for a story or stories about Tom Bombadil is much older than 1962, older than *The Lord of the Rings* (1954-1955), older even than *The Hobbit* (1937), for the titular poem in the 1962 "sequel" dates from February 1934 (when it was first published in *Oxford Magazine*).

The crucial question, of course, is what Bombadil and his pocket eutopia represent. This is a hard question because Tolkien (as he admitted in a 25 April 1954 letter to Naomi Mitchison) created Tom Bombadil as an intentionally enigmatic character (*Letters* 174). Within the works themselves, he seems to symbolize a nature deity. He is married to the daughter of the river, and after the four hobbits have been rescued from Old Man Willow, Frodo asks Goldberry about Bombadil. She begins with something gnomic: "He is, as you have seen him" (*FR* 122), but then amplifies that to: "He is the Master of wood, water, and hill" (*FR* 122) within a natural community of creatures in which each has independent being. "The trees and the grasses and all things growing or living in the land belong each to themselves," she says" (*FR* 122). In a sense, he seems to be responsible for a cooperative enterprise, an intentional community of two with innumerable acolytes. As he is a nature deity, the food is always plentiful at his house—as Bombadil says: "The table is all laden with yellow cream, honeycomb, and white bread and butter" (*FR* 118). Goldberry is, as one might expect, as much a part of nature as he is, and lovely because of that fact:

> Her long yellow hair rippled down her shoulders; her gown was green, green as young reeds, shot with silver like beads of dew; and her belt was of gold, shaped like a chain of flag-lilies set with the pale-blue eyes of forget-me-nots. About her feet in wide vessels of green and brown earthenware, white water-lilies were floating, so that she seemed to be enthroned in the midst of a pool (*FR* 121).

She is "as young and as ancient as Spring" and has a voice "like the song of a glad water flowing down into the night from a bright morning in the hills." It has the cadence of falling silver (*FR* 119).

Nevertheless, Tolkien himself is unusually helpful in answering this question of what Bombadil means—at least early in this character's creation. In a letter to his publisher, Stanley Unwin, dated 16 December 1937 (right after, that is, the publication of *The Hobbit*), Tolkien discusses the merits of the non-hobbit material he has just sent him. The majority of that was Silmarillion material, but he also sent Unwin his 1934 Bombadil poem. Now he asks "Do you think Tom Bombadil [...] could be made into the hero of a story?" but only after he has characterized him very specifically as "the spirit of the (vanishing) Oxford and Berkshire countryside" (*Letters* 26). Later in that long 1954 letter to Naomi Mitchison from which I quoted earlier, he talks of Bombadil as representative of "Botany and Zoology (as sciences) and Poetry as opposed to Cattle-breeding and agriculture and practicality" (*Letters* 179). In this way, he is "not an important person," but "he has some importance as a 'comment'" (*Letters* 178). Last and, perhaps, most importantly, he symbolizes someone who is a "natural pacifist," someone who has no desire to possess and who never experiences fear (*Letters* 179). With the bloody history of the twentieth century in mind (so much war and so much possessiveness and so much fear), these are surely cardinal virtues to Tolkien and to us. And that is enough I think, for Tolkien himself admonishes one of his numerous correspondents (Peter Hastings): "I don't think Tom needs philosophizing about, and is not improved by it" (*Letters* 192).

Lothlórien (also Lórien)

Originally called Laurelindórian ("golden song valley" in Quenyan) and termed "Golden Wood" and the "Hidden Land" in Westron as well as "Dwimordene" ("Haunted Valley") by the Rohirrim, Lothlórien is (along with Rivendell) the single most important pocket eutopia standing against the dystopian power of Saruman and Sauron in Middle-earth. Indeed, it is perhaps more important than Rivendell, for the latter is ruled over by someone who is only "half-elven" (Elrond) and the former by a Noldorin princess and the most beautiful woman of the house of Finwë, Galadriel. It is an elven realm as impervious to Sauron's power (without the One Ring) as Rivendell—and for the same reason. Where Rivendell had Elrond and the elven ring Vilya, Lothlórien has Galadriel and Nenya, a ring she was freely given at its creation. It is a ring (the "Ring of Adamant") which, as Legolas puts it, constitutes "a secret power" that "holds evil from the land" (*FR* 356, 329). With it, Galadriel may wisely guess at Sauron's plans, but her mind is ever closed to his. This pocket eutopia is deliberately modelled on Doriath and founded in the Second Age by Galadriel. It is located just west of where two rivers (Celebrant and Anduin) meet and itself contains two lesser rivers (Silverlode and Nimrodel). Three times in the Third Age, the wood is attacked by Sauron's forces (under the command of the Nazgûl) from Dol Guldur in southern Mirkwood. Three times those forces are defeated. So strong is Lothlórien that though it is surrounded by the forces of evil "on the land of Lórien no shadow lay" (*FR* 340). Truly eutopian, then, and Tolkien almost repeats the phrase within a page as if for emphasis: "On the land of Lórien there was no stain" (*FR* 341). It also represents hope as Galadriel believes that the acceptance of Gimli in Lothlórien—when dwarves and elves have been bitter enemies for many ages of the world—is "a sign that though the world is now dark better days are at hand" (*FR* 346). Gimli silently agrees, for when he first meets Galadriel he seems to look into "the heart of an enemy" but he sees there "love and understanding." Hope there is when Gimli is so transformed at the sight of her that he instantly remarks directly to her: "The Lady Galadriel is above all the jewels that lie beneath the earth!" (*FR* 347). This from the kin of Thorin Oakenshield is praise indeed!

Lothlórien plays a major role in *The Lord of the Rings* after the Fellowship succeeds in navigating Khazad-dûm even after it suffers the loss of Gandalf. It forms the principal matter of three chapters (VI-VIII) in *The Fellowship of the Ring*: "Lothlórien"; "The Mirror of Galadriel"; and "Farewell to Lórien." Tolkien takes the opportunity to describe this eutopian realm and its community of Silvan elves in considerable detail. We find out that it is under near constant, if minor, threat from orcs ("yrch" in Elvish) and wolves. We discover something of elvish architecture as the elves live on "flets" or "talans" (treehouses of a sort without walls or rails but with "a light plaited screen, which could be moved and fixed in different places according to the wind" [*FR* 335]). We are introduced to the delights of "lembas": a waybread definitely more sustaining and tastier than the dwarves' "cram" and more delightful even than the honey-cakes of the Beornings (*FR* 360-361). We are told that the heart of the forest lies in a section called the Naith and, within that, there is a sacred hill called Cerin Amroth, and that hill is, as Aragorn wistfully says, "the heart of Elvendom on earth" (*FR* 343). Its capital city (Caras Galadhon) echoes eutopia's concern with the environment, for it is called the "City of the Trees." We learn that Galadriel and Celeborn have dwelt together there "years uncounted; for ere the fall of Nargothrond or Gondolin" Galadriel "passed over the mountains." And it matters that Lothlórien may be a eutopian enclave of loveliness and grace and beauty, a place where nature is deeply honoured, but it is ruled by realists. They know that for years uncounted they "have fought the long defeat" (348). Sauron may be defeated, but the elves will fade and leave Middle-earth.

For the Fellowship (now only eight strong without Gandalf), the sojourn in Lothlórien is idyllic:

> They remained some days in Lothlórien, so far as they could tell or remember. All the while that they dwelt there the sun shone clear, save for a gentle rain that fell at times, and passed away leaving all things fresh and clean. The air was cool and soft, as if it were early spring, yet they felt about them the deep and thoughtful quiet of winter. It seemed to them that they did little but eat and drink and rest, and walk among the trees; and it was enough (*FR* 349).

Or in Sam's language: "Nothing seems to be going on, and nobody seems to want it to" (*FR* 351). And then this idyll is interrupted for a short while as Galadriel allows Sam and Frodo to look into her Mirror if they wish, a remarkable device which enshrines the eutopian principle of foresight. As Galadriel simply phrases it: "it shows things that were, and things that are, and things that yet may be" (*FR* 352). Notably the Mirror is embedded in nature at its loveliest. It is created by pouring water from the stream into a basin. The stream runs through a "deep green hollow" and the basin sits on "a low pedestal carved like a branching tree" (*FR* 352). In it, Sam sees the dystopian destruction of the Shire. In it, Frodo sees the Eye of Sauron (the personification of dystopian desire) searching for him and not finding him. Not quite. And in this episode, Galadriel, as this community's leader, is tested and passes the test. Frodo offers the One Ring freely to her and she rejects the offer, but in so doing she shows how rapidly eutopia can pass into dystopia even with the best intentions:

> In place of the Dark Lord you will set up a Queen. And I shall not be dark, but beautiful and terrible as the Morning and the Night! Fair as the Sea and the Sun and the Snow upon the Mountain! Dreadful as the Storm and the Lightning! Stronger than the foundations of the earth. All shall love me and despair! (*FR* 356).

She accepts eutopia and its corollary for the elves: "We must depart into the West, or dwindle to a rustic folk of dell and cave, slowly to forget and to be forgotten" (*FR* 356). The logic of dystopia is power; the logic of eutopia, acceptance: Galadriel wishes only that "what should be will be" (*FR* 356).

And as the Fellowship leaves, each is given a gift by Galadriel, and each gift is either an emblem of oneness with the natural world or a symbol of the love between good people. So, members of the Fellowship all receive warm and silky cloaks and hoods which render them invisible: "grey with the hue of twilight under the trees they seemed to be; and yet if they were moved, or set in another light, they were green as shadowed leaves, or brown as fallow fields by night, dusk-silver as water under the stars" (*FR* 361). These cloaks were made according to a simple principle that died for Tolkien with the Industrial Revolution: "we put the thought of all that we love into all that we make," says the "leader of the Elves" (*FR* 361). And so, Sam, ever the gardener, receives a box with earth in it from Galadriel's garden and a seed of the mallorn tree. And so, above all, Gimli is rewarded with three golden hairs from Galadriel's head because all he wants is something to have "in memory of your [Galadriel's] words to me at our first meeting" (*FR* 367).

Much as I love to talk of all things eutopian in the legendarium, it is important to look at the other side of the image of communities at one with nature. We need to talk of dystopias in Tolkien's mythology. Fortunately, it need not detain us long, for all the examples are cut from the same design if not from quite the same cloth. Brutalist architecture, unvarnished power, cruel mind.

Utumno, Angband, Thangorodrim

These three fortresses belonged to Morgoth; they were his creation and date from the time when he was known as Melkor. Utumno ("The Pit" in Quenya) was his first fortress and citadel. It was a huge underground complex in the north of Middle-earth and was built during the Spring of Arda. He threw up the Iron Mountains (or Ered Engrin) as a fence to protect it. It is enough to see the damage he did to nature to understand how much Melkor and everything he created defined dystopia for Tolkien:

> The evil of Melkor and the blight of his hatred flowed out thence, and the Spring of Arda was marred. Green things fell sick and rotted, and rivers were choked with weeds and slime, and fens were made, rank and poisonous, the breeding place of flies; and forests grew dark and perilous, the haunts of fear; and beasts became monsters of horn and ivory and dyed the earth with blood (*Silmarillion* 36).

There he bred balrogs and orcs (as bastardized elves) and spiders. There he imprisoned many and cruelly corrupted and enslaved them. There he was finally defeated by the Valar at the Second Great Battle and after the Siege of Utumno. Utumno was unroofed and broken, and so came to an end what J.E.A. Tyler has memorably called "the vast and dreadful reality of Morgoth's first realm" (671). As a result of that battle, Angband, Melkor's second great fortress ("Iron Prison" in Sindarin), was likewise destroyed—albeit not completely. It had been built some 150 leagues north of Menegroth. Its purpose was to guard Melkor from unexpected attack by the Valar and was ruled over by his lieutenant, Sauron. When Morgoth returned from his long imprisonment, he rebuilt Angband and it was not finally and wholly destroyed until the Great Battle at the end of the First Age in which the combined might of the Valar, the Eldar, and the Edain finally destroyed Morgoth for all time and remade the map of Beleriand. Thangorodrim ("Mountains of Tyranny" in Sindarin) was a three-peaked mountain above Angband created by the slag produced when the fortress was built. It was broken by the dragon Ancalagon the Black's falling on it during the Great Battle. That did not happen, however, until after Húrin was chained on its slopes for 28 years so that he could watch the destruction of the elves.

Dol Guldur, Barad-dûr

The first of these ("Hill of Sorcery" in Sindarin) was for almost two thousand years of the Third Age the most feared fortress of Sauron's besides Barad-dûr itself. It was located in the southwest reaches of Mirkwood and founded in about 1100 of that Age. The White Council drove Sauron from there in 2941, but not before he had tortured and killed Thráin II after five long years of torment. In 3041, the Nazgûl re-occupied it until Galadriel utterly destroyed it after the defeat of Sauron at the end of the Third Age. The second (Barad-dûr, "Dark Tower" in Sindarin) was the mightiest fortress of the Second and Third Ages. Located in the Ered Lithui (or "Ashy Mountains") in Mordor, it was first destroyed by the forces of the Last Alliance at the end of the Second Age but only after a seven-year siege. However, it could not be entirely broken for its foundations held strong as they were protected by the One Ring. At the end of the Third Age and with the destruction of the One Ring in the fires of Mount Doom, Barad-dûr was finally and permanently destroyed. It is a dreadful place, a "shadow-mantled fortress" with "cruel pinnacles" and a "proud and bitter crown" (*RK* 921, 924). And as it falls to destruction, Sam sees its "towers and battlements, tall as hills, founded upon a mighty mountain-throne above immeasurable pits; great courts and dungeons, eyeless prisons sheer as cliffs, and gaping gates of steel and adamant" (925).

Minas Morgul, Isengard, Orthanc

Minas Morgul was formerly Minas Ithil, a Gondorian fortress of great power and beauty built in 3320 of the Second Age and the place where the White Tree was kept. That is, before the Nazgûl took it over in 2002 of the Third Age and made of it a place of fear. So, "The Tower of the Moon" (in Sindarin) became the "Tower of Sorcery." The last two (Isengard and Orthanc) were similarly the creations of Gondor and lovely before Saruman perverted them with the same intent as Sauron and the Nazgûl had corrupted Minas Ithil. Isengard (or Angrenost) was a natural rock formation enclosing a valley no more than a mile wide. The Dúnedain cleverly fashioned the formation to make it nearly impregnable. There they built the Tower of Orthanc (500 hundred feet high and made of smooth, glossy, black stone). It is this Tower which Saruman took over through trickery and made of the entire site a military camp with dens and pits and armouries and caves. And there he used the Uruk-hai, a "superior" race of orcs created by Sauron, to try to break the Rohirrim. When Saruman was cast out of the order of the Istari (or wizards) by Gandalf in 3019 of the Third Age, Isengard and Orthanc returned to their rightful owner, Aragorn.

Some Reflections on Tolkien's Utopian Vision

So, I have toured and discussed many of the pocket utopias Tolkien created in his legendarium. What generalizations can be drawn from such a discussion?

To begin, the pocket eutopias. Several foci come to mind here: simplicity; order; friendship; love of the natural world; pity; and hope. Simplicity in the life the hobbits live in the Shire: good food and lots of it and conversation, and gift giving, and family. Order in the neatness of hobbit homes and the aesthetic beauty of the hidden elven kingdoms in the First Age (Doriath, Nargothrond, and Gondolin) and the Second and Third (Lothlórien). Friendship among the fifteen of Thorin and company who struggle to the Lonely Mountain and among the twelve who come back in *The Hobbit*. Friendship among the nine (and, later, eight) of the Fellowship of the Ring who achieve together the extraordinary: destruction of the One Ring in the fires of Orodruin. Love of the natural world in every pocket eutopia, but perhaps most spectacularly in Rivendell and Lothlórien. And then there are the qualities so striking in those who gain a victory over evil: pity and hope. The first of these is best illustrated in that early but vital conversation between Gandalf and Frodo before Frodo and his fellow hobbits leave the Shire. Frodo says it is a pity that Bilbo did not kill Gollum when he had the chance. Gandalf emphatically replies:

> Pity? It was pity that stayed his hand. Pity and Mercy: not to strike without need. And he has been well rewarded, Frodo. Be sure that he took so little hurt from the evil [of the Ring], and escaped in the end, because he began his ownership of the Ring so. With Pity (*FR* 58).

And pity is evident in all the pocket eutopias, pity for all the creatures damaged or killed by the evil that Morgoth and Sauron represent. And it is a vital quality, for, as Gandalf remarks right after his comments about pity, Gollum, he believes, "has some part to play yet, for good or ill, before the end, and when that comes, the pity of Bilbo may rule the fate of many [...]" (*FR* 58). And Gollum does. Without him, the Ring would never have been destroyed.

Had Bilbo killed him when he had the chance, the story would have been very different. It is as simple as that.

As to the importance of hope, that is symbolized in the Council of Elrond's decision to destroy the Ring, in Faramir's decision to let Frodo and Sam go after he captures them in Ithilien, and in Aragorn and Gandalf's decision at the Last Debate to challenge Sauron and give Frodo and Sam more time by having their army march to the Black Gate into Mordor. Pithily, Legolas summarizes their logic with this proverbial phrase: "*Oft is hope born, when all is forlorn*" (*RK* 859). And the narrative substantiates this belief in hope on two particular occasions. The Rohirrim are victorious against the odds at Helm's Deep, but Aragorn emphasizes that possibility before the final battle there when he says: "dawn is ever the hope of men" (*TT* 524). Later, the witch-king of Angmar would seem to have Gandalf at his mercy during the siege of Gondor: "Old fool!" he says to him, "Do you not know Death when you see it?" (*RK* 811). Gandalf does not reply, but nature emphatically does when a cock crows shrill and clear "recking nothing of wizardry or war, welcoming only the morning that in the sky far above the shadows of death was coming with the dawn." And at that moment the horns of the Rohirrim are heard: "Rohan had come at last" (*RK* 811). With the morning comes hope.

And now the pocket dystopias. They can be swiftly dealt with. They are characterized by isolation and cruelty and the lust for power and large-scale industrial production. Morgoth and Sauron and Saruman are utterly alone and friendless unless you count the odious and ultimately murderous Wormtongue as Saruman's friend. Morgoth is never anything other than cruel, but his chaining of Húrin to the slopes of Thangorodrim for 28 years stands out among his most appalling acts in this regard. Morgoth and Sauron and Saruman only ever want power. That wish is the entire purpose behind Morgoth's building of the massive fortresses of Utumno and Angband as well as Sauron's creation of the One Ring. And Saruman transforms Isengard and lays waste parts of Fangorn with only one purpose in mind: to create an unbeatable army of orcs. These are all the acts of beings intent for perverted reasons on creating an utterly dystopian reality.

Tolkien's Utopian Vision and Faery

I will finish by looking at two stories by Tolkien which explain well the particular qualities of his utopian vision. The first is *Leaf by Niggle*; the second *Smith of Wootton Major.*

Leaf by Niggle (originally titled *The Tree*) was first published in the *Dublin Review* in January 1945 and reprinted (with only minor revisions) in *Tree and Leaf* in 1964. It is a fascinating tale of a man named Niggle and his life and habits as a painter. It is clearly autobiographical (as Tolkien mentions in a letter to his aunt, Jane Neave, dated 8-9 September 1962) as it derives from his recollected anxieties about the writing of *The Lord of the Rings* (*Letters* 319-322). Very early on in the story, Tolkien describes Niggle's working habits:

> He had a number of pictures on hand; most of them were too large and ambitious for his skill. He was the sort of painter who can paint leaves better than trees. He used to spend a long time on a single leaf, trying to catch its shape, and its sheen, and the glistening of dewdrops on its edges. Yet he wanted to paint a whole tree, with all of its leaves in the same style, and all of them different
>
> There was one picture in particular which bothered him. It had begun with a leaf caught in the wind, and it became a tree; and the tree grew, sending out innumerable branches, and thrusting out the most fantastic roots (*Leaf* 73-74).

For the "whole tree" substitute the entire legendarium. For the "one picture in particular" think *The Lord of the Rings.* And for his attention to leaves at the expense of the tree, consider his habit of writing linear narratives punctuated by close attention to pocket utopias (both eutopian and dystopian). My focus on these in this essay derives, then, in part from Tolkien's working habits as imagined creatively in *Leaf by Niggle.*

Smith of Wootton Major is a late work by Tolkien. It was first published in 1967—only six years before his death. It grew out of an abandoned preface to an edition of George MacDonald's "The Golden Key," and it explores in a creative way many of the issues Tolkien covered in his seminal essay "On Fairy-Stories" (first published twenty years earlier). The story involves the making of a Great Cake every 24 years for a feast in the village of Wootton Major. In the story, we meet the King and Queen of Faery and visit their "perilous country" (*SWM* 257). It is an extraordinary country, and it is one which Smith comes to love and revere over a lifetime. Towards the end of the story, Smith realizes that his time in Faery is necessarily limited. So, Alf (the cook's assistant, who turns out to be the King of Faery) comforts him: the gifts one has "cannot belong to a man for ever, nor be treasured as heirlooms. They are lent. You have not thought, perhaps, that someone else may need this thing [a little silver star from the land of Faery]. But it is so. Time is pressing" (*SWM* 267). And so, the Queen of Faery comforts him too: "Better a little doll, maybe, than no memory of Faery at all. For some the only glimpse. For some the awaking" (265). For Smith, substitute Tolkien. For the star, think Tolkien's extraordinary talents as a creative writer. For a life in the land of Faery, consider that Tolkien spent a lifetime creating his legendarium (from 1914 to 1973). Tolkien was 75 when *Smith of Wootton Major* was published; he was just 22 when he wrote the poem which began it all, *The Voyage of Éarendel the Evening Star*. It was time, he knew to pass on the talent, and he did—to a whole generation of new writers. In essence, Tolkien founded the genre of modern fantasy. No wonder he felt *Smith of Wootton Major* was "An old man's book, already weighted with the presage of 'bereavement'" (*Letters* 389). No wonder, too, that in an essay on the story written after it was finished Tolkien asserted "this love of Faery is essential to the full and proper human development" (quoted in Scull and Hammond 2.947). Worth devoting a life to, then.

End Note

1 After I completed this essay, Hamish Williams published *J.R.R. Tolkien's Utopianism and the Classics* (2023). His focus is very different from mine, however: the utopian strain in Classical literature rather than that deriving from More's eponymous 1516 work. It is remarkable, in fact, how few scholars have examined the utopian strain in Tolkien. No book-length studies and fewer than half a dozen articles. There is Robert T. Tally Jr.'s 2014 essay. It looks at Tolkien and utopia but focuses more on fantasy. Alastair Whyte (2020) and Maria do Rosario Monteiro (1993) have written about utopianism and Tolkien; however, Whyte is concerned with imperialism and colonialism, and Monteiro focuses on Númenor alone. David Glover (1984) and Flora Liénard (2009) both make connections between Tolkien and utopia, but Glover's attention is on the connections between Tolkien and William Burroughs and Michael Moorcock in the 1960s, and Liénard's study discusses Tolkien's environmentalism in contrast with Charles Williams' fiction rather than Tolkien's utopianism per se.

Chapter Nine

Christopher Tolkien as Editor: The Perils of Kinship

Toby Widdicombe

Introduction

On 16 January 2020, Christopher Tolkien, the third son and third child of J.R.R. Tolkien and Edith Tolkien died at the age of 95. He had been named the literary executor of his father's estate when the latter died on 2 September 1973. He took the job with the utmost seriousness so that over the following 47 years he edited and produced almost all of the publications by J.R.R. Tolkien: from *The Silmarillion* (1977) to *The Fall of Gondolin* (2018). The purpose of this essay is to examine Christopher Tolkien's legacy and make clear, in ways that most Tolkien scholars are unaware of or have ignored, how mixed that legacy actually is. That mixed legacy results, as we shall see, from the dual nature of Christopher Tolkien's role as guardian of a reputation and editor of his father's posthumously published work as well as from significant weaknesses in the editing itself.

Let us look first at that legacy. After his father died, Christopher Tolkien began his work on his father's literary manuscripts with some low-hanging fruit: the very circumscribed "Guide to the Names in *The Lord of the Rings*" (published in *A Tolkien Compass* in 1976), and an edition (published in 1975) of J.R.R. Tolkien's translations of three Middle English poems (*Sir Gawain and the Green Knight*, *Pearl*, and *Sir Orfeo*).[1] This slight work was followed in 1977 by what many consider the son's most important achievement, *The Silmarillion*: a one-volume synthesis of his father's work on the story of the First Age of Middle-earth with materials, also, about the Second Age. Two years later (1979), he wrote the foreword and notes to accompany a selection of his father's artwork. In 1980, he published *The Unfinished Tales of Númenor and Middle-earth*. It's as if, having synthesized a history of the Silmarils he wished to finish off the task of presenting his father's legacy by publishing a collection of incomplete materials about the narrative arc of all three Ages in Middle-earth. Indeed, he indicates as much in the introduction to the *Unfinished Tales.* Just as he preceded the Unfinished Tales with a digression into his father's artwork, so he gets ready to undertake the massive task of presenting in all its complexity the evolution of the history of Middle-earth by clearing the decks. In 1981, he helped Humphrey Carpenter put together a collection of J.R.R. Tolkien's letters.[2] In early 1983, he published a collection of his father's important academic work that was hard to locate for modern readers: *The Monsters and the Critics and Other Essays.* Then, between 1983 and 1996, Christopher Tolkien produced his massive twelve-volume History of Middle-earth. Only 1991 and 1995 did not witness the appearance of a volume in the series. Then there is more than a decade of near silence from the extraordinarily industrious son before he undertakes more than a decade of completing his father's legacy. That completion involved two editorial tasks. The first was fleshing out the materials left by his father about the three major stories from The Silmarillion: Húrin; Beren and Lúthien; and the fall of Gondolin. The first appeared in 2007 as *Narn I Chín Húrin. The Tale of the Children of Húrin*; the second appeared in 2017 as *Beren and Lúthien*; the third in 2018 as *The Fall of Gondolin.* The second task was editing and publishing Tolkien materials that were not part of the legendarium but were important to an understanding of the development of his father's ideas. These were *The Legend of Sigurd and Gudrún* (2009), *The Fall of Arthur* (2013), and *Beowulf* (2014). The only other item of note during this period by Christopher Tolkien was his 2016 "Note on the Text" for *The Lay of Aotrou and Itroun* as edited by Verlyn Flieger.

There were others of Tolkien's works published between his death and 2022 which mention Christopher Tolkien's role in his father's legacy but do not include any work by him. Those are Douglas Anderson's revised and expanded edition of *The Annotated Hobbit* (2002); Alan Bliss's edition of *Finn and Hengest* (1982); and Carl Hostetter's *The Nature of Middle-earth* (2021). Last, there are six works by Tolkien, the father, from the same period which are totally free of work by or mention of Christopher Tolkien: *Bilbo's Last Song* (*at the Grey Havens*) (1974), revised and expanded, illustrated by Pauline Baynes, and republished in 1990; *The Father Christmas Letters* (1976), revised and expanded and republished in 1999 as *Letters from Father Christmas; Mr. Bliss* (1982); *Roverandom* (1998); *The*

Lord of the Rings fiftieth-anniversary edition (2004); and *The Story of Kullervo* (2016), edited by Verlyn Flieger.

Before we critique Christopher Tolkien's achievement, a little background on the man may prove useful as it pertains to his suitability for editing his father's works. Christopher Tolkien was a student at Trinity College, Oxford University in 1942 and then (after a hiatus due to the Second World War) from 1946 to 1948. He received two B.A. degrees: the first "he qualified for by war decree," and it was conferred in December 1946; the second (in English Language and Literature) was awarded in Michaelmas Term (Oct.-Dec.) 1948. It was a Third Class degree. He then immediately undertook a B.Litt. degree in Hilary Term (Jan.-Mar. 1949) with his thesis being an edition of the Old Icelandic saga, *King Heidrek the Wise*. The B.Litt. was conferred in October 1953 (Degree Conferrals Office). From the late 1950s through the early 1960s, he was a Lecturer in Old and Middle English and Old Icelandic. In 1963, he was elected a Fellow of New College, Oxford and Tutor in English Language as well as a University Lecturer in Early English Language and Literature. He held these academic posts until he retired in 1975, at the age of 51, to devote his life fulltime to the editing and publication of his father's work. Apart from an edition of his B.Litt. thesis, he also collaborated while a Lecturer and later Fellow with Nevill Coghill on editions of three of Chaucer's *Canterbury Tales*: "The Pardoner's Tale" (1958), "The Nun's Priest's Tale" (1959), and "The Man of Law's Tale" (1969). He was also awarded the Bodley Medal for his contributions to literature and scholarship. As Richard Ovenden, the Bodley's Librarian put it at the time: "Christopher Tolkien's contribution as a scholar and editor has been immense. Without his dedication and commitment, his father's works would not have reached such a broad public audience and without his erudition and scholarship J.R.R. Tolkien's work would not have been presented so fully and with such authority" (Onwuemezi). My sense is that the medal was awarded less for the quality of his work as editor and more in recognition of the Tolkien family's bequest of much of its father's manuscripts to the Bodleian in 1979 and with thanks for a job persistently done. The medal was awarded in 2016. Christopher Tolkien then published *Beren and Lúthien* in 2017, and writes in his Preface to that book that he believes—wrongly as it turned out since he published *The Fall of Gondolin* one year later—that it will be his last: "In my ninety-third year this is (presumptively) my last book in the long series of editions of my father's writings, very largely previously unpublished [...]" (16).

I have looked at the four works Christopher Tolkien published as an academic and have read reviews of them. They show competence in textual editing and a clear understanding of the discipline. He has one persistent weakness as a writer, and that weakness is evident in the work he did as editor of his father's work: his syntax is sometimes very complex (almost Miltonic actually) in ways that hamper the clear statement of meaning. It's as if Christopher Tolkien imagines that using commas to excess will clarify rather than muddy meaning.[3] This is a serious issue, in part because any lack of clarity when dealing with the complex textual history of his father's manuscripts will lead to ideas being mispresented to, or misunderstood by, the reader.

His experience, his training, and his knowledge of his father's work would seem to have made him the perfect person for the job. One could cavil that it is unusual for someone with only a Third Class B.A. and a B.Litt. to go on to become a University Lecturer. The Tolkien name no doubt helped, but then J.R.R. Tolkien himself became a Professor at Oxford University in 1926 on the basis of a First Class Honours B.A. degree from Oxford University awarded in July 1916. There are expectations then and expectations now. One should also note, perhaps more usefully, that four books in 15 years, all of them scholarly editions, is not a particularly stellar publication record for a senior academic. It is also worth making two other comments. First, neither the Icelandic saga nor the relatively well travelled land of Chaucer studies will have presented Christopher Tolkien with the multilayered manuscript problems evident in his father's work. Second, it is interesting that all the editions he published (the Icelandic saga and Chaucer's tales) are collaborative and that the standard model for some of what Christopher Tolkien produced after his father's death was collaborative with one collaborator (Tolkien) having more experience and clout than the other. We see this situation with *The Silmarillion* (1977) and the Carpenter edited *Letters* (1981), for example. I think it is evident (albeit disguised) in editions of J.R.R. Tolkien's work by other scholars too—as I will try to show.

Nonetheless, it is surprising how many difficulties the son's editions of the father's work raise given his background in knowledge and experience. We will now turn to that forty-year project of publishing that which his father had never been able to, but it is worth stressing one more time what was implicit at the beginning of this essay: Christopher Tolkien placed himself (perhaps it is fairer to say "was placed" given his role of literary executor in his father's will) in an unenviable, even impossible, position. He needed to be both the guardian of his father's legacy and the editor of another's man's literary achievement—a role in which disinterestedness should be writ large. One is powered by love and duty; the other by a wish to judge and preserve an achievement. And a third concern, unusual for most academic publishing, hovers at the edge of sight: profit. The family and its publishers make money—sometimes considerable sums—off every new Tolkien book, but every book needs to be packaged carefully and attractively.

The longevity and closeness of the dual role of guardian and editor is unexampled in literary history, and that longevity allows us to look at many examples of the problems Christopher Tolkien encountered. I'll begin by focusing on six pivotal moments between the death of his father in 1973 and Christopher Tolkien's last contribution to his father's memory, *The Fall of Gondolin* in 2018. The first is the moment of embarking on his (the son's) life's work: the edition of *Sir Gawain and the Green Knight*, *Pearl*, and *Sir Orfeo* (1975). The second, *The Silmarillion* (1977). The third, the selected *Letters* (1981). The fourth, the first volume of *The Book of Lost Tales* (1983). The fifth, the first of the three substantial First-Age tales (*The Children of Húrin* [2007]). The last, Christopher Tolkien's viaticum (*The Fall of Gondolin*).

The First Pivotal Moment (1975)

With the edition of the three medieval poems as translated by his father, one can see immediately how Christopher Tolkien makes significant editorial mistakes. These mistakes derive from the triple role (guardian of a legacy; dispassionate editor; garner of monetary profit) he had set himself once he accepted the literary executor position. Among the critical apparatus expected in such a book as *Sir Gawain and the Green Knight, Pearl, and Sir Orfeo*, Preface and

Introduction, for example, there are two sections that potentially confuse and one which certainly misrepresents the arc of the narrative in the edition. This muddiness comes, in the first case, from failing to make clear the exact roles of author (father) and editor (son). The three translations of the Middle English poems are immediately followed by a Glossary, an Appendix on Verse-forms, and an item labelled on the Contents page as "*Gawain's Leave-taking*." As far as the Glossary is concerned, Christopher Tolkien says at the beginning of the final paragraph of the Preface: "At the end of the book[,] I have provided a short glossary" (x). One may fairly assume, then, that the glossary is the work of *fils* not *père*. One would be wrong. At least I think so, but my confusion is due to Christopher Tolkien's ambiguity not a careless or casual reading by me. The headnote to the glossary reads (in part):

> This glossary provides no more than the meanings of some archaic and technical words used in the translations, and only the meanings that the translator intended in those contexts (which in a very few cases may be doubtful). In the stanzas describing the breaking-up [sic] of the deer he employed some of the technical terms of the original which are debatable in meaning, and in such cases (e. g. *Arber*, *Knot*, *Numbles*) I have given what I believe was his final interpretation (191).

Now it seems the glossary is J.R.R. Tolkien's work and not his son's, but is Christopher looking at a glossary created by his father or a glossary he (Christopher) creates from the translation? I am almost sure by the end that it is the former, but even as I type this I am riven by doubt. And if it *is* J.R.R. Tolkien's glossary, his son needed to have explained in some detail in the headnote itself how he decided on the "final interpretation" of what may be his father's words. Such an explanation is de rigueur in textual editing—as Christopher Tolkien would or should have known.

If the first error derives from a confusion of roles, the second comes from a wish to make money from the project or to publish as much of his father's work as possible. Christina Scull and Wayne Hammond trace the history of the project in their *J.R.R. Tolkien Companion & Guide* (2: 930-933). J.R.R. Tolkien began in 1959 by considering publishing a translation of *Sir Gawain and the Green Knight* on its own. By 1962, the idea had become to publish the *Gawain* poem and *Pearl* together, but J.R.R. Tolkien had not finished putting the typescript together by the time of his death. As his literary executor, Christopher Tolkien now decides to publish those two poems along with *Sir Orfeo*, which is not, incidentally, by the same poet as the one who wrote *Sir Gawain and the Green Knight* and *Pearl*, in one edition even though his father's translation of *Sir Orfeo* was long ago laid aside and even though his father apparently never wrote any explanatory material for it. So, the introductory material to the three poems becomes even more of a mishmash than it might have been. For the *Gawain* poem, the son stitches together two different pieces by his father. For *Pearl*, he takes the part of the introduction to E. V. Gordon's 1953 edition for which his father was responsible. For *Sir Orfeo*, Christopher Tolkien himself provides the introductory material. So, what we have in the edition of *Sir Gawain and the Green Knight, Pearl, and Sir Orfeo* is a rather confused salmagundi. It has, however, with the addition of *Sir Orfeo* become of publishable length.

The third error is a variant of the second and a classic academic one. Christopher Tolkien has three of his father's translations he considers worthy of being published, but he provides helpmeets with insufficient attribution. Here the son is thinking of his mass-market audience (does the profit motive rear its head?) and, so, provides an Appendix on the Verse-forms of *Sir Gawain and the Green Knight* and *Pearl*. After all, realistically, how many of the readers of all things Tolkienian will know much about a form of verse in a language at two removes from modern English? Given the fact that J.R.R. Tolkien edited the standard edition of *Sir Gawain and the Green Knight* (first edition 1925; revised 1967) it is surely reasonable to assume that the appendix is his. There is no indication in the appendix itself, but buried towards the end of the Preface is this comment: "Since a primary object of these translations was the close preservation of the metres of the originals, I thought that the book should contain, for those who want it, an account of the verse-forms of *Sir Gawain* and *Pearl*" (ix-x). And Christopher continues by stating that the notes are based on his father's own drafts and that "There is very little in these accounts (and nothing that is a matter of opinion) that is not in my father's words" (x). I find the double negative ("nothing ... not") confusing, and know from many years of academic writing myself that one person's fact is another's opinion. An example or two by way of clarification would have been helpful, just as it would have been useful for the editor to sort out more clearly what belongs in a Preface and what in an Introduction.

The fourth error derives not from a misconceived idea of audience or a poor turn of phrase or two but from a wrong-headed appeal to his father's memory. The edition ends with a two-page poem titled "Gawain's Leave-Taking." At first blush, a reader might assume that this is a newly discovered part of the manuscript by the *Gawain* poet as translated by J.R.R. Tolkien. That is not the case as the Preface points out: "On the last page will be found some verses translated by my father from a medieval English poem. He called them "Gawain's Leave-taking," clearly with reference to the passage in *Sir Gawain* where Gawain leaves the castle of Sir Bertilak to go to the tryst at the Green Chapel" (x). Then Christopher Tolkien continues: "The original poem has no connection with Sir Gawain; the verses translated are in fact the first three stanzas, and the last, of a somewhat longer poem found among a group of fourteenth-century lyrics with refrains in the Vernon manuscript in the Bodleian Library at Oxford" (x). It would have been helpful, then, to put the title in square brackets to indicate it was added by Tolkien's father. It would have been helpful to give a shelf mark for the Vernon manuscript (Bodleian Library MS. Eng. poet. a. 1). Above all, it would have been helpful to explain why it has been included in the edition if it has nothing to do with the *Gawain* poem besides his father's personal, mental connection. The answer, of course, is that it is by J.R.R. Tolkien. Not for the last time in his editorial career, Christopher Tolkien makes a judgment based not on sound editorial practice but on a mistaken view of his role. He sees himself as the preserver of his father's legacy even if this particular part of the legacy is minor indeed and, as presented, thoroughly confusing. There is a simple correction for the mistake—in this case at least. Move "Gawain's Leave-taking" to a place in the Introduction, give it some context, and speculate why his father saw this as specifically Gawain's taking leave. That would make something useful for a reader out of something minor.[4]

The Second Pivotal Moment (1977)

Two years after he published *Sir Gawain and the Green Knight, Pearl, and Sir Orfeo,* Christopher Tolkien edited his father's manuscripts about the First and Second Ages to produce *The Silmarillion.* The 1999 second edition of the book consists of three pieces of front matter in two sections: a Foreword (reprinted from the first edition); and a Preface to the second edition, which includes a reprinting of J.R.R. Tolkien's famous 1951 letter to Milton Waldman. In many ways, this book is Christopher Tolkien's greatest achievement as editor. The inclusion in the second edition of the Waldman letter is clever as it provides a coherent overarching narrative for the material in *The Silmarillion*, much of which will have been new to the general reader. Tolkien does a fine job of laying out the context for the First Age materials. He explains how he decided to present the Silmarillion story:

> On my father's death it fell to me to try to bring the work into publishable form. It became clear to me that to attempt to present, within the covers of a single book, the diversity of the materials—to show *The Silmarillion* as in truth a continuing and evolving creation extending over more than half a century—would in fact lead only to confusion and the submerging of what is essential. I set myself therefore to work out a single text, selecting and arranging in such a way as seemed to me to produce the most coherent and internally self-consistent narrative (vii-viii).

He correctly does not look entirely to smooth over the complexities of the story arguing that "[a] complete consistency (either within the compass of *The Silmarillion* itself or between *The Silmarillion* and other published writings of my father's) is not to be looked for, and could only be achieved, if at all, at heavy and needless cost" (viii). He wisely decides, also, not to burden "the book further with any sort of commentary or annotation" (ix). As to back matter, he provides five useful genealogical tables of elves and men (*Genealogies*), and a taxonomy of types of elves (*The Sundering of the Elves*). Then there is a "Note on Pronunciation;" an "Index of Names;" an "Appendix: Elements in Quenya and Sindarin names;" and a "Map of Beleriand and the Lands of the North".

This is exemplary, but there are three warning signs for the astute or the wary. First, the title of the book is misleading as it includes material outside the scope of the Silmarillion narrative itself: the creation of the world and the work of the Valar; the fall of Númenor; and his father's account, "Of the Rings of Power." That would have been easy, superficially at least, to fix with just a change of book title to *The Silmarillion and Other [Related] Writings*, but the tendency on the son's part to group together lots of somewhat disparate material between two covers had already shown up with *Sir Gawain, Pearl, and Sir Orfeo* and will show up again later on with the History of Middle-earth series. Second, there is no indication of the location of the materials he uses. That is understandable in 1977, when his father's manuscripts were in the possession of the Tolkien family and, so, private in every way, but by the time the second edition of *The Silmarillion* appeared in 1999 most but not quite all of the Tolkien papers had been housed in the Bodleian Library at Oxford University for two decades. So, Christopher Tolkien writes of his father's legendarium in these terms: "a large narrative structure" "far indeed from being a fixed text." Indeed, "the changes and variants, both in detail and in larger perspectives, became so complex, so pervasive, and so multi-layered that a final and definitive version seemed unattainable" (vii). Later, he writes that it was "my father's explicit intention" to combine the materials in the way his son does in *The Silmarillion*. However, he provides no information about the manuscripts or where his father's intention was made clear (orally or in writing), or, indeed, when. *The reader, then, is presented with materials they cannot verify should they wish to do so. They simply have Christopher Tolkien's version of his father's legendarium with no ability to examine it in an unmediated way.* This was a problem in 1977; it is a problem to this day. It is a problem throughout all the editing projects Christopher Tolkien undertook with his father's legendarium. The third warning sign is clear in the 1977 "Preface" to *The Silmarillion* when he ends the penultimate paragraph in this way: "There is indeed a wealth of unpublished writing by my father concerning the Three Ages, narrative, linguistic, historical, and philosophical, and I hope that it will prove possible to publish some of this at a later date" (ix). That later date was 1983 with the first volume in the History of Middle-earth series, and that series, as we shall see, has many problems with it—in idea and execution. Yet even in the 1977 "Preface," there is this ominous phrase: "the difficult and doubtful task of preparing the text of the book [*The Silmarillion*] [...]" (ix). The first adjective is undeniable and accurate; the second seemingly suggests the son was not even sure even after the book was published that his decision to provide a clean and straightforward narrative was a good idea. By the time the History of Middle-earth series began to be published, those doubts had manifestly grown to a certainty.

The Third Pivotal Moment (1981)

Before we get there, however, let us look at the third pivotal moment in the son's long engagement with his father's work: the publication in 1981 (four years after *The Silmarillion*) of *The Letters of J.R.R. Tolkien*. This case is a little unusual among the six pivotal moments I am discussing in that the son is not the titular editor of the collection. The title page reads: "The Letters of J.R.R. Tolkien. A Selection edited by Humphrey Carpenter with the Assistance of Christopher Tolkien." However, it is clear from the three-page introduction by Carpenter that Christopher Tolkien played a vital role in creating the book. I have talked in detail elsewhere in this book (cf. "For Want of a Biography") about the inadequacies of Carpenter's authorised biography of J.R.R. Tolkien, so I will not repeat those arguments here. I will simply say that the title page and the introduction to *Letters* show how seriously Christopher Tolkien took the job of protecting his father's legacy even if that meant inadequately depicting him through his letters. The title page says that the book is merely a "selection" of Tolkien's letters, a selection which was arrived at with the "assistance" of Christopher Tolkien. The first word begs the question: what percentage of letters was left on the cutting-room floor? The second disingenuously distorts the power relation between editor and assistant. The assistant (Christopher Tolkien) has the letters. As his father's literary executor, he has an absolute veto over what gets published. To that, add the age and life experience differential: Carpenter was 35 when *Letters* was published. He was a former radio journalist who had just begun to make a name for himself as a biographer (with the authorised biography of Tolkien no less). Christopher Tolkien was 57, a former don at New College and well-respected University Lecturer in a town (Oxford) where the Tolkien name would have had cachet even had the legendarium never been dreamed up. The two had also already worked together on the authorized biography of J.R.R. Tolkien, so the son had already shown how protective he was of his father's life. It would have likely been more accurate if the title page had read "a small selection" and the phrase "assistance of" had been "supervision by."

To his credit, Carpenter does describe in vague but illuminating terms what was (and has been to this day) lost by not publishing all the letters available to the family. J.R.R. Tolkien (always a gregarious man) wrote an "immense number" of letters. Carpenter then avers "it became obvious that an enormous quantity of material would have to be omitted" without indicating why (1). Let me apply some commonsense logic here. By 1981, Tolkien, the father, had become a hugely popular writer: *The Hobbit*; *The Lord of the Rings*; *The Silmarillion*. He was a millionaire when he died as a result of his legendarium. The general public would have snapped up a multi-volume *Complete Letters of J.R.R. Tolkien* almost without a second thought, and if expense were an issue a visit to a college or public library would solve that. Yet, Carpenter decides with the "assistance" of Christopher Tolkien to whittle down the number to just 354 letters to be published. Rather than provide the real reason (the Tolkien family through Christopher Tolkien wanted to create a particular image of their famous father and grandfather), Carpenter tries to argue (unsuccessfully, in my view) for the breadth of these 354 letters left standing and for the rightness of focusing on those letters which are about Tolkien's legendarium. He does, however, let slip a little about what has been left out: "Among the omissions is the very large body of letters he wrote between 1913 and 1918 to Edith Bratt," his fiancée and, later, wife (1). These have been omitted because they "are highly personal in character" (1). Given the desire felt almost as a need by many to understand as fully as possible the genius of Tolkien, I should have thought this characteristic would guarantee their publication *not* their omission. After all, Tolkien was the one who made the incredibly romantic decision to have "Edith Mary Tolkien, Luthien, 1889-1971. John Ronald Reuel Tolkien, Beren, 1892-1973" engraved on the tombstone of the burial lot he shares with his wife in Wolvercote Cemetery. It turns out, however, that the expurgation of letters does not end with a wholesale pruning. Even those letters which are included in the volume are subject to the use of ellipses to indicate material omitted. Carpenter states that ellipses are nearly always used to save space rather than "for reasons of discretion," but that claim raises the unanswered question: What sorts of discretion are we talking about?

In many ways, Carpenter's introduction has the clarity I would have liked to see persistently and not occasionally with Christopher Tolkien's editing. What Carpenter talks of is ambiguous, but he does, at least, talk about it clearly. Towards the end of the introduction, Carpenter goes into helpful and revelatory detail about the process of selection used by him and Christopher Tolkien in selecting the few letters that were finally published. It appears to have been a six-stage business:

1. Carpenter collects and transcribes all the letters.
2. Carpenter makes the first selection.
3. Tolkien comments on the selection and makes suggestions for change.
4. The changes are agreed on and made.
5. A radical cut in the number of letters is made by the process outlined in 2-4.
6. A "final procedure" is agreed on.

This is clear and yet puzzling. Is the transcription mentioned in stage 1 of all the letters or just those made after the first cut in numbers? If it is all of the letters, what has happened to Carpenter's unpublished transcriptions? How were the changes made in stage 4 "adopted" (stage 3)? Is the cut mentioned in stage 5 the same cut as that talked of at the beginning of the introduction or a second major culling? What is meant by the "final procedure" in stage 6? (I thought the process outlined in 1-5 is this "final procedure" and not a "preliminary" one.) It is as if Carpenter can read my mind (or any reader's mind) as he provides this summarizing statement: "The book [*The Letters of J.R.R. Tolkien*] as published therefore reflects my own taste and judgement rather more than his [Christopher Tolkien's], but it is also the product of our joint work; and I am very grateful to him for sparing many hours, and for guiding and encouraging me" (3). Based on the gratitude expressed at the end and on the power differential I talked about earlier, based too on the fact that not all the work was "our joint work," and based on Christopher Tolkien's "providing certain additional pieces of information" to the notes without being solicited, I suspect the final version of the letters "reflects" at least as much Christopher Tolkien's own taste and judgement. His taste and judgment, after all, explain the major excisions as well as the persistent steering away from the personal to the public. How much more satisfactory a collection of letters might we have had without the "assistance" of Tolkien's son? How much more satisfactory in 2024 than in 1981? Carpenter says this at the end of the introduction with arresting confidence: "there can be no doubt that much of Tolkien's correspondence still remains untraced" (3). This is now a world shaped by the internet. How much more successful would tracing these letters be these days than in those antediluvian times when *The Letters of J.R.R. Tolkien* was first published 43 years ago. Crowdsourcing comes to mind as a potentially winning strategy now, for example, that was not available then.

The Fourth Pivotal Moment (1983)

Two years after the appearance of the Letters, the first of the History of Middle-earth series appeared: *The Book of Lost Tales, Part I* (1983). In the interests of concision, I will focus in this part of the critique of Christopher Tolkien as editor on just the eleven-page "Foreword" with which the volume (and, indeed, the whole History of Middle-earth series) begins. I do have specific concerns about the annotations and commentary that accompany each story, but I will leave any particular discussion of those to some later date. In essence, the "Foreword" is a presentation of the reasons why Christopher Tolkien chose to produce the History of Middle-earth series (and in particular those volumes devoted to the Silmarillion narrative) after he had already published six years before and in one volume *The Silmarillion*. It is a quite fascinating argument as well as what its writer calls a "rather rambling discussion" (8).

After almost five pages of discussion about *The Silmarillion* and *The Book of Lost Tales*, Christopher Tolkien confesses: "The published work [*The Silmarillion*] has no 'framework,' no suggestion of what it is and how (within the imagined world) it came to be. This I now think to have been an error" (5). The multi-volume History of Middle-earth is his effort to atone for that error, to present in as much detail as possible the "fearsome jigsaw puzzle" of the Silmarillion manuscripts (10). It is clear from the "Preface" to *The Silmarillion* back in 1977 as I earlier pointed out, that Christopher Tolkien was not entirely happy with that finished book. Now in *The Book of Lost Tales, Part I*'s "Foreword," he uses the criticisms of three Tolkien scholars (Tom Shippey, Randel Helms, and Constance Hieatt) to buttress his decision to redo his editing of the whole history of Middle-earth. He uses Shippey and Hieatt to argue for the need to give significant background to the Silmarillion story; he uses Helms to discuss the relation between author and editor. And what will the revised version of the Silmarillion story (and, indeed, the whole legendarium) now look like? Christopher Tolkien makes this clear:

> [M]y intention is to give complete or largely complete texts, so that the books will be more like a series of editions. I do not set myself as a primary object the unravelling of many single and separate threads, but rather the making available of works that can and should be read as wholes (9).

The sequence of the tales with the Silmarillion will follow the "sequence of the narrative" and not the chronology of composition (10). Each tale will be followed by limited annotations and commentary.

As I interpret the "Foreword" and Christopher Tolkien's intentions, the same range of concerns I had with earlier pivotal moments in his editing of his father's work appears again. Only the details change. As guardian of his father's legacy, Tolkien continues to protect his father's manuscripts. He refers to "the tattered notebooks in which they [the Lost Tales] were written [and] were bundled away" (9) and the many manuscripts he has examined, which proved "intrinsically very difficult" to decipher (9). Again, as before, no shelf-mark information so that scholars could replicate or test (in the Tolkien Papers at the Bodleian) the son's interpretation of his father's work. No likelihood, even if access were feasible, of the results of any examination by other scholars being published or made widely available. As editor of another man's achievement, Christopher Tolkien is too close to his material—even talking at one point of "the author's vision of his own vision" (7). As editor, he also chooses, I think unhelpfully, to privilege linguistic studies over literary studies of the legendarium: "There are explorations to be conducted in this world with perfect right quite irrespective of literary-critical considerations" (7). This choice is behind the special access to his father's language manuscripts given to linguists and philologists in the 1990s, access which has rather skewed J.R.R. Tolkien's achievement in recent years.

As editor again, he quotes Helms' remark in *Tolkien and the Silmarils* (93) about "a long-standing problem in literary criticism: what, really, *is* a literary work? Is it what the author intended (or may have intended) it to be, or is it what a later editor makes of it?" (qtd. in "Foreword" 6). Christopher Tolkien does not appear to realize that this "problem" is stated as a false dichotomy by Helms. Any editor (*pace* Helms) has only three choices as long as competence is a given: they can attempt an edition which reflects the author's last, clearest, or best intention; they can attempt a heavily edited revision of the author's work for some particular and defensible reason; or they can attempt some sort of eclectic version of the work, an effort that privileges the editor or the author at particular moments and for particular, stated, reasons. The reality is that any version of the Silmarillion materials (whether it be *The Silmarillion* [1977] or the History of Middle-earth series [1983-1996]) will be viewed by one sort of reader or another as too difficult to read. Early in his "Foreword," Christopher Tolkien says as much and then appears to forget this insight: "it may be doubted whether any 'approach' to it [the Silmarillion materials] can greatly aid those who find it unapproachable" (2).

My clear sense from the "Foreword" is that Christopher Tolkien considered (or was persuaded by some Tolkien scholars to consider) the editorial strategies in *The Book of Lost Tales* and, by extension, the whole History or Middle-earth series as leading to a superior version of his father's legendarium in comparison to *The Silmarillion.* I firmly disagree. Yes, the reader is given more material to work with (albeit in Platonic terms still at three removes from reality) but at great cost, as Christopher Tolkien himself admits:

> An edition that takes account of such complexities, as this [*The Book of Lost Tales*] does, rather than attempt to smooth them artificially away [as *The Silmarillion* did?] is liable to be an intricate and crabbed thing, in which the reader is never left alone for a moment (10).

Despite Christopher Tolkien's best efforts with different font sizes for some of the supplementary material (notes, annotations, commentary and so on), *The Book of Lost Tales* and the whole History of Middle-earth series is at many moments that "intricate and crabbed thing" he feared creating.

I have one final conjecture to make which weakens Christopher Tolkien's work as editor further by causing him to make decisions for extrinsic reasons. I have already mentioned the profit motive with J.R.R. Tolkien's legendarium earlier in this essay. I wonder if it did not play into Christopher Tolkien's thinking on this occasion.[5] He talks in these terms of the *Lost Tales*:

> This edition of the *Lost Tales* in two parts is to be, as I hope, the beginning of a series that will carry the history further through these later writings [of the legendarium], in verse and prose; and in this hope I have applied to this present book an "overriding" title intended to cover all that may follow it, though I fear that "The History of Middle-earth" may turn out to have been over-ambitious (9).

At the end of the "Foreword," he brings up the bipartite form of *The Book of Lost Tales* one more time: "Lastly, the division of this edition into two parts is entirely due to the length of the *Tales*. The edition is conceived as a whole, and I hope that the second part will appear within a year of the first [...]" (11). The rest of books in the History of Middle-earth series are in the 450-500 length in pages. The first part of *The Book of Lost Tales* comes in at under 300 pages. Given that a combined volume of both parts would have been shorter by eliminating redundancies in appendices and indexes, was the two-part approach an effort to test (on the part of editor and publisher) reader interest in material which is in every way more difficult than *The Silmarillion* (1977)? Was it an effort to do so at less cost and with greater potential profit? Was the editor's adding a series title to the first volume even before the second part of *The Lost Tales* had appeared in 1984 an attempt to nudge opinion towards the positive, towards acceptance of the entire project? That is an unanswerable line of questioning but an important speculation.

The Fifth Pivotal Moment (2007)

Let us move on to the fifth of the six pivotal moments in the son's editing of his father's work. The History of Middle-earth series came to an end in 1996. Just over a decade later and after having already presented the legendarium materials in heavily, but nearly invisibly, edited form (*The Silmarillion* [1977]) and more lightly, but intrusively, edited form (*Unfinished Tales*, and the many volumes in the History of Middle-earth series), Christopher Tolkien brought out new editions of parts of the legendarium already presented to Tolkien's many fans. He decided, that is, to edit once again the major stories of the First Age, those dearest to his father's heart. *This time in a new way.* That decision bore fruit, first, with *The Children of Húrin* in 2007. This he followed up with *Beren and Lúthien* (2017) and *The Fall of Gondolin* (2018). With *The Children of Húrin*, the reader is presented with the fourth iteration of a particular First-Age story, and with the two later volumes it's the third go around. Presumably at getting it right.

As with *Sir Gawain and the Green Knight, Pearl, and Sir Orfeo* (his first go around as the editor of his father's work more than thirty years before), Christopher

Tolkien goes for the low-hanging fruit: the longest and most complete tale from the First Age. This allows him to try out his new editing strategies before he encounters the altogether more intractable works: Beren and Lúthien, and the Fall of Gondolin. This edition comprises Preface, Introduction, a note on pronunciation, three genealogical charts, two appendices, a list of names, and a note about the map which is folded into the book's end papers. As with *The Silmarillion*, he opts for a short preface rather than the long (and too revelatory?) preface in *The Book of Lost Tales*. As with the latter work, he remains preoccupied with the tales of the First Age being seen "by their repute as strange and inaccessible in mode and manner" (7). This edition of *The Children of Húrin*, appears, however, to be an effort to use some of the techniques in *The Silmarillion* on this one tale instead of the highly mediated approach in the History of Middle-earth series. As he remarks at the beginning of the Preface to *Húrin*:

> It has seemed to me for a long time that there was a good case for presenting my father's long version of the legend of the Children of Húrin as an independent work, between its own covers, with a minimum of editorial presence, and above all in continuous narrative without gaps or interruptions, if this could be done without distortion or invention, despite the unfinished state in which he left some parts of it (7).

He hopes that the focus on one tale will obviate the complaints of Shippey, Helms, and Hieatt about the supposedly unsuccessful *The Silmarillion* of 1977. I can't decide if Christopher Tolkien the editor is being disingenuous here or if he's simply mistaken. However, it is impossible to accomplish what he wishes and tries to do with *Húrin* "without distortion or invention." Impossible. The pendulum has swung back hard towards a syncretic approach once more, but Christopher Tolkien doesn't see that or won't acknowledge it.

In the process of constructing this "good case," Tolkien takes a very narrow view of his readership when he suggests there are those in the world of Tolkien's legendarium who only know of Beren and Túrin (his examples) because of their being alluded to in a description of Shelob in *The Lord of the Rings*. He even goes so far as to utterly misjudge his readers by claiming that *Húrin* opens a "window" onto "a scene and a story set in an unknown Middle-earth" (8). This comment would suggest, very oddly, that *The Silmarillion*, the *Unfinished Tales*, and The History of Middle-earth series had never been published.

These weaknesses when it comes to the role of an editor and the definition of readership are unusual in the litany of the mistakes of Christopher Tolkien as editor. We are once again in more familiar territory, however, when we see that he gets too close to his subject to be the dispassionate or disinterested editor that the complexity of Tolkien's work surely requires. Once more he uses the rhetorical swerve of inside knowledge to preface his comments on the legendarium: "When my father was a young man during the years of the First World War and long before there was any inkling of the tales that were to form the narrative of *The Hobbit* or *The Lord of the Rings*, he began the writing of a collection of stories that he called *The Book of Lost Tales*" (8). Yes, that gives him private (largely undivulged) knowledge, but it also means that as editor he cannot render fair judgment on the legendarium. That insider position, which Christopher Tolkien relishes and which provided the energy for him to work so assiduously on his father's manuscripts for almost 45 years, leads him further astray still as he sees himself as the heir apparent completing his father's three "Great Tales" of the First Age because his father could not:

> It thus seems unquestionable, from my father's own words, that if he could achieve final and finished narratives on the scale he desired, he saw the three "Great Tales" of the Elder Days [...] as works sufficiently complete in themselves as not to demand knowledge of the great body of legend known as *The Silmarillion* (10).

This is a reasonable editorial goal for Christopher Tolkien to aim for, but not if he thinks that goal can be achieved "without distortion or invention." That is surely a fool's errand and, on the face of it, *The Children of Húrin* is better than that as a book. At one point (in "Appendix 2: The Composition of the Text") Christopher Tolkien even seems for a moment to acknowledge the contradictoriness of his position when he admits "The text [*The Children of Húrin*] is nonetheless artificial, as it could not be otherwise: the more especially since this great body of manuscript represents a continual evolution in the story" (289). But the insight fades and the opportunity to do something different and more honest with his father's legendarium fades along with it.

Christopher Tolkien's being the heir apparent intent on finishing his father's work leads him to one even more egregious mistake deriving from his unavoidable closeness to his subject. He comments in the first appendix ("The Evolution of the Great Tales") on his father's repeatedly choosing to abandon parts of his legendarium. Actually, Christopher Tolkien comments on this characteristic, in this appendix, no less than *ten* times in eleven pages: 269, 270 (twice), 272, 273, 275, 278 (twice), and 280 (twice). He appears increasingly distraught at this paternal habit, so much so that in the last two of these ten comments he says: "grievously, he [his father] stopped, and never went further" and "he [his father] failed of his purpose" (280). These are strong words indeed. His closeness to his beloved father masks from him the very real likelihood that J.R.R. Tolkien may well have *intended* fragmentariness as part of his modus operandi with his legendarium. He had studied as a scholar the fact of incompletion in so many Anglo-Saxon and Middle English works (*Beowulf, The Battle of Maldon, The Canterbury Tales*, and so on); he may have been aware of its being almost an epic trope (Spenser's *The Faerie Queene* and Wordsworth's *The Recluse* immediately come to mind). Tolkien the father is on record as wishing throughout his life to complete "The Silmarillion," but in the nearly two decades between the publication of *The Lord of the Rings* (1954-1955) and his death in 1973 that never happened. He never even got close. Christopher Tolkien does not or, more likely, cannot see it—even though he was, like his father a scholar of the Anglo-Saxon and medieval periods.

The Sixth Pivotal Moment (2018)

Let us move on the last of the six pivotal moments: *The Fall of Gondolin*, which Christopher Tolkien the editor knows, at the age of 94, will be his last engagement with his father's profoundly important and moving legacy. (I will have less to say here as there is little new to say about Christopher Tolkien's editorial procedures after his more than 40 years as editor.) For obvious reasons, his "Preface" to *The Fall of Gondolin* is nostalgic and bitter-sweet, but it is also mutedly triumphant. Very much against the odds, Christopher Tolkien published in his lifetime all of the Silmarillion materials and managed to do so in various guises. So, gone is the long preface of *The Lost Tales, Part I* with its decision to disavow his editorial strategy in *The Silmarillion*, and as this is the third book in which the reader is treated to multiple successive narratives in one book (*The Children of Húrin* and *Beren and Lúthien* being the first two, of course) the need to justify is gone as well. That said, this "Preface" does have its peculiarities. There is the front-loading, in quasi-Biblical terms, of his father's story: "My father, as the Maker, ponders the large history [...]" (10). There is the poor logic, where Christopher Tolkien chooses to use the "same curious form" of presentation with *The Fall of Gondolin* as he had with the earlier First-Age stories in 2007 and 2017 because "it is certain that the present book is the last" (13). There is the consistent refrain of sorrow at his father's work habits, that refrain which was so characteristic of his discussion, more than a decade before, of how *The Children of Húrin* was composed. So, he talks in this "Preface" of J.R.R. Tolkien's "profoundly saddening abandonment of the last version of the *Tale*" (17). There is the refusal to give up entirely his disdain for his editing choices in *The Silmarillion* (even 41 years after its publication): "There was indeed *The Silmarillion* that I published in 1977, but this was composed, one might even say 'contrived' [...]" (11). There is the weak writing too when a little more care with comma usage and parallel construction would work wonders for clarity:

> To illustrate the transformations that took place as time passed nothing is more striking than the portrayal of the god Ulmo as originally seen, sitting among the reeds and making music at twilight by the river Sirion, but many years later the lord of all the waters of the world rises out of the great storm of the sea at Vinyamar (11).

And the ambiguity that comes from failing to define precisely what he means:

> Thus I retain *Ylmir* when it occurs for *Ulmo*, since it is a regular occurrence of a linguistic nature, but give always *Thorondor* for *Thorndor*, "King of Eagles," since my father was clearly intending to change it throughout (17).

Am I the only one who does not understand "of a linguistic nature"? Isn't language a universal, fundamental given?

Conclusion

The latter part of the title of this essay ("the Perils of Kinship") emphasizes the false position that Christopher Tolkien's lifelong relation to his father put him in as editor. The essay has branched out from there to look at his weaknesses as an editor and the role profit may have had in his decisions about what to publish and when. It has also looked at the persistent problem of access to manuscripts as well as restrictions on any right to publish. That restriction is most clearly addressed in a Tolkien work I have not spent time discussing because its editor was not Christopher Tolkien—at least not in a titular sense. That work is Carl Hostetter's *The Nature of Middle-earth* (2021), the latest publication in a long line of Tolkien books. In the "Foreword," Hostetter thanks, among others, Cathleen Blackburn (of Maier Blackburn) as the legal representative of the Tolkien Estate "for making publication of this book possible" (xiv) as well as, of course, Christopher Tolkien, who played a major supervisory role in the book's creation:

> Finally, my greatest gratitude is of course to Christopher Tolkien, who directly supplied me with most of the materials that have gone into this book and supported my idea to publish them in this manner. He was able to see and approve my book proposal, with a representative selection of my treatment and presentation of the texts, and my plan of the book as a whole, in the year before his passing (x).

So, in the third decade of the twenty-first century and almost fifty years after Tolkien's death, we have the following situation. Almost all of the imaginative writings of J.R.R. Tolkien have been published. Or have they? Tom Shippey remarked after Christopher Tolkien's death: "While [J.R.R.] Tolkien was very poor at finishing things, he also never threw anything away, so we don't know what's still unpublished. There may be some surprises yet" (Seelye and Yuhas). We *perhaps*, then, have all the imaginative writings of J.R.R. Tolkien in published form, but we can't know because we don't know what manuscripts there are in any full sense and we don't know what is housed where. We only know that the Bodleian has most and the Tolkien Estate some. And, as scholars, we don't know what we will be allowed to publish without (undue) interference as the Tolkien family's right of veto is absolute. Fans of Tolkien's legendarium do owe a debt of gratitude to his son's persistence and longevity in publishing versions of so much of his father's work regardless of how adequate those editions are from a professional point of view. That I want to make clear. The record of publication, however, has produced a whole range of problems partly because of the distorting quality of all mediation. In almost all cases, we only have what the son says his father wrote; we do not have what his father wrote in any verifiable form.

At the end of the Preface to *Beren and Lúthien*, Christopher Tolkien quotes his father's letter to him of 11 July 1972, the year after his wife, Edith, died: "But the story has gone crooked, and I am left, and *I* cannot plead before the inexorable Mandos" (17). Deeply, deeply moving: a husband's sorrow at the death of his wife of more than 50 years. Of course, it is in the nature of any lifelong achievement such as the legendarium to have "gone crooked." I only wish that his son had straightened it more than he did, or that the Tolkien Estate had allowed other, disinterested and more capable, scholars to have tried to do so, and if straightening proved not possible or sensible, I only wish his son would have described more effectively the nature of the crookedness.

End Notes

1 The publication, in *A Tolkien Compass*, of Christopher Tolkien's first editing work on his father's legendarium is one of two examples I will cite to show how fierce was Christopher Tolkien's guarding of his father's legacy. The "Guide to the Names in *The Lord of the Rings*" was published in the first edition of *A Tolkien Compass* in 1976 but removed from the second edition "at the request of Tolkien Estate, the legal owners of the text" ("Guide"). That is odd given the fact that Christopher Tolkien was in charge of the Tolkien Estate at the time both the first and the second editions of *A Tolkien Compass* were published. The second example (really of how litigious the Tolkien Estate is and can afford to be when it comes to the legacy of J.R.R. Tolkien) occurred when the Tolkien Estate "filed an $80 million lawsuit against Warner Bros. over the digital merchandising of characters from 'The Lord of the Rings' and 'The Hobbit.' The suit accused the company of causing harm to the Tolkien legacy. It was eventually settled on undisclosed terms" (Seelye and Yuhas).

2 The 1981 edition of *Letters* was republished in 1995 with a "new, expanded index." A new and expanded *edition* was published by William Morrow in 2023 in response to readers' wish to read more of Tolkien's letters. I discuss the *Letters* in this chapter under "The Third Pivotal Moment (1981)." I do not, however, talk about the 2023 edition as that postdates Christopher Tolkien's death.

3 I will offer just two examples from his first published work: his B.Litt thesis on the Icelandic saga, *King Heidrek the Wise*, published in 1960. (Later in this essay, I will present, in the text itself, an example or two from his editing of his father's work as that is the focus of my argument.) The first example confuses by inserting a participial phrase and a complex dependent clause between the subject and its verb: "Verse 75, containing a list of kings three of whom do not otherwise appear in the legend at all, while one of them (Gizur) is differently represented and may indeed not be the same person, is unquestionably in origin either a bit of a separate poem or else an isolated 'catalogue-strophe'" (xxii). The second confuses by trying to make too many statements in one sentence: "Some of the verses (such as 76, 81-6) are notable for their heavily-filled lines, comparable with the technique of *Hamðismál* and *Atlakviða*, probably the oldest of the Eddaic lays, while others are more meagre in verse-content and with less vivid expression" (xxii).

4 I have gone into such detail with *Sir Gawain and the Green Knight, Pearl, and Sir Orfeo* because the errors I describe there do show up repeatedly in Christopher Tolkien's extensive work on his father's legacy. So, this 1975 book (Christopher Tolkien's first after his father's death) is representative of much that happens between 1975 and 2018.

5 I will project forward in this discussion of the profit motive to the three individual editions of First-Age stories (*The Children of Húrin, Beren and Lúthien*, and *The Fall of Gondolin*). Uniquely, these editions feature a total of 25 colour illustrations by Alan Lee. In the "Preface" to *The Fall of Gondolin*, Christopher Tolkien acknowledges the work of this artist: "He has brought to this task a deep perception of the inner nature of scene and event that he has chosen from the great range of the Elder Days" (18). As paratext, the artwork should justify itself by commenting on the action described. (One thinks of the work of Pauline Baynes with *The Hobbit, Farmer Giles of Ham, Smith of Wootton Major*, and *The Adventures of Tom Bombadil.*) Lee, however, has a different remit apparently, "the great range of the Elder Days." With the last two of the separate tales, the illustrations are tagged to particular events; with the first this is not the case.
It would seem that Lee's art is in part an effort to stimulate sales of this new approach to the legendarium that the three edited tales represent. After all, Lee became famous among Tolkien fans as the conceptual designer for Peter Jackson's six legendarium films. All six of those films (2001-2003 and 2012-2014) had been released by the time *Beren and Lúthien* and

The Fall of Gondolin were published. Only *The Children of Húrin* (2007) preceded the cinematic release of *The Hobbit* trilogy. The result is that the artwork becomes an unacknowledged commentator on the action, almost a second editor choosing to emphasize one particular idea or another.

The decision to include Alan Lee's art was a good idea commercially. I am not sure it makes sense editorially.

List of Abbreviations

A&I — *Tolkien, Artist and Illustrator*. Wayne Hammond and Christiana Scull. Houghton Mifflin, 1995.

ATB — *The Adventures of Tom Bombadil and other verses from The RedBook*. J.R.R. Tolkien. All quotations are from the edition edited by Christina Scull and Wayne Hammond. HarperCollins, 2014.

B&L — *Beren and Lúthien*. J.R.R. Tolkien Edited by Christopher Tolkien. Houghton Mifflin, 2017.

Bio — *J.R.R. Tolkien, A Biography*. Humphrey Carpenter. Houghton Mifflin, 1977.

C&G — *The J.R.R. Tolkien Companion and Guide*, 3 vols. Christina Scull and Wayne G. Hammond. Houghton Mifflin, 2017.

DSM5 — *Diagnostic and Statistical Manual of Mental Disorders*, Fifth Edition. American Psychiatric Association, 2013

FR — *The Fellowship of the Ring*. J.R.R. Tolkien. Houghton Mifflin.1954.

GL — Gnomish Llexicon or "*i·Lam na·Ngoldathon*, The Grammar and Lexicon of the Gnomish Tongue." *Parma Eldalamberon*, No. 11. Edited by Christopher Gilson, Patrick Wynne, Arden R. Smith, and Carl F. Hostetter. 1995.

GS — *Green Suns and Faerie, Essays on Tolkien*. Verlyn Flieger. The Kent State University Press, 2012.

H — *The Hobbit or There and Back Again*. J.R.R. Tolkien. Houghton Mifflin, 1937.

Letters — *The Letters of J.R.R. Tolkien*. J.R.R. Tolkien. Ed. Humphrey Carpenter with the assistance of Christopher Tolkien. Houghton Mifflin, 1981.

LR — *The Lost Road and Other Writings*. J.R.R. Tolkien. Edited by Christopher Tolkien. Houghton Mifflin, 1987.

LT1 — *The Book of Lost Tales, Part One*. J.R.R. Tolkien. The History of Middle-earth, Vol. 1. Edited by Christopher Tolkien. Houghton Mifflin, 1984.

LT2 — *The Book of Lost Tales, Part Two*. J.R.R. Tolkien. The History of Middle-earth, Vol. 2. Edited by Christopher Tolkien. Houghton Mifflin,

OFS — "On Fairy-Stories." *The Monsters and the Critics and Other Essays*. J.R.R. Tolkien. Ed. Christopher Tolkien. Houghton Mifflin, 1984. 109-161.

PE — *Parma Eldalamberon, The Book of Elven-Tongues.*

Peoples — *The Peoples of Middle-earth. J.R.R. Tolkien. The History of Middle-earth*, Vol. 10. Edited by Christopher Tolkien. Houghton Mifflin, 1996.

QL — "Qenya Lexicon or "Qenyaqetsa" or "The Qenya Phonology and Lexicon" with "The Poetic and Mythologic Words of Eldarissa." *Parma Eldalamberon*, No. 12. Edited by Christopher Gilson, Carl F. Hostetter, Patrick Wynne, and Arden R. Smith. 1998.

QT — *A Question of Time: J.R.R. Tolkien's Road to 'Faerie'*. Verlyn Flieger. The Kent State University Press, 1997.

R *Roverandom*. Edited by Christina Scull and Wayne G. Hammond. Houghton Mifflin, 1998.

RK *Return of the King*. J.R.R. Tolkien. Houghton Mifflin.1955.

RS *The Return of the Shadow*. J.R.R. Tolkien. *The History of Middle-earth* Vol. 6. Edited by Christopher Tolkien. Houghton Mifflin Company, 1988.

S *The Silmarillion*. J.R.R. Tolkien. Edited by Christopher Tolkien. Allen and Unwin. 1977.

SD *Sauron Defeated*. J.R,R, Tolkien. *The History of Middle-earth* Vol. 9. Edited by Christopher Tolkien. Houghton Mifflin, 1992.

S&G *The Legend of Sigurd and Gudrún*. J.R.R. Tolkien. Edited by Christopher Tolkien. Houghton Mifflin, 2009.

SWM *Smith of Wootton Major, Extended Edition*. All quotations in this volume are from the edition edited by Verlyn Flieger. HarperCollins Publishers, 2005.

TFA *The Tolkien Family Album*. John and Priscilla Tolkien. Houghton Mifflin Co, 1992.

TOFS *Tolkien on Fairy-stories, Expanded Edition, with Commentary and Notes*. Edited by Verlyn Flieger and Douglas A. Anderson. Harper Collins Publishers, 2008.

TT *Two Towers*. J.R.R. Tolkien. Houghton Mifflin. 1954.

WR *The War of the Ring*. J.R.R. Tolkien. *The History of The Lord of the Rings Part Three. The History of Middle-earth* Vol. 8. Edited by Christopher Tolkien. Harper Collins Publishers, 1990.

Bibliography

Ahmed, Christine. "William Charles Mountain, J.P. and Grace Brindley Tolkien." *Amon Hen* no. 236, July 2012, pp. 11-13.

Allen, Frank James. "Mirror writing." *Brain*. 19 (2-3), 1896, pp. 385-87.

American Psychiatric Association. *Diagnostic and Statistical Manual of Mental Disorders, Fifth Edition*. American Psychiatric Association, 2013.

Amos, William. *The Originals, Who's Really Who in Fiction*. Sphere Books Ltd., 1985.

Anderson, Douglas. "Obituary: Humphrey Carpenter (1946-2005)." *Tolkien Studies*, vol. 2. Edited by Douglas A. Anderson, Michael D.C. Drout, and Verlyn Flieger. West Virginia University Press, 2005, pp. 217-24.

2006. "R.W. Chambers and *The Hobbit*." *Tolkien Studies*, vol. 3. Edited by Douglas A. Anderson, Michael D.C. Drout, and Verlyn Flieger. West Virginia University Press, 2003, pp. 137-147.

"*Smith of Wootton Major: Extended Edition* by J.R.R. Tolkien, edited by Verlyn Flieger." *Journal of Tolkien Research*. Vol. 2, iss. 1, Article 1, 2015. http://scholar.valpo.edu/journaloftolkien research/vol2/iss1/1.

Anonymous. *English Catholic's Vade Mecum*. London, G.J. Palmer, 1883.

Anonymous. *Every Woman's Encyclopædia*. volume 8, London, The Amalgamated Press, Ltd., 1910-1912.

Anonymous. "Hemispheric Lateralization." Boundless Anatomy and Physiology. Boundless, 05 Jul. 2016. https://www.boundless.com/physiology/textbooks/boundless-anatomy-and-physiology-textbook/central-nervous-system-12/functional-systems-of-the-cerebral-cortex-121/hemispheric-lateralization-657-10252/). Retrieved 20 Aug. 2016.

Auerbach, Erich. *Mimesis: The Representation of Reality in Western Literature*. Trans. Willard R. Trask, Princeton University Press, 2003.

Bair, Deidre. *Jung, A Biography*. Little, Brown and Company, 2003.

Bede. *The Ecclesiastical History of the English People*. Edited by Judith McClure and Roger Collins, Oxford University Press, 1994.

Bellamy, Edward. *Looking Backward: 2000-1887.* Ticknor, 1888.

Bettelheim, Bruno. *The Uses of Enchantment, The Meaning and Importance of Fairy Tales.* Random House, 1975.

Bills, D.M. and E. and W.R. Griffiths. *By Tram to Kinver: 1901-1930.* Elda, 1980.

"The Black Country Geological Society Newsletter " No. 35, October 1982. https://bcgs.info/pub/wpcontent/uploads/newsletters/BCGS_Newsletter035.pdf, accessed on 5/29/20222.

Blackham, Robert S. *Roots of Middle-earth.* Tempus Publishing Ltd., 2006.

Bliss, Alan J. editor. *Sir Orfeo.* Oxford University Press, 1954.

Bosworth-Toller, Joseph. *An Anglo-Saxon Dictionary.* Clarendon Press, 1882.

Bowers, John M. *Tolkien's Lost Chaucer.* Oxford University Press, 2019.

Brace, Keith. "Perspective: In the footsteps of the hobbits." *The Birmingham Post,* May 25, 1968.

Braun, Eric. *J.R.R. Tolkien: Epic Fantasy Author.* Lerner Publications, 2022.

Brewer, Rev. E. Cobham, LL.D., *A Dictionary of Phrase and Fable.* Cassell and Company, Ltd., 1923.

Bridoux, Denis. "Letting Images Speak for Themselves: Tolkien's Rebus Letter to Fr. Francis Morgan, August 8, 1904." *Beyond Bree.* October 2020, pp. 1-2, 11-12.

Brljak, Vladimir. "The Book of Lost Tales: Tolkien as Metafictionist." *Tolkien Studies,* vol.7. Edited by Douglas A. Anderson, Michael D.C. Drout, and Verlyn Flieger. West Virginia University Press, 2010, pp. 1-34.

Broomfield, Andrea. *Food and Cooking in Victorian England: a History.* Greenwood Publishing Group, 2007.

Brothers, Doris. *Toward a Psychology of Uncertainty: Trauma-Centered Psychoanalysis.* The Analytic Press, 2008.

Bruce, Alexander M. "The Fall of Gondolin and the Fall of Troy: Tolkien and Book II of *The Aeneid.*" *Mythlore,* vol. 30, no. 3, Spring/Summer 2012, pp. 103-115.

Bunting, Nancy. "1904: Tolkien Trauma, and Its Anniversaries." *Mythlore,* vol. 34, no.1, iss. 127, Fall/Winter 2015, pp. 59-81.

"... And What About Zanzibar? Or an Adult Fairy Tale Concerning Tolkien's Biographical Legend." *Mallorn,* vol. 58, Winter 2017, pp. 30-37. A version of this paper was given at Mythcon 2017.

"Checking the Facts." *Mallorn*, iss. 59. Winter 2018, pp. 52-56.

"Concerning Tolkien's Deadly Spiders, Part I." *Lembas*, vol. 38, no. 185, December 2018, pp. 201-211.

"Concerning Tolkien's Deadly Spiders, Part II." *Lembas*, vol. 38, No, 186, March 2019, pp. 213-24.

"J.R.R. Tolkien–Ambidexter!" *Beyond Bree*, October 2018, pp. 4-6.

"Reconsidering Tom Bombadil in *The Lord of the Rings*." *Hither Shore* 17. 2020, pp. 225- 246.

Reply to Noad's Comments on the article, "Checking the Facts." *Mallorn*, iss. 63, Winter 2022, pp. 36-42.

"Roverandom, an Autobiographical Reading, Part I." *Beyond Bree*, June 2016, pp. 3-6.

"Roverandom, an Autobiographical Reading, Part II." *Beyond Bree*, July 2016, pp. 6-8.

"Tolkien and the Boy Scouts." *Lembas Extra*, 2015, pp. 75-87.

"Tolkien in Love: Pictures from the Winter of 1912-1913." *Mythlore*, vol. 32 no. 2, iss. 124 Spring/Summer 2014, pp. 5-12.

Bunting, Nancy and Elizabeth Currie. "The 1911 Swiss Walking Tour: A Sentimental Education and Some of Its Fruits, Part I." *Beyond Bree*, May 2021, pp. 1-5.

Bunting, Nancy and Seamus Hamill-Keays. *The Gallant Edith Bratt: J.R.R. Tolkien's Inspiration*. Walking Tree Publishers, 2021.

Burns, Maggie. "Faces and Places: Jane Suffield." http://www.search.connectinghistories.org.uk/engine/resource/exhibition/ sequential. Downloaded 11/29/2008.

"Faces and Places: John Suffield." https://www.search.connectinghistories.org.uk/details.aspx?ResourceID=1386&ExhibitionID=1387&PageIndex=1&KeyWord=John%20suffield&SortOrder=2.

"John Suffield" birminghamhistory.co.uk/forum/index.php?threads/some-great-men-and-women-of-birmingham.40423. Downloaded 2/6/2011.

"Faces and Places: Thomas Ewart Mitton." http:www.search.connectinghistories.org.uk/engine/resource/exhibition/sequential. Downloaded 7/17/2009. https://www.search.connectinghistories.org.uk/Details.aspx?&ResourceID=1280&PageIndex=1&KeyWord=Thomas%20Ewart&DateFrom=0&DateTo=2022&SortOrder=0&ThemeID=0, accessed on 4/17/22.

"…a local habitation and a name…" *Mallorn*, vol. 50, Autumn 2010, pp. 26-31.

"Roland Suffield." *Amon Hen* no. 232 November 2011, p. 16.

"They Slept in Beauty." *Amon Hen*, no. 201, September 2006, pp. 11-12.

"An unlettered peasant boy' of 'sordid character'—Shakespeare, Suffield and Tolkien." *Mallorn*, vol. 49. Spring 2010, pp. 18-20, 22-23.

Burns, Marjorie. *Perilous Realms: Celtic and Norse in Tolkien's Middle-earth*. University of Toronto Press, 2005.

Byrne, Evelyn B. and Otto M. Pensler. *Attacks of Taste*. Gotham Book Mart, 1971.

Card, Orson Scott. "How Tolkien Means." *Meditations on Middle-earth*. Edited by Karen Haber, St. Martin's Press, 2001, pp. 153-173.

Carpenter, Humphrey. *J.R.R. Tolkien, A Biography*. Houghton Mifflin, 1977.

(in conversation with Lyndall Gordon). "Learning about Ourselves: Biography as Autobiography." *The Art of Literary Biography*. Edited by John Batchelor. Clarendon Press, 1995, pp. 267-279.

Carson, Rachel. *The Sense of Wonder*. Harper and Row, 1965.

Castell, Daphne. "Talking to a Maker of Modern Myths." *The Glasgow Herald*, 6 August 1966.

Chance, Jane. *'The Lord of the Rings': The Mythology of Power*. Revised ed. University Press of Kentucky, 2001.

Chance Nitzsche, Jane. *Tolkien's Art, A 'Mythology for England'*. St Martin's Press, 1979.

Cilli, Oronzo. *Tolkien's Library: An Annotated Checklist*. Luna Press Publishing, 2019.

Coghill, Nevill and Christopher Tolkien, editors. *The Pardoner's Tale*. Geoffrey Chaucer, George G. Harrap, 1958.

Coitir, Niall Mac. *Ireland's Trees—Myths, Legends and Folklore*. The Collins Press, 2016.

Collins, David R. *J.R.R. Tolkien: Master of Fantasy*. Lerner Publications, 1992.

Collins, Phil. *The Kinver Light Railway: Echoes of a Lost Tramway*. History Press Limited, 2012.

Colum, Padraic. *The Voyagers: Being Legends and Romances of Atlantic Discovery*. MacMillan Co., 1927.

Coren, Michael. *J.R. R. Tolkien: The Man Who Created 'The Lord of the Rings'*. Scholastic, 2001.

CORREALE, Robert M., editor. *Sources and Analogues of the Canterbury Tales,* Volume 2. D.S. Brewer, 2005.

CRANE, Christopher. "Early Drafts and Carbon Copies: Composing and Editing Smith of Wootton Major." *Tolkien Studies,* vol. 19. Edited by Michael D.C. Drout, Verlyn Flieger and David Bratman. West Virginia University Press, 2022, pp. 143-157.

CROCKETT, S.R. [Samuel Rutherford]. *The Black Douglas.* London, Smith, Elder and Co., 1899.

CROFT, Janet. "Tolkien's Faërian Drama: Origins and Valedictions." *Mythlore* vol. 32, no.2, Spring/Summer 2014, pp. 33-46.

DÁITHÍ, Ó hÓgáin. *An Encyclopaedia of Myth, Legend and Romance.* Boydell Press, 2006.

DAVIDSON, Alan, editor. *The Oxford Companion to Food,* 1st ed., 2014.

DERDZIŃSKI, Ryszard. "Mabel Tolkien baptized in …1891!" Friday, January 5, 2018, http://tolkniety.blogspot.com/, accessed on 10/5/2023.

DICKERSON, Matthew and Jonathon EVANS. *Ents, Elves, and Eriador: The Environmental Vision of J.R.R. Tolkien.* University of Kentucky Press, 2006.

DIJKSTRA, Bram. *Idols of Perversity, Fantasies of Feminine Evil in Fin-de-Siècle Culture.* Oxford University Press, 1986.

DOUGHAN, David. "In Search of the Bounce: Tolkien Seen through Smith." *Leaves from the Tree: J.R.R. Tolkien's Shorter Fiction.* The Tolkien Society, 1991, pp. 17-22.

DOUGLAS, Ann. *The Feminization of American Culture.* Doubleday, 1988.

DROUT, Michael D.C., editor. *J.R.R. Tolkien Encyclopedia, Scholarship and Critical Assessment.* Routledge, 2007.

DURIEZ, Colin. *Tolkien and Lewis: The Gift of Friendship.* HiddenSpring, 2003.

Tolkien and The Lord of the Rings. A Guide to Middle-earth. HiddenSpring, 2001.

EIDENVALL, Góran. "Trees and Traumas. On the Use of Phytomorphic Metaphors in Prophetic Descriptions of Deportation and Exile." *Images of Exile in the Prophetic Literature.* Edited by Jesper Høgenhaven, Frederik Poulsen, and Cian Power, Tübingen, Germany, Mohr Siebeck, 2019, pp. 217-269.

ELANSEA. See Alex Lewis and Elizabeth Currie.

ELWORTHY, Frederick T. *The Evil Eye: An Account of this Ancient and Widespread Superstition.* 1895.

Evans, Robley. *J.R.R. Tolkien (Writers for the 70's).* Warner Books, Inc., 1972.

Ezard, John. "Tolkien's Shire." *The Guardian*, Saturday, December 28, 1991.

F.A. "Ungrateful Guests." *Punch, or the London Charivari*, December 23, 1908, pp. 458-9.

Federal Reserve Bank of Dallas. "Time Well Spent." https://www.dallasfed.org/~/media/documents/fed/annual/1999/ar97. Pdf, accessed on 1/6/2024.

Ferrández Bru, José M. 'Uncle Curro': *J.R.R. Tolkien's Spanish Connection.* Luna Press Publishing, 2017.

Fimi, Dimitra. *Tolkien, Race, and Cultural History: From Fairies to Hobbits.* Palgrave Macmillan, 2009.

Fisher, Jason. "Galadriel." *J.R.R. Tolkien Encyclopedia, Scholarship and Critical Assessment.* Edited by Michael D.C. Drout, Routledge, 2007, pp. 227-228.

Flanders, Judith. *The Victorian House.* Harper Collins, 2003.

Flieger, Verlyn. "Fays, Corrigans, Elves, and More: Tolkien's Dark Ladies." *There Would Always Be a Fairy Tale: More Essays on Tolkien.* The Kent State University Press, 2017, pp. 165-177.

Green Suns and Faerie, Essays on Tolkien. The Kent State University Press, 2012.

A Question of Time: J.R.R. Tolkien's Road to 'Faerie'. The Kent State University Press, 1997.

Splintered Light, Logos and Language in Tolkien's World. Wm. B. Eerdmans Publishing Co., 1983.

There Would Always Be a Fairy Tale: More Essays on Tolkien. The Kent State University Press, 2017.

Freud, Sigmund. *Studies on Hysteria*, 1893.

Gardner, Angela and Neil Holford. *Wheelbarrows at Dawn: Memories of Hilary Tolkien.* ADC Publications Ltd., 2010.

Garth, John. "As under a green sea: visions of war in the Dead Marshes." *The Ring Goes Ever On: Proceedings of the Tolkien 2005 Conference: 50 years of The Lord of the Rings*, Vol. One. editor, Sarah Wells, The Tolkien Society, 2008, pp. 9-21.

Tolkien at Exeter: How an Oxford Undergraduate Created Middle-earth. Exeter College, 2014.

Tolkien and the Great War, the Threshold of Middle-earth. Houghton Mifflin, 2000.

GEIER, Fabian. "Leaf by Tolkien? Allegory and Biography in Tolkien's Literary Theory and Practice." *Tolkien's Shorter Works. Proceedings of the 4th Seminar of the Deutsche Tolkien Gesellschaft and Walking Tree Publishers Decennial Conference.* Edited by Margaret Hiley and Frank Weinreich, 2008, Walking Tree Publishers, 2008, pp. 209-232.

GIRARD, René. *Deceit, Desire, and the Novel.* Translated by Yvonne Freccero. Johns Hopkins University Press, 1988.

Things Hidden Since the Foundation of the World. Translated by Mark Bann and Michael Metteer, Stanford University Press, 1987.

GOODMAN, Ruth. *How to Be a Victorian.* Viking, 2013.

GORELIK, Boris. "'Africa ... always moves me deeply': Tolkien in Bloemfontein." *Mallorn.* vol. 55, Autumn 2014, pp. 5-10.

GRAFTON, Charles Chapman. *The Works of the Rt. Rev. Charles C. Grafton: A Catholic Atlas; or Digest of Catholic Theology.* Longmans, Green, 1914.

Great Britain. *[Parliament's] Accounts and Papers. Education (England and Wales)—(continued). List of Public Elementary Schools.* Volume LXXXIV. London, Wyman and Sons Limited, 1908.

GREEN, Richard Firth. *Elf Queens and Holy Friars: Fairy Beliefs and the Medieval Church.* University of Pennsylvania Press, 2016.

GREEN, Roger Lancelyn. "Recollections." *Amon Hen* no. 44, May 1980, pp. 6-8.

GRIMM, Jacob and Wilhelm. "The Juniper Tree." *Grimm's Fairy Tales.* 1812.

GROTTA-KURSKA, Daniel. *J.R.R. Tolkien, Architect of Middle Earth.* Running Press, 1976.

GRUEN, Arno. *The Betrayal of the Self: The Fear of Autonomy in Men and Women.* Translated by Hildegarde and Hunter Hannum, Grove Press, 1986.

GUEROULT, Denys. *Now Read On.* BBC Radio 4 (recorded 26 Nov. 1964, aired 16 Dec. 1970) *Minas Tirith Evening-Star*, vol. 8, no. 2, transcript.https://www.bbc.co.uk/programmes/p021jx7j, accessed on 1/6/2024.

"Guide to the Names in The Lord of the Rings." *Tolkien Gateway.* https://tolkiengateway.net/wiki/Guide_to_the_Names_in_The_Lord_of_the_Rings, accessed 28 July 2022.

HALIDAY, Charles. *The Scandinavian Kingdom of Dublin.* second edition. Edited by John Patrick Pendergast, Dublin, M.H. Gill & Son, 1884.

HAMILL-KEAYS, Seamus. "Tolkien in Buckland: An Analysis of the Evidence." *Brycheiniog: Cyfnodolyn Cymdeithas Brycheiniog /The Journal of the Brecknock Society* XLIX, 2018, pp. 91-107.

HAMMOND, Wayne G. and Christina SCULL, editors. *J.R.R. Tolkien, Artist and Illustrato*r. Houghton Mifflin, 1995.

'The Lord of the Rings', A Reader's Companion. Houghton Mifflin Company, 2005.

HANKS, Patrick. *A Dictionary of First Names.* Oxford University Press, 2006.

HEAD, Hayden. "Imitative Desire in Tolkien's Mythology: A Girardian Perspective." *Mythlore*, vol. 26, no. 1/2, Fall/Winter 2007, pp. 137-148.

HEELY, Joseph. *Letters on the Beauties of Hagley, Envil and The Leasowes with critical remarks and Observations on the Modern Taste in Gardening.* Baldwin, 1777.

HEMMI, Yoko. "Tolkien's *The Lord of the Rings* and His Concept of Native Language: Sindarin and British Welsh." *Tolkien Studies*, vol 7. Edited by Douglas Anderson, Michael D.C. Drout, and Verlyn Flieger. West Virginia University Press, 2010, pp.147-174.

HENRY, Mick. "There and Back Again? Tolkien's Brief Visit to Sussex in 1904." *Mallorn*, vol. 60, Summer 2020, pp. 31-32.

HEWSTON, Norman. *A History of Moseley Village*, Vol .1. Amberley Publishing plc, 2009. https://historicengland.org.uk/images-books/ publications/jubilee-ation/ jubilee-parks/, accessed on 5/5/2002.

HILEY, Margaret. *The Loss and the Silence. Aspects of Modernism in the Works of C.S, Lewis, J.R.R. Tolkien, and Charles Williams.* Walking Tree Publishers, 2011.

HILTON, James. *Lost Horizon.* Macmillan, 1933.

HOBB, Robin. "A Bar and a Quest," *Meditations on Middle-earth.* Edited by Karen Haber, St. Martin's Press, 2001, pp. 85-100.

HOLMES, John. "Harping on One-String in Middle-earth." *Music in Tolkien's Work and Beyond.* Edited by Julian Eilmann and Friedhelm Schneidewind, Walking Tree Publishers, 2019, pp. 359-385.

HONEGGER, Thomas. "Fantasy, Escape, Recovery, and Consolation in *Sir Orfeo*: The Medieval Foundations of Tolkienian Fantasy." *Tolkien Studies*, vol. 7. Edited by Douglas Anderson, Michael D.C. Drout, and Verlyn Flieger. West Virginia University Press, 2010, pp. 117-136.

HOOKER, Mark T. "Annotated Transcription of Tolkien's 1904 Rebus Letter to Fr. Francis." *Beyond Bree*, November 2020, pp. 2-5.

Iter Tolkienensis, A Tolkiennymical Road Trip from Buckland (Worcestershire) to The Ivy Bush (Carmathen, Wales). Llyfrawr, 2016.

"Journey to the Center of Middle-earth," *The Tolkienaeum, Essays on J.R.R. Tolkien and his Legendarium.* Llyfrawr, 2014, pp. 1-12.

Tolkien and Sanskrit, 'The Silmarillion' in the Cradle of Proto-Indo-European. Llyfrawr, 2016.

Tolkien and Welsh. Essays on J.R.R. Tolkien's Use of Welsh in his 'Legendarium'. Llyfrawr, 2012.

Tolkienian Glôssology or a Study of the Primitive Elvish Vocabulary of Tolkien's 'Qenya Lexicon' and Gnomish Lexicon from the Late 1910s, the Precursors of Quenya and Sindarin. Llyfrawr, 2020.

A Tolkienian Mathomium, A Collection of Articles about J.R.R. Tolkien and His Legendarium. Llyfrawr, 2006.

Tolkienotēca: Studies in Tolkiennymy; Or, Searching for the Origins of Elvo-Indo-European in Tolkien's Elvish Lexicon; With an Addendum to 'Tolkien and Sanskrit', and a Lexicon of Elvish Month Names. Llyfrawr, 2019.

Translating "The Hobbit" Into Afrikaans, Belarusian, Bulgarian, Czech, Danish, Dutch, Frisian, German Icelandic, Lithuanian, Norwegian, Polish, Romanian, Russian, Serbian, Slovak, Slovene, Serbian, Swedish, Ukrainian, and Yiddish. Llyfrawr, 2023.

Horobin, Simon. "J.R.R. Tolkien as a Philologist, A reconsideration of the Northernisms in Chaucer's Reeve's Tale." *J.R.R. Tolkien: Critical Assessments of Major Writers. Volume I Tolkien's Life–Writer and Medievalist.* Edited by Stuart Lee. Routledge, 2017, pp. 115-126.

Huttar, Ronald. "Tolkien's Magic." *The Return of the Ring. Proceedings of the Tolkien Society Conference 2012* Vol. I. Edited by Lynn Forest-Hill. Luna Press Publishing, 2016, pp. 175-186.

Jalland, Patricia. *Death in the Victorian Family.* Oxford University Press, 1996.

Johnson, A.E. "English Cave Dwellers of Today." *The Wide World Magazine: An Illustrated Monthly of True Narrative; Adventure, Travel, Customs and Sport;* vol. 13, April 1904 to September 1904, pp. 603-607.

Johnson, Judith. *J.R.R. Tolkien: Six Decades of Criticism.* Greenwood Press, 1986.

Jones, Leslie Ellen. *J.R.R. Tolkien: A Biography.* Greenwood Press, 2003.

Joyce, Patrick Weston. *The Wonders of Ireland and Other Papers on Irish Subjects.* London, Longmans, Green, and Company, 1911.

Kilcrease, Bethany. *The Great Church Crisis and the End of English Erastianism, 1898-1906.* Routledge, 2017.

Kilby, Clyde. *Tolkien & the Silmarillion.* Berkhamstead, Lion Publishing, 1976.

"Kinver Edge and the Rock Houses." https://www.nationaltrust.org.uk/kinver-edge-and-the-rock-houses, accessed on 5/29/2022.

"Kinver Rock Houses-The Original Hobbit Holes?" https://britainexplorer.com/listing/kinver-edge-rock-houses-the-original-hobbit/, accessed on 5/1/2015.

KLINGER, Judith. "The Fallacies of Power: Frodo's Resistance to the Ring." *The Ring Goes Ever On. Proceedings of the Tolkien 2005 Conference: 50 Years of 'The Lord of the Rings'* Vol. One. Edited by Sarah Wells, The Tolkien Society, 2008, pp. 355-369.

"Tolkien's 'Strange Powers of Mind': Dreams, Visionary History and Authorship." *Sub-creating Middle-earth: Constructions of Authorship and the Works of J.R.R. Tolkien*. Edited by Judith Klinger, Walking Tree Publishers, 2012, pp. 43-106.

KOUBENEC, Noah. "The Precious and the *Pearl*: The Influence of *Pearl* on the Nature of the One Ring." *Mythlore*, vol. 29, no. 3/4, Spring/Summer 2011, pp. 119-131.

KOCH, John T. *Celtic Culture: A Historical Encyclopedia*. ABC-CLIO. 2006.

LEE, Hermione. EDITH WHARTON. Alfred A. Knopf, 2007.

LEE, Stuart E. "J.R.R. Tolkien and 'The Wanderer': From Edition to Application." *Tolkien Studies*, vol. 6, Edited by Douglas A. Anderson, Michael D.C. Drout, and Verlyn Flieger, West Virginia University Press, 2009, pp. 189-211.

"'Tolkien in Oxford' (BBC, 1968): A Reconstruction." *Tolkien Studies*, vol 15. Edited by Michael D.C. Drout, Verlyn Flieger, and David Bratman, West Virginia University Press, 2018, pp. 115-176.

LEŚNIEWSKI, Michał. "The Question of the 'Round Arda': An Abandoned Idea, or Another Perspective on Tolkien's Legendarium." *The Ring Goes Ever On: Proceedings from the Tolkien 2005 Conference: 50 Years of 'The Lord of the Rings'* Volume Two. Edited by Sarah Wells, The Tolkien Society, 2008, pp. 353-359.

LEWIS, Alex and Elizabeth CURRIE. *The Forsaken Realm of Tolkien: J.R.R. Tolkien and the Medieval Tradition*. Medea, 2005.

Tolkien's Switzerland, A Biography of One Special Summer. privately published, 2019.

LEWIS-STEMPEL, John. *Six Weeks: The Short and Gallant Life of the British Officer in the First World War*. Weidenfeld and Nicholson, 2010.

LONG, Josh. "Clinamen, Tessera, and the Anxiety of Influence: Swerving from and Completing George Macdonald." *Tolkien Studies*, vol. 6. Edited by Douglas Anderson, Michael D.C. Drout, and Verlyn Flieger, West Virginia University Press, 2009, pp. 127-150.

"Faery, Faith and Self-Portrayal: An Allegorical Interpretation of Smith of Wootton Major." *Tolkien Studies*, vol. 18. Edited by Michael D.C. Drout,

Verlyn Flieger and David Bratman. West Virginia University Press, 2021, pp. 93-129.

"Pillaging Middle-earth: Self-Plagiarism in *Smith of Wootton Major*." *Mythlore*, vol. 32, no.2, Spring/Summer 2014, pp. 119-137.

"Two Views of Faerie in *Smith of Wootton Major*: Nokes and his Cake, Smith and his Star." *Mythlore*, vol. 26, no.3/4, Spring/Summer 2008, pp. 89-100.

Loughlin, Marie H. "Tolkien's Treasures: Marvellous Objects in *The Hobbit* and *The Lord of the Rings*." *Tolkien Studies*, vol. 16. Edited by Michael D.C. Drout, and Verlyn Flieger and David Bratman. West Virginia University Press, 2019, pp. 21-58.

Lynch, Doris. *J.R.R. Tolkien: Creator of Languages and Legends*. Franklin Watts, 2003.

MacDonald, George. "The Golden Key." *Dealings with the Fairies*. 1867.

There and Back. 1891. McAllister Edition (mcallistereditions@gmail.com). 2016.

Mahler, Michael W., S.J. "'A Land without Stain': Medieval Images of Mary and Their Use in the Characterization of Galadriel." *Tolkien the Medievalist*. Edited by Jane Chance. Routledge Studies in Medieval Religion and Culture, 2003, pp. 225-236.

Manlove, Colin. "How much does Tolkien owe to the work of George MacDonald?" *The Ring Goes Ever On: Proceedings from the Tolkien 2005 Conference: 50 Years of 'The Lord of the Rings'* Volume Two. Edited by Sarah Wells, The Tolkien Society, 2008, pp. 109-116.

Martsch, Nancy. "Tolkien Reading Day and 'Eyes Clear as Glass'." *Beyond Bree*, April 2021, p. 9.

McAlister, Caroline. *John Ronald's Dragons: The Story of J.R R. Tolkien*. Roaring Brook Press, 2017.

McIlwaine, Catherine. *Tolkien: Maker of Middle-earth*. Bodleian Library, 2018.

Mendelsohn, Daniel. "Epic Fail?" *The New Yorker*. October 15, 2018, pp. 87-93.

Mills, David. *A Dictionary of British Place-Names*. Oxford University Press, 2011.

Milton, John. *Areopagitica. A Speech of Mr. John Milton for the Liberty of Unlicenc'd Printing*. London, 1664. https://www.gutenberg.org/ebooks/608, accessed 8 July 2022.

More, Thomas. *Utopia*. 1516. Rev. ed. Edited and translated by Paul Turner, Penguin Books, 2003.

Morris, William. *News from Nowhere; Or, An Epoch of Rest Being Some Chapters from a Utopian Romance.* Reeves & Turner, 1891.

Nagy, Gergely. "The 'Lost' Subject of Middle-earth: the Constitution of the Subject in the Figure of Gollum in *The Lord of the Rings.*" *Tolkien Studies*, vol. 3. Edited by Douglas A. Anderson, Michael D.C. Drout, and Verlyn Flieger, West Virginia University Press. 2006, pp. 57-79.

Needham, Steven. *Biography of J.R.R. Tolkien.* Hyperlink, 2012. Ebook.

Neimark, Anne E. *J.R.R. Tolkien: Myth Maker.* Harcourt Brace, 1996.

Nesbit, Edith. "Five Children and It." *Strand Magazine.* 1902.

Neubauer, Łukasz. "'The Polish Inkling': Professor Przemysław Mrockowski as J.R.R. Tolkien's Friend and Scholar." *Mythlore*, vol 39, no. 1, 137, Fall/Winter 2020, pp. 149-176.

Noll, Richard. *The Jung Cult, Origins of a Charismatic Movement.* Free Press, 1994.

Onwuemezi, Natasha. "Christopher Tolkien awarded the Bodley Medal." *The Bookseller* (31 Oct. 2016). https://www.thebookseller.com/news/christopher-tolkien-awarded-bodley-medal 424211, accessed 25 July 2022.

Ordway, Holly. *Tolkien's Faith: A Spiritual Biography.* Word on Fire, 2023.

Tolkien's Modern Reading: Middle-earth Beyond the Middle Ages. Word on Fire, 2021.

Pamuk, Orhan. *The Naïve and the Sentimental Novelist.* Vintage Books, 2010.

Parker, Douglass. "Hwaet, We Holbytla...." *Hudson Review*, 9, 1957, pp. 598-609.

Patch, Howard Rollin. "Some Elements in Mediæval Descriptions of the Otherworld." *PMLA* vol. 33, no. 4, 1918, pp. 601-643.

Pearce, Joseph. "Heaven." *J.R.R. Tolkien Encyclopedia, Scholarship and Critical Assessment.* Edited by Michael D.C. Drout, Routledge, 2007, pp. 267-68.

Tolkien: Man and Myth. A Literary Life. Ignatius Press, 1998.

Pepetone, Gregory G. *Hogwarts and All. Gothic Perspectives on Children's Literature.* Peter Lang, 2012.

Phelpstead, Carl. "Myth-making and Sub-creation." *Companion to J.R.R. Tolkien.* Edited by Stuart D. Lee, John Wiley & Sons, Ltd., 2014, pp. 79-91.

Tolkien and Wales: Language, Literature, and Identity. University of Wales Press, 2011.

Pigott, B.A.F. *Flowers and Ferns of Cromer and its Neighborhood.* Jarrold and Sons, 1885.

Plimmer, Charlotte and Denis. "The Man Who Understands Hobbits." *The Telegraph*, March 22, 1968.

Ponty, Steve. *Middle-earth in Magic Mirror Maps of Wales … of the Wilderland in Wales … of the Shire in England*. Matador, 2014.

Potts, Michael. "'Evening-lands': Splengerian Tropes in *Lord of the Rings*." *Tolkien Studies* vol. 13, edited by Michael D.C. Drout, Verlyn Flieger, David Bratman, West Virginia University Press, 2016, pp. 149-168.

Priestman, Judith. *J.R.R. Tolkien, Life and Legend*. Bodleian Library, 1992.

Pryce-Jones, David. *Unity Mitford: An Enquiry into her Life and the Frivolity of Evil*. Dial Press, 1977.

Rabkin, Eric. "The Fantastic and Fantasy." *Fantastic Literature, A Critical Reader*. Edited by David Sandner. Praeger, 2004, pp. 167-171.

Rateliff, John D. *The History of the Hobbit*. (2 volumes: *Part One: Mr. Baggins and Part Two: Return to Bag-End*). Houghton Mifflin, 2007.

Ready, William. *The Tolkien Relation, A Personal Inquiry*, Henry Regnery Co., 1968.

Resnik, Henry. "An Interview with Tolkien," *Niekas* 18. Spring 1967, pp. 37-47.

Rhŷs, John. *Celtic Folklore: Welsh and Manx*, vol. 1. The Clarendon Press, 1901.

Early Britain. Celtic Britain. Society for Promoting Christian Knowledge, 1882.

"The rock houses of England's last cave people: Kinver Edge, Staffordshire." https://www.theguardian.com/travel/2020/oct/02/kinver-edge-black-country-to-tea-englands-last-cave-people, accessed on 5/29/2022.

"The rock houses that inspired Tolkien." https://www.amusingplanet.com/2017/10/the-rock-houses-that-inspired-tolkien.html, accessed on 5/29/2022.

Rose, Lionel. *The Erosion of Childhood, Child Oppression in Britain 1860-1918*. Routledge, 1991.

Rosegrant, John. "Mother Music." *Tolkien Studies*, vol 16. Edited by Michael D.C. Drout, Verlyn Flieger, and David Bratman, West Virginia University Press, 2018, pp. 111-131.

Ross, Jean W. "CA Interview." *Contemporary Authors, New Revisions Series*, vol. 13. Gale Research, 1984, pp. 100-102.

Ruud, Jay. *Critical Companion to J.R.R. Tolkien: A Literary Reference to His Life and Work*. Facts on File, 2011.

Ryan, John S. *Tolkien's View: Windows into His World*. Walking Tree Publishers, 2009.

SARGENT, Lyman Tower. "The Three Faces of Utopianism Revisited." *Utopian Studies*, 5.1, 1994, pp.1-37.

Utopianism: A Very Short Introduction. Oxford University Press, 2010.

SAUNDBY, Robert M.D. "An address on the Modern Treatment of Diabetes Mellitus, delivered before the Annual meeting of the Gloucestershire Branch of the British Medical Association at Cheltenham on May 15, 1900." *Lancet.* May 19, 1900, pp. 1420-1426.

SAYER, George. "Recollections of J.R.R. Tolkien." *Tolkien: A Celebration, Collected Writings on a Literary Legacy.* Edited by Joseph Pearce, Ignatius Press, 1999, pp. 1-16.

SCHOTT, Geoffrey D. "Mirror writing: Allen's self observations, Lewis Carroll's "looking-glass" letters, and Leonardo da Vinci's maps." *Lancet.* 34 December 18/25, 1999, pp. 2158-61.

"Mirror writing: neurological reflections on an unusual phenomenon." *Journal of Neurology, Neurosurgery, and Psychiatry.* 2007:78, pp. 5-13.

SCOTT, Walter. *Marmion*. Houghton, Mifflin, 1885.

SCOTT, William (of Stroubridge). *Stourbridge and Its Vicinity: Containing a Topographical Description of the Old Parish of Swinford, including the Township of Stourbridge; with the adjoining parishes of King Swinford, Kinver, Pedmore, and Halesowen; Observation on Hagley, Enville, Clent, &c.; Antiquities, Itinerary and Memorable Occurrences; and Memoirs Geological, Mineralogical, Botanical, &c. Illustrated with Plates.* J. Heming, 1832.

SCULL, Christina and Wayne G. HAMMOND. *The J.R.R. Tolkien Companion & Guide. Vol. 1: Chronology. Vol. 2: Reader's Guide.* Houghton Mifflin, 2006.

The J.R.R. Tolkien Companion and Guide, 3 vols. Houghton Mifflin, 2017.

SEELYE, Katharine Q., and Alan YUHAS. "Christopher Tolkien, Keeper of His Father's Legacy, Dies at 95." *The New York Times* 25 Jan. 2020. https://www.nytimes.com/2020/01/16/books/christopher-tolkien-dead.html. Accessed 28 July 2022.

SENIOR, W.A. "Loss Eternal in J.R.R. Tolkien's Middle-earth." *J.R.R. Tolkien and His Literary Resonances.* Edited by George Clark and Daniel Timmons, Greenwood, 2000, pp. 173-82.

SHAY, Jonathan. *Achilles in Vietnam: Combat Trauma and the Undoing of Character.* Touchstone, 1994.

SHIPPEY, Tom A. "Allegory Versus Bounce: Tolkien's *Smith of Wootton Major.*" *Green Suns and Faerie, Essays on Tolkien*. The Kent State University Press, 2012, pp. 170-178.

J.R.R. Tolkien: Author of the Century. Houghton Mifflin, 2001.

The Road to Middle Earth, Revised and Expanded. Houghton Mifflin, 2003.

"Tolkien and the *Beowulf*-Poet." *Roots and Branches: Selected Papers on Tolkien by Tom Shippey*. Walking Tree Publishers, 2007, pp. 1-18.

"Tolkien and the Gawain-Poet." *Roots and Branches: Selected Papers on Tolkien*. Walking Tree Publishers, 2007, pp. 61-77.

SHORTO, Russell. *J.R.R. Tolkien: Man of Fantasy*. Kipling Press, 1988.

SIMPSON, Eileen, *Orphans, Real and Imaginary*, NAL Penguin, 1987.

SITWELL, William. *A History of Food in 100 Recipes*. Little, Brown, 2013.

SLACK, Anna. "A Star Above the Mast." *Hither Shore*, vol. 4, 2007, pp. 177-187.

SLY, Debbie. "Weaving Nets of Gloom: 'Darkness Profound' in Tolkien and Milton." *J.R.R. Tolkien and His Literary Resonances: Views of Middle-earth*. Edited by George Clark and Daniel Timmons, Greenwood Press, 2000, pp. 109-19.

SMITH, Arden. "Book Review: *A Secret Vice: Tolkien on Invented Languages.*" *Tolkien Studies*, Vol. 14. Edited by Michael D.C. Drout, Verlyn Flieger, and David Bratman, West Virginia University Press, 2017, pp. 169-84.

SPENGLER, Oswald. *The Decline of the West*. Abr. Ed. 1932. Translated by Arthur Helps. Oxford University Press, 1991.

STERNBERG, Martin. "*Smith of Wootton Major* Considered as a Religious Text." *Tolkien's Shorter Works. Proceedings of the 4th Seminar of the Deutsche Tolkien Gesellschaft and Walking Tree Publishers Decennial Conference*. Edited by Margaret Hiley and Frank Weinreich, Walking Tree Publishers, 2008, pp. 292-323.

SZAFLARSKI, J.P., J.R. BINDER, E.T. POSSING, K.A. MCKIERNAN, B.D. WARD, T.A. HAMMEKE. "Language lateralization in left-handed and ambidextrous people: fMRI data." *Neurology*. 2002 Jul 23; vol. 59 (2), pp. 238-44.

TATTERSALL, Robert. *Diabetes, the Biography*. Oxford University Press, 2009.

TERR, Lenore. *Too Scared to Cry: Psychic Trauma in Childhood*. Harper and Row, 1990.

THOMAS, Charles. *Christianity in Roman Britain to AD 500*. Batsford, 1981.

Thomas, Clayton L. *Taber's Cyclopedic Medical Dictionary* 13th edition. F.A. Davis Company, 1977.

Tolkien, Christopher. "Note on the Text." *The Lay of Aotrou and Itroun together with the Corrigan Poems.* Edited by Verlyn Flieger, HarperCollins, 2016, pp. xi-xii.

editor. *The Saga of King Heidrek the Wise.* Thomas Nelson and Sons, 1960.

Tolkien, Hilary. *Black and White Ogre Country, The Lost Tales of Hilary Tolkien.* Edited by Angela Gardner. ADC Publications Ltd., 2009.

Tolkien, John F.R. and Priscilla. *The Tolkien Family Album.* Houghton Mifflin Co., 1992.

Tolkien, J.R.R. *The Adventures of Tom Bombadil and Other Verses.* 1962. George Allen & Unwin, 1969.

The Adventures of Tom Bombadil and other verses from The RedBook. Edited by Christina Scull and Wayne Hammond, Harper Collins, 2014.

The Ancrene Wisse: The English Text of the Ancrene Riwle. Oxford University Press, 1962.

Beowulf, a Translation and Commentary together with Sellic Spell. Edited by Christopher Tolkien, Houghton Mifflin, 2014.

Beren and Lúthien. Edited by Christopher Tolkien, Houghton Mifflin, 2017.

Bilbo's Last Song. Houghton Mifflin, 1974.

The Book of Lost Tales, Part One. The History of Middle-earth, Vol. 1. Edited by Christopher Tolkien, Houghton Mifflin, 1983.

The Book of Lost Tales, Part Two. The History of Middle-earth, Vol. 2. Edited by Christopher Tolkien, Houghton Mifflin, 1984.

"Chaucer as a Philologist: *The Reeve's Tale.*" *Transactions of the Philological Society.* 1934, pp. 1-70. reprinted with corrections in Tolkien Studies, vol. 6. Edited by Douglas Anderson, Michael D.C. Drout, and Verlyn Flieger, West Virgina University Press, 2008, pp. 109-71.

The Children of Húrin. Edited by Christopher Tolkien, Houghton Mifflin, 2007.

"*Eldarin Hands, Fingers* and Related Writings." Edited by Patrick H. Wynne, *Vinyar Tengwar* no. 48, February 2005, Tolkien Trust. pp. 4-26.

The End of the Third Age. The History of Middle-earth Part 4. (unnumbered vol. of the History of Middle-earth, first part of *Sauron Defeated.*) Edited by Christopher Tolkien, Houghton Mifflin, 1998.

"English and Welsh." *The Monsters and the Critics, and Other Essays*. Edited by Christopher Tolkien, George Allen and Unwin, 1983, pp. 162-197.

"The Etymologies." *The Lost Road and Other Writings, Language and Legend before 'The Lord of the Rings. The History of Middle-earth*, vol. 5. Edited by Christopher Tolkien, Houghton Mifflin, 1987, pp. 377-448.

The Fall of Arthur. Edited by Christopher Tolkien, Houghton Mifflin Harcourt, 2013.

The Fall of Gondolin. Edited by Christopher Tolkien, Houghton Mifflin, 2018.

Farmer Giles of Ham. Edited by Christina Scull and Wayne Hammond, Houghton Mifflin Company, 1999.

The Father Christmas Letters. Edited by Baillie Tolkien, 1976. Rev. ed. as Letters from Father Christmas. HarperCollins, 1999.

The Fellowship of the Ring. Houghton Mifflin, 1954. 1994.

Finn and Hengest: The Fragment and the Episode. Edited by Alan Bliss, HarperCollins, 2006.

"For W.H.A." *Shenandoah: The Washington and Lee University Review*, volume 18, No. 2, 1967, pp. 96-97.

"The Grey Annals." *The War of the Jewels. The History of Middle-earth*, vol. 11. Edited by Christopher Tolkien, Houghton Mifflin, 1994, pp. 1-170.

"Guide to the Names in *The Lord of the Rings*." *A Tolkien Compass*. Edited by Jared Lobdell, Open Court, 1975, pp. 153-201.

The History of Middle-earth [series]. Edited by Christopher Tolkien. 12 vols. Houghton Mifflin, 1983-1996.

The Hobbit or There and Back Again. Houghton Mifflin, 1937.

i·Lam na·Ngoldathon, "The Grammar and Lexicon of the Gnomish Tongue." *Parma Eldalamberon*, no. 11. Edited by Christopher Gilson, Patrick Wynne, Arden R. Smith, and Carl F. Hostetter, Tolkien Trust, 1995.

The Lay of Aotroun and Itroun. Edited by Verlyn Flieger. Houghton Mifflin Harcourt, 2016.

The Lay of Aotroun and Itroun. Edited by Aleksandar Mikić with assistance of Elizabeth Currie. Novi Sa, Serbia, Abraka Dabra, 2015.

Lays of Beleriand. The History of Middle-earth, vol 3. Edited by Christopher Tolkien. Houghton Mifflin, 1985.

Leaf by Niggle. Tree and Leaf. Unwin Books, 1964.

Leaf by Niggle. A Tolkien Miscellany. SFBC Science Fiction Printing. 2002, pp. 149-162.

The Legend of Sigurd and Gudrún. Edited by Christopher Tolkien, Houghton Mifflin, 2009.

The Letters of J.R.R. Tolkien. Edited by Humphrey Carpenter with assistance of Christopher Tolkien, Houghton Mifflin, 1981.

The Letters of J.R.R. Tolkien, Revised and Expanded Edition. Edited by Humphrey Carpenter with assistance of Christopher Tolkien, William Morrow, 2023.

The Lord of the Rings. Houghton Mifflin, 1955.

"The Lost Road." *The Lost Road and Other Writings, Language and Legend before 'The Lord of the Rings'. The History of Middle-earth*, vol. 5. Edited by Christopher Tolkien, Houghton Mifflin, 1987, pp. 31-104.

The Lost Road and Other Writings, Language and Legend before 'The Lord of the Rings'. The History of Middle-earth, vol. 5. Edited by Christopher Tolkien, Houghton Mifflin, 1987.

A Middle English Vocabulary: Designed for use with Sisam's 'Fourteen Century Verse & Prose'. Clarendon Press, 1922.

Mr. Bliss. 1982. HarperCollins, 2011.

The Monsters and the Critics and Other Essays. Edited by Christopher Tolkien, Houghton Mifflin, 1984.

Morgoth's Ring: The Later Silmarillion, Part One—The Legends of Aman. The History of Middle-earth, vol. 10. Edited by Christopher Tolkien, Houghton Mifflin, 1993.

Mythopoeia. Tree and Leaf: Including the Poem Mythopoeia. Houghton Mifflin Harcourt, 1988.

The Nameless Land. Realities: An Anthology of Verse. Edited by G.S. Tancred, Leeds, at the Swan Press and London, Gay and Hancock, 1927, pp. 24-25.

"The Name Nodens." Appendix to "Report on the excavation of the prehistoric, Roman and post-Roman site in Lydney Park, Gloucestershire." *Reports of the Research Committee of the Society of Antiquaries of London, 1932*. Reprinted in *Tolkien Studies*, vol. 4, 2007, pp. 177-83.

The Nature of Middle-earth. Late Writings on the Lands, Inhabitants, and Metaphysics of Middle-earth. Edited by Carl F. Hostetter, Houghton Mifflin, 2021.

"Nomenclature [of '*The Lord of the Rings*'] or Guide to the Names in '*The Lord of the* Rings." *The Tolkien Compass*, edited by Jared Lobdell. Open Court, 1975, pp 153-201. Re-edited by Wayne G. Hammond and Christina Scull, *'The Lord of the Rings" Companion*. Houghton Mifflin Company, 2005, pp. 750-82.

"The Notion Club Papers." Sauron Defeated, The End of the Third Age. The History of 'The Lord of the Rings' Part Four. The History of Middle-earth, Vol. 9. Edited by Christopher Tolkien, Houghton Mifflin, 1992, pp. 155-327.

"On Fairy-Stories." *The Monsters and the Critics and Other Essays*. Edited by Christopher Tolkien, Houghton Mifflin, 1984, pp. 109-161.

Pearl. A Tolkien Miscellany. SFBC Science Fiction Printing, 2002, pp. 309-40.

The Peoples of Middle-earth. The History of Middle-earth, vol. 12. Edited by Christopher Tolkien, Harper Collins Publishers, 1996.

Pictures by J.R.R. Tolkien. Edited by Christopher Tolkien, Houghton Mifflin, 1979.

Poems and Songs of Middle Earth. Caedmon TC 1231, 1967.

"Qenya Lexicon" or "Qenyaqetsa" or "The Qenya Phonology and Lexicon" with "The Poetic and Mythologic Words of Eldarissa." *Parma Eldalamberon*, No. 12. Edited by Christopher Gilson, Carl F. Hostetter, Patrick Wynne, and Arden R. Smith, Tolkien Trust, 1998.

The Return of the King. Houghton Mifflin, 1955. 1994.

The Return of the Shadow. The History of Middle-earth Vol. 6. Edited by Christopher Tolkien, Houghton Mifflin Company, 1988.

Roverandom. Edited by Christina Scull and Wayne G. Hammond, Houghton Mifflin, 1998.

Sauron Defeated. The History of Middle-earth vol. 9. Edited by Christopher Tolkien, Houghton Mifflin, 1992.

"A Secret Vice." *The Monsters and the Critics and Other Essays*. Edited by Christopher Tolkien, Houghton Mifflin, 1984, pp. 198-223.

The Shaping of Middle-earth: The Quenta, The Ambarkanta, and The Annals. The History of Middle-earth vol. 4. Edited by Christopher Tolkien, Houghton Mifflin, 1986.

The Silmarillion. Edited by Christopher Tolkien, George Allen and Unwin, 1977.

Sir Gawain and the Green Knight, Pearl, and Sir Orfeo. Edited by Christopher Tolkien, 1975. Ballantine, 1980.

Sir Orfeo. A Tolkien Miscellany. SFBC Science Fiction Printing, 2002, pp. 341-355.

Smith of Wootton Major. George Allen & Unwin, 1967. *Tales from the Perilous Realm*. HarperCollins, 2008, pp. 243-281.

Smith of Wootton Major, Extended Edition. Edited by Verlyn Flieger, HarperCollinsPublishers, 2005.

The Story of Kullervo. Edited by Verlyn Flieger, Houghton Mifflin, 2016.

A Tolkien Miscellany. SFBC Science Fiction Printing, 2002.

Tolkien on Fairy-stories, Expanded Edition, with Commentary and Notes. Edited by Verlyn Flieger and Douglas A. Anderson, Harper Collins Publishers, 2008.

The Treason of Isengard. Edited by Christopher Tolkien, Houghton Mifflin Company, 1989.

Tree and Leaf. Houghton Mifflin, 1965.

The Two Towers. Houghton Mifflin, 1954. 1994

Unfinished Tales of Númenor and Middle-earth. Edited by Christopher Tolkien, Houghton Mifflin Company, 1980.

The War of the Jewels. The History of Middle-earth vol. 11. Edited by Christopher Tolkien, Houghton Mifflin, 1994.

The War of the Ring. The History of The Lord of the Rings Part Three. The History of Middle-earth vol. 8. Edited by Christopher Tolkien, Harper Collins Publishers, 1990.

"Words, Phrases, and Passages in Various Tongues in *The Lord of the Rings*." *Parma Eldalamberon* no. 17. Edited by Christopher Gilson, Tolkien Trust, 2007.

Tolkien, J.R.R., E.V. Gordon, et al. *Songs for the Philologists*. Privately printed. 1936.

Tolkien, Michael H.R. "J.R.R. Tolkien: The 'Wizard Father'." *Mythprint* 11, no. 1, January 1975, pp. 3-4. Reprinted from *Sunday Telegraph*, 9 September, 1973.

Tolkien, Simon. "My Grandfather—J.R.R. Tolkien." *The Mail*. Sunday, February 23, 2003. Reprinted on Simon Tolkien's website, www.simontolkien.com/author.html, accessed 11/12/2020.

Tolkiengateway. http://tolkiengateway.net /wiki/Letter to H. Cotton Minchin_(16_April_1956), accessed on 5/5/2022.

Tyler, J.E.A. *The Complete Tolkien Companion*, Third ed. St. Martin's Press, Thomas Dunne Books, 1976.

UNWIN, Rayner. *George Allen & Unwin: A Remembrancer.* Ludlow, privately printed by Merlin, Unwin Books, 1999.

VENKATESH, Krishnan. *Frodo's Wound. Why the 'Lord of the Rings' Is a GREAT BOOK.* Mercer University Press, 2021.

VIVIAN, Lt. Col. J.L., editor. *The Visitations of the County of Devon: Comprising the Heralds' Visitations of 1531, 1564 & 1620.* Exeter, 1895.

WATKINS, Carl S. *History and the Supernatural in Medieval England.* Cambridge University Press, 2007.

WATTS, Victor, editor. *Cambridge Dictionary of English Place-names: Based on the Collections of the English Place-name Society.* Cambridge University Press, 2004.

WEST, Richard C. "A Letter from Father Murray." *Tolkien Studies,* vol. 16, edited by Michael D.C. Drout, Verlyn Flieger, and David Bratman, West Virginia. University Press, 2019, pp. 133-139.

WHEELER, Jill C. *J.R.R. Tolkien.* ABDO Publishing, 2009.

WHITE, Michael. *J.R.R. Tolkien. A Biography.* Little, Brown, 2001.

WICKHAM-CROWLEY, Kelley M. "'Mind to Mind': Tolkien's Faërian Drama and the Middle English Sir Orfeo." *Tolkien Studies,* vol, 12, edited by Michael D.C. Drout, Verlyn Flieger, and David Bratman, West Virginia. University Press, 2015, pp. 1-29.

WILCOX, Miranda. "Exilic Imagining in *The Seafarer* and *The Lord of the Rings.*" *Tolkien, the Medievalist,* edited by Jane Chance, Routledge, 2003, pp. 133-154.

WILLETT, Edward. *J.R.R. Tolkien: Master of Imaginary Worlds.* Enslow Publishers, 2004.

WRIGHT, Walter Page. *Popular Garden Flowers.* Doubleday Page & Co., 1911.

YouTube: BBC documentary "In Their Own Words, J.R.R Tolkien." First broadcast March 30, 1968. Uploaded April 26, 2011. https://www.youtube.com/watch?v=w9OG6GpisIQ.

About the Authors

NANCY BUNTING is a retired Ph.D. clinical psychologist who now lives in Northwest Arkansas. She has published on Tolkien in *Beyond Bree*, *Hither Shore*, *Lembas*, *Mallorn*, *Minas Tirith Evening-Star*, *Mythlore*, and *VII*.

SEAMUS HAMILL-KEAYS served over 30 years, world-wide, in the Royal Air Force retiring in 1987 from a Senior Scientific Lecturer post at the RAF College Cranwell with the rank of Squadron Leader. He obtained a Master of Arts degree in Celtic Studies, with Distinction, from the University of Wales in 2011. His property in the Brecon Beacons includes the site of the North Gate of the Buckland Estate. The exciting parallels between Brecon Buckland and J.R.R. Tolkien's Buckland in *The Lord of the Rings* created his intense interest in Tolkien's early life. His findings about Tolkien are found on his website https://www.talybont.com

TOBY WIDDICOMBE was educated at Cambridge University and the University of California. He has been a professor at the University of Alaska Anchorage for over thirty years after teaching at UC Irvine and UC Santa Barbara. His major research fields are American literature, Tolkien, textual studies, Shakespeare, and utopianism. He has published numerous articles and almost a dozen books including *J.R.R. Tolkien, A Guide for the Perplexed* (Bloomsbury).

Index

A

B

C

F

G

I

J

K

L

M

N

O

P

Q

R

S

Y

Z

Walking Tree Publishers

Zurich and Jena

Walking Tree Publishers was founded in 1997 as a forum for publication of material related to Tolkien and Middle-earth studies.

www.walking-tree.org

Cormarë Series

The *Cormarë Series* collects papers and studies dedicated exclusively to the exploration of Tolkien's work. It comprises monographs, thematic collections of essays, conference volumes, and reprints of important yet no longer (easily) accessible papers by leading scholars in the field. Manuscripts and project proposals are evaluated by members of an independent board of advisors who support the series editors in their endeavour to provide the readers with qualitatively superior yet accessible studies on Tolkien and his work.

News from the Shire and Beyond. Studies on Tolkien
Peter Buchs & Thomas Honegger (eds.), Zurich and Berne 2004, Reprint, First edition 1997 (Cormarë Series 1), ISBN 978-3-9521424-5-5

Root and Branch. Approaches Towards Understanding Tolkien
Thomas Honegger (ed.), Zurich and Berne 2005, Reprint, First edition 1999 (Cormarë Series 2), ISBN 978-3-905703-01-6

Richard Sturch, *Four Christian Fantasists. A Study of the Fantastic Writings of George MacDonald, Charles Williams, C.S. Lewis and J.R.R. Tolkien*
Zurich and Berne 2007, Reprint, First edition 2001 (Cormarë Series 3), ISBN 978-3-905703-04-7

Tolkien in Translation
Thomas Honegger (ed.), Zurich and Jena 2011, Reprint, First edition 2003 (Cormarë Series 4), ISBN 978-3-905703-15-3

Mark T. Hooker, *Tolkien Through Russian Eyes*
Zurich and Berne 2003 (Cormarë Series 5), ISBN 978-3-9521424-7-9

Translating Tolkien: Text and Film
Thomas Honegger (ed.), Zurich and Jena 2011, Reprint, First edition 2004 (Cormarë Series 6), ISBN 978-3-905703-16-0

Christopher Garbowski, *Recovery and Transcendence for the Contemporary Mythmaker. The Spiritual Dimension in the Works of J.R.R. Tolkien*
Zurich and Berne 2004, Reprint, First Edition by Marie Curie Sklodowska, University Press, Lublin 2000, (Cormarë Series 7), ISBN 978-3-9521424-8-6

Reconsidering Tolkien
Thomas Honegger (ed.), Zurich and Berne 2005 (Cormarë Series 8), ISBN 978-3-905703-00-9

Tolkien and Modernity 1
Frank Weinreich & Thomas Honegger (eds.), Zurich and Berne 2006 (Cormarë Series 9), ISBN 978-3-905703-02-3

Tolkien and Modernity 2
Thomas Honegger & Frank Weinreich (eds.), Zurich and Berne 2006 (Cormarë Series 10), ISBN 978-3-905703-03-0

Tom Shippey, *Roots and Branches. Selected Papers on Tolkien by Tom Shippey*
Zurich and Berne 2007 (Cormarë Series 11), ISBN 978-3-905703-05-4

Ross Smith, *Inside Language. Linguistic and Aesthetic Theory in Tolkien*
Zurich and Jena 2011, Reprint, First edition 2007 (Cormarë Series 12), ISBN 978-3-905703-20-7

How We Became Middle-earth. A Collection of Essays on The Lord of the Rings
Adam Lam & Nataliya Oryshchuk (eds.), Zurich and Berne 2007 (Cormarë Series 13), ISBN 978-3-905703-07-8

Myth and Magic. Art According to the Inklings
Eduardo Segura & Thomas Honegger (eds.), Zurich and Berne 2007 (Cormarë Series 14), ISBN 978-3-905703-08-5

The Silmarillion – Thirty Years On
Allan Turner (ed.), Zurich and Berne 2007 (Cormarë Series 15), ISBN 978-3-905703-10-8

Martin Simonson, *The Lord of the Rings and the Western Narrative Tradition*
Zurich and Jena 2008 (Cormarë Series 16), ISBN 978-3-905703-09-2

Tolkien's Shorter Works. Proceedings of the 4th Seminar of the Deutsche Tolkien Gesellschaft & Walking Tree Publishers Decennial Conference
Margaret Hiley & Frank Weinreich (eds.), Zurich and Jena 2008 (Cormarë Series 17), ISBN 978-3-905703-11-5

Tolkien's The Lord of the Rings: Sources of Inspiration
Stratford Caldecott & Thomas Honegger (eds.), Zurich and Jena 2008 (Cormarë Series 18), ISBN 978-3-905703-12-2

J.S. Ryan, *Tolkien's View: Windows into his World*
Zurich and Jena 2009 (Cormarë Series 19), ISBN 978-3-905703-13-9

Music in Middle-earth
Heidi Steimel & Friedhelm Schneidewind (eds.), Zurich and Jena 2010 (Cormarë Series 20), ISBN 978-3-905703-14-6

Liam Campbell, *The Ecological Augury in the Works of JRR Tolkien*
Zurich and Jena 2011 (Cormarë Series 21), ISBN 978-3-905703-18-4

Margaret Hiley, *The Loss and the Silence. Aspects of Modernism in the Works of C.S. Lewis, J.R.R. Tolkien and Charles Williams*
Zurich and Jena 2011 (Cormarë Series 22), ISBN 978-3-905703-19-1

Rainer Nagel, *Hobbit Place-names. A Linguistic Excursion through the Shire*
Zurich and Jena 2012 (Cormarë Series 23), ISBN 978-3-905703-22-1

Christopher MacLachlan, *Tolkien and Wagner: The Ring and Der Ring*
Zurich and Jena 2012 (Cormarë Series 24), ISBN 978-3-905703-21-4

Renée Vink, *Wagner and Tolkien: Mythmakers*
Zurich and Jena 2012 (Cormarë Series 25), ISBN 978-3-905703-25-2

The Broken Scythe. Death and Immortality in the Works of J.R.R. Tolkien
Roberto Arduini & Claudio Antonio Testi (eds.), Zurich and Jena 2012 (Cormarë Series 26), ISBN 978-3-905703-26-9

Sub-creating Middle-earth: Constructions of Authorship and the Works of J.R.R. Tolkien
Judith Klinger (ed.), Zurich and Jena 2012 (Cormarë Series 27), ISBN 978-3-905703-27-6

Tolkien's Poetry
Julian Eilmann & Allan Turner (eds.), Zurich and Jena 2013 (Cormarë Series 28), ISBN 978-3-905703-28-3

O, What a Tangled Web. Tolkien and Medieval Literature. A View from Poland
Barbara Kowalik (ed.), Zurich and Jena 2013 (Cormarë Series 29), ISBN 978-3-905703-29-0

J.S. Ryan, *In the Nameless Wood*
Zurich and Jena 2013 (Cormarë Series 30), ISBN 978-3-905703-30-6

From Peterborough to Faëry; The Poetics and Mechanics of Secondary Worlds
Thomas Honegger & Dirk Vanderbeke (eds.), Zurich and Jena 2014 (Cormarë Series 31), ISBN 978-3-905703-31-3

Tolkien and Philosophy
Roberto Arduini & Claudio R. Testi (eds.), Zurich and Jena 2014 (Cormarë Series 32), ISBN 978-3-905703-32-0

Patrick Curry, *Deep Roots in a Time of Frost. Essays on Tolkien*
Zurich and Jena 2014 (Cormarë Series 33), ISBN 978-3-905703-33-7

Representations of Nature in Middle-earth
Martin Simonson (ed.), Zurich and Jena 2015, (Cormarë Series 34), ISBN 978-3-905703-34-4

Laughter in Middle-earth
Thomas Honegger & Maureen F. Mann (eds.), Zurich and Jena 2016 (Cormarë Series 35), ISBN 978-3-905703-35-1

Julian Eilmann, *J.R.R. Tolkien – Romanticist and Poet*
Zurich and Jena 2017 (Cormarë Series 36), ISBN 978-3-905703-36-8

Binding Them All. Interdisciplinary Perspectives on J.R.R. Tolkien and His Works
Monika Kirner-Ludwig, Stephan Köser, Sebastian Streitberger (eds.), Zurich and Jena 2017 (Cormarë Series 37), ISBN 978-3-905703-37-5

Claudio Testi, *Pagan Saints in Middle-earth*
Zurich and Jena 2017 (Cormarë Series 38), ISBN 978-3-905703-38-2

Music in Tolkien's Work and Beyond
Julian Eilmann & Friedhelm Schneidewind (eds.), Zurich and Jena 2019 (Cormarë Series 39), ISBN 978-3-905703-39-9

Sub-creating Arda: World-building in J.R.R. Tolkien's Works, its Precursors, and Legacies
Dimitra Fimi & Thomas Honegger (eds.), Zurich and Jena 2019 (Cormarë Series 40), ISBN 978-3-905703-40-5

"Something Has Gone Crack": New Perspectives on J.R.R. Tolkien and the Great War
Janet Brennan Croft and Annika Röttinger (eds.), Zurich and Jena 2019 (Cormarë Series 41), ISBN 978-3-905703-41-2

Tolkien and the Classics
Roberto Arduini, Giampaolo Canzonieri & Claudio A. Testi (eds.), Zurich and Jena 2019 (Cormarë Series 42), ISBN 978-3-905703-42-9

José María Miranda Boto, *Law, Government, and Society in J.R.R. Tolkien's Works*
Zurich and Jena 2022 (Cormarë Series 43), ISBN 978-3-905703-43-6

Middle-earth, or There and Back Again
Łukasz Neubauer (ed.), Zurich and Jena 2020 (Cormarë Series 44), ISBN 978-3-905703-44-3

Tolkien and the Classical World
Hamish Williams (ed.), Zurich and Jena 2021 (Cormarë Series 45), ISBN 978-3-905703-45-0

Nancy Bunting and Seamus Hamill-Keays, *The Gallant Edith Bratt. J.R.R. Tolkien's Inspiration.* Zurich and Jena 2021 (Cormarë Series 46), ISBN 978-3-905703-46-7

Nólë Hyarmenillo: An Anthology of Iberian Scholarship on Tolkien
Nuno Simões Rodrigues, Martin Simonson, and Angélica Varandas (eds.), Zurich and Jena 2022 (Cormarë Series 47), ISBN 978-3-905703-47-4

The Songs of the Spheres: Lewis, Tolkien and the Overlapping Realms of their Imaginations
Łukasz Neubauer and Guglielmo Spirito (eds.), Zurich and Jena 2024 (Cormarë Series 48), ISBN 978-3-905703-48-1

Richard Z. Gallant, *Germanic Heroes, Courage, and Fate: Northern Narratives of J.R.R. Tolkien's Legendarium.* Zurich and Jena 2024 (Cormarë Series 49), ISBN 978-3-905703-49-8

Thomas Honegger, *Tweaking Things a Little. Essays on the Epic Fantasy of J.R.R. Tolkien and G.R.R. Martin*. Zurich and Jena 2023 (Cormarë Series 50), ISBN 978-3-905703-50-4

The Romantic Spirit in the Works of J.R.R. Tolkien
Will Sherwood and Julian Eilmann (eds.), Zurich and Jena 2024 (Cormarë Series 51), ISBN 978-3-905703-51-1

Nancy Bunting, Seamus Hamill-Keays, and Toby Widdicombe,
Celebrating Tolkien's Legacy. Essays by Nancy Bunting, Seamus Hamill-Keays, and Toby Widdicombe. Zurich and Jena 2024 (Cormarë Series 52),
ISBN 978-3-905703-52-8

Tolkien among the Theologians
Austin M. Freeman (ed.), Zurich and Jena 2025 (Cormarë Series 53),
(forthcoming)

Beowulf and the Dragon

The original Old English text of the 'Dragon Episode' of Beowulf is set in an authentic font and bound in hardback as a high quality art book. Illustrated by Anke Eissmann and accompanied by John Porter's translation. Introduction by Tom Shippey. Limited first edition of 500 copies. 84 pages. Selected pages can be previewed on: www.walking-tree.org/beowulf

Beowulf and the Dragon, Zurich and Jena 2009 , ISBN 978-3-905703-17-7

Tales of Yore Series

The *Tales of Yore Series* provides a platform for qualitatively superior fiction that will appeal to readers familiar with Tolkien's world:

The Monster Specialist

Sir Severus le Brewse, among the least known of King Arthur's Round Table knights, is preferred by nature, disposition, and training to fight against monsters rather than other knights. After youthful adventures of errantry with dragons, trolls, vampires, and assorted beasts, Severus joins the brilliant sorceress Lilava to face the Chimaera in The Greatest Monster Battle of All Time to free her folk from an age-old curse. But their adventures don't end there; together they meet elves and magicians, friends and foes; they join in the fight to save Camelot and even walk the Grey Paths of the Dead. With a mix of Malory, a touch of Tolkien, and a hint of humor, The Monster Specialist chronicles a tale of courage, tenacity, honor, and love.

The Monster Specialist is illustrated by Anke Eissmann.

Edward S. Louis, *The Monster Specialist*
Zurich and Jena 2014 (Tales of Yore Series No. 3), ISBN 978-3-905703-23-8

Tales of Yore Series (earlier books, presently unavailable)

Kay Woollard, *The Terror of Tatty Walk. A Frightener*
CD and Booklet, Zurich and Berne 2000 (Tales of Yore Series No. 1), ISBN 978-3-9521424-2-4

Kay Woollard, *Wilmot's Very Strange Stone or What came of building "snobbits"*
CD and booklet, Zurich and Berne 2001 (Tales of Yore Series No. 2), ISBN 978-3-9521424-4-8

Information for authors

Authors interested in contributing to our publications can learn more about the services we offer on the "services for authors" section of our web pages.

www.walking-tree.org/authors

Manuscripts and project proposals can be submitted to the board of editors:

Walking Tree Publishers
e-mail: info@walking-tree.org

www.ingramcontent.com/pod-product-compliance
Ingram Content Group UK Ltd.
Pitfield, Milton Keynes, MK11 3LW, UK
UKHW021857190726
13853UKWH00003B/1309